FROM THE NEW FREEDOM TO THE NEW FRONTIER:

A History of the United States from 1912 to the Present

FROM THE NEW FREEDOM
TO THE NEW FRONTIER:

A History of the United States

from 1912 to the Present

BY ANDRÉ MAUROIS

of the Académie Française

Translated by PATRICK O'BRIEN

DAVID McKAY COMPANY, INC.

New York

FROM THE NEW FREEDOM TO THE NEW FRONTIER: A HISTORY OF THE
UNITED STATES FROM 1912 TO THE PRESENT

© Copyright, 1962, by Jaspard, Polus et Cie, Monaco, et, pour
l'édition française, Presses de la Cité.
English transition © copyright, 1963, by George Weidenfeld and Nicolson, Ltd.

MANUFACTURED IN THE UNITED STATES OF AMERICA
VAN REES PRESS • NEW YORK

Preface

IN 1959, a group of editors of several countries had the idea that it would be interesting to publish a parallel history of the two giants of our time: the United States and the Soviet Union. In order that the analysis be as impartial as possible, they decided to request these two studies, not of an American and a Russian, but (perhaps in memory of Tocqueville who had first anticipated the emergence of the two nations and their rivalry) of two Frenchmen. It was proposed to me, therefore, to write a history of the United States from 1912 to 1960. The date 1912 was chosen, with reason, because it marked the beginning of the era of United States involvement in world affairs and would predate the Russian Revolution and the establishment of the Soviet Union by only a few short years.

I at first hesitated to accept. I had begun a life of Balzac that would require several years of research. Moreover, I knew that there existed many excellent American books on the period. Yet I was fascinated by the idea. I had long been involved with the United States. I was president of *France-États-Unis;* I attached an immense importance to the preservation of good relations between America and Europe; I knew that European public opinion poorly understood the United States. I believed it would be beneficial for a study to be done, and I was convinced it would be of more value to have it made by a man who loved the United States and who had made many long sojourns there.

My role was to offer a synthesis, destined for the average reader of numerous countries, of my readings, of my recollections, and of my conversations with eminent Americans. My contribution would not be to introduce new facts—this has been admirably done by American historians—but to organize and clarify the known facts. I had also the advantage of having been in the

United States at critical times (the depression of 1929-1933, the months that preceded the war of 1939, the crucial years 1941 and 1942). This permitted me to enrich the narrative with some personal impressions.

It is important, in order to judge this book fairly, to remember that the author was asked to address himself to an international public. This book is therefore not designed as a scholarly work; it is a book composed, with conscience and good faith, by a foreigner who has always been interested in the history of the United States and who has endeavored to present it with clarity, with affection, and without prejudice.

Contents

xi

FROM THE NEW FREEDOM
TO THE NEW FRONTIER:

*A History of the United States
from 1912 to the Present*

PART ONE

The State of the Union
before the First World War

IN no country does history ever move forward in one steady flow toward a perfect and unchanging state of balance. All nations go through their periods of difficulty, their hard times; they have their bouts of fever, their recoveries, and their relapses. The United States, at the end of the nineteenth century, was suffering from growing pains. The country had grown too fast; its population, industry, and technical ability had increased so rapidly that they had outgrown its institutions. These institutions now cramped the country like clothes that are far too small. The country needed a medicine that would really work; it needed far-reaching reforms. The Americans knew this. Many of them had come from Europe to live in a Golden Age upon an untrodden soil: they had found no more than an Age of Gilt. And yet they still passionately believed that one day everything would be for the best in this best of continents.

1

The new citizens, huddled in the slums or living on the farms of the Midwest, waited for their good fortune to come to them with a dogged, stubborn faith—fortune for themselves or at least for their children. "It's a great country," they said proudly. In spite of crises and in spite of injustice, the years before 1914 were years of hope. The trumpets of reform were sounding. What kind of reform? A return to Jeffersonian democracy; the setting of controls upon the country's economy; a fairer sharing of profits; a struggle against poverty and against the building up of those immense and artificial fortunes that were born of financial manipulation; and all this without discouraging boldness in enterprise or diminishing freedom. A long and heavy task. There were to be victories and setbacks and two world wars. "And at the seventh time . . . the wall fell down flat." But before the varying fortunes of this struggle are described, the circumstances that made it necessary must be brought to mind.

I

The country had grown too fast. The whole history of mankind had never seen such vast migrations. In one century, an almost empty continent, which had barely managed to feed half a million Indians, had been populated by another continent, Europe. In 1790, the United States had four million inhabitants, a fifth of these being Negro slaves; in 1840, there were seventeen million inhabitants, a growth largely brought about by natural increase—by the excess of births over deaths. This first population consisted almost entirely of English, with some Germans and Dutch and a few Frenchmen in Louisiana. These men had brought a nation into being. They had won their independence, established a tradition, and created an ideal.

Later, between 1840 and 1850, a great many Germans escaped from political persecution by crossing the sea, while at the same time the Irish, in their hundreds of thousands, fled before the potato famine. Why did these unhappy Europeans look upon America as a Promised Land? Partly because the land belonged to no one. There was a shifting frontier that moved westward every year, and by going to the far edge of the country, any man could become his own master. But the immigrants also came because they wanted freedom. In spite of a few brief revolutions, Europe had been oppressing the mass of the people since 1815. Those who left longed for a country where the citizens would be treated according to their abilities, not according to their birth; where law, rather than power and privilege, should rule; and where bold, enterprising men should have unbounded opportunities before them. Was the American dream no more than an illusion? Sometimes this almost seemed to be the case; but unshakable faith outlived these fears. The immigrants soon became part of their new country. The man who had just crossed the Atlantic and who did not even speak English, would still proudly say, "I am an American."

After 1880, the pattern of immigration changed. The Germans and the Irish no longer had the same reasons for leaving the countries they were born in; yet the building of the American railways and the industries that had been originally stimulated during the Civil War by the requirements of the army called for labor. Because of this, new waves came in from the poorer countries. In 1880, the population of the United States reached 50,000,000; in 1890, 62,000,000; in 1900, 75,000,000; in 1910, 91,000,000. This human tide flowed in from Italy, where the government, alarmed by the high birth rate, encouraged emigration, and also from Austria-Hungary and Russia. The Slavs were ill treated in the Austro-Hungarian Empire, and Czar Alexander III persecuted the Polish Jews. Slavs and Jews flooded in. Between 1840 and 1860, out of every hundred immigrants there were forty-three Irish and thirty-five Germans; between 1901 and 1910, twenty-eight Italians, twenty-seven Austro-Hungarians, and twenty Russians and Poles.

This new immigration raised serious problems. The America of the Founding Fathers had been Protestant; it had shared the Anglo-Saxon tradition; it had possessed a surprisingly high degree of culture. At the period of independence, the quality of the American political assemblies and the value of their debates had very much impressed the Europeans. Later, Germany and Scandinavia had provided the country with sober, hard-working, well-educated farmers. But the proportion of citizens born in the United States was rapidly decreasing. The old families had few children. "What does it matter?" said the Americans. "Im-

3

migration brings us children ready made and ready reared." No doubt it did; but these immigrants were very soon going to turn into citizens of a kind far harder to absorb than those who had come before them. Toward 1900, 27 percent of those over fourteen were unable to read or write. The newcomers did not know English, and they kept together in separate national quarters in the towns. An electoral campaign had to be conducted in sixteen different languages. In thirty large cities, more than half the children had foreign-born fathers. These groups differed not only by nationality, but also by religion. Catholic churches and parochial schools rose for the Italians, the Irish, and the Poles; and in 1886, James Gibbons, Bishop of Baltimore, became the first American cardinal. New York was the biggest Irish town in the world and the biggest Jewish town. The sum of these motley communities made up a great American city and one of the living centers of the national tradition.

According to one sanguine theory, America was a melting pot, and once the races had been run together, this crucible would pour out nothing but genuine Americans. There was some truth in this. In 1912, Arnold Bennett, going through New York by the elevated railway, was struck by the uniformity of the faces, clothes, and manners of the people he saw. These crowds, coming from such different origins, seemed mysteriously all of a piece. They spoke every kind of language, Yiddish, Italian, Greek, German, Polish. Yet both in their bearing and in their clothes, all these men looked alike. The American walked faster than other men and with a greater freedom. He wore not suspenders but a belt, which confines the body less. The influences of the climate and the country and of interbreeding all were tending to produce a single type. The immigrants shared in the American dream. How would it have been possible for them not to have believed in the common man, the man of the people? They were all common men themselves. How would it have been possible for them not to have praised tolerance? They themselves were all in need of it. They had left a wretched past behind them, and they were ready to take enormous risks to make themselves a happy future.

But the American dream insisted upon equality of opportunity. Take risks? Certainly. Work hard? Happily. Yet still, to keep this faith alive, it was essential that the risk should pay. For a long while, as the poor and enterprising immigrant saw it, the frontier opened onto the Land of Canaan. According to the American meaning of the word, the frontier was not a line between two countries, studded with posts and customs men, but a moving border between civilization and the uncultivated land. In 1862, the Homestead Act had granted 160 acres to anyone who would settle on them and work the land. And then the railway companies, who had been given vast tracts of land by the government, hurriedly sold them, as much to increase their working capital as to make travelers and rail-users for themselves.

So the westward rush grew faster. For a while, it ran up against the immense expanse of country that stretches between the Rocky Mountains and the Missouri. There the sparsely scattered towns were no more than outposts—a single street running between two short rows of one-story wooden houses. Immediately outside the towns began the plains, a treeless, grass-covered wilderness, swept by scorching winds in the summer and by snowstorms in the winter; a vast expanse upon which grazed the enormous herds of bison, popularly known as buffalo, that supplied the Indian tribes with their meat, their clothes, and their tents. Hunters set about destroying the bison, and the annihilation of the herds contributed to the destruction of the Indians. Then the Texas cattlemen realized that the grass of the plains, which had fed so many bison, might do the same for steers; and thus the Western Range was born.

Soon the moving herds hollowed out the cattle trails. "Western" films have made this picturesque life, with its feathered Indians and cowboys in ten-gallon hats with red handkerchiefs around the throat, revolvers at the belt, and lassos in hand, familiar to us all. Once the region was made peaceful, the stockbreeders were able to expand into the great plains instead of bringing their herds the whole wearisome journey from Texas. The meat and canning towns rose up. In the meantime, the farmers found that certain kinds of grain would grow in this kingdom of the cattle and that barbed wire would allow them to divide the grazing from the farm land. Great seas of Indian corn rose from the soil. Queen Grass became as powerful in the Middle West as King Cotton in the South.

Now the railway had brought an east-west axis into being, and

5

it was continually traversed by trains. The tide, which had needed two centuries to advance from the Atlantic to the Missouri, took only a few years to reach the Pacific shore. As early as 1890, the Director of the Census announced the end of the frontier. This did not mean that there was no more free land but rather that the great adventure seemed to be over. The frontier had played a part of the first importance on the formation of the national character. There, with danger right at hand, men helped one another; a feeling of goodwill was born—a feeling of the brotherhood of mankind. Women were respected because there were very few of them and those few were precious, and because in those unprotected regions, only a stern, unwritten law could shield them. There were hardly any of the social safeguards. The sheriff was still more of a fighting man than an administrator. Every man both thought and said, "I attend to my own business. Leave me alone." The frontier meant the possibility of tearing oneself away from the bondage of the old civilizations, of going forward into the empty land, and of reaching the highest rank in the new cities. The end of the frontier did not foretell the end of the migration of the European nations, but the end of a form of equality whose tradition was nevertheless to remain with America, and which Americans were to remember with a nostalgic longing.

II

By the beginning of the twentieth century, the contrast between this dream of equality and the inequality of real life was becoming frightening. During America's Colonial period, a kind of aristocracy had been formed. It was constituted on the one hand of the Southern planters, who made up a knightly feudal body, and on the other, of the outstanding families of New England, Philadelphia, and New York—long-established dynasties of merchant princes, whose manner of life was sober and circumspect and whose standing was quite unquestioned.

The aristocracy of plantation-owners in the South had been ruined by the War of Secession. In the North, big business had brought a class of nouveaux riches into existence, men with unimaginably vast incomes. Formerly the merchants and the shipowners of the East had built up their fortunes slowly, with all the healthy difficulties that are inherent in trade and shipping. But between 1860 and 1900, the government land grants, the formation of very large companies and the fantastic rise of their shares, the discovery of oil wells or of mines, had all enriched manufacturers and bankers with a speed that went beyond anything that had ever been known in Venice or Genoa, or even London.

Political and judicial authority was divided among the federal government (which had only a small share), the states, and the municipalities; this fragmentation of power and the weakness of the laws made things easy for the businessmen. Almost uncontrolled, they had been able to build up gigantic concerns, endowed with boundless privileges. This had enabled them to undertake great tasks and to equip and develop the country, but it had given them a dangerous amount of power. An aggressive, uncouth plutocracy dominated the former ruling class; and most unwisely this plutocracy did not allow any more than a thin trickle of the new wealth to filter down to the other classes. In 1900, one-eighth of American families possessed seven-eighths of the national fortune. Andrew Carnegie's yearly income, untaxed, was $20,000,000; the average American income was $500. It was said that the Astors owned between $250- and $300,000,000, the Goelets, $100,000,000, and Marshall Field of Chicago almost as much. As for the possessions of the Vanderbilts, the Goulds, the Rockefellers, and the Morgans, they were nearly incalculable. The millions rolled naturally toward them. Many of these enormous fortunes had been made in a single generation. Carnegie, the son of a weaver, had been a telegraph operator; Rockefeller, a clerk; Hill, the great railway boss, a clerk in a village grocery. Many of the lords of the economy had no ancestors but themselves.

Parvenus have always risen up in every country and at every period; but in Europe, they had always found an ancient aristocracy there to receive them at the top of the golden staircase— an aristocracy whose manners and tastes they did their best to make their own. Napoleon had tried to draw Louis XVI's nobility to his court. In America, this did not apply. The steel dukes, the beef barons, and the oil kings swamped the small upper class of merchants and shipowners that had originated in the Colonial and Federalist eras and were left essentially without guides. They did not know what to do with their superabundant fortunes,

7

so in the adolescent cities, they built Florentine palaces, châteaux of the Loire, or English manor houses. They bought everything that the Old World had for sale—old masters, furniture that had belonged to Marie Antoinette, tapestries with royal arms upon them, Chinese silks, Greek statues, and even well-born sons-in-law.

The wisest, such as Rockefeller and Carnegie, lived in comparative simplicity. Others made a show of their wealth and brought European performers, at great expense, to adorn their parties. James Hazen Hyde, the son of an insurance prince, turned the Sherry Hotel into a Grand Trianon for a ball. He brought the famous actress Réjane and her whole company from Paris for a single evening. At Delmonico's, Leonard Jerome gave a banquet for seventy-two friends, where the centerpiece of the table was a gleaming sheet of water with swans swimming in it, separated from the guests by golden bars. In the villas of Newport, more than one family had a large staff of servants under the orders of an English butler who did his utmost to teach his masters the customs of his native country. After a splendid entertainment at the château of Vaux-le-Vicomte, Louis XIV grew uneasy about the wealth of Fouquet, the minister of finance. Another sovereign, the American people, became uneasy at the beginning of the twentieth century about the entertainments given by a hundred overshowy ministers of finance.

Unless it can bring a meaningful society into being, wealth procures few lasting joys. Mrs. William Astor, the high priestess of New York elegance, with Ward McAllister had set the limits of an exclusive body, the Four Hundred—this was the number of guests that her own ballroom could hold. This chosen group of multimillionaires sought to connect itself with the older upper class by marriage, at first with the merchant princes of New England and then with the European nobility. In this way, more than one family of the Old World restored its fortunes. Miss Jenny Jerome married the Duke of Marlborough's cousin, Lord Randolph Churchill, and became the mother of the most illustrious of English statesmen; Consuelo Vanderbilt married the Duke of Marlborough himself; Anna Gould married first Boni, Comte de Castellane, and then the Duc de Talleyrand. An Astor raised herself so high "that she ended up by landing on the other side of the ocean in the English peerage" and in the British Parliament. Others chose rather to stay in their traditional surroundings. Pierpont Morgan reigned like a patriarch over his family, among the powerful, grave, complacent bankers.

Between the Four Hundred and the middle classes, there opened a chasm, wide and deep. The middle classes were made up of the professional men, the doctors, lawyers, teachers, and clergymen; of the smaller manufacturers, managers, and tradespeople. Some of them found it very difficult to live decently; the more skillful managed to achieve a measure of comfort. An income of $3,000 a year in 1900 was worth an income of $9,000 in 1950. Why? Because income tax did not exist, because the purchasing power of the dollar was higher, and because people needed less and managed on smaller budgets. Many women made their own clothes. A cook was paid $5 a week and a cleaning woman a $1.50 a day. It was among the middle classes that the Puritan virtues were best preserved. The well-to-do farmers copied this kind of life, but about 1890, well-to-do farmers were becoming rare.

The middle classes had about the same social position as they have today; but the condition of the workers was harder than it is at present. Laws, taxes, and wages had not yet been adjusted to the country's new wealth. The newly arrived, lost, and illiterate immigrants felt themselves powerless to defend their rights. Many of them lived in slums. We find the same words used by all the commentators of the time: filth, unsanitary conditions, lack of security. Giuseppe Giacosa, having visited an Italian quarter, wrote, "It is impossible to describe the mud, the stinking dampness, the disordered confusion of the streets." In the Jewish quarter of New York, Paul Bourget found hollow-cheeked, hungry-faced girls of fifteen who looked as old as grandmothers, and who had never eaten meat in their lives. Great political labors were necessary if the American dream was to become a reality.

In about 1913, an article in the *Atlantic Monthly* that described a small Eastern town showed that its classes remained entirely apart. There were the old families, the descendants of the men who had built the venerable stone church at the end of the eighteenth century. The members of this ruling class were not all wealthy, but they all shared in its hereditary standing.

There was only one manufacturer, a man who owned the largest factory in the town, who stood on an equal footing with the old families, and who was a director of the local bank. These patricians operated by means of the middle class, the lawyers and the businessmen who organized the political campaigns and who managed the elections, but who were not asked to "society" entertainments, nor to the dances at the country club. The aristocracy remained Protestant—increasingly Episcopalian —and its ideals, at least those it professed, were still Puritan. The middle classes, for the most part, were Baptist or Methodist. The working classes were completely isolated, and they lived "on the other side of the tracks"; they were nearly all recent immigrants, Italians or Poles, and they were nearly all Catholics. They seemed apathetic and resigned to grinding poverty. The whole structure of the little town called feudal paternalism to mind.

Between 1860 and 1891, the wage earner's standard of living had risen somewhat, but the economic crisis of 1893 depressed wages again, and they fell to about $500 a year. In the clothing industry, some women earned no more than $5 a week. The week's work was six days of ten hours each. Industrial accidents were common, protection inadequate.

The position of the workers grew better between 1900 and 1910. Some five hundred thousand employees worked no more than forty-eight hours a week, and four million, fifty-four hours. Thanks to new industries, such as the manufacture of cars, unemployment declined. But the purchasing power of the wage earners did not rise as fast as the national income (national income around 95 percent; wages a little less than 30 percent). The rich were still too rich, the poor too poor. The rich felt it themselves. In their old age, Carnegie, Pierpont Morgan, and Rockefeller became the benefactors of universities, museums, libraries, and scientific research. After a certain stage, what can one do with a fortune unless one gives it away?

But good works are not equality. The situation was of such a nature that it might have brought about serious disturbances, yet it will be seen that in America, the reforms were the product of a slow revolution that took place in order and freedom. There are many reasons for this choice.

1. *A revolutionary outbreak would have been unavailing in so heterogeneous a country.* A revolution in Paris might well be called a French revolution; but in the United States, where was a revolution to be made? New York was not the whole of America; Washington was no more than a little town full of civil servants; Chicago or San Francisco governed only a limited area, and even that they did not govern thoroughly. The newly arrived immigrants lacked boldness in a still unknown country. The native Americans, who were naturally pragmatic, distrusted European ideologies.

2. *The poor went on doggedly hoping for miraculous success.* And their hopes were kept alive by the prodigious expansion of America, the genuine cases of sudden enrichment, and the "success stories" the sentimental magazines delighted in publishing— and which, in any case, were true.

3. *Local patriotism insisted upon a sanguine outlook.* Every state and every town wanted to attract immigrants. The person who spoke ill of his own place was a traitor to the community. The bitter jealousy between neighboring cities, such as Minneapolis and Saint Paul or Dallas and Fort Worth, called for strict loyalty.

4. *The wage earners hoped to win political power.* The trade unions were gaining greater authority, and organized labor was becoming a force to reckon with.

In a democrary, the majority can peacefully alter the laws and transform the country. This warranted every kind of hope.

III

Furthermore, at that time, peoples' minds were diverted by the great changes in their manner of living. Mass production had brought new techniques within the reach of Americans with small incomes. The gas stove freed women from the dirty work of the coal fire; electricity did away with oil lamps; the telephone came into the home. Sewing machines helped with linen and clothes. Women bore fewer children. With their greater freedom, they demanded their share in public affairs and in amusements. Their very clothes changed. In the nineteenth century, their bodies had been bundled up in several layers of cloth and laced into corsets—the female body had been a mystery to men; but from 1900, although indeed skirts still remained long and trailing, it began to show its shape more freely. Yet customs and manners in the East were still very strict. A girl might not be seen in public with a young man unless she had a chaperone. At the Boston Athenaeum, a library and club, the women left at nightfall, because it would not have been proper to meet a gentleman between the bookshelves in the dusk.

The pace of life was growing faster. The New Yorker ran to jump onto the moving street car; the suburbanites ran to catch the 8:30; the housewives bestirred themselves to get their husbands' breakfasts ready. In 1914, there were over a million and a half cars in the United States, and a half million a year were being produced. For a long while, it had been a common saying that when a farmer made a little money, he bought a piano. Now when he was prosperous, he bought a Ford, which enabled him to carry his produce to the town. Workmen would go to their factories by car. The automobile created more unity among men than it did jealousies.

In this stirring, uneasy life, the young people in the towns hardly lived with their families any more. As soon as the meal was over, they would hurry out to see others of their kind. What could they have done in their parents' home? There was no room. Smaller places, which allowed people to do without servants, were being built now—this was the beginning of the age of flats. The old people regretted the happiness of living with their children and grandchildren; they regretted the days when dinner, which had taken a great while in the preparation, was savored and drawn out in the eating; when a Bible reading was followed by a long, slow talk with friends. Reasonable and just regrets. Life took on a superficial brilliance; manners grew more familiar, witticisms and wisecracks sharper and more pointed; but the mechanical era had produced nothing that could replace warm affection and solid friendship.

Freedom of movement transformed manners and customs. For a long time, Puritanism had repressed the extramarital longings of the flesh by making the satisfaction of them difficult. Where could an amorous pair hide themselves in a small community? But in the twentieth century, the motor car served as a private room; and city life allowed secrecy. Marriage was increasingly thought of as something convenient, not as something sacred. In some states, such as Nevada for example, divorce was easy. Disgruntled spouses went to take up domicile there, and the shaking off of matrimonial bonds became the principal industry of some towns—Reno among them. There had been an attempt at unifying the laws of the various states upon divorce, but this had failed.

Both men and women of the middle classes were greedy for amusements, some amusements, like tennis, golf, and swimming, being active, but many more passive—football matches between the great universities or the army and navy drew great crowds; so did professional baseball games. All through the country, people danced madly, either the forthright, strongly rhythmic dances (ragtime, foxtrot) that called to mind the religious dances of the Negroes, or else the slower, more voluptuous dances like the tango that came from Latin America. The "movies" had made their modest beginnings in little five-cent theaters called nickelodeons. Then real movie theaters opened, showing full-length films with orchestras to accompany them. Film stars came into existence, those gods and goddesses of an industrial mythology who provided countless lonely people with the illusion of love and adventure. Mary Pickford, "America's sweetheart," as they said in those days, charmed all America. Charlie Chaplin personified the humiliated and insulted of this world, the courageous poor man who stands up to the oppressor, masters fate, and goes off in the end, with his huge splayed-out shoes and his invincible stick, toward new battles on the horizon. The fashion, around 1914, was for serial films: at that time, for example, there was Pearl White appearing in *The Perils of Pauline*. The episodic tale, a human need ever since the time of the Greek bards, moved from the newspaper to the screen.

The people's avidity for a rapid succession of images, for syncopated music, for dancing, and cars contained within it a great longing for escape. Economic life, interspersed with those storms that were called crises, seemed, with its alternation of calms and squalls, as changeable and uncertain in its temper as the sea. Years of plenty were followed by years of unemployment and wretchedness, and the men in the street could not understand why. Glaring anomalies outraged common sense. In a country that had led the world in declaring the principle of free education, there were six million illiterates in 1900. Businessmen generous enough to leave their whole fortunes to a foundation would not go so far as to protect their own workers against accidents. In this strange, jerky civilization, there was much that was confusion, chaos, struggle, and yet men kept the beautiful American dream unbroken in their hearts. A great part of the country remained "firmly entrenched in the theory that this is the best of all possible worlds, and getting better by the minute . . . . There was a kindly God in the heavens, whose chief concern was the welfare, happiness, and continuous improvement of mankind though His ways were often inscrutable . . . ." And from this there arose among many a great spiritual conflict that turned to a need for escape and oblivion: among others it aroused a will to correct the faults of their civilization and to turn the dream into a reality.

IV

James Truslow Adams has called the second half of the nineteenth century the Age of the Dinosaurs: and indeed, just as monstrous reptiles, larger than anything that had gone before them or that was to come after, came into existence in Jurassic times, so, in this period, industrial combines of terrifying size multiplied in the United States. In the beginning, the rapid growth of industry had been quite healthy. It was a growth that was explained by obvious causes: the Civil War that in four years had hurried the economy on to a point it would have taken twenty years to reach in ordinary times; the growth of the population and therefore of needs; the building of the transcontinental railways that in its turn called for an immense production of steel. All this was useful, indeed essential, and a day was to come when the whole world would applaud America's industrial power.

But it soon appeared that one of the effects of the increased power of big business was going to be the subjugation of the state. The defeat of the South had delivered Congress into the hands of Northern politicians who were devoted to financial interests. Lands of inestimable value had been made over to the railway magnates; the manufacturers had been allowed protective tariffs that mounted higher and higher. A new class of "captains of industry" had come into existence. These were bold, clever men, with dash, toughness, and a remarkable capacity for work; but many of them also displayed a complete absence of scruples. In a few years, they had taken the control of the political institutions away from the agricultural majority of the country. They did not change the Constitution, but for a while, they did in fact seriously impede representative government.

What did they want? They thought of business, of economic life, as a war, in which the stronger—the man who won—was what counted. To begin with, these captains of industry had aimed at acquiring great wealth; they very soon had more money than they could spend. Nevertheless they carried on for love of the game and for love of power. For them, business was a religion that had its ritual and its theology, its high places and its own jargon. A historian has called them the robber barons and has compared them to the great medieval companies that plundered and despoiled the countryside. It would be more just to liken them to the great feudal lords who, before a central power was set up, saved Europe from anarchy. By their courage and their energy, most of them had rendered immense services; but, being too complacent about themselves and their success, they no longer perceived the immorality in some of their actions.

In 1912, Arnold Bennett visited the immense building of one of the great insurance companies. As he came nearer to the president's office, the splendor increased, the carpets grew thicker, the gilding and the mahogany more brilliant. The office itself, conceived in a spirit of stately prodigality, outdid all expectation. The president, an elderly man with a noble face, had the distant courtesy of a reigning prince. He described his work in founding and building up his firm: "My wife says that for ten years she never saw me."

Bennett asked what his amusements were and what he did with his evenings.

The president seemed taken aback. "Oh," he said carelessly, "I read the literature of insurance." A reply worthy of one of Balzac's heroes.

The great difference between an English and an American businessman, thought Bennett, was that the Englishman was in a hurry to get away from his work, the American to get back to it. For the American, business was not a task but a passion, and that was why he had made modern America. But he thought of this

America only in relation to his business, and that was why he understood neither its needs nor its dangers.

Since the end of the frontier, there was no longer any possibility of pioneering—the pioneer could no longer advance. Some people thought that imperialism would provide a solution and a new frontier; and under McKinley, the country briefly adopted this policy. The United States in 1898 annexed Hawaii, occupied Cuba, compelled Spain to yield Puerto Rico, Guam, and the Philippines. The fair-mindedness of the average American, however, condemned all conquest. The independence of the United States had been proclaimed in the name of the right of nations to dispose of themselves. How could the country reverse its decision? What was the point of trying to push the frontier beyond the boundaries of the country when the population of the United States was increasing so rapidly that any kind of gambling on a rise seemed guaranteed by the growth of human capital? For the new generations, new industries must be created; and thus the splendid forceful driving game could go on. Salvador de Madariaga y Rojo has compared this adolescent America to an immense nursery filled with the most wonderful toys. What kind of gigantic Father Christmas was it who invented skyscrapers? And what was he like, this little boy in Detroit who had the idea of giving all the other boys a real horseless carriage? But in the excitement of the game, the players sometimes forgot the rules.

In an agricultural society made up of small communities like the America of before 1860, a man's moral life is an integral part of his business. If he does wrong, he injures a customer, a neighbor whom he knows. On the other hand, when a giant corporation ruins its shareholders or its rivals, it does so by means of such complicated and anonymous maneuvers that ultimate success is enough to cover up the wrong. "There is nothing like distance for disinfecting dividends." Those who were guilty of these new sins against society for the most part both believed themselves to be, and intended to be, honest gentlemen.

Their deeds were impersonal and within the law. The spirit of the frontier and the laissez-faire tradition of Adam Smith agreed that business lords should not be interfered with; they should be left alone, whatever they did. What crime was there in grouping all the operations of an industry, the manufacture of

16

steel, for example, in one single organization, a trust that would control everything from the iron mines to the finished rail? It was a legal means of avoiding competition and a technical means of organizing the business on sound lines. What wrong did John D. Rockefeller commit in owning oil wells and pipelines and refineries and filling stations? Was it a sin to buy all the railways that served a given region so as to avoid a price war? Presently the country was to reply, "A sin? Not at all. But every monopoly soon becomes a danger to society, and it must be controlled."

Why? First, because there was a danger that the natural resources of the country might all be gathered into the hands of a few men answerable only to themselves. The doctrine of laissez-faire rested upon the assumption of free competition. But what if there were no competitors left? From 1882, Standard Oil's refineries received 90 percent of the oil produced. Secondly, because monopolies favored other monopolies. For example, the railways granted secret rebates to the oil trust, but when it came to carry agricultural produce, they made the farmers pay "all that the traffic will bear." And lastly, because big business had an unhealthy influence upon politics. Many municipalities and even states were found to be corrupted. The Supreme Court of Michigan reached the point of asking whether free government could subsist for long in a country where so small a number of men could own such enormous sums of money.

Toward 1900, the greatest fortunes were not the fruit of the rightful profits of an industry, but of skillful manipulation or market rigging. A holding company or trust would buy two or more companies and merge them, at the same time considerably increasing the number of shares—an operation that Wall Street called watering. Then these shares would be palmed off on the public, but, seeing that the concern was now overcapitalized, the shares would no longer yield anything. The promoters would double and triple their stake, if they did not multiply it ten times over; the banks would receive their commission; the shareholders would find that they were ruined. It was immoral; it was scandalous, but what could be done? It was laid down in the Constitution (the Fifth and Fourteenth Amendments) that the national government should not interfere with private property "without due process of law." Now a corporation, viewed as a

17

legal entity, a corporate body, enjoyed the same immunity as an individual; and this, for want of texts that would effectively protect the public, made the corporations inviolable.

The rapid development of industry called for capital, and during the Civil War powerful banking organizations had been formed. In this field, too, the Dinosaurs first fought and then merged with one another. Two Mastodons, the Morgan Bank and Standard Oil, ruled the market. Pierpont Morgan, a remarkable mathematician and a man with an exceptionally acute mind and a power of quick decision, had financed most of the railways; together with Carnegie, he had formed the United States Steel Corporation, and he was allied to the life insurance companies that disposed of immense quantities of capital. A very small number of men (the Money Trust) shared the places on the boards of directors among themselves, and they managed the savings of the American people, not always wisely.

There were no more conflicting interests. A chosen few, all on Christian-name terms, all grew richer in a body. "They were united by religion," said Bennett, "and it was not, as it would have been in England, golf." Wall Street pushed the price of shares to giddy heights. The American pot boiled merrily. From time to time it boiled over. In 1907, there was a panic that ruined the speculators. At that juncture, Pierpont Morgan and a few others saved the situation; but a country that can only be saved by the intervention of a few bankers is not likely to be saved for long; besides, it does not deserve to be. Public opinion began to react angrily against the methods of high finance. There were good minds that thought it essential to cut through this network of influences, these chains of boards of directors—in short, "to unscramble the eggs."

A government of the people, by the banks, for the Dinosaurs, could not last. No state in history has ever allowed the roads and the rivers to become private monopolies. How then could it be maintained that the railways, those rivers of steel, should escape from all control? The laws made in former times for an agricultural community could not have foreseen gigantic corporations. Technical progress had begotten a new society that needed new laws. In order to govern, a government must be stronger than any combination of private interests, so that its citizens may be equal before its courts. But the United States was a federation, in which the states remained jealously attentive to their rights, and in which the Constitution strictly limited the federal government's powers. To be able to deal with the trusts, it was necessary to find a legal solution that would allow Washington to step in.

The paradoxical excellence of the American Constitution lies in the fact that by shrewd interpretation it can be made to say almost anything one chooses. The Supreme Court bethought itself that the railways formed part of trade between states; this, according to the holy Constitution, was within the province of the federal government. The first movement of resistance was therefore the setting up of the Interstate Commerce Commission that had the power of regulating the rates. In 1890, the Sherman Anti-Trust Act was passed, and this stated that all contracts, all combinations in the form of a trust or otherwise, and all conspiracies to restrain commerce between states or with foreign nations, were illegal. In the beginning, the Sherman Act was but feebly applied by the Supreme Court; later it was to be of great value. By an odd distortion, however, it was first used against the trade unions that were accused of conspiracy against interstate commerce. For the wage earners, too, were uniting.

The unification of the workers was proceeding slowly, partly because they were influenced by the general climate of laissez-faire and partly because of the hostile attitude of the courts; but a far more important reason was that great numbers of them were ignorant, frightened immigrants. In 1886, the American Federation of Labor was born. Like the country itself, it was a federation in which the unions of which it was composed had a great deal of self-government. At first, it left politics entirely to one side, aiming at nothing but practical ends: higher wages, shorter working hours, security of employment, collective contracts, recognition of the unions by the law and the courts. This pragmatic, moderate attitude arose from the fact that the American workingman obstinately hoped that he would be able to make himself a reasonably pleasant situation within a system of free enterprise.

In 1886, Samuel Gompers became president of the American Federation of Labor, and he was reelected every year but one until his death in 1924. Gompers was born in London of Dutch-Jewish parents. When he was thirteen, he emigrated to America, where he worked in a cigar factory. He was straightforward and practical; he would not give up advantages at hand in favor of distant revolutionary aims. He was a thickset, bulky man with an air of authority. Talking to the French politician Edouard Herriot, he said, "I have my own philosophy and my own dreams, but first and foremost I want to increase the workingman's welfare year by year. We do not ask this workingman his political opinions, nor his religious beliefs . . . . The French workers waste their economic force by their political divisions . . . ."

Gompers advanced by short stages, aiming only at results that were easy to attain within a limited period. By these tactics, he gradually won over his long career important successes: the eight-hour day, the Saturday afternoon holiday, restrictions on immigration, and protection for women and children. He certainly upheld the unions in their strikes, and he certainly boycotted the industries that were hostile to trade unionism; but what he wanted above all were immediate, positive results; and these he obtained.

Intelligent employers wanted a rise in the workers' standard of living. In the new industries, new techniques, interchangeable parts, and the use of Taylor's methods of organizing and apportioning jobs allowed a very great and cheap production of goods. Mass production calls for mass consumption. Ford was about to discover a new frontier in the purchasing power of the wage earners, to whom a rejuvented industry offered happiness at bargain rates. In 1913, he instituted the assembly-line system. The car bodies passed slowly along on a belt in front of the workers, each of whom put one part in its place. The reduction in manufacturing cost was almost unbelievable. The basic price of the famous Model T fell from $950 to $360. At the same time, Ford raised the minimum daily wage from $2.40 to $5 and reduced the hours of work from nine to eight. This enraged the less prosperous or less discerning companies. One Indiana newspaper wrote, "Henry Ford thinks that wages ought to be higher and goods cheaper. We entirely agree with him, and we should like to add that summer ought to be cooler and winter hotter." The example of the Ford factory seemed to foretell a time of general prosperity. "The pursuit of happiness," which the Constitution held to be one of man's inalienable rights, was no longer modest and reasonable, as it had been in Franklin's day; it had become feverish and passionate.

Trade was no less changed and concentrated than industry. In the days of the small country communities, the general store supplied the village with everything. Then, with the development of the towns and the parcel post and the coming of cars, the mail-order houses appeared, as well as the chain stores with their many branches.

For their part, the farmers had scarcely profited at all from the country's increasing wealth. Yet agriculture had gone through a revolution quite as far-reaching as the revolution in industry. Vast new areas had been put under cultivation and machines had come into use—factors that had enormously increased production. Family farming, working for the local market, had been succeeded by industrial farming, working for the world market. Then as Europe, Canada, and Australia in their turn set themselves up with machines, production increased beyond consumption and prices fell shockingly. Wheat went down from $1.21 a bushel in 1879 to 61¢ in 1894; cotton from 50¢ a pound to 6¢ in 1893.

But the prices of farm machinery, of barbed wire, and all the products that the farmer had to buy were rising. The railways' tariffs for the farmers were too high, and the banks' interest on the money they had to borrow, exorbitant. The farmer ran into debt, mortgaged his farm, and then, unable to pay when the date came around, lost his land. From this there arose a deep dissatisfaction that showed itself in such movements as the People's party. The farmers called upon the government for loans at a low rate of interest, the nationalization of the railways, a greater volume of currency, and a double standard, based upon silver as well as gold, for any inflation would lighten the burden of their debts. Silver, a more abundant metal than gold, seemed to them the magic substance that would undermine the iniquitous wealth of the towns.

In 1896, William Jennings Bryan, a radical Democrat, had accused the banks of "crucifying mankind upon a cross of gold." At that time, the farms were more revolutionary than the factories. "You come to us and tell us that the great cities are in favor of the gold standard," said Bryan. "We reply that the great cities rest upon our broad and fertile prairies. Burn down your cities and leave our farms, and your cities will spring up again as if by magic; but destroy our farms and the grass will grow in the streets of every city in the country." The farmers roared their applause of the eloquent, naïve orator, arrayed in candid probity and white alpaca.

But politics vary according to a country's economy. From 1900 to 1910, the farmers had a succession of good harvests; the price of corn rose; and the discovery of new gold mines brought about the longed-for inflation. Now that farming was a paying proposition once more, the Middle West returned to its conservatism. In ten years, the gross income of the farms and the price of land went up by 100 percent. The Populist party melted away. This upward swing made the buying of land much harder. The number of small landowners went down; that of tenants rose. In 1914, nearly 40 percent of the land in the Corn Belt was rented. The agricultural problem was still the most disturbing in America, as it was everywhere else in the world. The division of the work among the people was changing fast. Because of machines and artificial manures, a much smaller number of countrymen could feed a much larger number of townsmen. Agriculture occupied a smaller and smaller proportion of the population. A movement from the land to the towns was at once difficult and necessary.

To sum up: no more profound change can be imagined than that which American life had undergone in fifty years. An agricultural society had yielded place to an industrial society. What this had been able to accomplish in half a century was almost miraculous; but the old basic concepts of states' rights and unyielding individualism were no longer suitable to the transformed country. The great body of citizens felt a strong desire for protection. Nevertheless, the Americans still had enough of the pioneer spirit to want the government to limit itself to governing and to leave the organization and command of the economy to private men or to companies. What they required of the state (and in this Gompers was as liberal as Pierpont Morgan) was that it should act as an arbiter, without itself taking over the direction of the economy. "The capitalists' right to unite for a legal object is the same as the workers' right to unite for a legal object. But all these agreements must be made in obedience to laws made for the good of all." This was the goal: it was to be the task of the reforming presidents to reach it—to reach it by many stages.

V

To what degree did the political structure of the United States at the beginning of the twentieth century allow a peaceful revolution? It was one of the most advanced countries, but it was ruled by an eighteenth-century Constitution that still retained all its great standing and that had changed little in its fundamental aspects in the last 120 years. While there had been significant amendments made, particularly right after the Civil War, these could be made only with the greatest difficulty, and the original text, permeated with the culture of Greece and Rome, was thought of as sacred. Everything called Ancient Rome to mind, from words like senator and president to the symbols on the coinage. The needs of America had grown to be quite different from those of the Founding Fathers; but the Founding Fathers had drawn up their Constitution with an ingenious ambiguity. The Nine Sages of the Supreme Court had assumed the right of interpreting it freely, and thanks to them, the flexible Constitution could bend without breaking.

In theory and in fact, the government of the United States remained federal. The nation was not a confederation that would have given all the power to the states; nor yet was it a unitary government, in which all the authority was concentrated in the national capital. The national and the local authorities divided the power between them. The Constitution distinctly specified the central government's powers—all those that were not given to it belonged to the states. No authority whatsoever might infringe the rights of the citizens as they were laid down in the Bill of Rights. The function of the Supreme Court was to see that this did not happen and to declare unconstitutional any law or any decision that violated the nation's charter.

By the middle of the first decade of the new century, owing to the interpretations of the Supreme Court, the powers of the central government in the twentieth century were greater than they had been before. For example, the central government now controlled transport between the states, the price to be paid for this transport, and, because of the "interstate commerce" ruling, every company whose operations were nationwide. The government also had a means of bringing pressure to bear on the states. This arose from the "grants in aid," sums voted by Congress for education or for road making. The states were not forced to accept these sums, since such undertakings were all within the sphere reserved to them; but if they did accept them, then they were obliged to comply with Washington's requirements as to their use.

Two parties, the Democrats and the Republicans, competed for power. But as Emerson said, these were parties made for the occasion, not based upon principle. There were no deep ideological differences between them. The Democrats were fond of calling themselves Jefferson's party, but Jefferson defended the rights of the states, whereas the Democrats of 1913 wanted to strengthen the federal government. There was a progressive wing of the Republican party, just as there was a conservative wing of the Democratic party. This was made up of the Southern Democrats, who would no doubt have been Republicans had it not been for the bitterness that the Civil War had left in the Southern mind. It was supposed that the Republican party, generally speaking, was tolerably well disposed toward big business; yet it was Theodore Roosevelt, a Republican, who was to prove one of the most active reformers. It was he who first broke up and prosecuted a powerful trust (Northern Securities). Pierpont Morgan's comment was, "The President has not behaved like a gentleman." As for the purely ideological parties, such as populism or socialism in the European manner, they never won more than nine hundred thousand votes in the presidential elections. America distrusts ideologies.

Reforms, in fact, are not accomplished in the United States by the triumph of one party over another, but by the formation of groups representing given interests (farmers, Catholics, Jews, planters, Negroes, ex-servicemen, miners) that take no notice of the division between parties. In a country made up of so many races, religions, cultures, and regions, it is essential to find a way in which groups divided by a thousand antagonisms can live, work, and deliberate together. This can only be arrived at by compromise. Everyone must accept the rules of the game, so that the country may be governed. The pieces in this game, in Washington, are not the parties but the groups, whose formation is insured by the lobbies—the intermediaries between the interests and the lawmakers.

Then what is the function of these two curious parties? In Europe, parties are there to divide men of differing political ideas into clearly defined bodies; in America, they are there to gather together, somehow or other, enough voters to win an election. It is because of the fluid nature of the ·parties and because of the very large numbers of uncommitted voters that the president can represent all the classes of the nation. He is directly elected by the people, and an Englishman would say that he was at the same time king and prime minister; a Frenchman would say that he owed his position to a plebiscite, like a Bonaparte. For the whole length of his term of office, he has "the divine right to govern wrong," even if his party is beaten in the elections and is in a minority in Congress. But he too must obey the rules of the game; for the American system includes a masterly balance of powers. The president has the right of veto; Congress holds the purse strings and may overrule the president's veto by a two-thirds majority; the consent of the Senate is necessary for the approval of treaties and for nominations to important posts; and the Supreme Court is the most powerful of restraints, seeing that there is no appeal from its judgments.

The complexity of this system of checks and balances is owing to the Americans' horror of all absolute authority: this is one of their essential characteristics. The nation was born from a revolt against the authority of the king of England. The states only accepted the federal government with marked dislike. The frontier kept alive a passionate love of equality. Very deeply rooted in the American consciousness is the idea that the authority of one man over another is a hateful thing, that it is praiseworthy to throw it off, and that one is called upon to help the weak who refuse to obey a tyrant. Men who have great power are obliged to excuse themselves by a display of popular manners. "They must act as one of the boys, glad-handed, extrovert, mindful of first names, seeing their subordinates in their shirtsleeves." It was John D. Rockefeller's stiff reserve, rather than his huge fortune, that caused him to be disliked by the American people, until a skillful public relations man put the matter right.

The president is the political head of the nation. He incarnates the people of the United States. "Let him win the admiration and the confidence of the country," said Woodrow Wilson, "and no other power can stand against him, no combination of powers can dominate him. If he interprets the nation's thought well, and stands up for it boldly, he is irresistible." As soon as he is elected, he should be respected by everybody, even by those who the day before were his opponents. He alone may say, "We, the people of the United States. . . ." And yet it happens that after some struggles the bitterness of defeat is so great that the president remains the object of lasting hatred.

As for the senators, they are in Washington what the cardinals are in Rome. As each state in the Union has but two senators, and as some great states have a larger population than some European countries, a senator has something of the appearance of an ambassador, speaking to the White House as equal to equal. "American senators," says the English writer Denis Brogan, "have the temperaments of prima donnas." They are particularly jealous of their right of approving treaties. In 1913, an amendment to the Constitution laid down that they should thenceforward be elected by direct suffrage instead of being chosen by the legislatures of their states. The intention of this measure was to keep big business or its nominees out of the Senate. *The history of the United States is a continual progress toward a greater participation of the people in the government.* For a long time the candidates had been chosen by the local "machines," or party committees, ruled by bosses, professional mercenary politicians. The "ticket," a list of the candidates for all the places, was put together by the professionals. The electors accepted this because many of them (new-fledged Americans) needed the machine, which helped and advised them, and because they did not know the candidates. About ten years earlier, Senator La Follette instigated direct primary elections in Wisconsin—elections in which the electors of each party themselves chose the party's candidates. After this, there were two successive elections, the one taking place within the party, while the other concerned the whole body of the electorate. The method, in varying forms, was gradually adopted by almost all the states in the Union. This weakened the power of the machine and consequently that of the vested interests and pressure groups. Events were to prove that the American people had both the power and the desire to choose a reforming president and to give him the means of governing.

VI

A revolution is a state of mind. It is ideas in motion that bring about the movement of crowds. The far-reaching American revolution of the twentieth century was above all the work of the middle classes. The mass of the people admired strength and did not expect businessmen or politicians to conform to the moral code of a Sunday school. The workers themselves did not hesitate to use violence against those who would not join their unions: iron girders fell upon nonunion men with remarkable frequency. But lawyers, teachers, journalists, and men in the upper reaches of business and management had learned a great deal in the last fifty years. Until 1860, the most usual kind of philosophy in the United States had been transcendentalism—the Utopian-romanticism of Frenchmen of 1848 mixed with German mysticism. It resembled a religion, a vague, easygoing, secular religion. "Emerson preached the loftiest idealism," writes Van Wyck Brooks, "but he never prevented a single one of his readers from devoting himself, as soon as the book was closed, to the swelling of his bank account." In short, think rightly, act rightly if you can, but let things go on, even if they go on badly.

This optimism was too frail to stand up against the furious blasts that sent whirlwinds of pioneers from one ocean to the other, often disappointed, between the years 1850 and 1890, and it was followed by a wave of pessimism. Darwin, whose ideas reached America rather late, taught that life was a struggle in which natural selection would sternly insure the survival of the fittest. His theories upon the origin of species shocked religious people; but the spectacle of the ferocious battles among the Dinosaurs gave strength to his teaching. The novelists seized upon it. Taking their admired Zola as an example, the American naturalists wrote "a pessimistic epic of human animalism." Upton Sinclair, Jack London, Frank Norris, Theodore Dreiser, who believed themselves to be realists and who in fact were romantics, described a dark and savage world. A journalist named Ida Tarbell brought out a severe account of Standard Oil. The public displayed a lively appetite for attacks of this kind. Many writers hurried to take advantage of the new, rich vein; and some of them wrote with neither discrimination nor measure.

One day, in a fit of anger, President Roosevelt called them the muckrakers. Roosevelt struggled against abuses: he did not like to have them exaggerated. But public opinion was behind the muckrakers. Their novels ran to editions of three and even five hundred thousand copies, and this was something new. Some of the popular magazines with huge circulations owed their success to muckraking; others, on the contrary, to sentimentality. Cinderella and Jeremiah fought for the public's favor. The newspapers too were now directed at the masses. Joseph Pulitzer made the *New York World* into a modern and progressive paper; William Randolph Hearst and Scripps built up chains of newspapers that covered the whole country. The great hosts of new readers had been provided partly by the increase in the population and partly by the progress of education.

For the native-born, as well as for the immigrant Americans, the greatest hope lay in their children. They wanted them to be educated and happy—educated and therefore happy. For the recently naturalized American, the child was a little god. The father spoke poor English or even none, and often he remained attached to the ways of his old country. The children, brought up in America, soon outstripped the parents. Here the father was not, as he was elsewhere, the guide and the model. The schoolmistress had much more influence. Foreigners visiting America were very much struck by the assured and confident air of the schoolchildren and the students as they came out of their classes. This was a country in which youth was king. The apparent disorder of the teaching that was provided for it, however, astonished a European. There was no controlling ministry of education at Washington and no common curriculum. The states retained the direction of the elementary schools and the high schools. Many of them had set up state universities. But besides these, there were also the universities founded by the churches or by private benefactors that were administered by trustees who chose the university's president themselves—a powerful figure, master in his own house. Harvard, Yale, Princeton, and several other colleges owned great wealth; they received donations and legacies, and they were subject to no authority other than that of the board of trustees. To a Frenchman, used to finding the same courses, the same examinations, and almost the same classes at the same hour of the day throughout his own country, all this variety was quite amazing.

In the nineteenth century, the European tradition had imposed a classical education, the humanities, upon America. Then changing needs had changed the curriculum. So long as most of the students had intended to become lawyers, doctors, teachers, or clergymen, classics had been suitable. But an expanding America called for engineers and agriculturists. Senator Morrill, a farmer from Vermont, brought in a law while he was a representative that set aside important sums of money for each state, raised by the sale of disposable land and devoted to the teaching "of agriculture, the mechanical arts, the related sciences, and the English language." These agricultural colleges, called by the students cow colleges, then came into being. Many colleges did no more than add a vague course in agriculture to their curriculum, so as to profit by the money; but this law also brought into existence some of the best technical schools in the world, such as the Massachusetts Institute of Technology. Some traditional subjects, particularly the dead languages, were neglected in the new colleges.

By the turn of the century, the official attitude toward education had come to approve of these innovations. "The aim of the school," said John Dewey, "is to prepare the pupil for real life." Manual work, handicrafts, and civic education by the use of freedom and organized games seemed as important as booklearning. "The school was a place where the child should learn life by living life." In the rural America of the early days, family and church had seen to moral training: in the overcrowded towns, this task became the responsibility of the school. More and more the American people came to believe that the hope of democracy lay in a vast system of free schools and in further education for the adults. Public libraries increased in number. The Chautauqua Alliance, a lecture society, brought the great speakers of the day to provincial audiences. Now that they had reached freedom, the great hosts of immigrants displayed a touching enthusiasm for culture. They wanted to know everything, and they had an artless faith in the experts.

The "new education" had its good aspects. It did develop a sense of responsibility in the child, and it set up a closer, more friendly relationship between teacher and pupil. Perhaps it left too much freedom of choice, however. It is an excellent thing to learn carpentry, dancing, and cookery; but the strict training of the mind by the old disciplines had produced great men. The new universities were too unequal. Some were as good as Europe's best; others were of the level of the better kind of secondary school in the Old World. The multimillionaires who were the benefactors of these institutions were often more interested in the neo-Gothic buildings and in the teams of professional athletes than they were in the work of the mind. Professors, scholars, and philosophers did not possess, in the eyes of the ruling class, the standing that they had at that time in Europe.

The education of women was an undeniable advance. In Colonial times, they had scarcely been taught as much as reading and writing and the household arts. Franklin advised that they should be shown how to use figures, "in case of widowhood." In 1837, a Miss Lyon opened a college for women, Mount Holyoke Seminary. "Educate the women," said Miss Lyon, "and the men will be educated." In 1865, the excellent women's college, Vassar, endowed by an exceedingly rich brewer, opened. As early as 1833, Oberlin College in Ohio, named after an Alsatian clergyman, had become the first college in the world to teach men and women together. By about 1914, all the Western universities were open to women. To some degree the East still remained faithful to the segregation of the sexes. There were some most distinguished women's colleges, but the old universities remained exclusively male. In fact, some young women were culturally well ahead of the young men. The American man, overwhelmed with work and business, made the dollars; his wife, having more time, became a founder or a member of literary groups, art clubs, and music clubs.

Before the First World War, starting back in Theodore Roosevelt's administration, the young men and women were filled with enthusiasm for an immense, positive, and constructive reform of the country. Toward 1912, the young people believed in the New Freedom that Woodrow Wilson, the Democratic candidate for the presidency, was preaching; and they no longer supported the muckrakers, whose attitude, after all, was merely negative; they believed in the new poetry, the new painting. These were happy years in which everything seemed possible. A "little renaissance" began in Chicago and then in New York; an eager group made Greenwich Village into an American Montmartre. "Little theaters" put on Eugene O'Neill's first plays. New magazines published Gertrude Stein; new galleries showed Matisse and Cézanne. The American public discovered D. H. Lawrence and Willa Cather, Chekhov, and Dostoevski. The great stores brought young postimpressionists from Paris to design their placards. New skyscrapers, freed from traditional ornament, rose into the air of the great cities. The world was filled with the intoxication of youth and of creation. In their certainty of making society new and young again, people escaped from the romantic-naturalistic revolt.

The religions too were in the movement. They were not losing ground, but rather gaining it. The registered members of churches and religious bodies in America numbered around thirty-eight and a half million in 1911, as against twenty-one and a half million in 1890. This was a remarkable phenomenon, when one reflects that the country was emptying into the towns, that Sunday was becoming a day for amusements, and lastly that the conflict between the theory of evolution and the Biblical account of the creation appeared to be insoluble. The underlying reasons for the expansion of the churches were, for the Catholic church, the flood of Irish, Italian, and Polish immigrants; for the Protestant churches, the emphasis that was set upon social Christianity. The Methodists, Presbyterians, and Baptists were very closely associated with the reforming intellectuals. In Baltimore, Cardinal Gibbons protected the trade unions. New sects, the Theosophists, the Christian Scientists, found many people to join them. The number of practicing Jews registered at the synagogues exceeded a million. Although the churches were separated from the state, they nevertheless had a very great influence upon public opinion. They attacked drink, prostitution, the exploitation of women and children as workers, and speculation. A positive crusade was launched against those twin plagues, privilege and poverty, by the women, the intellectuals, and the young people.

But there was one exception: the South. The South, since the Civil War, had always been too poor to organize the education of its people, white or black, and it scarcely shared at all in the country's great expectations. This was above all a rural poverty. A few prosperous cities had risen up around the mines or the oil wells, but those who chiefly profited from their industries were the Northern capitalists who had been attracted by the low wages of the South. In some of the totally ruined Southern states, ignorance brought about the election of "demagogues and buffoons" who shocked Washington. The South had retained an undying sense of distress from its appalling misfortunes in the past. There was fear of the Yankees and fear of the Negroes; and from this there arose, among the whites, those secret societies like the Ku Klux Klan. The descendants of the plantation-owners still longed for the romantic, chivalrous days that had gone. The men were honorable, brave, courteous; the women, beautiful and incomparably charming. They were all firmly convinced that *their* blacks were better treated than those in the North. But the Negroes, who were taught the egalitarian doctrine of the Bill of Rights, could not fail to be humiliated by the segregation to which they were in fact subjected, in spite of the nation's laws. The whole condition of the South set very difficult problems that only time, necessity, and perhaps generosity might one day solve.

VII

On March 4, 1913, Woodrow Wilson was inaugurated as president of the United States at Washington. The weather was fine. He appeared on the rostrum set up by the Capitol together with William H. Taft, the outgoing president. Taft was a very big, fair man, friendly and calm, and he had an infectious laugh that shook him "like a bowl of jelly." His friends called him Big Bill, and they loved him; but after they made him president of the United States in 1909, they found to their distress that he was primarily a clubman, in no way made to govern a democracy in a time of great changes, although they were peaceful. His presidency, coming after that of the energetic Theodore Roosevelt, had disappointed the masses.

Wilson's face looked stern. The aggressive jaw and the bony countenance spoke of an unbending determination. The blue-gray eyes behind the pince-nez could quickly grow threatening. Who was Wilson? He was a professor, and it was barely two years since he had first entered politics. He had been born in 1856, the son of a Southern Presbyterian minister of Scottish descent, and he had taught political science, constitutional law, and history. In the nineteenth century, it would have been unthinkable to choose such a man for the presidency—the America of the pioneers had little time for professors. But in 1912, a man who had no connections with the world of big business was reassuring, particularly as he was also an expert.

With his distinguished manners, his beautiful speaking voice, and the precision of his language, he had been an immediate success at Princeton. In 1902, he was chosen as president of the university by trustees who did not know him well. They had no idea how independent and stubborn they would find him. In the United States, the president of an important university wields great moral authority. Wilson strengthened his by making himself the champion of democracy in the university as opposed to the aristocracy of certain overexclusive undergraduate clubs. The trustees rose up against him; the liberal professors defended him. Wilson's character made any kind of argument very difficult. He was extremely sure of himself, proud of the clearness of his mind, and impatient of the least contradiction. People were astonished by his violence that could go to the pitch of grossness. He liked saying, "A Yankee always thinks he is right; a Scotsman *knows* he is right." Once, in a fit of temper at a friend's house, he actually smashed some vases. The next day he apologized; but, where friendship was concerned, he insisted upon nothing less than unconditional devotion. He therefore had few friends among his colleagues. He was very fond of reading his favorite poetry to women: they understood him; they admired him; and they did not argue. His conversation, sparkling with anecdote, was particularly brilliant for women, above all if they were attractive.

The rumor of a battle for democracy waged by the president of one of the most aristocratic of the old universities had reached the general public, and it earned Wilson a wide popularity. In 1910, the Democratic machine in New Jersey offered him the nomination for the post of governor. Happy to leave Princeton, where he had got himself into an impossible situation, not only over the clubs but also over the issue of establishing a graduate school that was not separated from the rest of the university, he accepted. As governor, he astonished and shocked the very men who had caused him to be elected. He turned out to be a remarkable politician and a most unserviceable servant of the machine. With the backing of public opinion, he defied the bosses. He paid them no further attention but went over their heads and spoke directly to the people, adopting the evangelical rather than the political attitude that he was to retain for the rest of his life. In order to understand Wilson, one must remember that he was a Presbyterian, that he believed himself to be inspired by God, and also that like his father, he had never been rich. He was not interested in the great men of the business world, nor did he respect them.

A gentleman from Texas, Colonel Edward M. House, a slight, fragile, intelligent, mysterious, affable man, undertook to make a president of the United States out of Wilson. Their friendship ripened during the presidential campaign of 1912. The two men were made for each other—a sympathy had sprung up at their very first meeting. House's soothing, bland manner and the fact that he was a perfect listener melted the distrust and coldness that surrounded Wilson like an armor. House's mental constitution and his want of physical strength made it impossible for him to act except by means of another man. "I was like a disembodied spirit seeking corporeal form," he says. In Wilson, he had found this form. Wilson, for his part, saw in House the rarest and most valuable thing in the world, an utterly dependable and totally disinterested man. House was the link between Wilson, a reticent, difficult, touchy man, and the outside world.

Bryan, who had great influence with the left wing of the party and who knew that he himself had no chance of election, swung to Wilson, who finally emerged as the Democratic candidate for the presidency.

At the time of the 1912 elections, Taft represented the conservative wing of the Republican party. The impetuous Colonel Theodore Roosevelt had created a new party from the progressive wing, and this divided the Republicans into two. "Roosevelt's tone was that of a fighting parson; Wilson already showed some glint of the spiritual quality of Lincoln. Roosevelt, with Biblical imagery and voice like a shrilling fife, stirred men to wrath, to combat, and to antique virtue; Wilson, serene and confident, lifted men out of themselves by phrases that sang in their hearts, to a vision of a better world. It was the Old Testament against the New, and the New won."

Wilson's was an upright campaign. He told his old friends in the South that having become a radical who meant to reform right down to the roots, he thought it but honest to warn them of it. But he promised that his methods would be conservative: democracy without demagogy.

Big Bill Taft, who had been chosen by the Republican convention and who very much wanted a second term, did not receive even a third of the votes. America firmly turned its back on the Old Guard. The Dinosaurs for the first time in many decades had lost the ability to make a president. Hope and power changed sides. The professor went to the White House. "What is he going to do there?" asked the politicians uneasily. The answer was simple: he was going to teach. His academic tone and his austerity would not allow him to enter into anything like familiar relations with the senators and journalists of Washington. "He loved humanity, but he could not stand men." It has been said that he had the temperament of a theologian; what appeared was above all the temperament of a moralist. In his view, the only basic distinction was that between right and wrong, and he, more fortunate in this than many men, always knew which was the right. He had said to one of his colleagues at Princeton, "I am sorry for those who disagree with me." And when he was asked why, he replied, "Because I know that they are wrong." Presently some men were to form the opinion that "since he had become Caesar, he had a tendency to believe himself to be God."

To pay for the move and to buy dresses for his wife Ellen and their daughters, Wilson had, for the first time in his life, to raise a large sum. "This citizen, who had been accustomed to dress carelessly and to polish his own shoes and who had never owned any vehicle grander than a bicycle was unchanged beneath his tall hat and his immaculate clothes when he stepped into the two-horse victoria that was to take him to his new home." Yet his family noticed his high spirits, the spring in his movements, and the gleam in his blue-gray eyes. His face seemed strengthened, more finely chiseled. A friend said, "God made him ugly, but Woodrow has made himself handsome."

On that March 4, a cheerful sun shone through the clouds above the stands. Fifty thousand spectators acclaimed the new president. Bryan, whom Wilson had, after some hesitation, appointed secretary of state, was also very much applauded. He was a people's politician, a supporter of popular rights, and he was happy in the thought that although he had not been able to reach the presidency, at least he was going to work with a man who was better qualified than himself to bring about the triumph of the policy they both believed in. The Chief Justice gave Woodrow Wilson a Bible; he took the oath and kissed the Holy Book. Then, observing that the police had made a cordon rather far from the rostrum, he said, "Let the people come forward"— words that seemed to be symbolic and that, in his mind, were so indeed. When this had been done, he addressed them without any party spirit, speaking about the duties of the citizens as much as their rights.

He extolled the strength of America and her prosperity, but he reminded them that wrong was still intermingled with right and that it was the duty of every man "to cleanse, to reconsider, to restore, to correct the evil without impairing the good. . . . The Nation has been deeply stirred, stirred by a solemn passion, by the knowledge of wrong, of ideals lost, of government too often debauched and made an instrument of evil. . . . This is not a day of triumph; it is a day of dedication. Here muster, not merely the forces of party, but the forces of humanity. Men's hearts wait upon us; men's lives hang in the balance; men's hopes call upon us to say what we will do. Who shall live up to the great trust? Who dares fail to try? I summon all honest men, all patriotic, all forward-looking men, to my side. God helping me, I will not fail them, if they will but counsel and sustain me!"

This was not the sublime voice of Abraham Lincoln, but the sentiments were lofty and the tone serious. The nation was pleased with the professor. Together they were going to try to build up a new America.

PART TWO

Wilson, the New Freedom, and the First World War

I. *Wilson, the reformer, lowers customs duties, reorganizes the banking system, and deals severely with misdeeds of the trusts.*

II. *Wilson and Bryan attempt a "moral" foreign policy. The facts do not fit it. Difficulties in Latin America.*

III. *Colonel House, Wilson's éminence grise, tries to prevent a European war. It breaks out in August, 1914. Wilson, though in favor of the Allies, hopes to remain neutral, but submarine warfare forces him to declare war on Germany in 1917.*

IV. *America, at first taken aback, soon gathers herself together in a huge effort of production.*

V. *America brings together a great army and has an important share in the victory. Wilson wishes for a peace of reconciliation and a League of Nations.*

VI. *America's position in the world completely changed by the war.*

MEN make plans; events turn the plans upside-down and sometimes even the very principles upon which they are based. Wilson most earnestly desired that his presidency should be a period of reform and peace. It began according to his wishes. Then there burst out a war in which, against his will, he was obliged to engage his country—a war that brought about so great a revolution in American manners and customs that the boldest prophet would not have presumed to foretell it. Many blamed Wilson for this war and for the peace that followed it. The truth was not so simple. He had tried to direct the world toward wisdom, order, and moderation. But what is one man in the face of the monstrous forces that had been let loose?

I

Woodrow Wilson's virtues were his honesty (from which he occasionally lapsed, however), his steadfastness, his devotion to an ideal that, though at first abstract, was to become more concrete under the test of actions. His weaknesses were an intellectual arrogance that rendered him impervious to the opinions of those he did not like and a violence that was all the more dangerous in that he vainly tried to hold it in. "Sometimes," he said, "I feel like the fire in a far from extinct volcano; and if it does not look as though the lava were about to overflow, that is because you are not high enough to see down into the crater where it is boiling."

He had been wrong in choosing Bryan as secretary of state, for although he owed him the presidency, Bryan was a muddled thinker and dangerously enthusiastic. Disraeli had once said that enthusiasm was the least desirable of qualities in an archbishop of Canterbury: it seems no less perilous in an American secretary of state. Bryan was strongly in favor of far-reaching social reforms, and upon this point Wilson and he were in agreement. But although the Secretary of State, a lyrical demagogue, was capable of stirring the American farmers when he spoke to them about the country's home affairs, he was largely ignorant of the foreign affairs that were now his responsibility. He believed that it was possible to maintain peace throughout the world by distributing peaceable tracts to the warlike nations. This was a dangerous degree of naïveté. At first, Wilson defended his secretary of state. He acknowledged the influence that this great sentimental child had over the crowds. However, he overwhelmed Bryan with his encyclopedic intelligence and very soon came to judge him incapable of holding such a post in such difficult times.

Colonel House was much nearer Wilson's heart and mind; and the friendship of these two men was to take on a historic importance. Had Wilson been deprived of House when he was at the White House, he would have been cut off from communication with the outside world. His eloquence moved assemblies; his reserve repulsed private men. Bryan chose to ignore facts that ran counter to his notions; House, in forming his views, took account of "things as they are." Presently everybody applied to him. That was the way to reach the President and by the most favorable side. The businessmen found House a reformer quite as determined as Wilson, but one who understood them better. To whomever he was speaking, the little colonel seemed to radiate warmth and affection. "Even when he was cutting your throat, he was still your closest friend." This supple intelligence made relationships easier; but it also gave rise to misunderstandings when the other party confused understanding with acquiescence.

The aim of the new Administration was at once clearly defined: it was to free the great body of the people from the excessive hold of big business and to free the individual from tyranny in all its forms. In order to accomplish this, Wilson, who had formerly been a conservative in the Southern manner, surrounded himself with ardent reformers. To act quickly and to overcome resistance, he decided from the beginning to direct the work of Congress himself. This was a great innovation. He had always taught that the president was to be the nation's political head. "Let him once win the admiration and confidence of the country, and no other single force can withstand him, no combination of forces will easily overthrow him. His office is anything he has the sagacity and force to make it." When, on April 6, 1913, he announced that he personally would read his message in session, a thing that no president since Jefferson had done, some senators raised cries of virtuous indignation. One regretted that this speech from the throne should be so tasteless as to recall the ceremonies of the British monarchy, from which America had freed herself by the War of Independence. The objection was absurd. The speech of a sovereign who is answerable to no one is merely a traditional rite; the speech of a president of the United States is a positive political action.

When he entered the Capitol, Wilson was aware of an atmosphere of tension and reserve. He was himself somewhat pale and disturbed, and he spoke for no more than ten minutes. He said (as quoted in *The Outlook,* April 19, 1913, p. 845), "I am very glad to have this opportunity to address the two Houses directly and to verify for myself the impression that the President of the United States is a person, and not a mere department of the Government . . . that he is a human being trying to cooperate with other human beings in a common service." Applause broke out when he had finished, and as he left the Capitol with his wife, he was laughing with pleasure at his success.

From his first days in office, therefore, Wilson strengthened the presidential power. It was a power that remained democratic and subject to the approbation of the legislature, but the President acted both as prime minister and as the head of his party. He called the leaders of the Democrats to his house and with them he arranged a program for the work of Congress—in short, he united the legislative and the executive powers in his own person. He answered critics by saying, "You forget that I have been appointed by the people to fill this office and to be the official head of the nation." He succeeded in compelling the acceptance of this unwonted attitude because he was far superior to the majority of congressmen both in mental power and in eloquence. They came to see him, determined not to allow themselves to be dominated; they came out convinced that what he did was itself dictated by the pressure of facts and that there was no alternative course of action. They submitted.

The essence of the New Freedom, according to Wilson, lay in taking the control of the economy out of the hands of a minority, thus giving every citizen a fair opportunity. As early as his first message, he asked for the reduction of the customs duties, "which cuts us off," he said, "from the trade of the world, violates the principles of just taxation, and makes the government a tool at the service of private interests." He did not go as far as free trade, but he wanted to force the American manufacturers to take the competition of the Europeans into account. The foreign products that competed with those manufactured by the trusts, such as steel and agricultural machinery, as well as most raw materials, were to be entirely free of duty. For other goods, the duty would be reduced on an average to 24–26 percent. The price of food and clothing, which had hitherto been kept at an artificial level, would thus be brought down.

These were wise measures, but, as one might have supposed, as soon as the new tariff was announced, a swarm of lobbyists descended upon Washington. The Senate was besieged by telegrams, letters, and articles. Some senators appeared to be impressed. Wilson set up an inquiry to oblige the opposing members to disclose the effects that the new law would have upon their investments and their private means. "We have the proof," he said, "that money without limit is being spent to support this lobby." A relentless publicity against the invisible government of Washington caused opposition to vanish as if by a miracle. Wilson turned himself into a lobbyist for the general cause, and the tariff was passed. Even his opponents admired the vigor of his political strategy.

In order to make good the deficit that this reduction caused, a federal income tax, made legal by the ratification of the Sixteenth Amendment, February 25, 1913, was levied. During 1913, when Wilson had taken office, the Underwood-Simmons Tariff Bill had been passed. As part of this bill, the government was authorized to raise a uniform tax throughout the country of from 1 percent to 6 percent on incomes of more than $4,000 ($3,000 for bachelors) without having to share the amount between the states of the Union in proportion to their population. This was a step the President took, small, but of the very highest importance, toward a larger federal budget and toward that redistribution of wealth that liberal minds so rightly thought essential.

The other field in which immediate action was necessary was that of banking. The old system, which was both out of date and inefficient, had been hurriedly set up in 1863 for the financing of the Civil War. Any group of five men who put up a certain capital sum and subscribed to Treasury bonds were then allowed to found a bank. The banks issued notes against the bonds deposited in Washington, and these notes, together with gold and silver certificates and a small amount of coin, made up the monetary fund.

From this there arose a paradoxical situation. The more the country grew and the more business expanded, the more notes in circulation there should have been. But prosperity had allowed the government to redeem the Civil War bonds; and the fewer the bonds, the fewer the notes, since the notes were backed by the bonds. Thus, at a time when more money was needed, it was disappearing—hence, deflation, dear money, fall in the price of agricultural products, and justifiable fury on the part of the farmers. Furthermore, the banks were almost entirely without connections among themselves. If one of them had a sudden shortage of liquid money, the banks in the neighboring regions could not come to its help. It had to go to the Money Trust of Wall Street, the most excessive of all monopolies. An inquiry by a Congressional committee showed that the country's entire credit system was in the hands of a very small group of men: J. P. Morgan and Company, the First National Bank, the National City Bank, Kuhn Loeb and Company, and a few others. Mr. George Baker, of the First National Bank, admitted to the committee that this was too great a concentration.

Question: Do you think that it would be dangerous to go farther?

Answer: I think it has gone far enough. In good hands, it would do no harm. If it fell into bad hands, that would be very bad.

Question: In bad hands it would ruin the country?

Answer: Yes; but I do not think that it could fall into bad hands.

Question: So that safety, if you feel that there is any safety in such a situation, in fact rests upon the human element?

Answer: To a large extent.

Question: Do you think that for a great country that is a comfortable situation?

Answer: Not entirely.

Two solutions for getting out of this "not entirely comfortable situation" were suggested to Wilson. The conservatives wanted a central bank, controlled by the great bankers; the progressives, led by Bryan, required the control of the circulation of money to belong to the state, that is, to the federal government—a daring idea in a pioneers' country made up of states jealous of their independence. On the advice of Brandeis, House, and Senator Carter Glass, Wilson decided that money should thenceforward be controlled by a Federal Reserve Board, appointed by the president. The country would be divided into twelve regions, each of which would have its Federal Reserve Bank. The federal prejudice was so strong that there was still something shocking about the idea of a central bank. Most of the country's banks were to affiliate themselves to this system and subscribe part of the capital. In exchange, the Federal Reserve Bank would rediscount their commercial bills that, together with the gold reserves, would serve as guarantee for the bank notes. The bankers automatically protested. Wilson clenched his jaws and held on. He won, and his law was passed, and the Federal Reserve system was established in 1913.

It has been said that the three advantages of the system all began with R—reservoir, rediscount, and regularization: reservoir, because the Federal Reserve Bank would act as a pool into which each of the affiliated banks might dip; rediscount of paper, so that the more business increased, the more notes the central bank, having commercial bills as guarantee, could issue, which would make the currency elastic; regularization, because the Federal Reserve system would try to stave off booms and prevent financial panics by changing discount rates. In times of excessive rise, it would be possible to curb lending; in times of depression, to encourage it. It was the most important banking reform that had ever been made in the United States.

There remained the question of the trusts. During his presidential campaign, Wilson had said again and again that all private monopoly was indefensible and intolerable. Now the Sherman Act had not put an end to the monopolies. Far from it. Wilson, who had kept Congress in session 260 days to deal with the questions of the tariff and the banks, recalled it after no more than a month's vacation to attend to the trusts. He hurried the reforms along—the only way of carrying them through. A new law, the Clayton Anti-Trust Act (1914) strengthened the Sherman Act that had been a "monster without any teeth." The Clayton Act forbade all agreements on prices that would tend to create a monopoly or to lessen competition. It no longer allowed manufacturers to oblige retailers to sell at a given fixed price or for anyone to belong to several boards of directors in concerns with a capital of more than a million dollars. The directors of the companies became personally responsible for breaches of the law.

The trade unions were exempted from these measures, and the courts were forbidden to issue an injunction ordering the workers to stop a strike "unless it should be necessary to prevent irreparable damage." Gompers, too optimistically as it turned out, called this law "labor's Bill of Rights." In business circles, it was received with bitter resentment. This professor had filled businessmen with deep mistrust at the time of the presidential campaign; now they sadly realized that the mistrust had been justified. But they had good lawyers, and they hoped to get around this law as they had got around the others before it. More than one senator thought, as they did, that the new law did not even "have teeth enough to chew pap." The Federal Trade Commission was established in the same years as a watchdog over business conduct.

All in all, the professor had not done badly in this first stage of his administration. He, a Democrat, had carried on the reforming work begun by the Republican Theodore Roosevelt, and in doing so, he had proved that the progressive spirit was not bound by the limitations of party. The country's advance toward the American dream was going on. The Dinosaurs were now reduced to the defensive. The President had shown himself a skillful politician and an effective man of action. He had not declared war on capital, but he did mean to rectify abuses. The masses and the liberals were with him. Since the Civil War, the essential aims of the nation had seemed to be financial success, the acquisition of wealth, and the production of material objects. Wilson, like those who had elected him, wanted something else. To him, as a historian, the American ideal was above all something that concerned men's hearts, individual independence, and the brotherliness of the frontier. He liked to think of himself as a pioneer of freedom, using his ax to cut down the trees that were choking their neighbors, and rooting out evil practices. Between 1901 and 1917, the America of laissez-faire had given way to a new country, the America of Teddy Roosevelt and of Wilson.

All things being considered, Wilson had guided the country intelligently and courageously. He had been eighteen months in power, and looking at the things he had done, he saw that they were good. Then, while he was looking, the war in Europe came to interrupt all that he felt still remained to be accomplished.

II

From the country's earliest days, the foreign policy of the United States had been contained in the single word "neutrality." George Washington, and Jefferson after him, had left the nation this advice: "It is our true policy to steer clear of permanent alliances with any portion of the foreign world." Jefferson warned on colonization in the Western Hemisphere. Nevertheless, isolationism had not in fact been even possible until after 1815. During the French Revolution and the Napoleonic wars, the United States had several times been obliged to take hostile measures, now against one side, now against the other, to protect American trade. The only treaty of alliance the United States had ever signed was that of 1778 with France, and the Americans were very much relieved when Bonaparte agreed to annul it in 1800.

After 1815, isolationism became nearly complete except for some isolated instances, such as Commodore Perry's opening up of Japan. The United States, turned toward the moving western frontier and wholly taken up with the problems of their own growth, lost all interest in Europe. The Monroe Doctrine repeated Jefferson's warning to the European powers that the American continents were not to be considered as subjects for future colonization. In fact, the United States could not at that time have upheld the Monroe Doctrine without the backing of the British fleet. But the United States did have English support, because England wanted to keep the economic opening up of South America for the United States and herself. Throughout the entire century, the Royal Navy ruled the seas, and until the presidency of Theodore Roosevelt, the Americans' voluntary isolation was broken essentially only by the brief interludes of the war with Spain and the occupation of the Philippines and Puerto Rico.

Theodore Roosevelt was the first to understand that a country as powerful as his must sooner or later assume worldwide responsibilities. He therefore wanted the country to be strong. In a speech made at the Minnesota State Fair, Sept. 2, 1901, he said, "There is a homely adage, 'Speak softly and carry a big stick; you will go far.' If the American nation talks quietly, and if at the same time, we maintain an adequate navy in a perfect state of training, the Monroe Doctrine will go far." Teddy Roosevelt had carried quite a big stick all the time he was president, but he had carried it behind his back. That had been enough to keep Germany away from Venezuela and Japan from California. Then Roosevelt grew bolder and tried extending the influence of his big stick to other continents. It was thanks to him that in 1905 the peace between Russia and Japan was signed. In 1906, at the Conference of Algeciras, his firmness helped to prevent a European war over Morocco. He had thus gone against the American tradition and had intervened in world affairs; but the immense

45

majority of the country, completely taken up with home politics, scarcely noticed it.

It appeared that Wilson knew infinitely less about Europe than Roosevelt. He had visited it only occasionally, and that as a tourist; he was ill acquainted with its history. Just before his inauguration he said to an old Princeton friend, "It would be an irony of fate if my administration were to be chiefly concerned with foreign affairs . . ." Fate was indeed ironic, bitter, and hard. Wilson and Bryan, his secretary of state, came to power fully inspired with the notion that the role of the United States was to give more impetus to the world along the path of virtue. They, like the messianic Czar Alexander I before them, believed they were carrying out a divine mission. Wilson wanted neither the selfish isolationism of the past, nor Roosevelt's realism, nor "dollar diplomacy." With Bryan, he announced that the New Freedom would be one of America's exports, and that their foreign policy would be founded not on interest but on justice. They were both convinced that democracy was a sufficient solution to all problems, providing that its principles were generally observed throughout the world. Furthermore, they were certain "that they knew better how to promote the peace and well-being of other countries than did the leaders of those countries themselves."

Unhappily they were both quite without experience. They distrusted the traditional diplomacy that would have been so useful to them. The State Department had been, in part, restaffed, and unfortunately restaffed, with political nominees, and the career diplomats were much overworked. The President, and even more the Secretary of State, believed that moral forces alone guided the world. Bryan thought that if the United States were to declare to all nations that it repudiated war and was ready to submit any dispute to an international court, then not only would America never be attacked, but it would also become the supreme spiritual authority.

Those who were realists in the Roosevelt manner replied that this would be a very beautiful idea in a perfect world, but that ours was not a perfect world, and that interest, pride, and fear play a larger part in the relations between countries than love and righteousness—hence the necessity for the big stick. Colonel House occupied a reasonably judicious position between the two viewpoints. Like Wilson, he was an idealist and a peacemaker; but in Texas, he had been familiar with the violence of the cowboy's life, with men quick on the draw, and with the wiliness of politicians. This had given him a clear common sense that coolly measured the possibilities of a situation or a negotiation and preserved him both from the extremes of enthusiasm and from the bitterness of disillusion. House believed in justice, but justice backed up by strength. "One thing I am sure of," he said, "and that is that if the United States had possessed an army and a navy that could have acted vigorously, it would have become the arbiter of the peace, and that without our losing a single man."

From the beginning of Wilson's presidency, Bryan and Wilson showed, in their manner of dealing with international problems, their preoccupation with morality. They multiplied arbitration treaties; they came to an amicable settlement with England on the question of the Panama Canal; they tried to reconcile China and Japan. In South America, they came up against harsh reality. Wilson had promised "nevermore would the United States seek to acquire by conquest one single foot of territory." Yet in Wilson's presidency, the United States Marines had to occupy Haiti and Santo Domingo. It was, of course, to put their finances upon a sound footing and to prevent anarchy— worthy aims; but Latin America saw no more than the fact of occupation, and it expressed its displeasure.

In Mexico, a revolution of the people in 1911 overthrew the dictator Díaz who had ruled for the benefit of the great landowners. These then set up another dictator, a mixture of bandit and military leader, with bandit predominating. Most of the European states recognized Huerta in order to protect their investments, and they asked Wilson to do the same. He refused. It would scarcely have been possible to imagine a man he would have liked less than Huerta, a brutal, unscrupulous tyrant. To an English diplomat who said to him, "When I go back to England they will ask me to explain your Mexican policy. Can you tell me what it is?"

Wilson replied, "I am going to teach the South American republics to elect good men."

He knew that this "educative" policy would displease the American capitalists who would have come to a perfectly satisfactory arrangement with Huerta. But the Mexican adventurer had filled

47

the President, and not without cause, with one of his habitual violent dislikes. This led him to take the extraordinary decision of making war upon Huerta as an individual. He landed marines at Veracruz, stating clearly that he was attacking Huerta, not the Mexicans. But the Mexicans, angered at the presence of foreign troops, resisted, and there were serious losses upon both sides. Wilson was horrified. He, the man of peace, had caused blood to flow. At his press conference, his face was the color of parchment. He was only saved from a real war by the mediation of the ABC powers (Argentina, Brazil, and Chile), who proposed the setting up of a constitutional government in Mexico. Huerta fled. The United States recognized Carranza, his duly elected successor.

All's well that ends well; but the event was important because it left deep marks upon Wilson's mind. By a hasty act he had caused fighting and bloodshed in Mexico. This rendered him exceedingly cautious. Furthermore, it was this unhappy business that first began the disagreement between the President and Henry Cabot Lodge, the Republican senator from Massachusetts. Lodge, a cold, reserved, cultivated man, one of Theodore Roosevelt's friends and a leading light of the Republican party, had great authority in the Senate. He belonged to that small but authentic class, the American aristocracy. Lodge and his friends took their tea in their beautiful houses, furnished with unerring taste; they collected rare books; and they deliberately ignored the existence of the Western senators, the trade unions, the big businessmen, and the corrupt politicians. When he spoke in the Senate, Lodge liked quoting classical authors, "as if they were personal friends . . . . Whenever Lodge looked in the mirror, he saw a statesman."

Although he was a man of his party, Lodge was on good terms with Wilson at the beginning of his presidency. He found the President somewhat naïve and ignorant of world affairs, but he thought that Wilson was doing his best, and he supported him. Lodge was scandalized when Wilson, speaking to the leaders of Congress, maintained that the invasion of Mexico had been an attack upon the person of Huerta. The Senator coldly observed that the intervention of the United States was legitimate only if it were made for the protection of American citizens and American interests. Wilson replied that such an attitude would lead to

48

a real war. Lodge scornfully remarked that in any case it was already war. When Wilson, frightened at what he had done, drew back, Lodge's scorn increased. He wrote to Theodore Roosevelt, "Wilson is obstinate in political measures, but in foreign relations, he flinches." The enmity between these two powerful men was to have serious consequences.

III

Colonel House, the President's closest confidant, aspired to play a beneficent part in world affairs. In particular, he believed in the necessity for an international organization to prevent war. His first idea had been the creation of a Pan-American league, but this had come to nothing because of the opposition of Argentina and Chile. He had then turned to Europe, where the rivalry of the English and German navies seemed to him exceedingly dangerous. Both these countries were courting the United States; but England, although the American people liked its democratic way of life, had the unfortunate memories of the War of Independence to overcome, while Germany made the Americans uneasy with her autocratic regime and her clumsy diplomacy. The nation, wooed by both, therefore generally tended toward neutrality.

The President admired the character, institutions, and culture of the English. Colonel House went further. He thought that a lasting worldwide peace should be based upon an alliance between the United States, England, Germany, and France. Later, perhaps, an international league might be created, if the Americans became militarily strong enough to insist upon it. The President received House's proposals for military preparation coldly; according to him, the United States ought to give an example of resolutely peaceful idealism to all nations, and he felt that American public opinion was against the sacrifices that these preparations would entail. Walter Hines Page, the United States ambassador in London, urged the President to come to Europe— "Nothing else would give such a friendly turn to the whole world." Wilson did not want to leave America, for Ellen, his wife, was mortally ill. But in May, 1914, he authorized House to make a semiofficial journey to Europe to sound out the great powers upon their intentions, and, if it seemed practicable, to act as mediator.

House went first to Berlin, where the American ambassador, James Watson Gerard, had arranged an audience with the Kaiser for him. One of the most intelligent of the English diplomats, Sir William Tyrrell, the permanent undersecretary of the Foreign Office, had advised him to tell William II that America and England had "buried the hatchet." Tyrrell thought that the understanding between the two great Anglo-Saxon nations would impress Germany. House saw Admiral von Tirpitz, who told him that the only way to maintain the peace was by terrifying any possible enemy by the possession of great armaments. This was no reassuring omen. As for the Kaiser, he declared that he wanted peace, but that Germany was threatened. The Kaiser spoke admiringly of England: America, England, and Germany, all nations of the same blood, ought to come closer together. France and Russia did not count. Besides, the German army was invincible, which guaranteed peace. These were scarcely very encouraging remarks.

In France, House was unable to accomplish much, as the country was in the middle of a ministerial crisis. Still, he thought that he could see that the feeling of the country was not warlike and that the government would not begin a war of revenge to win back Alsace-Lorraine. In England, the ministers seemed to him almost too easy in their minds; and the German ambassador was doing his best to keep them in that state. The complacent tranquility of the English disturbed House, and he wrote to Wilson, "London is entirely taken up with social events; it is impossible to get any farther at present. Nobody thinks of anything but Ascot, garden-parties and so on . . . while in Germany the watchword is to push on with industry, to glorify war . . . ." In another letter, he expressed the wish to see the great powers come to the help of "the weak and indebted peoples" and expressed his prophetic fear of a revolt among the underdeveloped nations. More than ever he believed in the necessity for a League of Nations.

While House was waiting for a precise message from Sir Edward Grey that he could transmit to the Kaiser, a young Serb named Gavrilo Princip assassinated the Archduke Franz Ferdinand, heir to the double throne of Austria-Hungary, and his morganatic wife, the Duchess Sophie of Hohenberg, at Sarajevo on June 28, 1914. Few men in Europe then foresaw that, because of the interplay of alliances, the consequence of this romantic couple's death would be a world war. At London, the news, which came at the time of the Irish crisis and during the riotous demonstrations of the suffragettes, caused no more emotion "than a tenor singing in the middle of a boiler-works." But the bomb was in place and its fuse was ticking. Russia mobilized. On July 28, Austria, in agreement with Germany, declared war on Serbia. In Berlin, James Watson Gerard, a man of good will, despairingly watched the great implacable wheels of fate turning: on his own responsibility, the Ambassador wrote to the German chancellor, "Your Excellency, can my country do anything? Is there nothing I can attempt to prevent this terrible war?" He had no answer. On August 3, Germany declared war upon France.

In America, the first feeling was stupefaction. War between great European powers in the twentieth century seemed an anachronism. Wilson was astonished at finding mankind so foolish. "Unbelievable," he said to his family. "It is unbelievable." On August 6, 1914, Ellen Wilson, his wife, died; with her there vanished the best of advisers. "Oh, my God," cried the President, "what am I to do?"

The war aroused an intense interest in the country, but an interest "that was like that of the devotees of the cinema." An extraordinary show was beginning: the Americans, the spectators, watched. Yet the closing of the Stock Exchange turned the spectacle into a reality. In those days, Europe held many American securities. The belligerents found themselves obliged to sell as quickly as possible, in order to have liquid resources and to be able to make purchases in America. It was essential to close the Exchange, at least for a time. Meanwhile, the President, as early as August 4, had proclaimed the neutrality of the United States. Two weeks later, he asked his fellow countrymen to be impartial "in thought as well as in deed."

In deed? Everybody agreed with that. In thought? That was not so easy. Practically all Americans of European origin had inherited hatreds and sympathies from their ancestors. In the West and the Middle West, these feelings had somewhat faded. In the East, they were still very much alive. The German-Americans had an undeniable influence in some regions. The Irish kept up their ancient bitterness against the English. A very great many other people, however, were favorable to England, because of cultural ties and the similarity of language and religion. Alliance with France was part of the American tradition; nobody had forgotten Lafayette and the French soldiers of the War of Independence. Soon public opinion condemned Germany. The Germans had invaded innocent Belgium and Serbia, and the Americans could not forgive it. Rightly or wrongly, the German troops were accused of atrocities. In short, the balance was in favor of the Allies. But in practical matters, the country was solidly behind the policy of neutrality.

Many people thought: If the Europeans are mad, that is none of our business. We have our own obligations; we are well on the way to taming the business world in our own country, and we are struggling against poverty and the slums. Do not let us be turned aside from these fundamental tasks by out-of-date quarrels. What is it all about? A student has killed an archduke. Does that justify letting death and destruction loose upon the world? We Americans have just accomplished a gigantic undertaking; in one century, we have civilized and populated a continent. Why should we go and hazard a noble dream in the uncertain battles of the European kings? To the Californians, China, with its four hundred million customers, seemed far more important than Europe. To the farmers and shopkeepers of the Middle West, international politics were no more than one paragraph in their newspapers, and that not always on the front page, either. Wilson, in asserting his neutrality, expressed the feeling of the mass of people.

But the people, like Wilson, were to learn that in a tightly organized, interconnected world, every great war soon becomes a world war. A whirlpool, as strong and senseless as the Maelstrom, had drawn the European powers in after Serbia and Austria. Presently the United States in its turn was to feel its terrible influence. Neutrality? Certainly—but is it possible for a country whose trade is international? The English had one great advantage over the Germans: they were masters of the sea, and they could blockade the German coast, seize all cargoes intended for Germany, and deprive that country of raw materials such as cotton, copper, and steel, and perhaps even of food. England applied this blockade far more strictly than the United States was willing to permit, seizing cargoes sent to neutral countries that resold them to Germany. What else could England have done? For the Allies, it was a question of life or death. But it was a policy that raised the old problem of the freedom of the seas.

Very soon Wilson received innumerable complaints from the frustrated American exporters. The cotton planters of the South would have liked to sell their cotton to all the belligerents. Some senators suggested an embargo on the munitions made for the Allies if they would not moderate the blockade. The President thought that such an embargo would be inconsistent with neutrality. An impartial arbitrator should not deprive one of the contestants of his only chance. Besides, he, too, considered the Allied cause the cleaner of the two. The invasion of Belgium, the burning of the library of Louvain, and the bombardment of Rheims Cathedral outraged the cultivated professor. He said that a war waged in this manner would set the world back three centuries. Germany's victory would be the victory of a brutal militarism, and it would forever put it out of his power to set up the code of international ethics that he dreamed of. He said to the British ambassador, "Everything that I love is at stake." The battle of the Marne, the first Franco-British victory, aroused a lively feeling of respect and hope in him, as it did in many of his countrymen. But however favorable his heart and his mind might be toward the Allies, he went on saying that he observed the strictest neutrality. Politically this was to his interest; and morally he liked to think that it was his duty.

It was a profitable neutrality. At the beginning, the business world had been frightend by the possibility of losing overseas markets. It was very quickly reassured. The purchases of the Allies went beyond anything that could have been imagined. In Europe, a great proportion of the workers had been turned into soldiers. Those who were still working worked for the war; and this war was using up, in destruction, all the wealth gathered together over a hundred years. Europe was in need of everything. All at once, America experienced an unbelievable industrial and agricultural expansion. Metallurgy was the first to benefit; then the chemical industry set itself to replacing the huge German concerns. In five years, the price of cotton was to rise by 400 percent and that of wheat by 300 percent. The excess of exports over imports reached $3,500,000,000. To pay for all these things, the Allies began by liquidating all the dollars they had, some two billion of them; and after that they had to borrow. In the meantime, the neutral countries of Europe were also buying. A river of gold flowed across the Atlantic. In America, wages and prices went up. On Wall Street, where the Stock Exchange had been opened again, shares reached fantastic heights.

Among some people, this prosperity bred a cynical materialism. The cabarets were filled until dawn; new dances were invented; the most expensive shops overflowed with customers. Among others, good will and charity overcame other emotions. Many American women worked for the wounded and the children. Huge sums were collected for the Red Cross, for Belgium, and Serbia. Young Americans volunteered to drive ambulances in France. And yet the idea that this was also America's war and that the freedom of the whole world depended upon its outcome only made its way slowly into people's minds. The President was quite popular in the South and beyond the Mississippi, but he was still loathed by the Eastern businessmen. The intellectuals of New York, Boston, and Philadelphia, who were for the Allies, thought him weak and spiritless and accused him of being a pussyfooter, of carrying on a velvet-glove policy. They maintained that the situation called for an energetic attitude, and Wilson seemed to them incapable of it.

With the battle of the Marne, Germany lost all chance of a quick victory, and she now set all her hopes upon an American embargo that would deprive the Allies of munitions. In 1915, the German government informed the American government that in default of such an embargo, the German submarines would sink Allied ships on sight. International law had always held that a merchant ship should not be sunk before the safety of the passengers and crew was assured. The Germans argued that a submarine could not surface without the risk of being sunk itself, and that in any case, submarine warfare was forced upon them by an illegal blockade that was starving their people.

Some members of the Cabinet would not have opposed the embargo. The President said to them, "Gentlemen, the Allies have their backs to the wall, and they have wild beasts to deal with. I shall not authorize, on the part of the United States, any act that might hamper them." Whatever the moral judgment on either the blockade or the submarines may be, it is a fact that the German attacks, which brought about the loss of human lives, struck public opinion much more forcibly than the seizure of merchandise by the English. This time, Wilson reacted promptly. If German warships caused the death of American citizens, the Government of the United States would be obliged to hold the Imperial German Government responsible and to take measures to protect the lives of its citizens.

It was a warning, but it was still vague. Measures? What measures? Skeptics maintained that Wilson's pacifism would be satisfied with notes; and, in fact, the first incidents called forth nothing more. On May 7, 1915, the English liner *Lusitania* was sunk without warning and 1,100 passengers were drowned, 128 of them American men, women, and children. In the United States, condemnation was practically unanimous. This huge collective murder, carried out in cold blood upon innocent victims, revolted the American conscience. From that day onward, it was certain that if the Germans continued, the United States would sooner or later break with them.

Later it was said that the Americans came into the war because they wanted to save their debtors and thus the money that was owed to them. But no government can make a free people decide to go to war over a question of money. Women and children killed: those are the things that can rouse a nation. Wilson could have declared war the day after the sinking of the *Lusitania,* and the country would have followed him, although Bryan, his secretary of state, had resigned, saying that his conscience did not allow him to sign the note to Germany. Was the President right in waiting? Probably. From a military point of view the country was not prepared, nor was it ready morally. A gust of rage does not constitute a policy. But Wilson uttered one unhappy phrase: "There is such a thing," he said, "as a man being too proud to fight." In his mind, this meant "too sure of his rectitude to need to convince others of it by force." But it was taken as a withdrawal, a climb-down. "The peoples of the Entente powers were contemptuous, the Germans reassured, the Americans humiliated." But Winston Churchill, that shrewd prophet, observed that from that time onward England's position was strengthened. Thenceforward the English blockade no longer aroused American protests.

What did Wilson hope for? Perhaps for peace in Europe.

House, his personal envoy, was negotiating in London, Paris, and Berlin. He soon understood that a quick solution was impossible. Neither of the two sides thought itself beaten. France wanted at least Alsace and Lorraine; Germany insisted upon French economic concessions, an economic suzerainty over Belgium, and upon colonies. As for the submarine war, the Germans would have agreed to spare merchant ships if the English had partly raised the blockade; but it was impossible to come to an understanding over the manner in which an agreement could be reached. House wondered whether it would not be better for America to join the war on the Allies' side: it was the only chance of gaining authority and of subsequently making a lasting peace based upon a League of Nations. He thought that if the Americans were to remain mere onlookers, the country's moral standing with either side would be nonexistent, and that once the war was over America would be without friends. This position would be unfortunate even if the Allies were to win; it would be disastrous in the case of a victory for German militarism.

In December, 1915, Wilson married again. Mountaintops are lonely places, and the White House, with his companion gone, had become a desert pinnacle for this man who could only open himself fully to a woman. As early as August, the people about him had whispered that a young widow, Edith Bolling Galt, was becoming a very close friend of the President's—she was already intimate with his daughters. When he made his declaration, she objected that it was not a year since Ellen Wilson had died. "I knew you felt that," he said, "but, little girl, in this place, time is not measured by weeks, months, and years, but by deep human experiences." He assured Colonel House that "his dear dead wife" would herself have approved of his plan—an expression consecrated by very long usage in such cases. In spite of the difference in age, they made a handsome couple, and the marriage appeared to give Wilson new energy.

Meanwhile the German and Austrian propagandists in the United States piled up gaffes and blunders. They did not merely hire spies to sabotage the munitions factories; on one occasion, documents were left on an elevated train that proved their complicity. Franz von Papen was the German military attaché. One of his letters was intercepted, and in it, he said, "I continually tell these fools of Yankees that they had better shut up." The effect can be imagined. All this encouraged the Americans to increase their aid to the Allies. At the beginning, the President had forbidden the banks to lend them money. Then, in May, 1915, Wilson told the bankers that although he could not officially contenance loans he was not opposed to them. In fact, these advances were necessary for the support of American industry, since the European buyers had exhausted their dollars. Morgan bravely stepped into the breach. He formed a syndicate that advanced $50,000,000 without guarantee to an Anglo-French financial mission. Other huge loans followed, but this time on solid security. It was to the interest of every class in the nation that the prosperity arising from Europe's buying should continue.

The persistence of the submarine attacks and the discovery of the plots in their own country exasperated the Americans. The President sent notes of protest; they were received with derision. The English papers said that no one since Job had showed as much patience as Wilson. For his part, he was torn with uncertainty. He wanted to bring about the reign of justice; he hated war. How could this dilemma be resolved? And in fact, even if he were to decide to break with Germany, what would that matter to the Germans? How many divisions could the Americans provide? The American general Leonard Wood said himself that the regular army of his country was roughly equal to the police forces of New York, Boston, and Philadelphia. Wilson opposed the idea of preparation for a long time. He said, "I will not make our young men lose the best years of their lives." Then, in 1916, he confessed that he had changed his opinion—that he was converted. "I should be ashamed," he said, "if I had not learned something in fourteen months. . . . I know that you count on me to keep the country out of the war. So far I have done so, and I swear to you that with God's help I shall continue to do so—if it is possible!" But he added that he had another duty, that of preserving the honor of the United States. "Do you want the whole world to say that this flag which we all love can be trampled upon with impunity?" These words proved that the ironic attacks upon his ineffectual notes had touched him to the quick; but his actions were not so brave as his words. He hesitated to ask a peace-loving Congress for the immense supplies of money that would be necessary, and he contented himself with half measures.

Then at last the seer found a doctrine that satisfied his reasoning mind—the doctrine of international organization. The nations, like individuals, should have their code of honor. "We shall fight for the things we have always carried nearest our hearts, for democracy, for the right of those who submit to authority to have a voice in their own government, for the rights and liberties of small nations, for the universal domination of right by such a concert of free peoples as will bring peace and safety to all nations." It was a "Declaration of Interdependence." Wilson's conscience would allow him to fight for this great cause.

There was to be a presidential election in 1916. Wilson was the only possible Democratic candidate; Charles E. Hughes, the former governor of the state of New York, was his Republican opponent. Wilson's friends chose as their slogan "He kept us out of the war." It was a weighty argument. The Democratic convention, against Wilson's expectations, cheered for peace—he would have preferred the acclamation of patriotism. The unions were for him, out of gratitude: "He has protected me and mine." The Republicans might have won if they had chosen Theodore Roosevelt as candidate; but the business world held his progressive attitude against him. Hughes was an uninspiring candidate; he did not take up a clear position on the subject of the submarine attacks. For a moment, when he gained the State of New York, he was thought to be the winner, but in the end, Wilson carried the day by 277 votes against 254 by carrying California by 4,000 votes. This he most certainly would not have done if Hughes had not alienated the politically potent Senator Hiram Johnson. Wilson owed his victory to the Middle West and the South. The three Ps—Peace, Prosperity, and Progress—had won.

As soon as he was reelected, Wilson renewed his pleas to the belligerents for a negotiated peace and asked them for their conditions. He thought this a favorable moment: the fronts were stabilized, and they both seemed unbreakable on either side. The replies were discouraging. Both sides kept up attitudes that were suitable only to conquerors. Wilson thought that the time had come when he too should specify the conditions under which the United States was prepared to cooperate to establish and to maintain the peace of the world. He wanted "a peace without victory" that would include government with the consent of the governed, limitation of armaments, and the security of the small nations. If all this was agreed to, America would solemnly adhere to a league for the maintenance of the peace. If the peace were an imposed, a forced peace, said Wilson, it would arouse such resentment that it would be founded on quicksand.

He was right; but the phrase "peace without victory" was not well received, even in America. Once again the President's enemies set him down as faint hearted. In Germany, a violent struggle was going on between the Kaiser and his civilian ministers on the one hand, who were in favor of some degree of moderation, and the soldiers and sailors, who said that they were certain of victory, on the other. Admiral von Tirpitz promised that if he were given complete freedom to use his long-range submarines, he would put an end to the war by annihilating the Allies' merchant fleet. He was supported by Hindenburg and Ludendorff, the army chiefs, and he carried his point. In the margin of an Admiralty document memorandum, the Kaiser wrote, "Now, once and for all, no more negotiation with America. If Wilson wants war, let him make it, and he shall have it." Tirpitz promised victory in six months, on condition of widening the theater of war and doing away with all restrictions upon submarine warfare.

What would Wilson do? The German government's abrupt volte-face aroused a dark fury in him. His jaws clenched, and this, in him, was as highly significant as the quivering of his calf had been to Napoleon. Wilson told House that he felt the earth had suddenly turned upside-down and that he could not find his balance again. On February 3, 1917, he broke off diplomatic relations with Germany and demanded Ambassador Bernstorff's recall.

Meanwhile, ships and merchandise were piling up in the American ports. The President was urged on all sides to arm the American merchant ships. He was still holding out when he received from Page, his ambassador in London, an intercepted message from the German foreign secretary to the German minister in Mexico. Germany offered Mexico an alliance, in the event of war breaking out between her and the United States. In exchange, Mexico would receive Texas, Arizona, and New Mexico. Japan was to be invited to join the anti-American coalition. The revelation of this harebrained plot insured the passage through the House of Representatives of the law authorizing the President to arm merchant ships. But even then the Senate was tied up in a filibuster led by Senator La Follette,

59

and the President eventually had to proceed by executive action, using a rediscovered 1797 statute as his authority.

This time Wilson found that he was at bay. House told him that he had indeed his back to the wall; but at the same time he assured him that the problems raised by a war would not be harder to deal with than those that he had overcome so well in home affairs. But it was essential to face up to the situation firmly. "In my opinion," said House, "the President had begun the game betting on the impossibility of a war; he had lost, he had simply lost; and the country would write up this mistake against him unless from then onward he carried on the war so as to win it." Wilson listened to him calmly, then discussed the terms of his message to Congress. He wanted to establish a very sharp distinction between the German people and the rulers who had led them to this disaster. He thus hoped to overthrow the government of the Reich, by raising its people against it. Since this war would be undertaken to save democracy throughout the whole world, the German people, like the other nations, would benefit from it. On March 15, the revolution that took the Czar from his throne seemed to set Russia in the democratic camp. This took away the fear of fighting for the despotism of the Romanovs. House urged Wilson to recognize the new Russian government, and the President did so, before any other nation. In March, five American ships were sunk by German submarines, and men were killed. The die was cast.

On April 2, the President assembled Congress and asked it to pass a resolution recognizing that as a consequence of the criminal actions of the German government, a state of war was in existence. His speech had no violence, no oratorical effects: he spoke with a severe dignity. "We have no quarrel with the German people. We have no feeling toward them but one of sympathy and friendship. . . . We desire no conquest, no dominion. We seek no indemnities for ourselves, no material compensation for the sacrifices we shall freely make. We are but one of the champions of the rights of mankind. . . . It is a fearful thing to lead this great peaceful people into war. . . . But the right is more precious than peace, and we shall fight for the things which we have always carried nearest our hearts. . . . To such a task we can dedicate our lives and our fortunes, everything that we are and everything that we have, with the pride of those who know that the day has come when America is privileged to spend her blood and her might for the principles that gave her birth and happiness and the peace which she has treasured. God helping her, she can do no other." It was a noble speech, in the great style of Lincoln. Both Republicans and Democrats cheered the President. Senator Henry Cabot Lodge shook him warmly by the hand.

Yet Wilson remained uneasy about the future. The evening before the decision he had said to Frank Cobb, the journalist, "Is there anything else that I can do?"

Cobb replied that Germany had forced his hand and that America could not stay neutral.

"Yes," said Wilson, "but do you know what that means? It means that we should lose our heads, along with the rest, and stop weighing right and wrong. . . . It means that a majority of the people in this hemisphere would quit thinking and devote their energy to destruction. . . . It means an attempt to reconstruct a peacetime civilization with war standards." He added that once the war was started, it would be a war and nothing more, and that there were not two kinds of war. "Conformity would be the only virtue, and every man who refused to conform would have to pay the penalty." All this was even more true than he supposed. But it was also true that there was nothing else he could do, and that if the German militarists won, the freedom of America would be in danger.

IV

The German rulers had accepted the risk of a war with the United States, not only because they believed that America was unable to raise and equip an army rapidly but also that even if the army came into being it could not be transported across the submarine-infested ocean. Their mistake was to overlook a great country's huge potential in men and treasure, its industrial power, and also its courage. The Allies did not make this mistake. The King and Queen of England attended a thanksgiving service at Saint Paul's for the United States' entry on April 6, 1917 into the war for freedom. In Commons, Asquith said, "I do not use the language of flattery nor that of exaggeration when I say that this is one of the most unselfish acts in history."

61

Yes, it was certainly an unselfish act. Consequently, at least some part of the nation was ill prepared to understand the need for this enormous effort. Wilson had for so long kept the balance even and had refused to rouse the people to the real dangers that threatened America in this conjuncture that at first the people were more astonished than enthusiastic. Wilson felt this, and as soon as war was declared he presented it as a crusade to make the world safe for democracy. The country paid dearly for its delay in military and naval preparation, first because it went into war with no armies and secondly because doubt and reserve still remained in the minds of many Americans.

One should remember the nature of this vast people, this melting pot in which all the nations of Europe had been mingled. Many of its citizens had been born in Germany, or of German parents. Even those who had no family ties with the German and Austrian empires felt ties of race—the Scandinavians, for example. Almost all of them were to prove loyal citizens; but all of them, even including those who admired French and English culture, looked with distrust upon the United States' disregard of the Founding Fathers' warning not to get involved in European quarrels. Had they not crossed the ocean and broken the virgin prairie to escape from the weight of the past? This feeling was at once made manifest by the refusal of the word "allies"—in this coalition the United States was to be an "associated power." Six senators and fifty representatives had voted against the declaration of war.

Nevertheless, a surprising degree of national unity was attained. In order to "educate" the citizens, a Committee of Public Information was set up; it sent 75,000 "four-minute men" throughout the whole country, and they made 7,500,000 speeches to 350,000-000 listeners. Writers and professors put themselves at the service of the war effort. They did their utmost to keep up a heady state of excitement and sometimes indeed they were excessively zealous. Anti-German feeling took on some pathological aspects—sauerkraut, for example, was renamed liberty cabbage. The law on spying led to the imprisonment of hundreds of people, many of them innocent.

The President had foreseen this madness only too clearly. At least he could do his best to make the country's war aims pure. To those Americans who still hung back and to the world he

62

offered the hope that after the war there would be created an international association of the nations for the maintenance of peace. The pacific idealists were thus induced to join in the war effort. A little later, on January 8, 1918, Wilson defined the Allies' objectives in a way that was, alas, too optimistic, but that satisfied the liberals. This was the famous Fourteen Points speech. It may be summed up thus: "We ask nothing for ourselves. We want the world to give men of good will safety and freedom. The peace must be negotiated publicly, with no secret treaties. In the future, navigation will be free on all the seas. Armaments will be reduced, economic barriers lowered, colonial questions fairly settled. . . ." The other points had to do with future frontiers, and they foretold a just and moderate settlement.

Cynics made game of these Tables of the Law given from the top of Sinai by a spectacled professor. "Fourteen points!" they said. "God Himself had only ten." Yet this moderation and lofti- ness of tone were telling. In Germany, the Fourteen Points helped to create a desire for peace that steadily increased as defeat followed defeat, and in America, a good conscience. Mean- while, as it always happens in wartime, propaganda was doing its work. One aspect of it had to do with pleasant feelings— *"Lafayette, nous voici!"* and "The union of the English-speaking peoples"; and another aspect of it encouraged collective hatred and hysteria. In some states, rigorous laws set witch hunts afoot. A German name exposed very good citizens to the most unjust suspicions. Civil liberties were endangered, just at a time when the country was going to war to protect them. In more than one community, direct action took the place of the law. It was pos- sible to hear clergymen advising that those who made un- American remarks should be hanged. Injustice and intolerance almost obligatorily accompany any war, civil or foreign. The face of American democracy was sometimes hideously distorted. But the vast majority of the people was now united behind Wilson.

It was fortunate that this was so, for in this unprepared country, the task seemed terrifyingly huge. The government of Washington was much less centralized than that of London or Paris. New instruments had to be created. Wilson had a clear view of the requirements: "It is not an army that we must train and shape for war," he said, "it is a nation. To this end, our people must draw close in one compact front against a common foe. But this cannot be if each man pursues a private purpose. ..." And indeed, industry was in a chaotic state. The President set about reorganizing it. His Cabinet secretaries, who were politicians chosen not long since for entirely political reasons, were inadequate for this immense task. A War Industries Board was set up, and its chairman was a Wall Street banker, Bernard M. Baruch. Its function was to share out resources, to lay down an order of priority according to the nation's needs, to distribute labor, and to advise the government on buying prices. This work was exceedingly well done, and Bernard Baruch became the economic dictator of the country, without ever making a wrong use of his power. He relied upon the leaders of the business world, the heads of the great firms, and they had the wisdom, in this moment when the country had need of them, to forget their grievances against Wilson. Some of them even consented to come and work in Washington for a dollar a year—they were in fact called dollar-a-year men.

The same concentration was necessary in agriculture. There was not only the country and the army to feed, but the Allies as well. France had lost part of her farm land and a great many of those who could work it. England, even in peace time, imported a large proportion of her food. But now Argentina and Australia were becoming inaccessible—the voyage was too long for so reduced a merchant navy. And the Dardanelles were closed, which meant that the Russian wheat no longer came. Wilson called in a California engineer, Herbert Hoover, an excellent organizer who had signalized himself as early as 1914 by his success in managing the aid to the Allies. This round-faced, practical, energetic man was far from sentimental himself, but he had the art of arousing the feelings of others—a most valuable qualification in a task that entailed asking everybody to work and to make sacrifices. He did wonders: he bought the wheat harvest in advance, and he persuaded the whole country to become gardeners. Two million wartime kitchen gardens sprang up, some on the tennis courts of the rich, some in the backyards of the poor. There were meatless days and wheatless days that were voluntarily respected. Children were not allowed sugar with their cereal, and they were told, "Mr. Hoover would not like it." As a result, the United States had a surplus and was able to send half a million tons of sugar to France; and the wider result was that in 1918, the country exported twice as much food as it had in 1914, in spite of a bad harvest.

The question of fuel was treated with the same earnest attention. It was a difficult problem. There had to be more trains because of the needs of the army and the Allies. Coal was in short supply. It was necessary to stop every Monday those factories that were not working for the war. In 1918, Marshal Foch cabled, "If you do not keep up your supplies of petrol, we shall lose the war." The Americans voluntarily gave up using their cars on Sunday. The roads emptied. Food was strictly controlled under the direction of Herbert Hoover. As for the railways, which, in the United States, belonged to many and often competing companies, they agreed to be temporarily placed under the sole authority of Secretary of the Treasury McAdoo. And then ships to replace those sunk by the submarines were called for—ships to carry food, munitions, and armies. For a while shipbuilding was held up by an argument between those who thought ships should be made of wood and those who preferred steel, but in the spring of 1918, Charles Schwab of Bethlehem Steel was appointed director general, and he overcame the difficulties. Half a million tons of German shipping had been seized, and these ships were put in order. In September, 1918, the Shipping Board controlled 2,600 vessels. As for the workers, their unions agreed to give up the right to strike, for the time being, in exchange for an eight-hour day and the recognition of collective bargaining.

Enormous sums of money were needed for these gigantic efforts. The war cost the American people some $35,000,000,000, of which taxation provided a third. Basic income tax was raised by 4 percent, and a supertax varying from 12 percent to 65 percent imposed. Companies paid between 20 percent and 60 percent on their war profits. In the meantime, four Liberty Loans and one Victory Loan were launched with great publicity and with the assistance of film and opera stars and wounded heroes just back from the front, and they brought in $21,000,000,000. It is reckoned that 65,000,000 citizens bought these bonds. Until that time, the United States' public debt had been negligible; now it became heavy. Wall Street and the bankers had cooperated disinterestedly; for although they certainly did not like Wilson, they did approve of his foreign policy. It has been said that this was because the President, by declaring war, had yielded to their economic fears. This does not appear to be the case. It was far more in their interest to go on delivering goods to the Allies against security than to enter a war that must necessarily entail heavy taxes, give the federal authority a power that they were not accustomed to, and make the President, whom they knew to be their opponent, into a temporary dictator.

V

Many people had supposed that America's role would be that of helping her associates by supplies of money and goods and by the support of her fleet, but that no American army would be sent to fight in Europe. As early as the American declaration of war, Wilson knew that the Allies were at the end of their strength. French and British missions arrived in Washington. Lord Balfour led the English; René Viviani, a former premier, and Marshal Joffre, the French. House went to see them. He liked Joffre. "He seems to have a well-balanced mind—the kind of general that France needs at a time of superhuman effort." Later France had a permanent envoy, André Tardieu, an officer, historian, and journalist, a very cheerful, brilliantly intelligent man who had a great success. The first, most insistent demand of the English and the French was, "Let the American troops come right away." They were indispensable, both for forming a reserve and for the moral effect of their coming.

But the standing army of the United States was very small, at the most 300,000 men, counting the National Guard and the reserves. The secretary of war, the peace-loving Newton D. Baker, had done nothing to prepare for the recruiting of large bodies of men. It was obvious that only conscription would supply them. England had tried the voluntary system, but it had deprived the country, on the home front, of its most useful men. Congress hestitated. Ever since the Civil War, except for the brief interlude of the Spanish-American War, the United States had detested any militarism in any shape or form. Wilson and Baker had the wisdom to overcome their personal dislike of it, and in May, 1917, Congress voted for conscription. One month later, ten million men between the ages of twenty-one and thirty were registered on the lists. They had all come forward with no difficulty or resistance, in a wave of civic conscience. Later, in 1918, the age limit was raised, and twenty-four million men were registered. This was a reservoir of soldiers so great that it seemed to guarantee victory. Naturally, many of those on the rolls were never called up, either because they were unfit for service or because their work was necessary in America. The total of the men and women in the armed forces was to reach 4,800,000 in November, 1918.

It would not have been possible to do without these precious reinforcements, for a second revolution had taken Russia out of the war, and this allowed the Germans to bring many divisions back to the French and Italian fronts. The military experts did not think that the war could end before the summer of 1919, and they therefore advised that the American army should not be sent overseas until the spring of that year. Theodore Roosevelt offered to take over four divisions of volunteers at once. Wilson refused; he needed all the officers in America to train the troops. A commander in chief had been appointed: this was General Pershing, a man of fifty-seven who had fought in Cuba, the Philippines, and Mexico. He arrived in Paris on July 14, 1917, to set up the headquarters of the AEF, the American Expeditionary Force. The first American soldiers were frantically welcomed by the people of Paris. They went right through the city, going to Lafayette's grave in the Picpus cemetery. Some women put wreaths of flowers around their necks, others fell on their knees as the column marched by. In this little group of sturdy soldiers, the Parisians saw the promise of coming victory.

In the meantime, a first army of a million men was training in the United States. Equipping it was not easy. The regular army had no more than two thousand machine guns and six hundred pieces of light artillery. The American factories were not set up for supplying heavy guns, still less tanks and aircraft. Industry turned to these problems, but until it could solve them, French and English factories had to fill the gap. Out of the thirty-five hundred guns the American army possessed, only five hundred were made in America. At the time the United States came into the war, the German submarines were sinking 881,000 tons of shipping a month. During 1917, they sank 6,500,000 tons, while the Allies built no more than 2,700,000 tons. "They will win," said Admiral Jellicoe to the American Admiral Sims, "unless we can stop these losses—and stop them soon." In April, 1917, there was only two months' food for the civilian population in England. The Allied and associated navies took energetic measures. American destroyers patrolled the seas about the British Isles; and ingenious Americans advocated the method of escorted convoys and a barrier of mine fields between Scotland and Norway. These methods worked so well that after April, 1918, the losses never exceeded two hundred thousand tons a month. Two million American soldiers were carried over to Europe, half by English and half by American ships, so well protected that only two were torpedoed. At the end of the war, there were two thousand ships and five hundred thousand sailors in the American navy; and it was partly because of this force that the victory was gained as early as 1918, whereas the Allies had only reckoned upon a final result in 1920.

A supreme war council had been set up, and it was to sit at Versailles. Lloyd George tried, through House, to get the United States to be a member of it. Wilson agreed to send a soldier, not a political representative. Clemenceau and Pétain accepted this point of view. The military command, in an emergency, was to make the necessary decisions. For want of a unified command, the initiative was left to the Germans. The situation remained extremely dangerous. General Pétain told House that the French losses amounted to 2,600,000 men. He had 108 good divisions left, and of these, eight were to go to Italy. In France, therefore, there were a hundred divisions of eleven thousand men apiece. In Flanders, the English had sixty divisions. The Germans had as many as the French and English together on the western front, and they were going to bring back fifty-two divisions from Russia. General Pétain asked for a million Americans for 1919, with a million in reserve: "A million *soldiers*, not a million men," he insisted. To reach these figures, two divisions had to be brought to France every month until May, 1918, and thereafter three a month. The English and the French wanted the Americans to be amalgamated with the Allied forces from their arrival, by regiments or even by companies—that was the way to teach them quickly. Pershing did not respond favorably to this idea. He said that the system would have unfortunate repercussions both on the morale of the army and that of the American people; the soldiers wanted to fight under their own flag. From Washington, Tardieu supported Pershing. "If your aim is a permanent amalgamation . . . you will fail," he said. "It is not only the American command that will be against it, but the government, public opinion, and the force of circumstances." He suggested a compromise that was adopted. Six divisions of American infantry would *provisionally* reinforce the French and English; subsequently the American army would be entirely independent again.

An American sector therefore had to be created. Where was it to be? The English felt that they should defend the Channel ports; the French that they should cover Paris. The Americans should therefore come into action farther in the east. An excellent solution was found. Everything was governed by the question of supply and transport. Now the French ports in the northwest were used by the English troops, who had bases at Le Havre, Boulogne, and Calais. The only ports that were still available and that were capable of dealing with large ships were Saint-Nazaire, Rochefort, and La Pallice, while Nantes and Bordeaux could receive troop transports. Very fortunately, the railway lines going from these ports to Lorraine were scarcely used at all by the French army. By improving them, the American army could make good lines of communication between the southwest and the northeast, by Bourges, Nevers, Châteauroux, and Dijon, with a subsidiary base at Marseilles. And upon this battlefront, running from the Argonne forest to the Vosges, there was an ideal terrain for offensive operations. Here the enemy was covering Lorraine and the Saar, his great metallurgical center. For a successful attack, the Saint-Mihiel salient, which flanked both the Nancy and the Verdun fronts, had first to be reduced. Pershing asked Pétain to allot the sector to him, and this was done.

On March 21, 1918, the reinforced Germans broke the Allied front at the junction of the French and English armies, on the Somme. Once more the ominous processions of refugees were seen upon the roads, and for a moment it was even feared that the war might be lost before the Americans could get into action. Clemenceau, Lloyd George, and Orlando sent Wilson a cable telling him of their anxiety. Wilson then authorized Marshal Foch, who had been appointed supreme commander, to employ the American divisions. The Second Division and the United States Marines went successfully into action to help the French troops at Château-Thierry and then thrust the enemy out of Belleau Wood. When the attacks in Champagne were launched, eight American divisions came successfully into action between Rheims and Soissons. By August 10, the danger that had justified the amalgamation was over at last, and the American First Army, under Pershing's direct command, could take up its position around the Saint-Mihiel salient. In September, this army took the salient, capturing 16,000 prisoners and 443 guns. The victory, quite apart from its tangible results, gave the American army an awareness of its superiority. Now that it was beyond the barbed wire, it had freedom of maneuver again, and it took the Sedan-Mézières line as its objective. In October, Foch, by a series of thrusts, broke a great part of the German defenses from the Channel to the Vosges. Thanks to the American contribution, the superiority of the Allied side was now unquestionable. The Germans were weakening every day. The difference in strength could not but increase, and there was no longer any hope for the Germans. On October 3, 1918, Prince Max of Baden, the German chancellor, accepted President Wilson's Fourteen Points as a basis for negotiations.

The armistice conditions were what they had to be, effective guarantees against any resumption of hostilities; but, from the very nature of an armistice, they were provisional. It was now a question of learning whether the peace was to be Woodrow Wilson's peace or the peace of Georges Clemenceau.

A few words on the relations of the United States and the Russian Revolution should be added. The separate peace between Germany and Russia had been a very great danger to the Allies, and in 1917–1918, the Allies asked Wilson to authorize a Japanese intervention in Siberia and to support a Franco-British landing in the north of Russia. He stood out for a long while, but in June, 1918, he finished by unenthusiastically accepting Marshal Foch's decision upon this point. Furthermore, a Czech corps, which was attacking in Siberia, also called for the support of the United States. Wilson, like all Americans, had a sentimental prejudice in favor of the little nations. He said that he was ready to send seven thousand men, not to open a second front in Siberia, but to guard the Czechs' lines of communication. When the Japanese, who had landed in Manchuria, wanted to use these American troops, General Graves, who was in command of them, stated that he had received orders from the President not to interfere in Russian interior politics in any way whatsoever. At the time of the Paris Conference, Wilson again said that the Allied intervention in Russia seemed to him both a failure and a mistake. The American troops were withdrawn in January, 1919; but their presence had aroused a lasting resentment in the minds of the leaders of the Russian Revolution.

VI

The war had completely changed America's position in the world. All the other powers except Japan came out of the cataclysm weakened or altogether ruined. The United States emerged not only whole, but immeasurably strengthened. Its losses in men had been slight—53,000 killed as against the European powers' 8,500,000. Before 1914, America had needed European capital; in 1918, Europe owed the United States $10,000,000,000. The changes at home were no less great. For the first time, the federal capital had really guided the country's economic and financial life. Rigorous controls and enormously heavy taxes had been imposed and working conditions had been improved. Many sectors of American industry now led the world. The United States had learned how to do without Europe for chemical products; and although the American aircraft factories were young, they were doing well. Was this extraordinary increase in wealth owing to a wiser policy? Perhaps: but it was above all due to a privileged position. America was a distant nation, guarded by two oceans, and so she was able to enter the war later than the others—a war which by then had already done its worst. Fate, rather than men's will, had come into play; and its play had been in America's favor.

PART THREE

The Period of Disillusion

THE war was won, and now a peace had to be made. The United States undertook this difficult task with a burning desire for justice. In 1917, the country had agreed to give up its splendid isolation, partly because the freedom of the seas was threatened, but even more, and indeed principally, because its president had held this war up as a crusade for a better world. Wilson had not always been in favor of the idea of a League of Nations, and House had had some difficulty in winning him over. Now he was entirely for it, and he made it his own. The Fourteen Points, which, in his opinion, defined a just peace, henceforward became his gospel; and in this gospel he was the Messiah. He went to the peace conference certain that he would guide and sanctify it.

73

I

He appeared to have a strong position. Not only had he rallied the American nation by holding out noble aims, but the hopes of the liberals of the entire world rested upon him. The Germans had given up the struggle earlier than they were compelled to do by the military situation because Wilson's Fourteen Points promised them an honorable peace and a bearable future. It was at his call that they had thrown out their emperor and proclaimed a republic. He benefited from "a moral influence unequaled in history." He alone could speak to all nations, friendly, enemy, or neutral, over the heads of their politicians, and this moral strength also had behind it incomparable military force. "No philosopher had ever had such weapons to coerce the great ones of this world." Wilson's welcome in London and Paris went beyond anything that had been expected. "It was not human," says a witness, "it was superhuman." The cheering crowds saw in him the spiritual leader who, coming from a New World, would bind up the wounds of the Old.

This was how he saw himself. For him, more than for anybody, the Fourteen Points were the Divine Law, upon whose basic tenets no compromise whatever was admissible. Up until then, the American political tradition, inherited from Anglo-Saxon forebears, had been empiric. Americans did what they could, when they could. This was Lincoln's attitude toward slavery. Free the slaves? Yes, said Lincoln, but gradually, step by step. Wilson had Lincoln's good will, but not his patient pragmatism. He wanted freedom, justice, and everlasting peace; but he wanted them absolutely and immediately, according to his own program, and he took no account of the passions of an ancient continent riddled with history and disrupted by war. The brilliant economist John Maynard Keynes, who was one of the many English delegates at the conference, speaks of the surprise of the Europeans at this unwonted personality. They knew that he was aloof and obstinate, but they expected him to be an exceedingly well-informed professor who would intellectually dominate the scene. The real Wilson filled them first with astonishment and then with irritation.

74

"The president was not a hero or a prophet; he was not even a philosopher, but a generously intentioned man with many of the weaknesses of other human beings." He had neither the worldly wisdom nor the immense knowledge of Clemenceau or Balfour, nor Lloyd George's Celtic intuition that allowed him to detect the remotest echoes of an idea in the minds of those who were about him—Wilson had none of this sensitivity. Now the men he had to deal with were Clemenceau and Lloyd George: the first a ferocious, misanthropic patriot who wanted safety for his country and not the unlikely, nebulous salvation of mankind; the second a politician who judged everything by the number of votes that it would win or lose in England. "The Old World's heart of stone might blunt the sharpest blade of the bravest knight-errant. But this blind and deaf Don Quixote was entering a cavern where the swift and glittering blade was in the hands of the adversary. . . . " An unequal combat.

What did Wilson look like to the other leading figures of the conference? A nonconformist minister. He did not think as a politician, still less as a man used to business, but as a theologian. His one article of faith was the League of Nations. He was attached to the other thirteen points, no doubt; but if his Covenant, that mystical bond between all the nations of the world, were accepted, then all the rest would follow without any difficulty. The setting up of an international court would allow frontiers and injustices to be put right later. International law would become what ordinary law had been for so long—a standing tribunal, and a lasting, a permanent authority. A world police force would keep the peace. All aggressors would be punished. Might would put itself at the service of right. It all seemed clear and simple to him. The European liberals, who were also full of hope, thought that Wilson was going not only to bring a detailed plan for the League of Nations but also a program that would embody the Fourteen Points within this plan. When in fact the details were reached, it was quite obvious that his schemes were nebulous. "He had no plan, no scheme, no constructive ideas whatever, for clothing with the flesh of life the commandments which he had thundered from the White House. He could have preached a sermon on any of them or have addressed a stately prayer to the Almighty for their fulfillment;

but he could not frame their concrete application to the actual state of Europe." So it was said of him.

The President had against him, therefore, both his own character and the character of his partners in the debate. Furthermore, he was far from being unreservedly supported in his own country. In 1918, he had made the mistake of turning the Congressional elections into a party matter—a very great mistake during a time of war and general solidarity. He had some extremely bitter enemies among the Republican senators. It seems that Wilson must have forgotten that he needed a two-thirds majority in the Senate to have the treaty that he brought back ratified, for he arrogantly dismissed the objections of those who were against the inclusion of the League of Nations in the treaty, holding it to be incompatible with the American tradition. As was reported in *The New York Times*, March 5, 1919, "When that treaty comes back," said he to the Republicans, "gentlemen on this side will find the Covenant not only in it, but so many threads of the treaty tied to the Covenant that you cannot dissect the Covenant from the treaty without destroying the whole vital structure." The scornful, subtle Henry Cabot Lodge smiled blandly and bided his time.

Many people thought that Wilson ought to have included some Republican senators in the American delegation to the conference, in order to make them parties to the decision taken. He excused himself by saying that he did not choose to compromise them in this way, seeing that they were the men who would have to judge the treaty; and to accompany him he picked Colonel House, his other self; General T. H. Bliss, Robert Lansing, the secretary of state; and a solitary Republican, Henry White, who was an experienced diplomat but who had no political prestige. It was an obvious error. He could have taken either Elihu Root or Taft, men of far greater weight. The American delegation, therefore, did not represent the American people. The 1918 election, which had swung in favor of the Republicans, had proved that Wilson was no longer a prophet in his own country. When Theodore Roosevelt asserted that the Fourteen Points "had no relation to the feeling of the masses in the United States," that impenitent realist was saying something that was at that moment only too true. The tragedy of the American delegation in Paris was that it represented "what

America had felt profoundly in 1915 and would again feel profoundly in 1922. They did not, however, represent what America was feeling in January, 1919." The President, wrapped in his private communication with his maker, was unaware of this inconsistency.

He was equally unaware of the deep misunderstanding between himself, the allied powers, and the Germans. The Allied countries had only accepted the Fourteen Points in a softened "interpretation" of them by House, whose mind was incomparably more supple than Wilson's. According to this semiofficial commentator the expression "open covenant" did not exclude confidential diplomatic negotiations; "freedom of navigation" did not do away with the right of blockading; "removal of economic barriers" would not prevent a discreet protective tariff; and "disarmament" was only a general principle. It was not that Colonel House had deliberately sought to nullify the Fourteen Points, but it must be admitted that by carrying conciliation to excess he had involved them in "the most undesirable obscurity." The Germans took them at their face value. The Allies accepted them only in House's sweetened version.

House's excuse was that before the armistice he had had the impression that Clemenceau and Lloyd George would never accept them at all, which might have led to a separate peace between the United States and Germany—a disastrous state of affairs. This rupture had been avoided, but at the price of a dangerous ambiguity that was made worse by the existence of secret treaties signed by Great Britain and France guaranteeing territorial acquisitions for Italy and Romania—acquisitions that were contrary to the spirit of the Fourteen Points.

At the beginning of the war, it had been said of Sir Edward Grey that he was Parsifal in a poker game. In Paris, Wilson, a theologian who believed himself to be infallible, confronted a gathering of inimical freethinkers.

II

The Conference of Paris, unlike the Congress of Vienna, did not dance. It worked; but it worked in an unhealthy atmosphere. "American military police," wrote Harold Nicolson, "stood side by side with the policemen on the Champs Élysées. . . . For those few weeks, Paris lost her soul. The brain of Paris, that triumphant achievement of western civilization, ceased to function. The nerves of Paris jangled in the air . . . ." Yes, Paris was in a state of nervous agitation. The rumors that filtered through disturbed the city. Day after day, Clemenceau, in his black frock coat and gray suede gloves, came to take his place in silent irritation at the table of the four great powers. Nothing existed for him except France—for him, France was what Athens had been for Pericles. After so many invasions, it was essential, at any cost, to insure her safety. Clemenceau was a cynic; "he had one illusion, France; and one disillusion, mankind." Now standing in his path he found this ally, a fanatic who supposed himself to have been chosen by God to represent the voiceless masses of the world. Lloyd George was trying to save the British fleet and empire; Orlando, to gain Fiume for Italy; Clemenceau, to make sure of the left bank of the Rhine as an outer fortification. A spectacled Presbyterian minister sternly held up the Fourteen Points against them. They very soon became exasperated.

The French and English papers at first held back out of respect, but presently they began to scoff and even to grow cruel. Wilson was vulnerable and sensitive, and this hurt him. "Mr. Lloyd George and M. Clemenceau had, from this point of view, splendid elephant hides. Mr. Wilson retained the skin of a schoolgirl." The slightest stroke wounded him. He might have softened the journalists and even perhaps have brought some of them over to his side if he had had any human relations with them, but he shut himself away more and more in his certainty of being right. "He seemed," said his Secretary of State, "to consider opposition as a personal offense." Even his own delegation had but little contact with the Oracle. "Now Paris was very unlike Delphi." The Oracle of Paris, instead of trusting in his holy power, should have consulted his experts. He preferred to confine himself to a simple, single belief in the League of Nations. To get the Covenant accepted, he would compromise on other points. Like many theologians when they find reality and dogma coming into conflict, he too interpreted the sacred texts. So subtle were his glossings over that he succeeded in convincing himself; but liberal opinion in every country took fright when it realized that "Wilsonism was leaking everywhere, and that the ship in which we had so trustfully embarked, was letting water in from the top." The best minds in Europe, minds that put the future above revenge, had counted on Wilson to make sure, not of a peace without victory, but of a reasonable and lasting one. As soon as it became clear that, as his own country was not behind him, he could not enforce such a peace, and that the New World was not going to lay the ghosts of the Old, those who had put their trust in the American principles hurried back in panic to the old European idols, to the balance of power and an equilibrium based upon strength.

Young, independent-minded liberals who had done great things during the war expected great reforms from the peace; they were bitterly disappointed. One of them, the twenty-eight-year-old William C. Bullitt, had gone to Russia by Wilson's orders, and he had there obtained reasonably favorable conditions for the Allies from Lenin. When he came back, the atmosphere had so changed that the President did not even see him. Many of the younger men in the delegation resigned. Others said that resignation was about as useful a gesture as that of a mosquito attacking a battleship. One of the idealists, Adolf Berle, says that in the room at the Crillon in which this discussion took place, there was a vase of flowers: Bullitt handed out the red roses to those who resigned, as a badge of honor, and he scornfully threw the yellow jonquils to the others.

The Americans were not the only people to be disillusioned. Keynes and Nicolson, Englishmen with clear and liberal minds, blamed the concessions that Wilson made upon the other thirteen points in order to save the Covenant. It must be allowed that the Conference of Paris was deficient in that it did not prepare the way for the essential reconciliations—very far from it indeed. If it were desired that Germany should become sincerely democratic and that a war of revenge should be avoided, then at least the German Republic should have been allowed to live. Now nobody, not even Wilson, seemed capable of understanding the problems that obsessed Hoover, the American in charge of supplying Europe with food, that is to say, the utter impossibility of Germany's paying the reparations that were required of her and also the peril of total famine in that country during the coming winter. Instead of dealing with these immediate dangers, Wilson placed his hopes in the activities of a League of Nations that did not yet exist but that, in some undetermined way, was to resolve the difficulties.

Yet it must be admitted, when one considers the obstacles in his path, that he did get some results. No doubt there were absurdities in the new frontiers—there was an Austria and a Hungary that could not be economically self-sufficient, and a Polish corridor that ran across Germany, the seed of future wars sown in Europe's upturned soil. But Wilson had stood out against Italy over the question of Fiume, and he had induced France to grant that the fate of the Saar should eventually be determined by a plebiscite. There were injustices and there were stupidities, but they were fewer than there would have been without Wilson. Then again, from January 25 he secured the inclusion of *his* League of Nations in the draft treaty, and that in spite of Hoover and Lansing, who were ready to give it up to make negotiations easier, and in spite of Clemenceau, who thought the idea of permanent peace a dangerous and childish dream. To the objection "Your assembly will be dominated by the small nations, who will have the majority without having the strength," Wilson replied with the creation of a Permanent Council of nine members, the five great powers always having seats upon it. The aim of the League of Nations would be the preservation of its members' territorial integrity and political independence. It was to be made complete by an International Court of Justice, an International Labor Office, and a Council of Mandates, to be responsible for the administration of territories entrusted for the time being to various powers. This was an ingenious and original solution to the problem of disposing of the colonies taken from the former enemies until their political maturity should allow them to become independent.

As Wilson saw it, the essential principle of the international organization was to be collective security. Nations should treat one another according to the same moral rules that govern the relationships of private men. If one of them were to break the laws recognized by all civilized people, then the whole human community should oblige it to behave properly. This was a completely new idea in the history of our planet—the Holy Alliance and the Congress of Berlin had reference only to exclusive groups, without any universality. It was an idea that had a future at least, as the course of history was to prove. If one confines oneself to the events that happened during his lifetime, it is reasonable to speak of Wilson's failure and Wilson's tragedy; but is is a great error to overlook the fact that he brought a new concept of collective morality into international life. Without Wilson, the evolution of human society would have been different. Better or worse? Each man must judge for himself.

As soon as he had had his Covenant approved by the Conference of Paris, thanks to the support of Lord Robert Cecil, Léon Bourgeois, and General Smuts, the President made a rapid journey to the United States to sign various laws and, of much greater importance, to win over the Senate and public opinion to the support of his plan. On House's advice, he invited the members of the Congressional committees on foreign policy to dine with him at the White House. They came, headed by Lodge, and Wilson answered all their objections with a serene courtesy. The senators' great stumbling block was that the United States might find itself in a war because of a decision of the Council of the League of Nations, without the approval of Congress. There was a great deal of talk about the difference between a moral and a legal obligation. A legal obligation implied a penalty; a moral obligation left room for free opinion. Wilson later said to House, "Your dinner was a failure as far as getting together was concerned." He observed bitterly that Knox and Lodge had remained completely silent at table. House replied that even if the meeting had not mollified and persuaded the senators, it had had a good effect upon the public. It is by no means sure that he was right.

On March 14, the President came back to Paris. The atmosphere there was not good. The newspapermen were becoming more and more facetious about Wilson, who, according to them, took himself for the Messiah: there was the story of his leaping overboard from the ship that was bringing him back and crying, after they had fished him out, "And yet *He* used to walk on the water!" But, as he had wished, the League of Nations became Article One of the treaty of peace, and he succeeded in having the decision on the total amount of the German reparations delayed. Clemenceau and Lloyd George insisted upon astronomic sums that, said Keynes and Hoover, could not be and never would be paid. Wilson granted that France should exploit the mines of the Saar for fifteen years. Clemenceau wanted the left bank of the Rhine to be separated from Germany and made into a buffer state—Wilson and Lloyd George refused. Clemenceau accepted a compromise—the Rhineland should be occupied for fifteen years as a pledge for reparations, and France's security should be guaranteed by a triple mutual defense treaty signed by England, France, and America.

This was against Wilson's principles, which were opposed to any more individual alliances, and the negotiation was a severe trial to both his patience and his conscience. He even thought of breaking off the talks. He sent a message to America asking on what date the liner *George Washington* could be sent to Brest. Did he really mean to leave the conference? Or was he merely copying Disraeli's maneuver that had succeeded so well at the Congress of Berlin? Was it bluff or a genuine intention? And if it was bluff, did it work? One does not get that impression. During the days that followed the sending of the telegram, it was Wilson who made concessions, rather than the others, The Italian ministers, Orlando and Sonnino, also threatened to leave the conference. They had prevailed to the extent of acquiring a German-speaking part of the Tyrol (the Brenner Pass), but they also wanted the Dalmatian coast and Fiume. Wilson would not give way on this point, because he said that the new state of Yugoslavia had to have access to the sea. Lloyd George, who regretted the Treaty of Rome, did not support Orlando. The Italian left, and then came back again.

The Treaty of Versailles, the result of four months of talks and compromise, had very serious defects. When Hoover was shown the document, on the night of May 7, he said that he was certain that it contained the seeds of a future war. "If peace is wanted," he cried, "a choice must be made: either reduce Germany to such a degree of poverty and impotence that it is impossible for her ever to make a move; or allow a free government to make the nation into a peaceful member of the human family."

The treaty accomplished neither the one thing nor the other. In Central Europe, it could only breed revolution or else militaristic reaction. As a Frenchman, Jacques Bainville, has said,

"Its harshness was too gentle, and its gentleness too harsh." At dawn, Hoover left the Crillon for a walk, and in the still deserted streets he met Keynes and General Smuts. Some kind of telepathy or shared anxiety had drawn all three of them from their beds. They agreed that the economic consequences of the treaty were Germany's ruin; furthermore, nothing had been provided to restore the financial position of France and Italy, both heavily in debt. As for its political consequences, since Germany was being dismembered and irredentist blocs being brought into existence on her frontiers, it was clear from European history that in the past a situation of this kind had invariably bred an intense desire for reunification that culminated in a warlike explosion.

Keynes said that he was amazed at the four great powers' inability to feel concern at the dangers of famine and poverty. They had treated reparations and debts as though they were a problem in theology or electoral politics, or as though they were primarily concerned with revenge, and they had appeared to pay no attention whatever to the nations' economic future. They had preferred the straw of mere words to the corn of real things. And yet in Keynes's eyes the question was easy enough. In Europe, there was a very numerous population that was used to a high standard of living, a standard that it could only maintain by importing food and raw materials. But it was being deprived of the financial means of doing so. This was condemning it either to die of hunger or to revolt. "Men will not always die quietly." Wilson had been told these things, but it seemed to him that it would be easy to put the damage right, since the Americans would be the dominating power both in the League of Nations and the Reparations Commission, thus allowing them to correct any injustices. That America might stay out of the League was a thought that never for a moment entered his mind.

Thus, on June 28, 1919, in the Hall of Mirrors at Versailles, there was signed a treaty charged with disappointment and heavy with threats. House, with Lloyd George and Sonnino on either side of him, went up the great staircase, lined with guards with their sabers at the salute. The ceremony lasted for an hour. When everybody had signed, the guns roared out. "I felt some pity," says House, "for the Germans, sitting stoically motionless on their chairs. I would have liked more chivalrous simplicity . . . .

After the signing, we went into the park, where the great fountains were playing for the first time since 1914. Aeroplanes crossed
the sky; salvoes of artillery boomed out . . . . An immense,
unforgettable spectacle . . . ." But a splendid setting of the
stage does not necessarily mean that a masterpiece is being
produced.

Wilson had to sail the next day for the United States, there
to secure the ratification of the treaty by the Senate. From
House's diary, June 29, 1919: "My last talk with the President
leaves me uneasy. I urged him to approach the Senate in a conciliatory state of mind. If he treats the senators with the same
attention and thoughtfulness as he treats his foreign colleagues
here, all will be well. To this he answers, 'House, I have discovered that in this life you can never get anything worth having without fighting for it.' I protested against this opinion
and reminded him that Anglo-Saxon civilization was founded
upon compromise." But already Wilson was no longer paying
attention to what House said.

As soon as he was back, Wilson presented the treaty to the
Senate, and his speech upon this occasion was in his grand
manner: "The stage is set, the destiny disclosed. It has come
about by no plan of our conceiving, but by the hand of God
who led us into the way. We cannot go back." But the treaty
of which he was speaking was the treaty that he had imagined,
the treaty of his dead hopes; and with this the real treaty had,
alas, but few points of resemblance left.

III

The President was full of hope. Nonratification, he
thought, would bring about a diplomatic void, an emptiness
that was almost inconceivable. He had asked the senators to
wait for his return before beginning the debate: they had not
obeyed. A lively opposition had become apparent, an opposition voiced not only by Lodge, but also by the die-hard isolationists, Hiram Johnson of California, William E. Borah of
Idaho, and James A. Reed of Missouri. They were sincere men,
and they thought that if the United States were to join the
League of Nations it would violate the sacrosanct tradition

84

based upon Washington's injunction against involvement in European quarrels. The new Covenant would, when it was a question of defending an attacked member state, put Congress under the orders of the Council of the League. The Council could also intervene in America, which was contrary to the Monroe Doctrine. Furthermore, Great Britain would have six votes in the Assembly, since the Dominions were considered as separate states, while the United States would have but one. All these things seemed to them unacceptable.

Other groups of Americans made their dissatisfaction known. The German-Americans, who had behaved as good citizens throughout the war, thought the treaty absurdly harsh to Germany and Austria; the Italian-Americans thought that Italy had been unfairly treated; the Irish regretted that Wilson had not stood up for the cause of Irish independence at Versailles. Well-known liberals were against the treaty, holding it to be "an inhuman monster," a thing jointly begotten by cynicism, hypocrisy, and revenge.

As early as the summer of 1919, it was possible to foresee the positions that would be taken up in the Senate. Twelve to fifteen die-hard isolationists would vote against the treaty if the League of Nations appeared in it in any form whatsoever. Forty-three of the forty-seven Democrats would follow Wilson. The great majority of the Republican senators were in favor of ratification, but with certain amendments to safeguard American interests. It seemed possible, with a little diplomacy, to find enough common ground for a two-thirds majority (sixty-four votes) to agree upon. This was a policy that implied the making of concessions, but it would have taken care of the future. Lodge's position was not clear. At one time, he had himself been a supporter of collective security. His activities seemed to have no other aim than that of working against the President. To gain time, he read all the 264 pages of the treaty aloud, which was permitted by the rules of the Senate. His obstruction lasted for two weeks.

Why did Lodge hate Wilson? For it was the President, and not the treaty, that the Senator from Massachusetts was attacking, even at the risk of spoiling his own life. Was it the contrast of two opposing temperaments? The irritation of one highly cultivated man at the sight of another, equally cultivated but completely different in his reactions? The vexation caused in a justifiably proud statesman by those messages that seemed to be uttered from Mount Sinai? Ambition to be president in his turn? It was certainly not intellectual conviction, for as early as 1915, Lodge had said, "The great nations must be so united as to be able to say to any country, 'You must not go to war.'"—which was the very essence of the Covenant. But when Wilson appeared, on August 19, before the Senate committee that he had invited to the White House, he felt that his great work was threatened. At the beginning of September, he announced that he would undertake a great tour of the West to appeal to the country and to induce the body of electors to bring pressure to bear on the senators.

His physician, Admiral Cary Grayson, who knew the unsatisfactory state of the President's health and who was aware of the risks involved, opposed the tour with all his strength. He asserted that the President's life would be endangered, and he advised a long rest, far from Washington. Speaking in a tired voice to Joseph Tumulty, his secretary, Wilson said, "I know I am at the end of my tether, and I am willing to make whatever personal sacrifice is required, for if the treaty should be defeated God only knows what would happen to the world as a result of it. In the presence of the great tragedy which faces the world, no decent man can count his own personal fortunes in the reckoning." What a different Wilson this was from the vigorous, alert, and still youthful man who had come to the White House in 1913. Tumulty now saw before him a white-haired old man, exhausted, but stubborn.

The doctor and the secretaries began to prepare itineraries that would provide the President with long rests. He refused them. For him this was to be a mission, and it was not to be turned into a holiday trip. He had never seemed so worn and depressed as when he took his place in the special train. He was to make a hundred speeches in less than a month, and he had not had the time to prepare them. Yet the journalists who traveled with him were struck by his splendid form when he was speaking to the crowds; for all that, the President was suffering from violent headaches and an immense tiredness could be seen in his face. Against all expectation, the farther west they went, the more people came to hear him, and the more enthusiastic they were. The diehards,

Senators Borah and Johnson, followed in his tracks and cried down the League of Nations, but it was clear that the majority of their hearers were not with them. It really seemed that Wilson was going to triumph over his enemies. But on September 26, 1919, at four in the morning, after a stirring speech at Pueblo, Colorado, he had a severe attack. It was impossible to go on with the tour. Admiral Grayson ordered a return to Washington. There, he suffered a stroke that resulted in a partial paralysis, and he languished at the White House for many months. The champion of collective security was reduced to a state of impotence. Sitting, wrapped in shawls and rugs in his armchair, he had difficulty in following what was happening at the Capitol, but he spoke of nothing but *his* treaty. His illness had made him more emotional and irritable than ever. Nobody saw him. His wife and his doctor were the only lines of communication with the outside world.

It was Lodge, relentless in his opposition to Wilson, who drew up the committee's report. He proposed that the Senate should approve the treaty, but with reservations and amendments. The United States should not comply with Article X of the Covenant, either by sending soldiers or by punishing an aggressor in any other way, except with the approval of Congress; the United States alone would be the judge of its obligations and of whether it chose to accept arbitration; it would not be bound by the treaty unless at least three of its four chief associates accepted these reservations. Thus Lodge, cleverer than the diehards, pretended to accept the treaty while in fact he was killing it. During the long debate that followed, nothing was neglected that might draw the public attention to the dangers of overexact engagements, to the injustice of the treaty, and to the absurdity of a superstate that would reduce American freedom to nothing. Once again, the isolationists were preaching 100 percent Americanism.

Meanwhile ugly rumors about the President's mental condition were spread abroad. A delegation from Congress was allowed into the White House, and they were obliged to acknowledge that though Wilson was very ill his mind was perfectly clear. One of his worst enemies, Senator Albert B. Fall, said to him as he took his leave, "Well, Mr. President, we have all been praying for you."

Wilson looked at him and asked, "In what sense, Senator?"

The President refused to accept Lodge's reservations. He said that they would reopen the whole question of the League of Nations with all the powers concerned with the treaty. On November 18, he stated that in effect the amendments annulled the treaty and he asked the Democratic senators not to vote for them. The next day, November 19, the amended treaty was rejected by fifty-five votes (the Democrats and the diehards) as against thirty-nine. "The greatest victory since Appomattox," said the diehards. "The greatest defeat for the peace of the world," replied a few wise men.

It still seemed possible, by using the pressure of public opinion and by accepting some slight changes, to save at least the United States' membership in the League, which would take care of the future of the world. Colonel House urged the President to relieve himself from the responsibility and to give the Senate a free hand; Wilson would not move from his position of all or nothing, and he did not answer House's letters—without knowing why, House had fallen into disfavor. Bryan and most of the Democratic senators advised a compromise: "Something rather than nothing." The English and the French were worried, and they begged Wilson to reconsider the question. Sir Edward Grey was sent to Washington to do all that he could to bring about a reconciliation with Lodge. Wilson refused to see him, and the President was offended when Grey said that the League of Nations could not succeed without the United States and that the Allies accepted Lodge's reservations.

The danger was apparent to many people in the country. Twenty million citizens signed a petition for a compromise. But Wilson would do no more than bitterly criticize those who had murdered his treaty: "It's dead and lies over there. Every morning, I put flowers on its grave." Public opinion was so moved that the Senate declared itself ready to reopen the debate. At this point, the slightest concession might have insured victory. Wilson, who was getting better, would not give an inch. "I can stand defeat. I cannot stand retreat from conscientious duty." It was essential, he said, either to go fearlessly into the League and accept the responsibilities of doing so, or else to withdraw, with what grace was possible, from the great concert of powers that had saved the world. In March, 1920, there was a new vote:

the last. Wilson had forbidden the Democratic senators to vote for the treaty altered by the reservations. In obedience to him and against their own judgment, twenty-three Democrats voted with the diehards, and the treaty was definitively rejected, by failing to obtain the necessary two-thirds majority, with forty-nine votes for and thirty-five against. Seven Democrats voting in the other direction would have brought the United States into the League of Nations, but the senators of his party were afraid of Wilson. He said that the presidential election of 1920 would be a plebiscite that would vindicate his stand.

There now remained a separate peace to be made with Germany and Austria-Hungary. On May 15, 1920, Congress adopted a resolution on these lines: the President vetoed what he considered "an ineffaceable stain on the gallantry and honor of the United States." The House of Representatives did not override the veto, and the United States continued to be at war with Germany until July 2, 1921, when the state of war was officially ended by a joint resolution of Congress. In late August, 1921, separate peace treaties were signed with Germany, Austria, and Hungary that were quickly ratified by the Senate. Thus the tragedy was brought to its consummation. The Franco-Anglo-American treaty of guarantee was never signed—a great injustice to France, who had only accepted the new frontiers upon this condition. The League of Nations came into being without the participation of the government that had fought so hard to have it accepted, and, of course, without any American guidance. It was a terrible misfortune for Europe that needed fresh blood to give it new health and vigor, and for America too, that was deprived of a unique chance of learning the duties that her strength henceforward laid upon her. Allotting the blame would, in this place, be the most futile of tasks. Both Wilson and Lodge had shown themselves to be dangerously stubborn. The isolationists had understood nothing of the changed face of the world. The American nation deserved no blame whatever: It had accepted the perils and the costs of the war, and it would have accepted the duties of the peace, had they been clearly laid before it.

IV

The disillusionment was immediate and painful. America had flung herself into this war with such unselfish ardor that the bankruptcy of Wilsonian idealism caused a cynical reaction. The country had wanted "to make the world safe for democracy" and had believed it was doing so. Now America found herself alone in the world and saw Europe more isolated than ever. At home, the situation was no less disappointing. Neither the Administration nor Congress had made any plans for reconversion.

The men of the left said that the wartime economy had shown that antitrust legislation was perhaps not the right road for social progress. The war had made a national direction of the economy necessary. The War Industries Board had controlled the whole of production, had insisted upon agreements and priorities, and had suspended the Sherman Act against the trusts. The United States had become a cooperative community. An economy based on needs had taken the place of an economy based on profits; the general interest had been substituted for private interest. This was a triumph for the radicals, in the American sense of the word, the most progressive minds. If a kind of state socialism had worked so well in wartime, they said, why not keep it on in time of peace? In the spring of 1919, the radical weeklies, *The New Republic* and *The Nation,* foretold an economic revolution: it was to be orderly, of course, and constitutional, but it was to go deep; there was to be a guaranteed minimum salary as a right, and the right of work for all. But as early as May, the conservative forces in Congress and even in his own Cabinet obliged Wilson to put an end to controlled economy. He had tried to carry on the War Industries Board under the name of the Industrial Board, but it had been a total failure.

The majority of public opinion was in favor of a return to the past. The pioneering frontier tradition was against governmental controls. The soldiers had only one desire and that was to get home as soon as possible. Soon there were four million ex-servicemen looking for jobs. The demobilization of industry was as chaotic and haphazard as that of the army. The business-men had but one idea: to shake off the wartime controls and to return to "normalcy." Immediately after the armistice, prices were freed; in 1920, the railways given back to their private companies and the army and navy contracts canceled. The dollar-a-year men in charge of the war services closed their desks and went off for a few days' relaxation in Florida before going back to their own factories. Some offices in Washington were closed so abruptly that the chiefs had to lend the typists the money for their railway tickets home. The fact that in spite of this mad haste, wartime prosperity was able to carry on for some time and the ex-servicemen were easily reabsorbed proved the wealth and the vigor of the country.

It is true that in 1919 the nation went on spending far more than duties and taxes brought in. Some of this money went to the Allies in the form of loans that allowed them to continue buying in the United States. The whole of Europe lacked rail-way engines and rolling stock, gasoline, cotton, and food. The continent was a huge market, but it was insolvent. Other sums went to the ex-servicemen, as demobilization gratuities. They all bought civilian clothes, causing a boom in the textile in-dustry. Innumerable subsidies, for the building of ships, houses, and so on, kept the country's economy turning at full speed. The car industry had been at least partially taken up by the army's demands during the war. It was now overwhelmed with private orders. With a dangerous ease, the banks granted loans on the security of Liberty Bonds, and many of their clients used the borrowed money for speculation. Prices soared, and as is always the case in such circumstances, shopkeepers and con-sumers bought more than they needed, for fear of having to pay more tomorrow.

This sudden rise of prices was very hard on the workers. Real wages had risen a little during the war, but the move-ment had been limited by controls. The abrupt disappearance of the War Labor Board, which had acted as an arbitrator in the question of wages, left employers and workers free to fight it out among themselves. Both sides did their utmost to wring all the profit they could from the present prosperity. In 1919, there were a great many strikes, involving several million workers. Their aims were higher wages and shorter working hours (the steel industry still worked twelve hours a day) and the recognition of collective bargaining. Most of these claims were reasonable and the behavior of the union leaders moderate. John L. Lewis, for the miners, ended a strike with the words, "We are Americans; we cannot fight against the government." But there were more revolutionary agitators who waved the red flag. Bombs were thrown, and others were sent through the mails. The American Federation of Labor disavowed the violence of the Industrial Workers of the World. At Boston, the police force itself, hit by the rise of prices, went on strike. Calvin Coolidge, the governor of Massachusetts, until that time a comparatively unknown figure, said that "There was no right to strike against the public safety by anyone, anywhere, any time." His firmness earned him a sudden stature throughout the nation.

For at that time, many Americans were showing a dread of the "red peril" that, in a country where the socialists were so moderate, was surprising. The veteran of the party, Eugene Debs, was put in prison. The Russian Revolution was held up as an example, but in America, the Communist party did not represent a thousandth part of the adult population. Yet the ex-servicemen had come back from the war in a fighting mood. Violence had become habitual to them. They insisted upon repressive action, and, in an emergency, they took care of it themselves. Many states passed laws against "criminal unionism." The Civil Liberties Union had continually to defend citizens accused of "radicalism," a word that had formerly been uttered with much favor by the American intellectuals, but which the nervous tension of war and the fear of a revolution had given a new and sinister implication. An English journalist wrote, "I shall never forget the feverish condition of the public mind in the autumn of 1919 . . . Property was in an agony of fear, and the horrid name "radical" covered the most innocent departure from conventional thought." Wilson, who was somewhat better, although he still dragged his leg and spoke with difficulty, did his best to calm the attorney general, A. Mitchell Palmer, who had taken fright the day a bomb burst in his house, and who already saw the flames of revolution, like a prairie fire, threatening every American house and licking the altars of the churches. "Palmer," said the President, "do not let this country see red." In freedom's own mother country, freedom of speech was in danger.

Life in the army, far removed from their family, and the savagery of the fighting had had a profound and demoralizing effect upon the youth of the country. The war was over: it had not brought about the kingdom of Heaven upon earth. There were many who wondered whether it had not been a great mistake to get into it at all. They wanted to forget the whole nightmare. But how was it possible to get back to a state of innocence? Now, in the light of their experience, in the light of what they had gone through, the morality and the faith that they had formerly been taught seemed to be a pack of lies. Everything, this savage struggling, this disorder, the aborted peace, gave them the feeling that the world was devoid of meaning. They had to escape.

In the political field, escape took the form of neo-isolationism. From now on, the veterans vowed to become 100 percent Americans again and to leave Europe to stew in its own accursed juice. Among the young, the vogue was for the glorification of pleasure, particularly sexual pleasure taken "here and now," in defiance of any moral code and of old-fashioned taboos. In *The Sun Also Rises* and *A Farewell to Arms,* Ernest Hemingway was expressing a realistic reaction against the "hypocritical" idealism preached during the war and also against the prudery of the days before the war. He showed the free and dashing life of American young men (and women) liberated, in Europe, from the rigid protection of their families—young people who would never again accept the "respectable" life of former times. In his novels, Scott Fitzgerald described the moral and spiritual deliquescence of the "lost generation," for whom "all the gods were dead, all wars dishonored, all beliefs shaken." He told mothers of families who were still living in Victorian times that their daughters let dozens of young men kiss them and that they were not afraid of going to the utmost lengths. William Faulkner set down the decay of another false ideal, that of the old Southern aristocracy that was now degenerate. In 1924, Henry L. Mencken, together with George J. Nathan, founded the *American Mercury,* a rebellious monthly, the "lost generation's Bible," in which he ridiculed religion, democracy, and stupidity.

This was not only a revolt of the intellectuals. For the ordinary public, escape consisted of losing all interest in a now discredited

93

idealism and in seeking a tangible, immediate happiness in a material world. New inventions, such as the car, the radio, and the airplane, created new needs and longings. The young people of the universities called Freud to witness that all neuroses came from the complexes brought about by sexual repression. Puritanism was accursed. The motor car provided clandestine couples with safe and mobile hiding places. Dancing took on new aspects, which the churches denounced, speaking of "syncopated embraces." Emancipation was the watchword, whether it referred to sensuality, votes for women, or the right to drink. The prohibition of alcoholic liquor had already been made part of the law in some states before the war, but it was only in 1919 that the Volstead Act, the legal implementation of the Eighteenth Amendment, came into force. By this law, the making, the transport, and sale of all alcoholic drinks were forbidden throughout the whole territory of the United States. Anything that contained more than $\frac{1}{2}$ of 1 percent came under this heading. It meant that wine and beer, the ordinary drinks of a great many immigrants, were forbidden. An insane experiment.

How did so rigorous a law come to be passed? A powerful association, chiefly composed of women, called the Anti-Saloon League, along with other similar groups, had caused it to be adopted little by little, state by state. The South had welcomed it at once, because there were few immigrants there and also because its rulers thought that alcohol, by encouraging violence, helped to make the Negro question more dangerous. Manufacturers were in favor of prohibition (for others) as a means of lessening the number of accidents at work. The greater number of cars on the roads emphasized the danger of drunken drivers. Henry Ford said, "The speed at which we run our motor cars, operate our intricate machinery, and generally live, would be impossible with liquor." In other words, it was better to be drunk with speed than with alcohol. And then the restrictions during the war had accustomed people's minds to accepting strong, violent solutions. Many sincerely thought that prohibition would deliver America from a scourge.

When laws are not "the necessary relations that arise from the nature of things," they are almost never obeyed. The effects of prohibition were very unlike those that the worthy ladies of the Anti-Saloon League had expected. Not only did those who ordinarily drank desire to obtain their alcohol at all costs, but those who had scarcely drunk at all before now began to do so. For young people, the speakeasy, hidden in a basement or behind a shop, and the hip flask because symbols of their defiance of society. More was drunk in the towns than in the country, more in the East than in the West, more among the wealthy classes than the poor. The saloon had been squalid; the speakeasy was smart. Cocktails took the place of wine—or added themselves to it. Good citizens had their alcohol delivered to them in their homes by bandits. Libraries were turned into well-hidden bars. Until that time there had been no such thing as a cocktail party: it now became a common form of entertaining. An immense trade in alcohol was set up to supply the demand. The bootlegger became a professional. Sometimes he redistilled industrial alcohol, sometimes he imported his wares from Europe or Canada, sometimes he distilled for himself. The profits from this illegal traffic were so great that the bootleggers were able to buy the complicity of the police, and their great wealth gave them political influence. They formed themselves into gangs that, by threat, violence, and often by murder, seized the monopoly of breaking the law in their own area.

The gangsters were later to create other monopolies, especially in the great cities, such as Chicago. These barons of the underworld levied tribute upon gambling houses, brothels, and dance halls, and even upon such peaceful concerns as laundries, garages, fish markets, and dairies. The victims had to accept their protection—their very costly protection—or else run the risk of violence that might go as far as murder. For example, a racketeer invented a dairymen's association and required every milk store selling milk to belong to it, paying a heavy subscription for the privilege. If any vendor refused, an "education committee" would get into his shop and smash everything. This preliminary warning was usually enough. If it were not, the gangsters came and killed. The newspaper headlines spoke of a "wave of crime." Was it really worse than it had been before the war? It would be nearer the truth to say that in the United States, public safety had always been more hazardous than it was in Europe. According to insurance statistics, there were sixteen times as many murders in America as in England. This was explained by the youthfulness of the country, by the existence of a drifting population, and also, after the war, by the excellence of the wrongdoers' weapons.

English newspapermen in America were astonished to see money belonging to the banks being carried in armored cars guarded by armed men. A day was to come, after two wars had revived violence in Europe and after the motion pictures had made these ways familiar, when the same precautions became necessary both in London and in Paris. The gangsters' work was made easier by the car and the machine gun. Furthermore, the police forces of the various states of the Union were at that time ill prepared for cooperation. Presently, the policemen grew tired of risking their lives to arrest men who were then acquitted because of political influence. They adopted the habit of shooting any gangsters they caught in the act.

The sinister and at the same time ridiculous Ku Klux Klan was the most spectacular of the attempts at dealing out a private (and unjust) justice. The new Klan was founded in 1915 by a certain Colonel William J. Simmons in Georgia, and it attracted weak minds by its childish ceremonies and uniforms. During their raids, the members wore long white robes and hoods. In the name of Americanism, the Klan was against the Negroes, the Jews, the Catholics, foreigners, and the liberals who protected these minorities. Its chiefs called themselves Kleagles and Goblins; Simmons was the Imperial Wizard. The Klan grew until it had four and a half million members, and in the South, the Middle West, and on the Pacific Coast, it had real political power. In theory, the Klan was an association of all those who believed in "pure Americanism." In fact, in the South, its chief object was to terrorize the Negroes. The Klansmen were sworn to secrecy, and this made direct action—even murder—far easier. A Negro would be taken into the woods and "given a lesson." As it might be expected, ordinary criminals made use of the Klan. Burning down a house and chalking K.K.K. on the ground was an almost certain way of escaping punishment. As had happened at the time of the red panic, a movement that had its origins in fear begot more fear. Violence bred violence. The war had done a great deal of harm to the old, virtuous America of Washington and Lincoln. The great majority of Americans preserved the traditional virtues. It was a minority that perturbed the country's life.

V

Shakespeare himself never thought of anything more tragic than Woodrow Wilson's end. For more than a year, the ghost of a president ruled America. From time to time, a draft bill or a veto, signed in a trembling hand, would emerge from the White House, now an impenetrable retreat. The presidential election of 1920 was coming near: more than ever Wilson wanted to make it into a solemn referendum by the people on the League of Nations. Some hoped that he would stand again himself, since he was the Covenant personified; but the state of his health made this utterly impossible. McAdoo, his son-in-law, and the heir to the throne by marriage, would willingly have taken the succession. "He is not fit for it!" said Wilson, angrily. But who was to be chosen? At the Democratic convention in San Francisco, there were gathered under the same label men of entirely opposite views: there were Southern conservatives, who still voted Democrat out of hatred for the Yankees; the professional politicians of the machines; fanatical demagogues, "farmers' politicians," and bimetallists like Bryan; and lastly, cultivated liberals in the Wilsonian tradition.

It was one of these, Governor James Cox of Ohio, who was nominated. He stated that he was in favor of ratifying the Covenant; so did the candidate for the vice-presidency, the young and eager Franklin Delano Roosevelt, the assistant secretary of the navy, who had done wonders during the war.

For a time, the Republicans thought of Hoover, who would have been a good choice—he had proved that he was an exceptional administrator. They might have nominated General Leonard Wood or Nicholas Murray Butler, the President of Columbia University. But it appeared to them that after Wilson, the country was tired of outstanding minds for whom Congress was merely a rubber stamp. They considered Warren Gamaliel Harding, the senator from Ohio, the most average American and the most reassuring of men; they chose him.

Harding was an unimportant politician. But he looked like a president: "Tall, well built, with his handsome face set off by a fine head of silvery gray hair, he wore his conservative clothes with distinction." In his acceptance speech, he avoided taking up a stand on the League of Nations. "What America needs at present," he said, "is not heroics but healing, not nostrum but normality." And indeed, what the majority of the electors wanted was a return to laissez-faire, a final abandoning of the crusade that had brought nothing but ingratitude and bitterness, traditional isolationism once more, and business activity.

By the adoption of the Nineteenth Amendment in 1920, the women had become electors, but this made no alteration whatever in the respective strengths of the two parties. Harding won an overwhelming majority—16,152,000 against 9,147,353. "It was not a landslide, it was an earthquake." Coolidge, the governor of Massachusetts, became vice-president. There had been a time when the masses shared Wilson's faith in a free and peaceful world: now they forswore this noble aspiration. Clever propaganda had disgusted them with their victory by hinting that they had only been fighting for the bankers. Friendship for the former allies gave way to a vague pity for the former enemies. Wilson, deeply embittered, said that the American nation had given up "a fruitful leadership for a barren independence. . . . We had a chance to gain the leadership of the world. We have lost it and soon we shall be witnessing the tragedy of it all." This grim prophecy was only too true.

Meanwhile life was slowly coming back into the prophet's deadened limbs. On March 4, 1921, with great difficulty, he was able to accompany his successor to the Capitol. In the carriage, Harding did not know what to say, and he told a harmless story about elephants. The retiring president burst into tears. He had reached his end. When he returned to private life, Wilson never left Washington again, but lived on there in the utmost privacy. On Armistice Day in 1922 and 1923, he appeared on his balcony and said a few words to the crowd. He spoke of the shame of America's remaining outside the League. At last, in 1924, he died, after a long and painful agony. Not long before, he had made great and splendid plans, and he had almost carried them through successfully; he died defeated, having seen all his hopes brought to ruin.

As early as his inauguration, Harding declared that the United States "sought no part in directing the destinies of the world." And not content with staying out of the League, Harding pretended that it did not exist. Congress raised the customs tariffs, insisted upon the total repayment of war debts, and limited immigration. They forgot that if the safety valves are not allowed to work the boiler may blow up.

Harding was ignorant of this fact. He was a small-town politician—as Wilson said, he had "the bungalow mind." "For Harding exuded the atmosphere of a sleepy Ohio town—the shady streets, the weekly Lodge meetings, the smoking-room stories, golf on Sunday mornings, followed by a fried chicken dinner, and an afternoon nap." In forming his Cabinet, he mingled able men (Charles E. Hughes as secretary of state, Andrew W. Mellon at the Treasury, Hoover in charge of commerce, H. A. Wallace in the Department of Agriculture, and John W. Weeks as secretary of war) with poker-playing friends from his native state. He also picked Taft for chief justice. Alice Roosevelt Longworth, Theodore Roosevelt's daughter, was shocked at the sight of packs of cards all over the President's desk at the White House, tall glasses of whiskey (in the middle of prohibition), the air heavy with cigar smoke, and the "Ohio gang" sitting about with their vests unbuttoned and their feet on the table. Harding was not an evil man. He set the socialist Debs free and even received him kindly. But he had not the least understanding of business. If someone came to see him to speak of foreign policy, he would reply, "You and Jud Welliver get together . . . he handles these matters for me." If the business was finance, he would say, "I can't make a damn thing out of this tax problem."

Those who had voted for Harding in the hope of seeing prosperity maintained were thoroughly disappointed. In 1921, prices declined severely, the index falling from 193 in 1920 to 163 in 1921 (1913=100). The number of unemployed reached 4,754,000. There were a hundred thousand bankruptcies in the year. Four hundred and fifty thousand farmers became insolvent and lost their farms. What were the causes of this depression? The year before, Wilson had begun a new financial policy. Taxes had been raised, and the government's income now exceeded its expenditure. The army's purchases had stopped. The bankers had raised the rates of interest. Europe, with its supplies cut off, no longer had the means of buying the American harvests. There had to be a general deflation, and it did indeed take place. Now

99

the psychological effect of deflation is to stop buying. The consumer says to himself, "It will be cheaper tomorrow," and he waits. Many shopkeepers canceled their orders. Then there was a reaction from this excessive stagnation—purchasing, after all, could not be put off indefinitely. The crisis was very short. From the beginning of 1922, production began to rise again. The workers' purchasing power (real wages, on the basis of 1914 equaling 100) reached 113 in 1922 and 119 in 1923. The hurricane had blown itself out. Harding had had nothing whatever to do with either the depression or the recovery.

Yet the high customs barriers that the government so willingly granted the manufacturers helped to make foreign trade more difficult. Foreign countries that can neither export nor borrow are clearly unable to import, still less repay their debts. Wilson had uttered a warning full of sense: "If there ever was a time when America had anything to fear from foreign competition, that time has passed. If we wish to have Europe settle her debts—governmental and commercial—we must be prepared to buy from her." But it was the same with this question as with that of German reparations: it seemed that those who were dealing with the matter had never thought about even the ABCs of economics, or else that, for ignoble, vote-catching reasons, they deliberately ignored them. It would be difficult to imagine a more stupid economic policy than that of the years that followed the war. The refusal to help the workers to improve their standard of living meant a cutting down of the number of consumers. Although the unions had increased their membership during the war, rising from 2,647,000 in 1914, to 3,368,000 in 1918, they still only accounted for an eighth of the working population. It must be emphasized again that these unions were in no way revolutionary; but a struggle had begun between the principle of the open shop —that is to say, the factory being open to all workers, union members or no—and that of the closed shop, the factory being forbidden to hire nonunionists.

It was a legitimate dispute. Unfortunately, the manufacturers and the government on the one side and the unions on the other carried on their arguments in an intolerant manner. The "red panic" had died away, for want of anything to keep it going, but the campaign to suppress all "radicalism" went on. Patriotic organizations (the National Security League) appointed themselves guardians of Americanism. Teachers were required to take an oath of loyalty; history books were censored; those unfortunate people who had foreign names were treated as suspects. These were not the criminal activities of the Ku Klux Klan, but the spirit was the same. The Supreme Court, which had been set up to insure that every man enjoyed the rights that the Constitution guaranteed him, displayed weakness as soon as "sedition" or "criminal unionism" were mentioned. On several occasions two of its members, Mr. Justice Holmes and Mr. Justice Brandeis, had to dissent vigorously from the majority to defend the rights of free opinion and free speech. In 1921, the Sacco and Vanzetti case stirred the whole world. These two Italians were accused of murder. Their guilt was a matter for the jury alone. But they were known to be anarchists and troublemakers, and it very quickly became apparent that because of their opinions they were going to have no chance of an impartial trial. Their case then became a symbol, for the entire world, of the struggle for civil liberties.

Another aspect of the period, which sometimes took on the appearance of racial prejudice, was the restriction of immigration. On this point, the employers and the workers were in agreement. Before the war, industry had been in favor of immigration, since it supplied docile labor accustomed to low wages. During the war, on the other hand, millions of Europeans wanted to leave their ruined countries. In 1919, the number of newcomers had gone down to 141,132; in 1920, it leaped up to 430,001. In 1921, a law was passed reducing each nation's quota to 3 percent of the number of its nationals present in the United States in 1910. This was a severe discrimination against the southern and Slavonic nations, since their immigration was recent. The quota favored the oldest immigrant groups, the Anglo-Saxons, the Scandinavians, and the Germans, and the law was made in response to an obvious desire to safeguard the traditions of the long-established Americans. In 1924, the quotas were reduced to 2 percent of the number of nationals present in the United States in 1890. In 1929, this law was reinforced by another that set a maximum of 150,000 immigrants, maintaining the system of quotas. The result was that the yearly number of entries fell to 100,000 (for some quotas were not used) ; and from this figure the number of those who left for Europe—sometimes equally great—had to be deducted. America no longer welcomed the downtrodden and humiliated refugees from the Old World. The great adventure of the peopling of one continent by another had thus come to an end.

Although foreign policy was of very little interest to President Harding, a foreign policy was nevertheless necessary. His was above all negative. America turned in upon herself. She had not wanted to join the League of Nations. She did not want anything to do with the Russia of the Soviets. Other nations, observing the stability of the Communist regime, had recognized it, out of realism, in spite of ideological differences. The United States, frightened by the red bogey, would not do so, and this had the disadvantage of creating a hostile atmosphere between the two countries. On the other hand, a conference of the Pacific powers, meeting in Washington in 1921, seemed to produce some positive results. Several treaties were determined upon at this conference. One was an agreement between five powers (United States, Great Britain, Japan, France, and Italy) for a "naval holiday" in the building of capital ships, the relative tonnages being fixed at 5, 5, 3, 1.67, and 1.67 respectively. Another was a four-power treaty by which the United States, Great Britain, Japan, and France bound themselves to respect their respective rights in the Pacific. And a nine-power treaty guaranteed China's territorial integrity and the "open door" in trade. At the time of their signature, these pacts were thought of as a success. Later they were decried as having weakened the American position in the Pacific by preventing the navy from making bases at Guam, Samoa, and so on. But anyone can be wise after the event.

VI

Harding's tragedy was the weakness that prevented him from breaking with his old poker-playing friends from Ohio—friends to whom he had entrusted posts that carried financial responsibility. Some of them abused it. Stern watchfulness is the only remedy against corruption. Harding, a "regular guy," trustful by nature and faithful to his friends to the point of rashness, was no man to impose discipline. "I cannot hope to be one of the great presidents," he said, "but perhaps I may be remembered as one of the best loved." He was above all one of those who was most deceived. Colonel Charles R. Forbes, set at the head of the Veterans' Bureau, stole several hundred thousand dollars before being locked up in a more suitable place. Colonel Thomas W. Miller, the Alien Property Custodian, accepted money for upholding unjustifiable claims, and he too was convicted. Jess Smith, one of Harding's old companions, set up in Washington as the protector (for a fee) of those who chose to break the law on prohibition. He killed himself in the flat he shared with Daugherty, the attorney general. It was a curious friendship, that between a swindler and the chief legal officer; but Daugherty was no more than a dubious go-between, violent and embittered in politics, dishonest in business.

According to William Allen White, Albert B. Fall, the secretary of the interior, looked like a cheap, obvious faker. "I could scarcely believe my eyes." Fall was reminiscent of the cowboy politicians of 1860. He displayed an unlimited contempt for reform and for human nature. An exceedingly wealthy oil-magnate, Edward L. Doheny, who had made great contributions to Harding's campaign fund, presented Fall with a satchel containing $100,000 in notes, and this "out of pure friendship," as he put it. Now it so happened that Fall, in agreement with the Secretary of the Navy, was able to dispose of the vast naval oil reserves of Elk Hills and Teapot Dome. He granted Elk Hills to Doheny and Teapot Dome to Harry F. Sinclair, without their having been put up for bids, on the pretext that in time of war the navy could use them. When rumors began to circulate in Washington, Fall swore upon oath that there was not the least connection between the grant and the satchel with $100,000 in it. This hardly convinced anybody at all.

The year 1923 began badly for the President. Congress was threatening many of his favorites with inquiries. Cramer, Colonel Forbes's adviser, had killed himself. Mrs. Harding, known to her friends either as "the Duchess" or as "Ma," suspected that her husband had a mistress who was getting into the White House by the back stairs. Furthermore, the President was speculating on Wall Street, and he owed his brokers $180,000. It was scarcely surprising that he should sleep badly and that his heart should be giving him trouble. Under the influence of belated scruples, he told those of the group who had survived the

103

various scandals that he was giving up poker and liquor. In order to get away, he determined to make a journey in the northwestern states and in Alaska. At first he intended to take with him only the members of his own circle. Then, perhaps because he felt a great need for the advice of an upright man, he invited Hoover. The Secretary of Commerce had just won a great success—the reduction of hours of work in the steel industry from twelve to eight. He accepted, but he very soon regretted it; for Harding, anxious to escape from his own thoughts, wanted to play bridge from morning till night. By the end of the journey, Hoover was sick of bridge for the rest of his life.

One day after lunch, Harding hesitantly said to Hoover, "If you knew of a great scandal in our administration, would you for the good of the party and the country expose it, or would you bury it?"

Hoover at once replied, "Publish it! And at least get credit for integrity on your side." Harding remarked that this might be politically dangerous. On the return journey, he grew more and more nervous. At Seattle, in the course of a speech on Alaska, he suddenly dropped the notes that he was reading and clung to the desk. Hoover had to take over. Harding was to have spoken at San Francisco, and Hoover had taken the opportunity of adding to the speech some remarks on the International Court of Justice and on the United States' desire to cooperate with the rest of the world in the maintenance of peace. But the President's physician said that Harding had eaten some crabmeat that had disagreed with him and that he had to stay at the hotel in San Francisco for a complete rest.

The truth was that Attorney General Daugherty had been hurriedly called to Seattle to account for his doings. This painful interview had convinced Harding that all his closest intimates, Forbes, Fall, and Daugherty, had betrayed him. Was it so surprising that he should have had a heart attack? For that was the diagnosis of the specialists. The crabmeat had little to do with it. Nor had poison, in spite of the rumors that at once began to spread abroad. Would he live? It was scarcely likely. The doctors told him the truth, and perhaps it comforted him. He was aware that if he survived, he was headed straight for public scandal and domestic disaster. One evening, while Mrs.

Harding was reading to him, he died suddenly. His body was brought back to Washington, and at every station crowds (who as yet knew nothing) gathered to sing his favorite hymn. It was only when the scandals of his administration became public that his popularity evaporated. But was he indeed very blameworthy? The electors had chosen him because he was the most average American. Their mistake had been in wishing to entrust a more than human task to this average man, and in wanting a return to the normal in an essentially abnormal period.

On the night of the second to the third of April, 1923, the news came suddenly to Vice-President Coolidge, who had gone to spend his holidays at his father's farm in Vermont. By the light of a lamp held by Mrs. Coolidge, who had hurriedly put on a dressing gown, Mr. Coolidge senior, who was a justice of the peace as well as a respected country storekeeper, administered the oath of office to his son, on the old family Bible. The nation loved this little scene, so very much after the manner of the Founding Fathers. It was reassuring to think that the least moral president in the history of the United States, the president with the most undesirable set of friends, was to be succeeded by a Yankee and a Puritan.

PART FOUR

Boom and Depression

NOW began the time of wild extravagance. The flock, under its silent, Puritan shepherd, believed that the kingdom of Heaven had settled down in North America. A "new era" was beginning. Every year there would be more cars, more washing machines, more radios. On Wall Street, shares would perpetually go on rising, so that one day everybody would be rich. For everyone, employer, clerk, and workingman, would speculate and win. For a long while, the steadily rising curve of stock prices seemed to justify these hopes. The country was intoxicated by success, and its hero was the businessman: he appeared better qualified to give the country moral guidance than the artist or the philosopher. Spiritual values were left to one side. Profit and yield became the gods of the tribe.

Then suddenly, like a plane in an air pocket, the market collapsed, and despair was as disproportionate as the people's confidence had been before. The fall, like the rise, went much too far. It was not true that prosperity had been no more than an illusion. It had been justified by new techniques, by the application of scientific methods to the management and direction of undertakings, by the intelligent work of all, by abundant energy, and by the great size of the market. It was to come again. The trouble lay largely in people's minds. What had been lacking was not industry, nor knowledge, nor good fortune, but common sense, self-control, and the moderating activity of an intelligent government. All things being considered, America came out of this wild adventure wiser than she had gone into it, better prepared to accept new ideas and essential measures. Adversity is not without its uses.

I

In the United States, the president must be a symbol. If he has been well chosen, he embodies the wishes and the thoughts of the Americans. If he fails in this, he no longer fulfills his function, and the country is without a guide. In 1912, an idealistic nation had wanted a teacher of ethics—Wilson had been the man. Then the ideal set up by him had been degraded, and this had caused a materialistic reaction. Hence Harding, the symbol of "normalcy"; but Harding had been a grave disappointment. In an honest country, scandal is infinitely remote from normality. Calvin Coolidge, made president by the failure of a diseased heart, was exactly the man that the America of the twenties wanted. This may seem strange; for at a time of prodigal abundance, when Wall Street was bursting with wealth and pride, it was surprising to see a colorless, sparing, pious man in the White House. It seemed like an atavistic reversion to the earliest days of the Republic—"the survival of a spiritual race that had almost passed from the earth." William Allen White entitled his biography of Coolidge *A Puritan in Babylon*: there is no better summing up of the situation.

License, speculation, ostentatious display in the great cities;

in the White House, the "family portrait," the Puritan from Vermont, thin, tight-lipped, pale, distrustful.

Calvin Coolidge had sand-colored hair, blue eyes, and the most outstanding nasal accent that New England had ever produced. It was said that "cow," as he pronounced it, was a four-syllabled word at least. But why should he not have drawn out his words? He said so few of them. By nature, by education, and perhaps because he had nothing to say, he had always been laconic. When he entered politics and observed that the brevity of his remarks was thought amusing, he turned what had been a weakness into a rule of conduct. He possessed a kind of negative humor, and his fooling amused nobody more than himself. He knew that his silences were useful to him. When he spoke, he had no fear of the commonplace, and by sheer force of platitude, he acquired a sort of originality. "Work and save, save and work": such was the text of one of his microscopic speeches. Mrs. Coolidge, a charming and unassuming woman, still, after a long married life, thought her husband an impenetrable mystery. Had this mystery been pierced, there would have been found, not emptiness, but the wan, shriveled image of a very old ideal.

Coolidge had no ambition to be, like Wilson, a leader who would force through a program. He preferred following—and upholding. He was honest, and sometimes he was sentimental. He advised the country to be faithful to the ancient traditions of honor, courage, honest work, and well-filled days that had made the nation what it was. He sincerely believed that these virtues were to be found above all in the world of business. "This is a business country," he said, "and it wants a business government." At this juncture, that was exactly what the nation wanted to hear. But paradoxically, it had no wish to see the White House occupied by one of those powerful bankers or captains of industry with a jutting chin, a huge neck, and the eloquence of a high-pressure salesman who were then the real leaders of the country. After so many dramas, the nation was reassured by an unobtrusive president who went to church every Sunday before his short trip on the Potomac, "like a God-fearing countryman."

At a time when deeds, if not words, were cynical, it was a

pleasure to hear the President say in a speech at Wheaton College in June of 1923 that the nation with the greatest moral power will win; there is only one form of political strategy, and that is to try to do the right thing. "We do not need more material development, we need more spiritual development. . . . We do not need more law; we need more religion. We do not need more of the things that are seen, we need more of the things that are unseen." Such were Coolidge's sermons. In fact, he rather favored, by his policy, the pursuit of visible objects. Who would have dared criticize him? "So completely did he win over the country that, if the President had declared that a straight line is the shortest distance between two points, one wonders if editorial pages would not have paid tribute to his concise wisdom."

Wilson too had delivered moral speeches to the American people. But he had tried to guide the nation, to lead it up to regions so high that the air there was difficult to breathe. Coolidge, on the contrary, justified the most mundane pursuit of happiness. He neither tried to reform nor to instruct his fellow citizens. He confirmed them in their prejudices, and at the same time, by his obvious integrity, he reassured them as to the purity of their intentions. William Allen White, who knew the President well, had an affection for him, although he found his icy silences disconcerting. Others were harder on him and said that he was not a great president, nor even a good one.

In his family life, Coolidge showed himself capable of senti-ment, or rather of sentimentality. In his public life he was "al-most a pathological case," cold, sour, and with a strange horror of human contact. His probity was unquestionable. The magnates of the banks or industry would never have been able to buy him, but there was no need for them to do so. He was instinctively devoted to them; he believed in the Hamiltonian doctrine of the faultlessness of the rich, the wise, the virtuous, and not in Jeffer-son's or Wilson's kind of democracy. Compassion was not his strong point. "If a man is out of a job, it's his own fault," said Coolidge; and his style was made up of aphorisms of this nature. Not long before, when he was vice-president, he had taken on the duty of dining out every evening, with Washington's great host-esses. As he never said a word at these entertainments, someone asked him why he accepted so many invitations. "Got to eat some-where," he replied. He would probably have been happier as a clergyman in a country village in the seventeenth century than as president in the White House in the twentieth.

And yet when the question of reelection came up in 1924, he decided to stand. He was so popular that his nomination by the Republican party was a foregone conclusion. Out of a feeling for economy (economy of both time and expense), he cut the convention as short as he could. What was the point of appealing to the electors' emotions? Since the end of the war, the country had not recovered its ability to feel political enthusiasm. No doubt there was one wing of the party that was still progressive, and Senator La Follette called for the nationalization of the railways, of hydroelectric power, and of public services, and for the right of having some of the decisions of the Supreme Court, which was very much against the trade unions, annulled by Congress. But the Republican convention's state of mind was that of Coolidge. At the very first ballot, it gave the incumbent president 1,065 votes as against 34 for La Follette, and then it broke up in that gray atmosphere of apathy and dismal constraint that always seemed to emanate from Coolidge.

The Democrats did not have a ghost of a chance. In the eyes of the electors, the Republican party meant prosperity. A leader like Wilson might, it is true, once more have brought over the progressive Republicans, the independents, and the unions to the Democratic side. But the Southern wing of the party came out in favor of prohibition and of the Ku Klux Klan, while the Northern wing spoke up for the unions and hoped to win the Negro vote. The convention was therefore hopelessly split. William McAdoo, backed by the South and the West, struggled against Al Smith, the Catholic governor of New York, for ninety-five ballots. At the ninety-sixth, they both withdrew and a compromise candidate was agreed upon: he was John W. Davis, a business lawyer; he was an intelligent and upright man, but as the greatest bankers were his clients, he could scarcely have the appearance of a champion of the working classes. Al Smith would no doubt have been a better candidate than Davis; he would have carried on a violent campaign based upon the scandals of the Harding Administration. Davis was not a man to use weapons of that kind. The progressives, looking upon both the big parties as corrupt and reactionary, formed a third party and nominated La Follette, as a gesture.

It was an uneventful campaign. Coolidge limited himself to promising economies and the reduction of taxes. He won 382 electoral votes, as opposed to Davis's 136. "Normalcy" had not even had to fight: it was supreme on either side. Coolidge's obvious honesty had won the party forgiveness for the sins of Harding. He was installed on March 4, 1925, and his inauguration speech was the first that was ever broadcast. The nation was pleased at hearing that slow, grating, nasal voice asserting that the American people had at last reached "a state of happiness rarely seen in the history of mankind." He stated that his administration would not intervene to change so perfect a state of affairs. Far from his mind was any intention of hindering or embarrassing those who had succeeded. No making of rules for industry. Coolidge considered that his function was to reduce public spending and taxation and thus to create conditions that would allow every man a chance of success. "We are not without our problems, but our most important problem is not to win ourselves new privileges, it is to maintain those we already have." It was a negative program—it was that program that the powerful rulers who had made Coolidge wanted. "They wanted as little government as possible, at as low cost as possible." As for Coolidge himself, he was convinced that by doing little and letting the masters of the economy have a free hand, he would be serving the country very well. The consequences were to show that the method was not without its risks.

II

Les Affaires sont les Affaires: business is business. This is the title of a French play by Octave Mirabeau, and it means that business is war—war in which there is no such thing as a foul blow. That was certainly not the official moral doctrine in the United States during the twenties. One had to make money, of course, otherwise the machine would have stopped working, but the desire for profit was not to be the prime mover of the economy. According to the new prophets, the real aim was to fulfill a social function. For them a great shop was a church, the owner a priest, and the "service" of the customer a kind of worship. Businessmen's clubs (Rotarians, Elks, Kiwanis) gave their weekly luncheons a ritual character. Business was there discussed with both unction and mysticism. The business executive became a kind of ecclesiastical dignitary. Holy Scripture itself provided texts that justified this philosophy. For some time, the nonfiction best seller was a book on Christ by Bruce Barton called *The Man Nobody Knows*. In this work, one learned that Jesus had been "a great executive." He had chosen twelve men "right at the bottom of the business ladder," and He had knit them into a model organization that had conquered the world. His parables in the Gospels were "the most powerful advertisement of all time." In short, Jesus of Nazareth was the founder of modern business. "Serve thy neighbor as thyself" was the salesman's slogan in the twenties.

The masters of the economy prided themselves on being aware of their responsibilities. In some cases this was true. Edward A. Filene, the owner of the biggest department store in Boston, shared his profits among his employees. Many had grasped that mass production, which required great numbers of buyers, also called for high wages. Henry Ford wanted low selling prices and a continual rise in the standard of living. The purchasing power of the workers was in fact increasing, but more slowly than profits. In 1914, there had been 4,500 millionaires in the country; in 1926, there were 11,000 of them, and an advance guard of billionaires was visible in the distance. Yet the masses could now own things that not long before had seemed quite out of their reach. America's standard of living astonished Europe. What did this prosperity mean? Was America benefiting by Europe's ruin? Or was the prosperity caused by the exceptional conditions provided by her continental market and her wealth in raw materials? Was it perhaps the scientific organization of work, the multiplication of machine tools, the intensity of research? Europe might cry out against some aspects of this civilization: she could not deny its successes.

It was not all the industries that were prosperous, however. Textiles, coal mining, and shipbuilding were only working at half strength. The farmers were sending out distress signals. There were whole regions, such as New England, the South, and the farming states of the Middle West, that did not share in the national euphoria. But there were some flourishing new manufactures. The automobile was the queen. In 1927, the launching of the new Ford (Model A) was a national event, and the mounted police had to be called out to control the crowds who came to gaze upon the new goddess. In 1919, there had been 7,576,888 cars; in 1929, there were 26,502,508. Filling stations rose up all over the country. In the towns, red and green traffic lights came into existence. Together with cars, the making of tires became a flourishing industry. Propelling himself in an automobile was now one of man's inalienable rights.

Immediately after the car came the radio. The sales of receiving sets went from $60,000,000 in 1922 to $842,000,000 in 1929. Pessimists said, "The public will soon get tired of it." They were wrong. These invisible friends who came to talk to everyone in his own home soon became indispensable. So many men and women are so very much alone. In a country where the newspapers were more local than national, the radio became a powerful means of unification and of education, too. Advertisers provided the listeners with excellent concerts. Appreciation of the better kind of music spread.

There was prosperity also in the industries that made such electrical household devices as refrigerators, vacuum cleaners, and washing machines; in artificial textiles, in telephones, and in films. The banks were prosperous; so were the insurance firms and the chain stores. Business took on new forms. Not only were the masses spending their earnings with an open hand, but they were also buying on credit—buying those things that publicity had made so desirable. Before the war, only objects that were meant to last a lifetime, such as houses, for example, were bought on installments. Since the war, everything could be paid for by the month. Furniture shops said to young newly married couples, "You furnish the girl; we furnish the home." Presently the funeral parlors were to advertise, "You die; we do the rest." A car, a radio, a refrigerator, washing machine, piano, record player, engagement ring with its traditional tiny diamond—anything would do to open an installment account. Often the farmer's tractor was worn out before it was paid for. Was this easy credit a good thing or not? It let young people enjoy things at the time when they wanted them most, but it burdened the family budget for a long while afterward; and above all it created, throughout the country, a debt amounting to several billion dollars, which, in a time of crisis, was to give rise to very serious dangers.

Another very marked tendency in business during the twenties was concentration. The Supreme Court had given up applying the antitrust laws, and the government would not strengthen them. In the course of this decade, there were many mergers in all industries, in the banks, and particularly in the public utility companies that looked after such things as water, gas, and electricity. In 1925, sixteen groups controlled 53 percent of these concerns. In many industries, there was a return to the practice of setting up holding companies—a dangerous practice, because it gave the real power in important firms to a small number of men who, for their part, were not risking their own capital. Concentration also spread to the distributive trades. Not only was there an increase in the number of branches of the Atlantic & Pacific Tea Company, and of the five- and ten-cent stores, but everywhere there were to be seen new chains of groceries, drugstores, candy stores, and cigar stores. These shops, working together and on a national scale, bought better and sold cheaper, which was to the public's benefit; and it appeared that the standard of quality would be better looked after. But the small shopkeepers suffered from this competition, just as they suffered from the competition of the huge mail-order firms such as Sears, Roebuck or Montgomery Ward, whose catalogues reached the most remote farmer. In trade, as in industry, big business was taking the place of the individual.

When, through some remnant of caution, the concentration did not take the form of a trust or a holding company, it assumed a new shape—the trade association, a grouping of manufacturers in the same industry, who came to friendly agreements to share out the market or to fix prices and wages. The Coolidge Administration took care not to upset these arrangements. The President enjoined the Federal Trade Commission to be an adviser to industry, a helper, not a controller. The good aspect of these understandings was that they favored the standardization of spare parts—the number of kinds of bolt, tube, electric plug, and so on, were limited. The success of this attempt at unification was principally due to Herbert Hoover, the secretary of commerce, a clear-minded, strong, and able man. Hoover agreed, with the Europeans, that personal taste should be left entirely free as regards art or fashion, but individualism rightly seemed to him absurd in the matter of the caliber of pipes. He substituted a simple orderliness for a very expensive state of chaos. This was one of American industry's strong points.

Coolidge's own economic policy was a mass of contradictions. The President agreed with Hoover when the Secretary of Commerce urged the American manufacturers to export, but he maintained a customs tariff that shut out foreign products. Now the European countries, which were already in debt, could only buy by exchanging their own wares for American goods or by finding loans in the United States. The latter was the method that was chosen. The final effect was that the exports were financed by the American taxpayer, since it was clear to any reasonable man that the international debts never could be paid. More logically, some of the great American firms, Ford, International Harvester, and Standard Oil, built factories in Europe.

Andrew Mellon, the secretary of the treasury, ruled over the country's finances. He was a seventy-year-old Pittsburgh banker, and he had deplored the policies of Bryan and Wilson in their time. Like Coolidge, he thought that the government of a business country should cooperate with the business world and not crush it with taxes. He was a fragile, distinguished man, enormously wealthy, and he collected the finest pictures in the world with the intention of leaving them to the American nation. But although he was personally generous, he maintained that government was business and that it ought to be carried on according to business principles, that is to say, economically. He wanted a balanced budget, the repayment of the debts, and the lowering of the supertax that he thought too great a burden for the great fortunes. If it exceeded 25 percent of the income, said Mellon, it was no longer taxation but confiscation, and this resulted in the discouragement of all fresh initiative. A budget intended to relieve the millionaires could scarcely be a popular one, however. The progressives in Congress stood out against Mellon, and for some time they compelled Coolidge to maintain the supertax. But the stubborn and able Mellon granted abatements and repayments to some taxpayers.

The danger of lowering taxes, like the excessive facility of credit, was that by increasing the amount that people could spend, it encouraged inflation. When the means of buying increase faster than the production of things to be bought, a rise in prices is inevitable. During the period of Coolidge and Mellon, there were some spectacular booms. It was then that the real estate speculators made unbelievable fortunes. The motor car enabled thousands of the newly wealthy to discover California and Florida. Until 1920, Miami had been a little, rather marshy tropical town of thirty thousand inhabitants. Suddenly it was invaded by the speculators. Twenty-five thousand agents sold plots of land, promising the buyers profits of $100,000—profits that some of them did in fact realize. Soon the spectacle of Florida called to mind the gold rush of the previous century in California. The whole coast was turned into a Riviera, a transformation to which the climate was favorable; Florida was nearer New York than the Pacific Coast, and confidence in the Coolidge prosperity incited men who a little while before had been quite sensible to commit follies. But was it really folly? We can now see that Florida's progress has justified the enthusiasms of that time. But these were premature. For two or three years, people spoke of nothing but plots bought for $1,000 and sold for $200,000, and of the Friendly Sun and Fairy Cities —it was a riot of capital letters. Then the buyers became fewer and payments harder: a cyclone hastened the disaster. A man who had sold a piece of land for $3,000 and who had been breaking his heart because successive buyers had then paid $6,000, $9,000, $12,000, saw his plot come back to him, all the subsequent owners having gone bankrupt one after another. The Florida boom ended in catastrophe.

But at least it was not an irremediable catastrophe, since the peninsula of the sun kept its beauty; besides, it only ruined some not very agreeable speculators. A far more serious case was that of the farmers. Between 1922 and 1927, a million men were forced off the land, and those who remained were none the better for it. The net income of the average farmer had fallen to less than $800 a year, against $1,300 for the teacher and $1,650 for the civil servant, other poorly paid groups of men. The farmers, who fed the nation, no longer received even 10 percent of the national income. It is true that after a war the position of agriculture is almost always bad: war causes unusually great requirements and unusually great production; then, as soon as peace comes, an agricultural crisis comes with it.

But in the past, recovery had often been rapid. In Coolidge's time, the distress went on and on. Why? (a) The high prices paid during the war had encouraged farmers to break new ground and to provide themselves with modern machines. They therefore produced more—too much. Hence a drop in farm prices (40 percent from 1920 to 1927). (b) Meanwhile the industrial products bought by the farmers, such as clothes, tools, manures, rose by about 30 percent. (c) Local land taxes increased; so did mortgage rates. The farmers, made bold by the high wartime prices, had borrowed heavily. (d) The restriction of immigration made labor scarce and wages high. (e) The consumers' tastes were changing. They ate less meat, less cereals, more vegetables and fruit. The fashion among women was to remain thin. During the war, the farmer had got into the habit of overproduction. He no longer knew how to readjust himself.

The desperate condition of the farmers necessarily had political repercussions. In Congress, a Farm Bloc won a protective tariff against imported foodstuffs; but it was absurd to defend what was normally an exporting industry by a customs barrier. Laws were passed to regulate slaughterhouses and to make farm loans easier. These are the usual sops; they never resolve agricultural problems. In the end, financial help from the government appeared to be the only remedy. Congress passed the McNary-Haugen Act in both 1927 and 1928: this provided for the purchase of farmers' surpluses, which the government would sell abroad at the world price, while for their home sales the farmers would be protected by the tariff. The government's losses were to be made good by an equalization tax. Coolidge vetoed this law both times, saying that it would make overproduction worse still, that it would give rise to frauds without number. The West and the Middle West strongly resented his action. Coolidge knew very little about the land, and he accepted the unhappy state of the farmers with resignation: "Well, farmers never have had money," he said. "I don't believe we can do much about it. But, of course, we shall have to seem to be doing something; do the best we can without much hope." This was economic defeatism. A two-thirds majority in the Senate was needed to override the veto. It was almost obtained, but not quite. The law did not pass, and the farmers' discontent increased.

There was another group that did not feel it had its share of the prosperity—the trade unions. The government's policy with regard to them was without any question reactionary. They were denied rights that prewar administrations had recognized. The federal courts almost reverted to the point of view of just after the Civil War, when the formation of a union was held to be conspiracy. The courts issued strikebreaking injunctions, and the unions were made responsible for losses. Some industries "paternally" set up their own unions, supported by the management. The Supreme Court upheld the "yellow dog contracts," by which a worker undertook never to join a union. In short, the retrogression was quite obvious; and in this case too there was deep discontent. Coolidge attached little importance to these feelings and serenely preserved his faith in the religion of laissez-faire and in the inherent virtues of big business.

To a superficial observer, he seemed to be right. Most of the Americans, if their standard of living was compared with that of other nations, appeared prosperous. But it was finance and industry that were profiting from the increase in the national income much more than the workers and the farmers, and that was where the danger lay. In 1929, out of twenty-seven and a half million American families, six million (or more than 21 percent) had incomes of less than $1,000 a year; twelve million (or more than 42 percent) less than $1,500, and twenty million (or 71 percent) less than the $2,500 that was then considered necessary to live decently. The thirty-six thousand richest families had an income equal to that of the twelve million who earned less than $1,500 a year. To an impartial eye it was clear that such inequality must sooner or later lead to great changes.

III

During the twenties, the United States had a schizophrenic foreign policy. Two strong currents of feeling tore the country apart. On the one hand, people were disgusted by the war and its results; they did not want to have any further part in European affairs that damaged the unity of the country by dividing its different racial groups against one another. They therefore wished to keep away from international organizations.

On the other hand, the country's conscience was not easy. Wilson's visions of worldwide peace were not forgotten, and people understood that a great nation, the strongest of all, could not always adopt Pilate's attitude, when the fate of the world was at stake.

These opposing currents gave rise to great weakness. There was an attempt at having the International Court of Justice accepted, but it was accompanied by such reservations that the United States would not have been bound by the Court's decisions. There was a disarmament conference at Washington, but critics pointed out that during the preceding year, America had spent 174 percent more on her fleet than she had in 1914.

There was at least one precise and immediate question that called for a prompt solution, and that was the problem of German reparations, complicated as it was by Europe's debts to America. Germany, by the Treaty of Versailles, had agreed to pay reparations that were insanely beyond the country's possibilities. Naturally, she had not kept her promise. She did not want to do so, nor was she able to do so. To force her, Poincaré had occupied the Ruhr; Germany had replied with passive resistance and the extreme devaluation of her money. The mark had fallen to something like absolute zero; Germany's finances had been systematically disorganized. There appeared to be no solution.

In this case, the United States' intervention was reasonably constructive. Officially, America refused to interfere in this European problem: unofficially, certain eminent Americans (Charles G. Dawes and Owen D. Young) were authorized, one after the other, to preside over a commission to gauge Germany's ability to pay and to draw up a scheme for the settlement of the reparations. Meanwhile, to save Germany from total bankruptcy and from a revolution, America lent $2,475,000,000 to the German government and to private concerns, during the period between 1924 and 1930. During the same period, the Germans paid the Allies $4,470,300,000 in reparations and the Allies repaid debts to the United States amounting to $2,606,340,000.

It was a somewhat ridiculous merry-go-round. No doubt the Allies had borrowed from the Americans during the war; but they observed that the money had been spent in a common undertaking. Washington had granted generous terms: repayment over sixty-two years, with interest scarcely rising to more than 2 percent. But that was not the question. The insoluble problem was still that of the movement of money at a time when America would not import European goods. The elementary principles of economics were being neglected. So long as the United States lent money to Germany, the wooden horses could go on turning, without anyone being the richer. If the Americans grew tired of lending, the movement would stop. This was perfectly clear; yet still the want of realism persisted. The problem was explained to Coolidge, and he replied, "They hired the money, didn't they?" It was a typical Coolidgism, but it was not sensible. The question was not whether they had borrowed the money or not, but whether they had any means whatever of repaying it. In the end, nobody paid America, and Uncle Sam was very unfairly renamed Uncle Shylock. It would have been better to have given up these irrecoverable debts and thus to have gained some friends.

In Latin America, the United States made worthy attempts at the difficult task of improving relations. Dollar diplomacy, which consisted of protecting American financial or commercial interests, if necessary by landing the marines, could not but wound the pride of the other American republics. In Mexico, a new government was making things difficult for American shareholders. Some of them asked President Coolidge to intervene. "Now look on the other side of the picture," said Coolidge. "Here we are the most powerful nation in the world. At this moment we have special representatives in Europe as well as all our diplomats urging reduction of armaments and preaching peace. The world of today would harshly condemn us if, despite our attitude, we should go to war with a neighbor not nearly our equal. What do you suppose people in years to come would say? Powerful United States crushing powerless Mexico. Don't you think it is better for us to find another way to handle the situation?"

He dealt with it by sending an intelligent, tactful representative, Dwight W. Morrow, to Mexico, to bring about a reconciliation. Thus, as William Allen White observes, Coolidge was "a curious mixture of moneylender and Samaritan," pitiless to European debtors, a good neighbor to Mexico, a harsh one to Nicaragua. In that country, a revolution had started up against the United States' financial protectorate. Coolidge supported the opposition that declared itself pro-American. He landed the marines, saying, "We are not making war on Nicaragua any more than a policeman on the street is making war upon the passers-by." This was a tolerably incoherent policy; but some allowances must be made for Coolidge. It was far from easy to reconcile neutralism, the defense of an ideal, and dollar diplomacy.

In 1928, the Kellogg-Briand treaty was signed: the laboring mountain had produced its mouse.

Frank B. Kellogg was the American secretary of state, Briand the French foreign minister. Between them, they had undertaken to outlaw war. Fifteen powers and then, by successive accessions, sixty-two, solemnly bound themselves never again to have recourse to war as an instrument of national policy. Some sanguine minds (Kellogg and Briand among them) sincerely believed that this was the most important international event in history, even more important than the League of Nations. They forgot, however, that the treaty did not contain any clause whatsoever that provided for the least penalty for the infraction of any of the obligations undertaken. It expressed pious hopes: it provided nothing that might justify them. In those days, the Americans, as well as many Europeans, would not admit that in international politics an obligation without penalty for nonobservance was worthless. It has been wittily said that strength and policy can no more be separated than marriage and sex: both sex and strength can be sublimated, but neither can be cast out.

The inefficacy of the pact was obvious as soon as real cases arose—cases such as Japan's attack on Manchuria in 1931, and the resurgence of warlike parties in Germany. When these things happened, nobody invoked the Kellogg-Briand Pact: its uselessness was too well known. Sumner Welles, later undersecretary of state, was even of the opinion that the pact had been a danger. It had given the Americans the impression (a) that they were sheltered from any war when in fact their position, in a world in turmoil, was growing more and more perilous; and (b) that they had done all that their ideal required of them; whereas in reality they and all the other signatories had done no more than set down a lot of high-sounding words once more.

IV

The end of Calvin Coolidge's presidency was marked by a financial frenzy. Since 1924, everybody in America had been speculating. Rich and poor, employers and workers, everybody bought shares and borrowed money to buy more. The banks had lent $3,500,000,000 to the brokers to enable them to carry their clients: these loans were secured on shares, but shares at an artificially high price that made the backing risky. The Federal Reserve System ought to have put on the brakes by practicing a policy of dear money; but it was feared that if interest rates were raised in the United States, it would attract capital and thus ruin Europe even more. In January, 1928, Coolidge, far from braking, put his foot on the accelerator by declaring, against all precedent, that the loans were not too high. This was giving the boom the White House's endorsement.

But Coolidge was proud of *his* prosperity and of *his* bull market. Not that he seemed to want to be reelected: on the contrary, in an ambiguous Coolidgism he had stated, "I do not choose to run for president in 1928." Nevertheless, he did want the election year to be a splendid one, for the sake of his party. In the eyes of the electors, the great statesman is the one who is in power when everything is going well. Now the fever was increasing, and it kept up the general euphoria. Woolworth, Radio Corporation of America, General Motors, all the stocks in the market climbed straight upward. Nobody took any notice of yield or the real value of a concern anymore. That sort of caution was quite out of date. All one had to do was to buy, and then the next day one found oneself richer than one had been the day before. Stock exchange, quotations, shares—that was the one topic of conversation throughout the country. There were prudent specialists who sounded the warning, but it was no use. According to an old and sensible rule, a share was worth about ten times its annual yield; but niggling maxims of this kind no longer counted. "The market banked not only upon the future, but the hereafter."

It was during this mad whirlwind that a president had to be chosen. The Republican convention scarcely hesitated at all.

The secretary of commerce, Herbert Hoover, had been a great success in that post, as he had been in all the others that he had held during the war. He came from Iowa, and he was of Quaker stock—a guarantee of sober responsibility. Even as a young man he had been one of the most outstanding of American engineers; the English had employed him; the Chinese and the Russians had consulted him; and everywhere he went he left behind a vivid impression of intelligence. The work that he had done during the war was much praised in Washington and abroad. He had thrown himself into it heart and soul, not passionately, since he appeared to be a cold, reserved man, but with a wonderful efficiency. He had done his best for Belgium, and then for the whole of Europe, whose arts and whose cities he loved so well. The selfishness, the stupidity, and the short-sightedness that he had witnessed at the peace conference had utterly revolted him. He had come away from that "furnace of hate" disgusted with the foreign nations, and he had devoted himself in his Department of Commerce to the prosperity of America. Brandeis considered him "the biggest figure injected into Washington life by the war."

Louis Brandeis and Franklin D. Roosevelt would have liked to make Hoover the Democratic candidate for the presidency as early as 1920; but, being much attached to the business world, he preferred to belong to the Republican party. The Democrats were in favor of the state's interference in business, and they seemed to him tainted with a kind of socialism. He was against the reactionaries and at the same time against the reformers, and what he wanted was "rugged individualism." He thought that the very widely spread possession of shares—some big concerns had two thousand stockholders—had so diluted ownership in the United States that this had solved the problem of classes. All that mattered was that the leaders, the managers, should be aware of their financial and moral responsibilities. For his part, he was conscious of his to the highest degree, and he injected his vigor into the entire government. It was said of him that he was secretary of commerce and under secretary and all the assistant secretaries. Coolidge alone did not care for him much and made ironic remarks about this "wonder boy" and this "miracle worker." But who has ever liked his successor? Hoover was nominated, with scarcely a dissenting voice. When he heard the news, Coolidge would not eat his lunch, but went to lie down. There was a hidden ambition behind his impassive face.

At the Democratic convention, Al Smith, the Catholic governor of New York, was chosen on the first ballot this time. He, too, was a product of the American dream. He was the son of Irish working people; he had been a fishmonger; and he had been brought up in New York in the Tammany Hall atmosphere; he was a good speaker, and he had climbed all the successive steps until he was governor of his state. He was an able politician, but he was universally believed to be honest. For many sons of immigrants, his example was another proof that an American may start from nothing and yet reach any height. He was known to be a tolerant man, against the censoring of ideas or books. As governor, he had approved of Sunday games and the Sunday opening of movie theaters. For him, and against the wealthy Protestant society, he had not only the Irish but also the Latins and the Jews. The Protestants counterattacked. Since Al Smith was against prohibition, they nicknamed him Al(cohol) Smith and spread the completely untrue tale that he was always drunk. Cartoonists drew his cabinet-to-be, with the Pope and twelve priests sitting in the White House, while Al Smith handed around the drinks. Smith protested against so un-American a campaign and tried to awaken the electors to a sense of the importance of reform. He also tried to win over the businessmen by making John J. Raskob of General Motors chairman of the Democratic party.

It was no use. Who was thinking about reform at a time of such happiness? The late twenties was a period of success in many fields. Thornton Wilder had published *The Bridge of San Luis Rey;* Warner Brothers brought out the first big talkie; Walt Disney the first Mickey Mouse. Wall Street was at its highest. All that was wanted was to run on in the same current without changing anything and to keep the Republicans in power, for they alone had the recipe for that splendid dish, prosperity. Hoover spoke "with a kind of ecstasy" about the absolute perfection of the economic system: "We in America today are nearer the final triumph over poverty than ever before in the history of any land. . . . We have not yet reached the goal, but, given a chance to go forward with the policies of the last eight years, we shall soon with the help of God be in sight of the day when poverty will be banished from this nation." He won 444 votes, against 87. It seemed that the Republicans, and with them the business world, had a new eight-year lease.

But, although the situation appeared to be healthy enough in the hands of "the great engineer," it was in fact filled with danger. Speculation, encouraged by Hoover's triumphant election, had gone completely mad. Many Americans who had never owned a share in their lives before the war had, during the course of it, purchased Liberty Bonds; this had made them familiar with the idea of a fortune on paper, with banks, and with brokers. Big firms had distributed shares to their workers. As prices continually rose, everybody took to gambling—it was such an easy way of making money without working! Nobody spoke of anything but Stock Exchange quotations. "In eighteen months, Montgomery Ward had gone from 132 to 466, General Electric from 128 to 396, Radio from 94 to 505!" How then could a man fail to be certain of the future? All that was needed was to buy, buy, buy, and everyone would become a Rockefeller.

The big men of the business world would have been saints if they had not shorn this woolly flock that pressed forward so eagerly to the shears. The magnates played every trick they knew —the issue of new shares, splitting of existing shares, issue of bonds that could be turned into shares. The risk was sold, and at a very high price, to the utterly defenseless small investor; the profit was kept for the little group with inside information. Every time a merger was announced, it was followed by a rise. Why? God knows. Formerly it had been thought astonishing if a million shares changed hands on the Stock Exchange in one day; in 1929, the daily turnover was four or five million. This could only end badly, very badly; but who dared say so? It was in the interest of some to keep the boom going. Others, with Hoover among them, were afraid of starting a catastrophe if they were to utter their doubts. As for the speculators, if they were reminded of the lessons of experience and of disasters in the past, they replied, "That has nothing to do with it. This is a new era."

And yet the danger stared them in the face. In the first place, there was the overvaluation of all the concerns that were capitalized to fifty times their yield, and sometimes more; then the distress of the farmers who for want of money were now almost entirely ceasing to be consumers of industrial products; the improper sharing of profits (26 percent of the income going to 5 percent of the citizens in 1929), which produced the same effect, since it did not raise the purchasing power of the masses sufficiently; and the dangerous lack of balance in international exchange that depended wholly upon free gifts from the United States. In addition, many industries were not doing at all well—and how could they have flourished, with a shortage of consumers at home and abroad? It was obvious that it could not last. The Federal Reserve Bank might have raised the discount rate, but it seemed that the speculators were ready to pay any price at all for money, and Mellon did not want the government to find itself obliged to offer a high rate for its own Treasury bonds. The market was behaving like a car that had gone mad and that could only be stopped by a terrible accident.

"Prosperity will have no limits," said the new experts. "Never sell in an expanding country. Don't play for the fall against your own country." A whole nation was keeping its ears open; every piece of gossip became a tip. An Arizona stockbreeder might buy shares in a mine in Wyoming without even knowing what metal it produced. Was it metal at all, anyhow? What did it matter? The thing to do was to buy, buy, buy, that was the thing, then follow the lovely rise of the quotations on the ticker tape. The very intellectuals were contaminated: "Literary editors whose hopes were wrapped about American Cyanide B, lunched with poets who swore by Cities Service and, as they left the table, stopped for a monment in the crowd at the broker's branch office, to catch the latest quotations." At last the Federal Reserve decided to raise the bank rate. It did no good. The American had rediscovered his pioneering instinct. Anyone who had been confident between 1870 and 1900 and had bought land on the frontier had won. Today the frontier ran along the foot of the banking citadels in Wall Street. What a man had to do was to buy, buy, buy, and buy.

V

In September, 1929, the financial experts were still asserting that the situation was fundamentally sound; but the precursors of the storm were already visible in the sky. Several times the market had dropped: each time it had recovered. On September 26, the Bank of England raised the bank rate, to stop the damaging flow of gold to New York. Millions of dollars returned to Britain. In London, an important financial house, the Hatry group, went bankrupt, and this brought a great many shares into the market. Who was going to take them up? The small investors had reached their limit; the big men were discreetly beginning to get rid of important blocks of shares. On Wednesday, October 23, 1929, Wall Street was overwhelmed with a sudden flow of selling. Dealing was so massive that the stock tickers could not work fast enough. The tape was 104 minutes behind. The next day, October 24, 1929, was to be known in the history of the Stock Exchange as Black Thursday. Thirteen million shares changed hands. It was no longer a recession; it was a panic.

Why did it happen on that day rather than any other? Why does a house that has been tottering for ten years fall down? Because it has reached the end of its resistance. The structure of investment had been unsteady for a long time; the crash was inevitable, since many speculators had been gambling on margin, without money enough to pay in case of need. On that Black Thursday, they did not even fix a bottom rate for their brokers. All that mattered was to limit the disaster—"Sell at the best price you can get." The floor of the Exchange echoed with the despairing cries of the sellers: there were no buyers to reply. That evening, some of the pillars of the market, men who had so often saved the situation, quietly met in the office of Thomas Lamont, a member of the Morgan Bank and one of the sages of Wall Street. They decided to form a stabilizing fund of $240,000,000, so that they might come in as buyers and thus stop the panic. This little defense seemed to be holding its own for three days. But the others did not close in behind it.

In vain, the President said, "The fundamental business of the country, that is, the production and distribution of commodities, is on a sound and prosperous basis." He was not believed, because the pricing of shares and the dealing in them, which had become the country's other fundamental business, was certainly not on a sound footing. "There is nothing to justify this nervousness," asserted the experts once more. "The worst is over. The panic is only a kind of hysteria." But this same hysteria brought crowds of terrified small investors converging on Wall Street, stupefied at having lost, in one day, what they had considered a solid fortune. The Stock Exchange was like a madhouse or a menagerie on fire. There was the roaring of lions and tigers: lunatics seized one another by the throat shouting "Steel!" or "Radio!" as they rolled together on the ground. From the West, the Middle West, the North, and the South, there came orders to sell. On the twenty-ninth, the whole market fell again. This time the bankers did not try to support it. You cannot stop a tidal wave with a broom. The collapse went on through November. By about the middle of the month, the losses totaled $3,000,000,000, and most shares had lost 40 percent of their value. The prosperity that the experts had thought everlasting had vanished.

For President Hoover and his government, this was as grave a political as it was a financial disaster. It was not Hoover's fault that the bottom had fallen out of the market. But the philosophy that he professed was not of a kind to comfort the victims. It was not that he was without sympathy for those who were ruined by the crisis, but his rigid principles required him to intervene as little as possible. He thought that direct action by the government on the economy would discourage that spirit of initiative that had made America what she was. It was up to each community to shift for itself: "A voluntary deed is infinitely more precious to our national ideals and spirit than a thousandfold poured from the Treasury."

Perhaps so; but the stock market panic was quickly joined to a worldwide depression. In the history of mankind, such things had happened before: the sixteenth century had seen places as far apart as Lyons, Augsburg, and Venice all shaken by the same financial earthquake. But this went beyond the others. From 1929 to 1932, banks failed everywhere, currencies collapsed, factories closed, and everywhere there was unemployment. The

Canadians burned the wheat that they could not sell; the Bra-
zilians their coffee. In Germany, a wave of misery brought in
Hitler and his madness. The European crisis made the American
crisis even worse. In the United States, factories shut their gates;
purchasing power dropped; the numbers of unemployed increased. From 1929 to 1932, the national income fell from 87.4
to 41.7 billion dollars; the true personal income from $681 to
$495. Wages dropped by 40 percent; dividends by 57 percent.

The depression had profound social consequences. People married later; there were fewer births (in 1929, 1,232,000 marriages;
in 1932, 981,903). Many colleges and schools closed. In some
states, the sums devoted to education were cut by 30 percent.
States and cities hastily improvised some sort of social assistance,
but a very primitive one. Then, with their money running out,
they had to suspend their payments. The buying of such things
as cars and jewels fell off, but old cars were at a premium and
the consumption of gasoline did not decline. A curious, but
understandable, phenomenon was that the artificial silk industry
remained prosperous: women sacrified everything else to their
underclothes. People did not give up the radio or cigarettes,
either—these were things that helped them to put up with unemployment and sadness.

Gradually the misery spread: hundreds of thousands of unemployed wandered about the countryside looking for some kind
of work. Entire families set off for the West, in the hope of being
employed in the harvests or the picking of fruit; others built
shanty towns in the outskirts of the cities, and they called them
Hoovervilles, in mockery. Long queues formed in front of the
places where charitable institutions handed out food: these were
the breadlines. Bankers, stockbrokers, and ruined speculators
jumped out of twentieth-story windows. Will Rogers wrote,
"You had to stand in line to get a window to jump out of." The
story went that receptionists in the hotels would ask, "You want
a room for sleeping or jumping?"

In 1930, the number of unemployed mounted in a geometric
progression. In the streets of New York, there were hordes
of young men to be seen, each standing by a basket of apples,
sadly repeating, "Buy an apple . . . buy an apple." The evil was
all the worse because the Administration did not want to admit
that it existed. Hoover was the prosperity president. How could

his term be the reign of unemployment? There was no escaping the fact that millions of people were suffering from hunger, but the official standpoint remained, "Above all, no state intervention! Do not let us commit the error of the English dole. If there is unhappiness to be assuaged, let private charity look after it."

It took the unemployed themselves a long time to understand what had happened to them. When they had been sent away from the factory they had been told "It is a temporary crisis." To begin with they had spent their savings, then they had sold their life insurance. When they had nothing left, and when the towns themselves had had to give up paying their employees, then indeed people had to turn to the federal government. How many unemployed were there at the worst of the depression? It is almost impossible to say. In some parts of that huge continent, statistics were rudimentary. Harry L. Hopkins, the head of the Federal Unemployment Service, gave a figure of four million destitute *families* for 1932, which would amount to fifteen or twenty million mouths to feed. A new social type emerged, the unemployed white-collar worker—architect, lawyer, teacher, doctor. How could an architect's office take on young men when so few had the money to build any more?

Hoover went on saying that the country was healthy—an observation that became true in the long run; and that prosperity "was around the corner"— an observation that was made far too soon. Out of respect for his principles, he tried to act as little as possible. If it were absolutely necessary that something should be done, he thought it wiser to help the banks and industry than the unemployed. If production started up again, the unemployed would be reabsorbed. He preferred giving the farmers, who were suffering from a drought, food for their animals rather than provide them with help for themselves. When the ex-servicemen of the great war, who had neither work nor money, insisted upon the immediate payment of their bonus and organized a march on Washington, the President considered the threat of an outbreak intolerable. He sent General Douglas MacArthur with tanks and machine guns to break up the "Bonus Army" and burn the rebels' camp. The public was shocked by this harshness. The veterans had done wrong in their obstinate harassment of the government, but they deserved sympathy and consideration.

Yet the President was not without humanity. Far from it, as

he proved during the war. But for him individualism was a religion. The welfare state was an abominable heresy in his eyes, and one step in that direction would lead to socialism and idleness. Before his time, great undertakings had been set afoot for the making of dams and the production of hydroelectric power: he was against these schemes. In his view, such enterprises did not enter into the functions of the state. To come to the help of the distressed farmers, he had authorized the setting up of a Federal Farm Board, endowed with $500,000,000, that could lend farmers money so that they might sell their harvests better. This board even went so far (against Hoover's principles) as to buy wheat and cotton. In spite of these measures, by the end of 1931 wheat had fallen from $1.04 to $0.39 and cotton from 17¢ to 5½¢. The government lost $180,000,000 on the operation. The lobby of the major industries had obtained a customs tariff that raised a great wall of China around the United States. How could the rest of the world possibly buy American agricultural produce? So what was to be done? Reduce sowing? Limit production? Here again Hoover's unyielding old-style liberalism forbade compulsion, and only half the farmers complied with the voluntary restriction.

In short, the depression was growing deeper and deeper. Finally Hoover overcame his scruples and imposed the authority of the state in measures for increasing great public works and for the creation of a Reconstruction Finance Corporation that was allowed to borrow $1,200,000,000 to lend to firms in danger—railways, insurance companies, building firms, banks, and so on. There is no doubt that this institution was of the greatest value. The strange thing is that Hoover, although he had made this concession, was still opposed to direct help for the unemployed. The Democratic Congress, elected in 1930, made life hard for him and accused him of doing "too little and too late." To this he replied that Congress was indulging in mere demagogy at the expense of the unfortunate, and that his administration had made the greatest efforts ever known to put an end to the depression. This had become true: but even these efforts turned out to be inadequate. More factories closed, and the number of unemployed increased.

For men like Hoover and Mellon, the position was inexpressibly painful. They had preached the scientific organization of government and business, and a balanced budget. But the depression was unbalancing the budget to a wild degree. Abroad, the crisis was turning the world upside-down. The Kredit Anstalt of Vienna, one of the greatest of all banking concerns, had had to suspend payments. Great Britain had abandoned the gold standard, and the pound sterling had fallen from $4.37 to $3.40. In France, money had lost four fifths of its value. In Germany, the old mark was utterly worthless. In America itself, some people were beginning to wonder whether it would not be necessary to devaluate the dollar, in order to lighten the burden of debts. In all periods of history, battles between creditors and debtors have produced great political dramas. Now the speculators had borrowed $7,000,000,000 to buy shares, at present of little value; the farmers had increased their mortgages; the manufacturers had borrowed to increase an excessive production that no longer found any purchasers. How was this enormous score to be wiped out? On his own authority, Hoover had decreed a worldwide moratorium for war debts and reparations; but he would not have dared pronounce a moratorium in his own country.

The Administration's foreign policy remained timid. In September, 1931, Japan occupied Manchuria. China appealed to the United States and to the League of Nations. But the Western countries, completely taken up with their financial crises, were scarcely minded to embark upon any distant adventure. Henry L. Stimson, the secretary of state, tried to persuade Hoover to take up a strong attitude, and he asked for economic sanctions against Japan. Hoover, influenced by public opinion, which was overwhelmingly in favor of peace and isolationism, and certain too that England would not cooperate in such a policy, refused Stimson's plan. All that he could consent to was moral coercion. Is it wise, in foreign affairs, to adopt a moral attitude when one has no intention of backing it up by force? Perhaps it is, if it is only a question of satisfying public opinion. It is certainly not, if it is results that are wanted. The nation that it is desired to stop is irritated in vain, and in its anger and at the same time its certainty of acting with impunity, it redoubles its boldness. Japan, "with graceful irony," attacked Shanghai. Hoover and Stimson limited themselves to "not recognizing" the results of the aggression. They did not recognize them, but they tolerated them.

This feeble policy was later to encourage war between the United States and Japan.

VI

In 1932, the presidential election had to take place. The Republican party was in a very poor position to face this critical year. The farmers and the unemployed were more than discontented. It did not go so far as an outbreak or rioting; the revolutionary parties did not gain ground, except perhaps among the intellectuals; but a great section of the country felt a strong resentment against an Administration whose one idea seemed to be that if prosperity could be restored at the top, it would filter down to the base of the pyramid by itself. This was considered to be an inhuman policy. Hoover maintained that it was already succeeding, and in fact the curves were going up a little. His party knew that the retiring President was unpopular, but there was nothing that they could do except support him.

The Democrats, on the other hand, had a very strong position. What was easier than blaming their opponents for all the misfortunes that had befallen the country? They prescribed vigorous changes in the economic policy, and they took care not to say exactly what they should be. Yet they did say that prohibition should be done away with by the abrogation of the Eighteenth Amendment, and they were in favor of revision of the tariff and the antitrust laws. It was, in short, a fairly commonplace platform, and radical minds (*The New Republic*) thought it lukewarm and inadequate; but after the Democratic convention, the nature of the party's candidate changed everything. This was Franklin Delano Roosevelt, governor of the State of New York, who had done so very well as assistant secretary of the navy during the World War.

In those days, he had been a splendid athlete, a handsome man with an infectious smile. Then an attack of poliomyelitis had paralyzed him from the waist down. Any other man would have spent the rest of his days in a nursing home. With a more than human courage, he had tried to reeducate his deadened limbs, and he had gone on with his political career, helped by his wife, who was also a Roosevelt, his cousin Eleanor. With his legs encased in iron braces and leaning on two sticks, he learned to walk again. Far from overwhelming him, his handicap had raised him above himself. When he had been chosen by the convention, he flew to Chicago to accept the nomination, and he announced his policy: "I pledge you, I pledge myself to a new deal for the American people." This "new deal" was to become a chapter of essential importance in the history of the United States.

During his campaign he attacked the out-of-date methods of his opponents: "Mistaking the sound of the ticker for the pulse of business, the government at Washington does nothing to restore the purchasing power of fifty or sixty million Americans who live in our little towns or on our farms. . . . For want of the farmers' dollars business stops and industry suffers. No country can be at the same time half bankrupt and half solvent . . . ." For a long time, he had been advising a juster—and wiser— sharing out of the national income. Hoover had tried to help the high and mighty lords of the economy; Roosevelt pleaded for "the forgotten man, at the bottom of the economic pyramid." His task was easy. His opponent, elected as the president of prosperity had, through the workings of fate and possibly also his friends' mistakes, become the president of wretchedness.

The sight that the country presented served Roosevelt's cause better than the finest speeches. The dismal word "depression" echoed throughout the whole of the United States. On the Stock Exchange, shares were no longer either bought or sold. Depression. A broker earned no more than $15 a day, and out of that he had to pay his staff. Depression. Prices plummeted straight down. The great stores, to attract unwilling customers, advertised "dramatic" sales. Depression. The most brilliant students could not find jobs when they left the universities. Depression. In the New York subway, one of the spaces reserved for advertisements showed an enlarged check "for a chicken dinner every Sunday" signed by the Republican party. And across it was written "Payment refused. Return to drawer." At the San Francisco Commonwealth Club, Roosevelt said that although the fundamental principles of democratic capitalism were still sound, the country needed to adapt the existing economic organizations to the service of the citizens. Hoover alone understood that under these somewhat dreary platitudes a positive revolution was preparing and that Roosevelt's New Deal would strike the rugged individualism of which he was the champion a mortal blow. The retiring President's speeches were many and well conceived; but between ten and fifteen million unemployed were an eloquent answer to them.

The result was not in doubt. Roosevelt carried the day in all the states but six, obtaining 472 electoral votes against 59. In Times Square, the crowd rejoiced all night long. They blew trumpets and rang bells: young men sang; girls danced. The excited and happy people hopefully waited for the promised New Deal. Unfortunately four months had to pass between the election and the installation of the new President at Washington. It was an unfortunate delay. The production index fell to its lowest level; unemployment increased even more; the banks let it be known that they could not hold out much longer; the foreign countries announced that it would not be possible for them to pay the sums due in December. To reestablish the international economic situation, Hoover sought Roosevelt's cooperation. But the President-Elect remained aloof. Why should he share in the responsibility before he had the power to apply his own ideas?

PART FIVE

The Peaceful Revolution

FRANKLIN D. ROOSEVELT's long presidency is without any doubt the most important period in the history of twentieth-century America. When his first term began, it was reasonable to wonder whether the United States' political and economic structure was not on the point of total collapse. It was a time when the people of many countries, feeling that they could no longer govern themselves, accepted authoritarian regimes. Was the complexity of modern life and the necessity for a guided economy—essential if the country were not to lurch from crisis to crisis—compatible with the delays and the hesitations of democracy? Many doubted it. Experience alone could give the answer.

I

The situation grew rapidly worse during the dangerous four months' interregnum that the Constitution of the United States then required—a period during which the old President no longer wanted to make decisions and the new one had not the right to do so. Because loans on real estate were no longer repaid nor even the interest due upon them, hundreds of local banks ceased to function. Because the great bankers had madly lent billions to South America and to Germany, and because these sums were frozen, the New York banking system was giving way. Scandals finally destroyed the public confidence. The small depositors took fright and withdrew their money. Throughout the country, frightened people were hoarding gold. In the city of Baltimore alone, the public silently took out $6,000,000 a day.

In February, 1933, the State of Louisiana proclaimed a bank holiday. Ten days later, the Governor of Michigan had to close the banks; as early as March 1, Alabama, California, Idaho, Kentucky, Mississippi, and Tennessee followed his example. In Detroit, the automobile capital, the manufacturers no longer knew how to pay their workers. A millionaire, unable to change $10, had to borrow a nickel from an unemployed man to telephone his wife. In New York, the bankers never left their offices. "Great was their anguish of mind and long the ashes of their cigars," wrote *Time*, a youthful, impertinent, brilliant magazine. They hastily had provisional notes printed, to satisfy the requirements of depositors who had gone out of their minds. At Salt Lake City, the Mormons issued a local currency. Stamps, telephone blanks, Mexican dollars, anything would answer as a means of payment. On the very eve of the new President's inauguration, Governor Herbert Lehman had to close the banks of New York, the financial capital of the country, for two days. The president of prosperity ended his term in an atmosphere of panic.

At Washington, the new President stepped out of his train into a mass of melting snow. Everywhere he found confusion and alarm. Eugene Meyer of the Federal Reserve Board advised the closing of all banks. The retiring President disagreed. Roosevelt declined to do anything until he was actually in power. According to custom, he should have dined at the White House, but Hoover was in no mood to invite him. The most he could be persuaded to do was to ask Roosevelt to tea. This proved but a dismal entertainment: "We are at the end of our string," said Hoover, "there is nothing more we can do." Some people thought that the whole economic system was going to collapse, and that Roosevelt might be the last president the United States would ever see.

The next day, Saturday, March 4, 1933, was overcast and ominous: squalls of icy rain swept down; the blast of ruin was blowing through the nation's mind. The hundred thousand Americans who had gathered toward noon in front of the Capitol to watch the ceremony stood there silently. Many of them wondered how they would find the money to get home. According to Arthur Krock, the correspondent of the *New York Times,* the atmosphere was that of a town beseiged in time of war. There was very little applause when the two Presidents went by. Hoover, gloomy, with his eyes cast down, made no response to the occasional shouts. Roosevelt considered that these last moments of the term belonged to the outgoing president, and he sat there motionless, smiling.

Why should the spectators have shown any enthusiasm? They had cause for nothing but despair. One worker out of four was unemployed. Fathers of families were turning over rubbish heaps to find something to eat. Farmers had to protect themselves against people were were stealing their milk on the roadsides. On the horizon, the dawn of a revolution was to be seen. An important Chicago lawyer, Donald Richberg, said, "There are many sign to show that if a legal authority does not take action, a new form of authority, perhaps an illegal one, will arise and act."

Yes, there was the fear of revolution, unless Roosevelt did something. But what could he do? The most powerful businessmen admitted that they had no remedy nor even any plan to suggest. At last the moment for the ceremony arrived. Chief Justice of the United States Charles Evans Hughes gave Roosevelt a family Bible, and the new President took the oath upon it. Then Roosevelt spoke. "This is a day of national consecration," he began. The time had come for a frank and bold disclosure of the truth, the whole truth. "So first of all let me assert my firm belief that the only thing we have to fear is fear itself—

nameless, unreasoning, unjustified terror which paralyzes needed efforts to convert retreat into advance. . . . In such a spirit . . . we face our common difficulties. They concern, thank God, only material things. Values have shrunk to fantastic levels; . . . the means of exchange are frozen in the currents of trade; the withered leaves of industrial enterprise lie on every side; farmers find no markets for their produce. . . . More important, a host of unemployed citizens face the grim problem of existence, and an equally great number toil with little return. Only a foolish optimist can deny the dark realities of the moment."

In his chair, the citizen Hoover, the ex-president, listened without any pleasure: he frowned. The people of the square listened to the fine voice and smiled skeptically. After three years of crisis, the most utterly devalued commodity in the United States was enthusiasm. The word "ballyhoo" was in everybody's mouth. Many in the audience were both cynical and embittered; but at all events none could deny that the speaker was eloquent. He went on to explain that nature was still lavishing her gifts upon America. The factories and the fields were still there. Abundance was still at the door, but out of obstinacy and incompetence the managers of the economy had failed in their task. "The money changers have fled from their high seats in the temple of our civilization. We may now restore that temple to the ancient truths. . . . This nation calls for action and action now. Our greatest primary task is to put people to work." Now the public, listless at first, unfroze: cheering broke out, and went on. This was the language that the American people had wanted to hear.

Yet some were distrustful of what these noble phrases might conceal. "The thing that emerges most clearly," wrote Edmund Wilson, "is the warning of a dictatorship." But in Roosevelt's mind, there was no question of dictatorship at all; his feeling was much more that the nation's misfortune was going to allow him to reknit and recast the American community. A serene faith was to be seen on his handsome face; and at such a moment, this calm confidence was not without its value. While the President was actually speaking, telegrams filled with dangerous news were being handed about behind him. The new Secretary of the Treasury had to leave the ceremony for a moment to answer an urgent message. Never had a President been inaugurated in such dramatic circumstance. Twelve to fifteen million unemployed, the farmers seething, banks closed, all the chief supports of the economy collapsing one after another amid the sound of curses —that was the background that might be glimpsed in the lowering twilight of that winter's day, behind the long star-spangled banners.

II

The nation had listened to the inauguration speech on the radio and had liked it. Half a million listeners wrote to the White House. They all said that the President had given them hope again. "People are looking to you almost as they look to God," wrote one of them. During those first weeks even his political opponents hoped for Roosevelt's success, although they wondered where he would lead them. His failure would mean disaster for all. At this juncture, it was Roosevelt or nothing. In a mystic way, his crippled condition identified him with the suffering nation. The courage with which he had overcome his handicap already served as an example. After so many mean, glum visages, his generous face was encouraging, full of promise, charming. When he had said "My friends," he had said the words in such a tone, with such sweetness and strength, that everybody had understood their truth and had grasped that he was going to try to do for them what others had not done.

What was there behind this smiling mask, behind the veil of humor, charm, and good temper that he liked to wrap around himself? It is not easy to tell, for Roosevelt deliberately kept up an appearance of easiness, and he almost never acknowledged that he was bored or irritated. Robert Sherwood, the playwright, who was an excellent judge of men and who knew the President well (he sometimes wrote his speeches) admitted that he had not been able to penetrate what he called "his heavily forested interior." The President could switch on at will the famous smile that lit up his whole face. It was possible to imagine that one made out reserves beyond this: very great maneuverability and a strength that might prove pitiless; but all that remained well hidden behind conventional good manners. He had many friends, but few of them were very close to him and even those were not admitted to his innermost confidence. The men he liked to surround himself with were those who did not attempt to violate this sanctuary.

No one could foresee what his reactions would be. His closest collaborators did not know how he would decide: on every question he would ask two or three of them for schemes, read and compare them, then make his decisions with a sometimes horrifying rapidity. The President's admirers said that quickness of decision proved quickness of mind, that in any case Roosevelt was not stubborn, and that if a method did not answer, he abandoned it without regret. That was true. He knew that he was fallible. "We will make mistakes . . . . Theodore Roosevelt said to me one day. 'If I can be right 75 percent of the time, I shall come up to the fullest measure of my hopes.' " He himself said to his chief assistants, "Suppose a truck driver was doing your job; 50 percent of his decisions would be right, on average. You aren't a truck driver. You've had some preparation. Your percentage is bound to be higher."

He did not like delegating too much of his authority; he did like setting off one man's power against another's. This was partly to keep a tight control over everything and partly because he had a secret liking for confusion. He proceeded by intuition rather than by reasoning; he gauged tempers, measured the reactions of public opinion, and bided his time if he felt that the business was not ripe for action. When his instinct told him that delay was called for, then the snap decisions gave way to long-drawn-out temporization, so long that in the end time did away with the problem. "He knew, from hard experience, that a person could not regain health in a day or a year; he had no reason to suppose that a nation would mend any more quickly." He had a very sick country to look after, and he showed infinite patience. This sometimes irritated the young men he had chosen to work with him; but it also allowed him to overcome resistance. It was compromise that he sought rather than struggle, and he often quoted Al Smith's remark, "If you can get the parties in one room with a big table and make them take their coats off and put their feet up on the table and give each one of them a good cigar, you can always make them agree."

Once he had taken a decision, he kept to it. "I do not have

to do it your way, and I will tell you why. The reason is that although they may have made a mistake, the people of the United States elected me president—not you." From that moment the charmer, who had seemed so pliable, became unbelievably authoritative. Frances Perkins, who was his secretary of labor, has said that he was the most complex man she had ever known. Henry Morgenthau, Jr., one of his intimate friends, writes, "Roosevelt is an extraordinarily difficult person to describe . . . weary as well as buoyant, frivolous as well as grave, evasive as well as frank."Robert Sherwood considered his character not only multiple but contradictory. The President was both hard and soft, capable of Christian charity and of unjust malice, now a cynic and now a believer. His ideas were sufficiently advanced for some to condemn him as a traitor to his class and to describe him as a Red in the White House; but in fact he was "a profoundly old-fashioned person with an incurable nostalgia for the very 'horse and buggy era' on which he publicly heaped so much scorn."

By nature he was kind, a sincere humanitarian, particularly since his illness, and he know how to reach the hearts of simple people. A week after his inauguration, he gave his first fireside chat over the radio. He used the expression "My friends" again, and he showed his wonderful skill in employing the first person plural. "Confidence and courage are the essential ingredients for the success of *our* plan . . . Together, *we* cannot fail." The word "chat" was a remarkably happy choice: it implied neither speech nor address, but a simple, friendly conversation that would bring every family into the White House. There was nothing better calculated to reawaken confidence. Presently all America spoke of the new regime as the New Deal; and it was indeed an attempt at a new dealing out of the cards of opportunity and income so that each man might find work again and that purchasing power might be fairly shared.

In fact, there were to be two New Deals. The first was that of the years 1933–1934, the time of the President's honeymoon with Congress, rich in bold, unquestioned decisions. Those were the days when the memory of the dangers undergone did away with factious discord, and when big business, so thoroughly battered by the crisis, lined up with the farmers and the workers under Roosevelt's banner. During this period, he exercised, for all intents and purposes, the vast powers that a president has in time of war, and he was able to try some radical experiments. Then, when the danger was over, people began to leave the temple. The second New Deal began toward 1935, and this time the business world and the Republican party united in bitterly accusing Roosevelt of autocracy and demagogy, thus obliging him to ally himself, in a new, more homogeneous, more reformist coalition, with the groups traditionally associated with a progressive policy. He was then led to take those socialistic measures that the men who in the beginning had supported him as the country's savior would never have accepted.

To bring back confidence after a disaster, spectacular deeds are called for. Roosevelt knew this by intuition. To stop the run on the banks, he paradoxically used the most radical of measures. He closed them all—at first until March 9, and then for a further period. It was an astonishing week. Hotel managers sent pages around to the churches to exchange checks for the collection money. In Detroit, the big stores offered to sell their goods to the farmers by barter—three sets of children's clothes and three pairs of shoes for one sow. The organizers of a boxing match let people in on the same principle, and they paid for their seats in cigars, combs, cakes of soap. On March 5, the hoarding of gold was forbidden by decree, with a penalty (after a period of grace) of ten years' imprisonment and a fine of $10,000. This energetic measure at once brought some billions of dollars into the government's hands. From that day on, the curve started to rise. The bank holiday turned into a national amusement. The embarrassment of the rich consoled the poor for their misfortunes, and the rich clearly understood that this apparent ruin was not to be taken seriously. It was an adventure: it was no longer a heart failure. People were living in a mad world, but life was going on; the President was at his work, giving orders, threatening the bad citizens; and the country, always eager for incident and novelty, was already raising its head, like a horse that feels a bold rider on its back and strong hands on the reins.

III

The president of the United States is responsible to the country as a whole; and during Roosevelt's terms he most decidedly dominated the whole scene. And yet to govern, the president needs a team. In ordinary times, this is provided by the Cabinet. In the case of Roosevelt, who wanted to accomplish new things, and to accomplish them quickly, the team consisted not only of the cunning old foxes of politics but also of young intellectuals, full of ideas and schemes, who made up what was called the Brain Trust. Intellectuals at Washington! Even Wilson, although he was himself a professor, had been more faithful to the traditions of the place. Congress gazed with some uneasiness upon these infant prodigies, almost all of whom had actually written books. The old senators ironically called the section where the Brain Trusters lived the "campus"; they spoke with a tart benevolence of "these delicious professors," whom Franklin would one day regret having brought to Washington.

The Cabinet properly so called was of quite an ordinary composition. The secretary of state was Cordell Hull, an upright veteran senator from the mountains of Tennessee, a man whose principles sometimes conflicted with the President's more opportunist policies; but Roosevelt always had the last word. At the Treasury, there was William H. Woodin, an important Democratic manufacturer who played on the guitar. The secretary of agriculture was Henry A. Wallace of Iowa, regarded by many as a visionary with a hankering for the policies of the extreme Left. In charge of the Department of the Interior there was Harold L. Ickes, a tough man with a biting tongue, nearly always at odds with authority. Roosevelt appointed a women secretary of labor—this was Frances Perkins, who had worked with him as a welfare worker when he was governor of New York. The postmaster general was the Tammany leader Jim Farley, an excellent political organizer to whom Roosevelt owed his election; but he took little interest in the New Deal and in the end he left the team.

The Brain Trust was more picturesque. The ideas and above all the men had been provided by Raymond Moley, a professor at Columbia University. As adviser on agricultural questions he had proposed his colleague at Columbia, Rexford G. Tugwell; and for financial matters, Adolf A. Berle, Jr., of the faculty of law, also at Columbia. Moley was a specialist in political and criminal law: he had literary gifts, and he prepared some of Roosevelt's speeches. Among the professors, he was the one who liked to affect realism: "I don't tilt at windmills," he said. The other Brain Trusters acknowledged his authority, and at the beginning of the reign, he had great power. *Fortune* told how a friend, who had come on a political mission to Washington, said to Roosevelt, "Franklin, there is something I should like you to do for me . . . Would you try to get me an appointment with Moley?" Rex Tugwell, the undersecretary of agriculture, a handsome man with prematurely gray hair, was capable both of boldness and intellectual discipline. "The revolutionary," said he, "is the man who wants to blow up the station and stop the trains until another has been built. The liberal wants to rebuild the station while the trains still go on running."

Adolf A. Berle, Jr., another of the Brain Trusters, was "an infant prodigy of infant prodigies." He had left Harvard at the age of fifteen, in knee-length pants. With his tormented, mysterious face, he looked the most "radical" (in the American sense) of all Roosevelt's advisers. He had written a remarkable book on the modern corporation, that is to say, the great joint-stock company. Was it to be run for the profit of the shareholder? Or, as had happened up until that time, for the profit of a few banking magnates? "Neither the one nor the other," replied Berle. "Big business must, like the Bank of England, the Bank of France, think of itself as a state service, at the same time preserving its autonomy." In short, he wanted to direct the economy toward a kind of corporate collectivism, nevertheless keeping freedom of action. Roosevelt did not go so far as that. With regard to businessmen, he did not have the same hostile prejudices as Wilson, who had thought of many of them as robbers. Roosevelt, brought up among them, thought that it was their wits rather than their morals that were at fault.

Side by side with this group of professors, he had installed some men of a very different kind. Harry L. Hopkins was a fragile young man from Iowa whom Roosevelt had discovered when he was governor of New York and when Hopkins was looking after the distribution of relief there during the crisis of 1929–1932. He had made a conquest of the governor, and when Roosevelt became president, he entrusted Hopkins, as we shall see, with immense responsibilities. Many of Roosevelt's friends were doubtful of Hopkins, regarding him as an intriguer, or as Robert Sherwood put it, as "an Iowan combination of Machiavelli, Svengali, and Rasputin." But Roosevelt liked him, trusted him, and upheld him against all and sundry. Many of the Brain Trusters wearied Roosevelt; Hopkins never did. He appeared nonchalant, but in fact he was always sharply on the watch, and "with an almost feminine sensibility," he divined the President's moods. Later Roosevelt's extreme, and no doubt excessive, confidence in Hopkins was to play a part of the first importance in world politics.

Lewis Douglas, the director of the budget, was a good choice. His father owned copper mines, and he himself was a great sportsman, brave, and amusing—he had been decorated for gallantry in the World War. Douglas thought that a balanced budget was a country's greatest strength, and that the balance should be accomplished less by heavy taxation than by economy. The President said that he was in agreement with these principles. It remained to be seen how they could be reconciled with the need for "priming the pump."

As for General Hugh S. Johnson, to whom Roosevelt entrusted the reorganization of industry, he was a retired soldier, fifty-one years old. He had made his mark during the war in preparing the mobilization. He was a friend of Bernard Baruch, and he had worked for him. The General was well known for the harsh realism of his remarks, his capacity for work, and his energy. "What is so ridiculous about these three wretched years that we have just gone through," he said, "is that they are an affront to common sense. Thousands of people without a roof over their heads in cities full of empty houses; millions hungry in front of full granaries; millions without enough to wear right by mountains of cloth—it is too foolish! It is like a child's tale. It is as if some bad fairy had thrown a spell and turned America into a Sleeping Beauty." Johnson was sentimental, romantic, and immoderate; but he was efficient.

There was nothing more remarkable than this team made up of professors, soldiers, and politicians, brought together by the chance of personal contact. Coming from New York, Maine, or California, they were now all settled together in Washington, there to coordinate their efforts and their plans. For ten years, they had all been criticizing the men in power. Then Roosevelt had come and said to them, "You have censured: you have made plans. Now you are in power. Carry out your plans and set the country on its feet again." They were delighted and somewhat afraid.

IV

The first three months of the New Deal have been called the Hundred Days. They were a hundred days of miracles. The President recalled Congress for an extraordinary session and sent it bill after bill. Congress met again on March 9 and passed the new banking laws almost without discussion. Both Houses passed them by majorities in which Republicans voted with Democrats. The first aim was to save the banking system — to save it and not to overturn it. Afterward, some radicals regretted that Roosevelt had not taken advantage of the opportunity to nationalize the banks. Tugwell had thought of a system of postal banks, administered by the state, but Roosevelt wanted to create a climate of confidence very quickly indeed. For this he needed the bankers just as he needed the people, and the bankers asked nothing better than to cooperate with him. The money changers came back to occupy their high places in the temple, and many of them were to be seen in the corridors of the legislature. Will Rogers said that the President was marvelous: he took a complicated subject like banking and made it comprehensible to everybody, even the bankers.

When the banks reopened, the worst of the danger seemed already over; gold was flowing in; the depositors' confidence had come back. Credit is a state of mind. Since things were going so well, the President decided to keep Congress sitting and to get it to pass other urgent measures. He carried on the work of lawmaking at a breakneck speed. In his electoral program, he had promised economies. It is common form to promise them, but not to make them. Yet now the President proposed cutting ex-servicemen's pensions, the salaries of the Congressmen and of all federal employees. This time a part of the Democrat majority jibbed: the ex-servicemen represented a very important part of the electorate. But there were enough Republicans in favor of the measure to carry it through. Naturally enough, it caused another veterans' march on Washington a little later. But Roosevelt's tactics of soothing by kindness answered far better than Hoover's. He met the leaders, caused the ex-servicemen to be comfortably housed, sent military bands to play for them, had them looked after by army doctors and dentists, and lastly asked Mrs. Roosevelt to visit their camp. "Hoover sent the army; Roosevelt has sent his wife," said one veteran. Spending was in fact to increase far more rapidly than the savings; but the effect of shock had been produced.

One of the causes of the disaster of 1929–1932 was prohibition, that baneful law. It was forced upon the men of the great cities, upon the workers and the intellectuals by puritanical farmers and women brimful of worthy intentions; and it had led to the formation of dangerous gangs. It had diverted to the pockets of the bootleggers the vast sums that should have come into the treasury. Above all, it had deprived the whole country of a necessary safety valve. The President did not have the right to abolish prohibition. It had come into being through an amendment to the Constitution, and it could only be done away with by another amendment. But he had the legal power of authorizing, by decree, a change in the percentage of alcohol—a decree that made the sale of light beer possible, "three point two beer." It seems astonishing that the sale of a yellowish, frothing liquid could make such a difference in the life of a great nation. Huge income for the state. Important numbers of unemployed taken on by the brewers and the allied industries. In 1933, a single factory was to make eight hundred and fifty million bottles. To turn out forty million barrels and crates, hundreds of sawmills were set up at the edge of the forests. The pretzel and salted biscuit factories worked day and night. There were aprons needed for the waitresses, iron tables for the pavements, green plants for the beer gardens. Later, wine was to follow too. A powerful instinct took back its place in the country's economy.

Bank holidays, economies, three point two beer—these spectacular measures might lead to convalescence. But before any complete recovery, it was essential to restore a certain purchasing power to the unemployed. How? The Brain Trusters caused the adoption of two kinds of measures, the one set temporary and meant to bring about an immediate relief; the other lasting and corresponding to the new requirements and to the progress of mechanization.

Temporary measures. The federal government placed $500,000,000 at the disposal of the states for unemployment relief. A Civilian Conservation Corps (CCC) was formed and two hundred and fifty thousand young men were sent into the forests. They were recruited like soldiers, fed and lodged in camps, and paid a dollar a day. By 1941, over two million youths had passed through its ranks. The plan of work was to provide for reforestation, the fighting of forest fires, and the prevention of floods. Furthermore, the President caused Congress to authorize him to spend $3,300,000,000 on public works—roads, ships, and postal services. Lastly, he had himself given full powers to devalue the dollar to the extent of half its gold value.

He devalued slowly, throughout the whole of 1933, and he did not go as far as the authorized limit. The inflation pleased the farmers, whose private debts were thereby lightened, without displeasing the manufacturers, since it raised the value of their stocks and stimulated buying. It charmed Wall Street by the promise of a long period of active business. It saved the insurance companies. In the long run, it quietly transferred $2,000,000,000 from the creditor class to the class of debtors. This transfer might very reasonably have angered the bondholders, possessors of bonds, debentures, and deposit accounts, who saw the purchasing power of their savings diminish. But this moneyed class was much less numerous in the United States than it was in France. Furthermore, the rich, who saw their bank accounts decline in value, reckoned upon restoring the loss by buying shares and by taking advantage of the certain rise. Roosevelt stabilized the dollar in January, 1934, at $35 to the ounce of gold, that is to say, at 59.06 percent of its value before 1933. Inflation is, in fact, like general paralysis, a disease whose first symptom is euphoria: it only the secondary effects that are painful. The devaluation had had little influence upon increasing exports because the European nations hurriedly aligned their currencies on the dollar: it had vexed the conservative Democrats, but during the Hundred Days it had helped to revive men's courage.

Lasting measures. How were the unemployed to be given work again? How were the consumers to be given back that purchasing power that would allow them to buy the products they needed and that were in existence? Roosevelt and his advisers thought they had found the solution in a law, the most controversial of all the new team's undertakings. This was the National Industrial Recovery Act, the NIRA for short, and its aims were: to shorten the hours of work, so that the progress of mechanization should be taken into account; to establish a minimum wage; to authorize, and even to encourage, trade associations among manufacturers of the same kinds of goods in order to fix prices in relation to the cost of production, to limit excessive competition, and to stabilize prices and wages. Also in article 7 (a) of the Act, labor was guaranteed the rights of collective bargaining. These results were to be reached in agreement with the manufacturers who, with the consent of their workers, were to set up a code for their industry. The industries that agreed to cooperate would be given a badge, the Blue Eagle, with the motto *We do our part.* Unwilling manufacturers would find themselves without a license to continue their production.

General Johnson was entrusted with the administration of the NIRA. He went into action with all the showy festivities and publicity that had been used for launching the war loans. Manufacturers and trade unionists from all over the country hurried to Washington to work out the codes. The cotton industry was ready first. It proposed a forty-hour week and a minimum wage of $12 in the South, $13 in the North. The session took place in the tropical heat of Washington. In his shirt sleeves, General Johnson presided over a meeting of employers and workers that showed a generosity and an enthusiasm very much in the style of the "night of August 4."* William Green, the president of the American Federation of Labor, spoke of "the encouraging attitude" of the cloth manufacturers. Nevertheless, difficulties arose. One manufacturer got up and explained that his materials were made of cotton and silk mixed: he asked that he should not be bound by the regulations of the cotton code.

"Then you will take the silk code?"

"No. We need a special one, a cotton and silk code."

* The reference is to the night of August 4, 1789, when, in the French National Assembly, the nobles and clergy gave up their privileges. [Translator's note.]

Was General Johnson going to be overwhelmed with a flood of codes? Moses himself, in such a position, said *Time,* would have had to climb Sinai again and again.

A journalist said to Johnson, "It is not going to be easy."

"Sure," he replied, "in two months, the air will be thick with dead cats," and he was not mistaken.

Behind the NIRA, there was the idea that the antitrust laws had helped to bring about the disaster and that it would be better to have cooperation among the manufacturers under governmental control. A blanket code to cover all industries for a provisional six months was promulgated in July: it forbade the employment of children (which was very rare, in any case), limited the hours of work, and fixed a minimum wage. Soon the great majority of the manufacturers and the workers had accepted the Blue Eagle. But the dead cats, foretold by General Johnson, came flying in from every side. The consumers railed against the codes, whose natural effect was to raise prices; the workers said that their employers evaded them; the small manufacturers maintained that the codes favored their big competitors. The NIRA did in fact improve the condition of the workers, particularly the Negroes; and by lessening the hours of work, it helped the unemployed to find jobs. Later on, nothing but its disadvantages were seen, but at the critical moment this vast effort, with Johnson's flamboyant zeal urging it on, gave the industrial system the shot in the arm that it needed. Then, like all stimulants, this one ceased to be effective. General Johnson did not stand criticism well. Bernard Baruch, who was very fond of him, never thought that he was made to be a "number one man," a leader. Beneath his aggressive manner of speaking, there was a deep unsureness and a want of capacity for sustained effort. But in any case, whatever the perils and the merits of the NIRA may have been, the question became merely academic in 1935, for the Supreme Court ruled that the codes constituted an illegal use of the federal power over interstate commerce and that the President had exceeded his authority in assuming legislative functions that belonged only to Congress.

What was to be done for the farmers, crushed between the rising mountain of their mortgage debts and the avalanche of falling prices? As in the case of industry, the new team proposed remedies, some temporary and some permanent. *First stage.* Before anything else, it was essential to stop evictions by the creditors. To this end, the state would take over part of the mortgages. Federal bonds carrying interest at 4 percent were issued and given to the farmers' creditors in exchange for their frozen mortgages. The creditors lost a certain amount of interest, but they recovered their capital. The farmers became the state's debtors, and they were allowed to repay over a long period. *Second stage.* Aim: to raise prices to a level that would allow the farmers to carry their fixed expenses. This was to be accomplished partly by inflation (devaluation of the dollar), and partly by a reduction of the area put under crops and by a compensating bounty, the necessary money being provided by a tax payable at the mill in the case of wheat, and at the spinner's in the case of cotton.

Naturally, the Agricultural Adjustment Administration (AAA) was attacked as quickly as the NIRA. Every action causes a reaction. Its opponents said that a Malthusian agricultural economy, at a time when many were not eating enough to satisfy their hunger, was absurd. The rise in agricultural prices affected consumption, while the rise of industrial prices hit the farmers. The restriction of production in America stimulated agriculture abroad, and exports remained as difficult as ever. But all things taken into account, by the end of 1934 the farmer's purchasing power as compared with the figure of 100 for the most fortunate period had moved from 55 to 70. This was not yet prosperity: it was poverty somewhat alleviated. The evictions of bankrupt farmers in fact ceased to a very large extent from 1934 onward. As regards agriculture, the New Deal went very far along the road of a planned economy. The government itself undertook the regulation of production and prices, the provision of credit for the farmers and the protection of the soil against erosion; and it was the consumer who paid the cost of these services. Agriculture now had the advantage of an expensive form of protection, and this seemed perfectly just to the farmers, since industry had always been protected by customs barriers. The policy was far from orthodox, but it worked.

Finally, the Brain Trust had come to power with very exact ideas about the reform of the banks and of Wall Street. In a book that he published at the time of his election, the President had pointed out that two of the chief reasons for the crash of 1929 were: (1) the confusion that had arisen between investment banking and deposit banking. He thought that a deposit bank, if it were to give its customers impartial advice, should never undertake the functions of an issuing house. (2) Irresponsibility of the issuing bankers. Roosevelt considered it scandalous that it should be possible for shares to be distributed among an uninformed public by men who had not made even the most elementary investigations. Two laws in the new team's program were to make good these deficiencies. One made the bank (or the broker) who issued a share answerable for the truth of the information given to the public in the prospectus; the other forbade any person (or firm) who sold shares to receive money on deposit, and established mutual insurance for deposits under $5,000.

In 1934 Congress rounded off these laws by the very important creation of the Securities and Exchange Commission (SEC) that was made up of five members appointed by the President and confirmed by the Senate, and that had the duty of giving information to uninformed subscribers, and even to those who supposed themselves informed. Every sale of stock that was made in several states, thus making the transaction interstate commerce, or that was made through the mail (these factors bringing it under federal authority) had to be thoroughly justified to the commission. The SEC made the companies fill out questionnaires covering all useful points of information, and their replies could be seen by any applicant for shares. The commission had the power of preventing the manipulation of any stock and the gaining of unfair profits by corporate insiders who were aware of facts unknown to the general public. The commission was also to supervise those holding companies that allowed the control of immense combinations to be acquired at the cost of very little capital: in case of need it could forbid them. The gigantic, and irrational, monopolies of public utilities (gas, water, electricity) were to disappear within five years. Naturally these strong measures were violently criticized: it was said that it was up to the shareholders to think about what they were at, and that nobody could protect fools against themselves. But was it true? Architects put up parapets to prevent people falling off.

While these new laws should have time to produce their

effect, it was necessary to come to the help of the unemployed. This was Hopkins' task, an immense task into which he threw himself with passion and prodigality. "Money flies!" said the *Washington Post,* in a melancholy headline. "The five hundred million dollars granted to Harry Hopkins for direct aid to the states will not last a month if Harry Hopkins goes on at the pace he set yesterday, spending more than five million dollars in his first two hours."

Hopkins replied, "I shall not last six months here, so I might as well do what I please."

Roosevelt had ordered him to relieve the unemployed quickly, without distinction of race, religion, or political opinion; he had obeyed his orders with all his heart, and this soon brought him into conflict with the politicians of the party, such as Farley, who wanted to use the relief funds to reward "deserving Democrats."

Hopkins very quickly came to understand that relief as such was of far less value than a job, even a poorly paid one, that would keep up a man's spirit, give him back his self-confidence and keep him fit for work. In his attempts at finding work for the unemployed, he met with opposition: the unions were afraid of the competition of badly paid labor; the conservatives said that plain, direct charity would cost less and that the schemes for public works would increase the public debt. But the workless, for their part, preferred Hopkins' way. Sherwood tells the story of an old man who had been given a relief check and who took to sweeping the streets of the little town of his own accord, saying, "I want to do something in return for what I get."

All these acts of the Hundred Days, the embargo on gold, the devaluation of the dollar, help for the farmers, and the industrial codes, lightened the intolerable burden that their own foolishness had placed upon the producers' backs, to increase the consumers' purchasing power, and thus to put the unemployed back to work again. Many thought that these Hundred Days would end in a Waterloo; but to form a fair opinion, one must remember the tragic disorder that Franklin Delano Roosevelt had inherited. On taking power, he had said that the country wanted bold experiments, and that above all something had to be attempted. His friends, "the professors," had thought over the possible lines of action for a long while, and they brought him ready-made plans, which explains the astonishing impression of speed at the beginning of the Administration. One cannot help calling to mind, as one writes the history of these three crowded months, the Biblical account of the Creation. The first day, the Brain Trust put an embargo on gold; the second day, it peopled the forests; the third day, it created the three point two beer; the fourth day, it broke the bonds that tied the dollar to gold; the fifth day, it set the farmers free; the sixth day, it created General Johnson, and then, looking upon what it had made of America, it saw that it was good.

But it could not rest on the seventh day. Fear, greed, and political passion were already distorting the steel and cracking the concrete arches of the splendid skyscraper of economic theory that the new team had built up in record time. "The difficulty," said one of the young members of the team to the writer of this book on a baking June day of 1933 in a Washington garden, "the difficulty is that this is a real world." Now the real world never accepts the lines that reason wishes to give it without altering them somewhat. To begin with, the convalescence had seemed utterly astonishing: for after July, 1929, the curve of industrial production had dropped from 114 until it reached 54 in March, 1933, the date of F.D.R.'s inauguration; from that day, it had risen in a sudden leap, reaching 58 in April, 68 in May, and 78 as early as the end of June. Prices rose. Cotton went from 6½¢ to 10, and then to 12¢. Wall Street followed the upward trend. U. S. Steel climbed in a few weeks from twenty-two to fifty-eight, General Motors from ten to thirty. But the very success quickly bred ingratitude. As soon as the steel industry had two million tons on its order books, as soon as the farmers saw wheat at a dollar, the fugitives turned around and began cursing their savior. From the beginning of June, grave difficulties made their appearance. The devaluation was disapproved of, even by a friend like Bernard Baruch: "We're raising prices for the benefit of a small proportion of the population: the unemployed, debtor classes—incompetent, unwise people . . . It can't be defended, except as mob rule."

On the international plane, a conference was to meet at London for the consolidation of European currencies. The gold standard and customs tariffs were to be discussed. But the New Deal, delighted with the results that it had obtained on the national plane, was prepared neither to stabilize the dollar nor to lower tariffs. Roosevelt, MacDonald, and Herriot nevertheless decided to keep to the date they had set. Cordell Hull, the secretary of state, came to London and talked of the possibility of stabilization with the English and French. These conversations gave rise at once to a wave of pessimism among those who were in favor of inflation in the United States. "Stabilize?" protested Wall Street. "That would mean the bottom falling out of the market again." "Stabilize?" cried the farmers. "That would be cotton at 5¢ once more."

The American delegation in London seemed to be divided. As soon as Cordell Hull pronounced the forbidden word "stabilization," the New Dealers protested. Europe made game of this inconsistency. F.D.R. sent Raymond Moley to preach the true gospel to the Europeans; but then Moley in his turn was disavowed. Thus the last attempt at reestablishing monetary stability broke down in complete disorder, and thus began that anarchy and that vicious financial circle in which each nation fixed the value of its own currency and in which there were reprisals after every devaluation. "The Europeans' anger took the form of blaming the Americans for everything," writes Allan Nevins, "and there is no doubt that Roosevelt was responsible for this collapse. . . . Constructive action in London might have greatly improved world morale." On this occasion, F.D.R. was shortsighted; but then he was in a difficult position.

The disarmament conference at Geneva was no greater success. Hitler was now in power: he recalled his delegates. On the other hand, the USSR seemed to be adopting a more conciliatory attitude. After talks with Maxim Litvinov, the Russian foreign minister, the USSR was given diplomatic recognition in 1933. In exchange for the United States' recognition of the USSR, Russia undertook to abstain from propaganda in America, to guarantee religious liberty for Americans in Russia, and to negotiate a settlement of debts. This last negotiation in fact came to nothing. But on the other hand, the Roosevelt Administration was more successful in Latin America. By force of tact, and even of humility, Cordell Hull finally overcame the South Americans' distrust, and a collective security covenant was signed. "Thus, by the time Hitler's threats had ended hopes of peace in Europe,

the Roosevelt Administration had laid the groundwork for friendship and mutual defense in the Western Hemisphere. Consider-
ing the long background of mutual distrust, the Good Neighbor
Policy was a remarkable achievement."

V

The mid-term Congressional election fell in November,
1934. It was an important election, for it would measure the
popularity of the first New Deal. Roosevelt made ready for it
with a book, *On Our Way,* in which he reviewed the achieve-
ments of his administration. "Some people described that policy
as revolutionary," he wrote, "perhaps it is." But if it was a
revolution, it had been a peaceful one. Roosevelt had not attacked the business world: he had done his best to get it to
cooperate with him, to reform it, and control it. Besides, if the
American people did not approve of his policy, they had a
simple means of reversing it—the voting paper. What had the
government undertaken to do? It had undertaken to put an end
to the excessive privileges of a small, all-powerful group and to
distribute the national income more fairly. And in fact the
country's economy, which had been on the edge of ruin in 1933,
was now in a better state. The farmers' income, for example, had
risen from $2,285,000,000 at the end of 1932 to $2,993,000,000
at the end of 1933. Industrial production had increased, and
this increase had been purchased by the consumers. The President was therefore determined to carry on in the same way.

But he was violently attacked, both from the Right and from
the Left. On the one hand, a conservative rebellion united the
important Republican businessmen and some powerful Democrats, such as Al Smith and John W. Davis. The NIRA had
angered all the manufacturers, great or small. The codes irked
and hampered them, and the unions' new freedom to organize
in an independent fashion rendered them uneasy. The Republicans attacked the New Deal for its contempt of states' rights
and for its federal bureaucracy—its "alphabet soup bureaucracy."
Their newspapers came out strongly against "this succession of
incoherent remedies, which had begotten economic chaos." The
President had spoken of economies. But the different kinds of

relief now reached $5,000,000,000, and the public debt had doubled.

The Left reproached the New Deal with having neglected the sharecroppers, the marginal farmers, and the old people in need. The most desperate of them were ready to follow wild men like the novelist Upton Sinclair, who was candidate for the governorship of California; like Dr. Francis E. Townsend, who wanted to give every unemployed person over sixty years of age $200 a month (the Townsend Clubs soon had five million members); like the well-known Father Charles E. Coughlin of Detroit, a Catholic priest who preached inflammatory sermons on the radio; or like the demagogic governor of Louisiana, Huey Long, who had set up a local dictatorship with the help of strong-arm men and who was promising every family a house and $2,500 a year.

So as the elections of 1934 came nearer, it had to be admitted that treacle had taken the place of the honey in the New Deal's honeymoon with the nation. Roosevelt had to choose between those who were discontented on the Right and those who were discontented on the Left: he unhesitatingly chose the Left, and with a remarkable agility, he recast his platform and got rid of those advisers who were more conservative than himself. He appealed to a combination composed of farmers, workers, the lower reaches of the managerial class, and the unemployed, and he offered them a bold program, intended to improve their standard at the expense of the budget and to redistribute the wealth of the country. The November elections gave Roosevelt's party an astonishing majority: 319 representatives out of 435 and 69 of the 96 senators. No president since Jefferson and Andrew Jackson had been so massively approved.

In spite of this electoral success, the dead cats continued to fly. Everything was going better, but nothing was going really well. Had the national income increased by 25 percent over that of 1933? Yes, but it was still forty billion dollars below that of 1929, and each dollar was worth less. Had the number of unemployed gone down by two million? Yes, but it was still infinitely too high. The Supreme Court took up a position against the New Deal and declared many of the new laws and agencies unconstitutional—an attitude that gave rise to much uneasiness and impatience. Was the country in favor of the reforms? Yes, it was; but many of the reforms remained at the planning stage. Irresponsible demagogues were making exaggerated claims, and their popularity showed that the American masses wanted changes that went far deeper.

On the Detroit radio, Father Coughlin thundered against modern capitalism and international bankers. Every week he received eighty thousand letters. For a long while, this turbulent priest had supported F.D.R., but toward 1935, he felt that he was strong enough "to gamble his own magnetism against that of Roosevelt." Dr. Townsend, the champion of old-age pensions, also took up a position against the President. As for Huey Long, now a senator from Louisiana, he had brought his overbearing ways, his ambition, and his hatreds to Washington. Roosevelt considered him one of the most dangerous men in America; and he was in fact a real menace. Coughlin and Long inevitably called up Fascism and Nazism. They did not suffer from the same neurosis as Hitler, but they were playing the same game, and like the European dictators they founded their power upon the dissatisfied shopkeepers, the workmen, and the farmers whom the depression had driven out of their minds with fear and who were against the banks, the big companies, and the unions all at the same time. Huey Long was perfectly capable of starting a right-wing radicalism. Roosevelt wrote to his ambassador in Italy, "We too are going through a bad case of Huey Long and Father Coughlin influenza. The whole country is aching in every bone."

All this uneasiness and disturbance grew threatening; and it became even more so when Roosevelt, at the beginning of 1935, seemed to be in a very hesitant state. Not only did he see himself attacked on two fronts, by the businessmen on one side and the demagogues on the other, but even his own advisers were no longer in agreement among themselves. Raymond Moley announced, "The New Deal is practically complete." Rex Tugwell's opinion was diametrically opposed: "This battle for a New Deal is not yet over; indeed, I suspect it has just begun." By now the President was doubtful of the NRA experiment; the nation did not seem to him ripe for planned industry. One of his favorite advisers, Brandeis, did not like plans that reached out too far. "Why should anyone want to go to Russia when one can go to Denmark?" he asked.

The first New Deal team, brought in by Raymond Moley, had

mostly come from Columbia University. It was made up of professors with generous, purely theoretical ideas upon the refashioning of society and its coordination. Toward 1935, a new team was formed, brought in by Felix Frankfurter of Harvard, and made up of lawyers. Once again, Roosevelt changed. Two young men, Tom Corcoran and Benjamin Cohen, became his intimates and wrote his speeches. The combination of an Irishman and a Jew struck the popular imagination. But Cohen and Corcoran were not comic characters. They knew what they wanted; they did not believe in long-term schemes; they liked dealing with each problem as it came up. They insisted upon the necessity for increasing purchasing power as quickly as possible. The ideal, said Corcoran, would be to have a huge squadron of airplanes fly over America, scattering dollars, and anyone who needed them would pick them up. This was reminiscent of Keynes's teaching: the public debt should increase in the years of the lean kine; the treasury would get it back in the years of the fat ones.

For Harry Hopkins, it was all that he could have wished. He called his team together. "Boys," he said, "this is our hour. We've got to get everything we want: a works program, social security, wages and hours, everything—now or never." He obtained the President's consent for a whole series of measures of the first importance. Ickes, the secretary of the interior, and some others, warned Roosevelt of Hopkins' prodigality; but Hopkins had an easy, wayward charm that worked upon the President. Neither Hopkins nor Roosevelt was an ideologist. They both liked action and risk.

An enormous sum, close on $5,000,000,000, was set aside for the Works Progress Administration (WPA), which had the intention of employing millions of the jobless—the numbers it employed did in fact reach 3,238,000 by November, 1938. Between 1935 and 1941, the WPA spent $11,000,000,000 on 1,410,000 projects, from the building of airports to frescoes, for the WPA employed painters, musicians, actors, and writers. For example, the best series of American guides was published in this way. There were other administrations to look after the marginal farmers and rural electricity. The National Youth Administration employed the students, both in order to help them and to prevent them from competing with the adult workers. In 1940, 750,000 students earned from five to thirty dollars a month as stenographers, assistants in libraries, laboratories, schools, and so on. Altogether, these projects were a triumph for Harry Hopkins. The mass of public opinion was behind them. A poll by *Fortune* showed that 76.8 percent of the persons questioned thought that "the government should see to it that every man who wants to work has a job."

Naturally, all this cost a very great deal. One day, in Iowa, his native state, when Hopkins was explaining the virtues of the deficit to a crowd a voice arose: "Who's going to pay for it?" Hopkins stopped, took off his coat and rolled up his sleeves, while the crowd watched him in silence. Then in a voice that cracked like a whip he cried, "You are!"

Taxes brought in part of the necessary money. In 1935, Congress raised the supertax to 31 percent for an income of $50,000 and to 75 percent after $5,000,000. The tax paid by companies was also increased. But the mass of the citizens saw more advantage than peril in these new schemes. The country, by salvaging millions of workers, was providing itself with a reservoir of labor that was to be invaluable in time of war. The social effects were immense: the unfortunate had the feeling that at last the government was taking care of them. The less openly admitted political effects were, in the long run, very deep. To begin with, Hopkins had prided himself on his impartiality: "Politics has no business in relief." Then the bosses made their dissatisfaction plain. Hopkins was a realistic idealist. "He had," says Joseph E. Davies, "the purity of a Saint Francis of Assisi combined with the sharpness of mind of a racetrack tout." He gave way, just as far as it was essential to survive. It was too tempting, for the local politicians, to favor their personal friends, at a time when dollars were being handed out by the billion. No government can either hope or claim to legislate for saints.

But the law that Roosevelt himself considered the New Deal's supreme accomplishment was that which dealt with Social Security and which was signed in August, 1935. "If, during this long and arduous session, the Senate and the House of Representatives had done nothing more than pass this Bill, the session would be regarded as historic for all time." It must be remembered that until this time the United States had been far behind Europe. The idea that each man was the guardian of his own

162

fate was very strong, and few states had attempted to insure some degree of permanent security for all. The new law allowed: (a) the federal government to help the states (on a 50 percent basis) to provide for the needs of the aged, of sick mothers and children, and of the blind; (b) to set up a national fund for old-age pensions, fed by the contributions of employers and wage earners; (c) to finance, using the same methods, an insurance against unemployment, varying according to the state, but in the neighborhood of $15 to $18 a week for twelve to twenty-six weeks a year. Roosevelt had every reason to call this a historic law. It put an end to two centuries of fierce individualism.

As the Supreme Court had ruled General Johnson's NRA and his codes unconstitutional, the cooperation between business and the government came to a stop. Strict regulation took its place. Several laws governed the hours of work, forbade child labor, and established a minimum wage. Manufacturers were forbidden to favor certain clients at the expense of others: every rebate had to be justified by a genuine saving on the cost price. The merchant marine and the airlines were put under federal control. The first New Deal had encouraged industrial associations: the second took up the struggle against monopolies once more. In 1938, the President appointed Professor Thurman Arnold assistant attorney general, with the mission of seeing that the antitrust laws were obeyed. Arnold's operations were particularly prudent and far less spectacular than those of Theodore Roosevelt and Wilson before him.

It was the Supreme Court, too, that put the farmers' fate in the balance again. The laws of 1933 and 1934 had markedly improved the agricultural position. The farmers' income had risen from $2,285,000,000 in 1932 to $5,052,000,000 in 1935. The relationship between agricultural and industrial prices had moved from 61 percent to 86 percent. But in February, 1936, the Supreme Court declared the Agricultural Adjustment Act (AAA) unconstitutional: (a) because the sale of farm produce was not necessarily part of interstate commerce, since many of the sales took place locally; (b) because Congress had created taxes levied at such places as the mills and textile plants for the benefit of the farmers, whereas the Constitution said that a tax was to be "for the general welfare." This was a narrow and partisan reading of the sacred text. It was clear that often a majority of the

Supreme Court had decided to kill the New Deal. Roosevelt had to have recourse to a whole arsenal of new laws. In February, 1938, a new AAA was voted into existence, an AAA intended to create "an ever normal granary" by having the surplus of plentiful years bought by the government and put upon the market in the years when the harvest was poor. If the surpluses became excessive, the government might sell them for the benefit of the poor or the schools or to favor export. These surpluses were to prove most valuable during the Second World War. Later they weighed heavily upon the American taxpayer, but in 1938, Roosevelt could see no other solution; and by adopting it he prevented a catastrophic disaster, for the harvest of 1937 had set up a dangerous abundance.

VI

The position of the labor unions needed strengthening, and this was done. The well-known article 7 (a) of the NIRA guaranteed the right to form unions without intimidation or employers' influence, and the right of collective bargaining. When the Supreme Court declared the NIRA unconstitutional on May 27, 1935, F.D.R. put all his influence behind Senator Wagner's act, which confirmed these guarantees and which furthermore brought into existence a body as important in its way as the Interstate Commerce Commission: the National Labor Relations Board, a commission of five members that had the power of defending the workers (and the employers, too) against all abuses.

Fortified by these measures, the unions increased their numbers and their power immensely, gaining 1,307,000 new members between 1933 and 1936. But they made this growth at the expense of their unity. A small, aggressive minority appeared in the American Federation of Labor, and it was led by John L. Lewis, "a leonine man with a stentorian voice and command of a virile, Elizabethan vocabulary." Lewis found solid support in the New York clothing industry. Sidney Hillman, the president of the Amalgamated Clothing Workers, was a Lithuanian who had come to America when he was twenty and who had then provided himself with an education. For him, unionism went far beyond making demands upon employers: he saw it as a constructive force, creating its own banks, its own insurance, art schools, and newspapers. At his side, there was David Dubinsky, who had organized the workers in the ladies' garment industry in the same manner. Hillman was eloquent, Dubinsky homely and sarcastic; but, together with Lewis, these men made up an irresistible team.

The conservative majority of the American Federation of Labor, together with its president, William Green, believed that the unions ought to be "horizontal," and that they should group the qualified workers of all the industries. Lewis wanted each industry (cars, cement, aluminum, metallurgy, etc.) to have its own industrial union. The struggle led to Lewis' secession. He formed the Committee for Industrial Organization (CIO) as a rival to the American Federation of Labor, and between March and October, 1937, he recruited nearly a quarter of a million members. There followed a period of violent strikes, sit-down strikes, in which the workers barricaded themselves in the factories. The great industries (General Motors and U.S. Steel) treated with the CIO. Roosevelt, who did not want to lose either of these two bodies of electors, handled both the AFL and the CIO with consideration. The National Labor Relations Board proved its worth by taking care of these innumerable conflicts and solving three quarters of them. The highest point of the New Deal's efforts in this field was the law of 1938 that established a minimum wage beginning at 25¢ an hour (it is five times as much today) and a maximum of forty-four hours in the working week. Interstate commerce was forbidden to any industry that employed child labor.

The year 1936 was to be a presidential election year, and the business world, uncertain how it would turn, hesitated to make investments. The President did his utmost to reassure them: "I don't believe in abandoning the system of individual enterprise. The freedom and opportunity that have characterized America's development in the past can be maintained if freedom and opportunity do not mean a license to climb upward by pushing other people down." To a letter asking him for "a breathing spell and a recess from further experiment," the President answered, in agreement with Moley, that the fundamental program had been accomplished and that in fact the time for the breathing space had come. In this way, the sky cleared on Roosevelt's right; and on his left he was no longer encumbered by Huey Long, who had been killed at the age of forty-two by a young doctor. From a moral point of view, Roosevelt of course cried out against this murder; but it was nevertheless useful to him politically. Meanwhile the left wing of the party protested against the idea of a "pause." According to his usual tactics, the President lavished contradictory appeasements, now to the Left, now to the Right.

Once he had been chosen by acclamation as the Democratic party's candidate, F.D.R. reaffirmed his declaration of war against the "economic royalists," who had brought about the rule of "an industrial dictatorship." He ended, "This generation of Americans has a rendezvous with Destiny. . . . We are fighting to save a great and precious form of government for ourselves and for the world. . . . I accept the commission you have tendered. . . . I am enlisted for the duration of the war."

The campaign of the Republicans, who had chosen as their presidential candidate Governor Alfred M. Landon of Kansas, was based upon opposition to the paternalism of the New Deal, to the welfare state, to the idea that Uncle Sam could play the shopkeeper, the manufacturer, the patron of the arts, and the stockpiler of the country's harvests; that he could be an estate agent and that he could subsidize theaters or publish books. True Americanism, they said, consisted of thinking that every man who worked hard would reach the top. But "rugged individualism" was out of date. Landon had almost all the means of reaching the public on his side—he had 85 percent of the newspapers and the radio, dominated by the advertisers. On the other hand, labor actively supported the President. John L. Lewis and Sidney Hillman set up a League for the Reelection of Roosevelt. They owed him a debt of gratitude, and they knew that his defeat would mean a setback for their movement. Landon's campaign was subsidized by big business, so the unions subsidized Roosevelt. Lewis offered him a check for $250,000. "No, John," said Roosevelt, "I don't want your check, much as I appreciate the thought. Just keep it and I'll call on you, if and when any small need arises." Lewis then grasped that the campaign was going to be very much more expensive. The Democrats also successfully mobilized the liberal intellectuals, the women, the Negroes—all the minorities. It was now no longer the old Democratic party, based upon professional politicians and committees, but a powerful combination of the weak to win justice in the American fashion, legally. Throughout the country, Roosevelt was welcomed with immense enthusiasm. His automobile was surrounded by crowds shouting "Thank you, Mr. President! . . . God bless you! . . . You saved my home." For his part, Landon counted on the average American. He was certain that the very flatness of his speeches—their banality—would be a virtue in the eyes of the electors: "The American people have always been fearful in the end of a *great* man."

A new extremist party, the National Union for Social Justice, brought together the followers of Father Coughlin, Dr. Townsend, and Huey Long, and it carried on a Hitlerish campaign that angered everybody, most particularly the Catholics. This party reckoned on winning 9,000,000 votes: it barely obtained 882,000. Landon had 17,000,000; Roosevelt 28,000,000. The Socialists received 188,000 votes; the Communists, 80,000. Roosevelt had 523 electoral votes as against 8 for Landon. It was the most overwhelming political victory in the history of the United States, and it was the New Deal's triumph.

The New Deal's *political* triumph, for a legal obstacle still remained. In 1937, the Supreme Court seemed determined to prevent the President from governing. Four out of the nine judges were reactionaries who were still living in the nineteenth century and who showed so constant a hostility to all humanitarian legislation that they were called the Four Horsemen of the Apocalypse. Chief Justice Hughes often voted with them. They perpetually referred to the words "interstate commerce," and they used the expression in its most limiting sense. It was intolerable that the entirety of the legislation upon labor should depend upon judges who were profoundly versed in the law but profoundly ignorant of industry and who interpreted the Constitution in a manner that favored their own social prejudices. Quite obviously the Founding Fathers had never decided that a Detroit mechanic should work a forty-eight-hour week. The huge power that four or five obstinate old men wielded without any control was contrary to common sense.

The only cure would have been to pack the court and thus to make certain of a majority. But this could only be done either by the passage of time, which would bring deaths or retirements, or else by the appointment of new judges. Deaths were unusual; retiring was still optional; the making of new judges disturbed the Senate. In February, 1937, Roosevelt nevertheless suggested adding up to a minimum of six new members to the Supreme Court, to deputize for those who declined to retire at seventy. The bill raised a storm of protest, and for the first time F.D.R. lost control of Congress. Even some of the liberal Democratic senators themselves said that the President was trying to subordinate the judiciary to the executive and that the Supreme Court, that sacred tribunal, must remain untouched. There was a drop on the Stock Exchange. Ex-President Hoover publicly rebuked his successor. Roosevelt replied, "We must take action to save the Constitution from the court and the court from itself." But he was obliged to change his bill to the point of emasculating it. For a moment it seemed that he was beaten. Then suddenly the whole aspect changed. By five votes against four the Supreme Court accepted the essence of the new labor laws. What had happened? The Four Horsemen had remained in the nineteenth century. But Chief Justice Hughes and Justice Owen J. Roberts had gone over to the liberal minority. Why? We now know that Roberts had made his decision long before. As for Hughes, he no doubt rightly considered that if the Supreme Court, against the great majority of the nation, opposed laws that were desired by all, it would sooner or later be brought low. "Thus the President had lost the proverbial battle but won the war."

In 1937, fearing a new wave of speculation, the government suspended all inflationary measures. It cut the numbers employed by the WPA, tightened credit, and announced the end of the policy of unbalanced budgets. This brought immediate results: a minor crisis threatened to take place. F.D.R. did not overstress his point but set his influence working in the other direction. The industrial production index had fallen from 119 (the August, 1937, figure) to 81 in May of 1938: it rose to 101 in December, 1938. Thus it was proved that it was possible to stop a depression if action was taken in time; but the machinery for doing so was complicated and the cost high. Furthermore, the world situation was growing most disturbing: Hitler was roaring, threatening, invading. With this dangerous future in sight, it was of the first importance to muster all the country's strength. In his message to Congress in January, 1939, the President said, "We have now passed the period of internal conflict in the launching of our program of social reform. Our full energies may now be released to invigorate the processes of recovery in order to preserve our reforms." All in all, he could be satisfied with his work: he had brought about many of the reforms that he had announced in 1932, and he had brought them about without a violent revolution, by democratic methods.

Not everything was for the best in the best of all possible worlds, but the purchasing power of the masses had increased, and above all they had regained confidence in their laws and in their government. Roosevelt had shown that, without giving up its freedom, a system of free enterprise is capable of imposing discipline and sacrifices upon itself, and of righting a ship that had taken a dangerous list. It had, perhaps, been a costly experiment, but it had left behind it an immense capital in new buildings, dams, and schools, and above all, it had put the nation back to work. The New Deal had not made America a socialist state; nor yet had it maintained the laissez-faire regime beloved of Coolidge. Its originality consisted in its refusal to turn political life into a conflict between two ideologies. Two abstract words can be in absolute opposition. Life insists upon more subtle shades, upon varying proportions and mixtures. "In a world where revolutions just now are coming easy," says Adolf Berle, "the New Deal chose the more difficult course of moderation and rebuilding." Roosevelt and his team had created a controlled capitalism. Would it work? Some thought it would not; but presently the war was to put it to a savage test, and it came out of it with flying colors.

PART SIX

The United States
before the Second World War

THAT crucial year, 1939, the year that stood like a lull between two vast upheavals, the depression and the war. The autumn of the New Deal's life was now beginning. Roosevelt and his friends had undertaken to bring about a peaceful revolution: they had succeeded, creating an economy midway between anarchistic capitalism and rigid state control. The New Deal had made its mistakes; but no omelet was ever made without eggs being broken. It had warded off the most immediate perils; it had made use of taxation to remedy inequality; it had supported the unions to counterbalance the power of the great companies; it had striven to keep up the purchasing power of the unemployed. The famous English economist Keynes could say to Roosevelt, "You represent all those who believe in the possibility of orderly change." The change had been far reaching: yet public order had not been disturbed.

It was a new country that the President was governing in 1939. For the first time, the American state had assumed the responsibility for insuring a relative degree of security for all its citizens. The degree was still far too low, but at least the principle had been acknowledged. Washington had become the economic capital of the country. Many powerful agencies were looking after the unemployed, the farmers, and relations between employers and the employees. The money that the reforms had called for had been found by raising the income tax and by permitting a certain lack of balance in the budget. In short, the movement that Theodore Roosevelt and Wilson had begun had accomplished many of its aims, and it had now reached a stage at which it could rest. The Age of the Dinosaurs was fading away into oblivion. The businessmen grumbled, but they accepted the controls imposed; the men in the street and the poor had, to a considerable extent, obtained what they had been asking for. After an immense effort, the country was recovering its breath again.

Although the presidential election was still a long way off, it was the one topic of conversation. One great question outweighed all the others: Would Roosevelt win a third term, in spite of tradition? He was reaching the age of fifty-eight, and he had gone through six grueling years. His handsome face was more lined than it had been, and his thinning hair was going white at the temples; but he was still high spirited and active, and his smile still charmed the newspapermen at his press conferences. As a relaxation from his strenuous work, he had his dog Fala, his stamp collection, two films a week, and his holidays at Hyde Park, the Roosevelts' family home. His friends adored him, although they did not always understand him; his enemies hated him with an incredible bitterness. He was the people's idol, but some circles detested him with a violence that went as far as hysteria. An elderly Fifth Avenue hostess, a pleasant, cultivated woman, said to the writer of this book, who was in America at that time, "I would rather see the whole planet blow up than give that man a third term!" It was surprising to see such a mad intensity of feeling.

But in spite of Roosevelt's popularity with the masses, it

172

seemed possible that the political pendulum might swing back again. Already the 1938 elections had brought a less docile Congress to Washington. The Dinosaurs, a species in the process of mutation, henceforward evoked not so much fear as a kind of ironic concern.

Every year the Gridiron Club, the newspapermen accredited to Washington, gave a dinner at which a very bold and free-speaking revue was acted before the President. In 1939, the theme was the struggle of King Arthur (F.D.R.), the Knights of the Round Table (the Cabinet), and the Sorcerers (the Brain Trust) against the dragon Business. Poor Business had been so mauled by the Knights that he was practically dead. He was brought into the banquet hall, covered with bandages and adhesive tape. "I am afraid," said one of his tormentors anxiously, "that we may have hit this old dragon too hard: he is going to die on our hands."

"That is just what I am always telling King Arthur," replied Sir Henry le Morgue (Morgenthau), "but it doesn't seem to worry him—he only smiles. Between you and me, now that it has been going on for six years, even the people are tired of the harsh treatment dealt out to poor old Business."

Henry le Morgue advised that the dragon should be given a potion called Appeasement to keep him going, but the wizards and the sorcerers of the New Deal, Eccles the Echo, Tommy the Cork, and Benny the Cone, were dead against this and wanted to kill Business without further ceremony. Finally King Arthur decided that Business should have a respite until 1940. "And now you, Knights, watch over him, and you, Sorcerers, leave him in peace." The dragon, suffering and battered, began to move off, and at that moment the king gave him one last kick, "So that you shan't forget who is your master, Business."

Was it accurate satire, and was the dragon, after six years of disfavor, really at the point of death—a death that America did not want? At this critical juncture, we must take our bearings.

I

Before anything else, we must once again call to mind the tragic circumstances in which the President had come to power—a panic-stricken nation, fourteen million unemployed, little relief or none, the states and many of the cities without money to feed the hungry, the night shelters besieged, the managing classes with nothing to manage, banks shut. In 1933, the country was heading straight for very serious social trouble and perhaps even for a violent revolution—a revolution desired by very few, but one that an absence of leadership would have made possible. "The elevator was on the ground floor." It was impossible to go lower. It has been said that if at that moment Roosevelt had asked all the citizens to stand on their heads in the middle of a public square to save the country, all, from the banker to the laboring man, would have done so without argument.

And he did ask them to do so: that is to say, he did induce them to do the contrary of what they had always done. Won over by the teaching of the young economists of the Brain Trust, the President maintained a thesis that ran more or less like this: Up until now our country's prosperity has been made by a willingness to take risks, by individual initiative, and by speculative investment in the new industries. But a frontier has been reached. Physically, the march toward the west has come to an end. In industry, production has increased faster than consumption. In the present state of affairs, the American state, rather than encourage the building up of capital meant to finance new undertakings, must for a while increase the buying power of the mass of the people. This means taxes upon incomes and upon companies, the raising of wages, and above all massive relief for the unemployed, the aged, the sick, and all those who, deprived of everything, can buy nothing. This was what was called the Three Rs program—Relief, Reform, Recovery. Urgent forms of relief, then far-reaching reforms, and finally the cure.

In fact, after six years of treatment, the patient was surviving and even seemed tolerably hearty. When one traveled through the America of 1939, one saw no more of those pitiable apple sellers; on the contrary, one had the pleasure of finding the strange, picturesque, baroque, sanguine America of the days of prosperity. Everywhere trains and hotels were crowded with travelers; everywhere new suburbs were being built; everywhere universities and colleges were refusing students for want of room. In Iowa, as in Texas or in Oklahoma, the swelling cities proudly pointed out the shining lights of their skyscrapers among the stars of the night sky. These cities were building museums, maintaining symphony orchestras. There were some groups that still led a wretched life—the "poor whites" of the South, some of the Negroes, the Puerto Ricans, and the unhappy denizens of the Bowery in New York, for example—but the popular movie theaters were crammed, the cheap restaurants could scarcely contain all their customers, and the crowds were better dressed than ever they had been before.

No, this was certainly not a society in its death throes. The opponents of the New Deal asserted that only the daily injections of government subsidies kept the patient going, that many so-called workers were being paid by the state for doing jobs that produced nothing, that Washington was sowing dollars in billions all over the country so as to harvest votes in the 1940 elections, and finally that America could not go on playing this ruinous game for long. "Priming the pump," as Roosevelt had put it at the time of his inauguration, was still valid enough; but pouring out a limitless supply of water from a cistern that was certainly not a bottomless one seemed a disastrous method to the New Deal's enemies—a system bound to come to a fatal end.

They added (and this was true) that there were still between nine and ten million unemployed; they affirmed that the depression was not over; and they emphasized the fact that when the government had tried to reduce subsidies in 1937, the immediate consequence was the beginning of an economic crisis. According to them, it was the natural vigor of the country alone, and not Roosevelt's legislation, that had put an end to the panic. This, however, does not have to be accepted as gospel. Some of the worst defects that had weakened the American economy were, by 1939, thoroughly cured. Speculation was now obliged to obey strict rules and to give the public honest information; the farmer, somewhat better supported and maintained, was a consumer once more; a first draft of a system of social security had raised the purchasing power of the poorest class; and the well-protected unions had won higher wages for their members. All this had been done through the ordinary legal means of the country's institutions, without any sacrifice of fundamental liberties. The accomplishment deserved gratitude and admiration.

America seemed to have reached economic maturity. For a long while, enterprising immigrants, seeing boundless natural resources at their disposal, had given themselves up to complete and total individualism. Every man for himself, and the frontier for all. Like the spoiled child that it was, the country had suffered the governmental controls of the First World War with an ill grace, and as soon as the fighting was over it had hurried back to isolationism, as much for the nation in the world as a whole as for the individual in the nation. And, like a spoiled child again, it had believed in the possibility of making money without working for it, and it had believed that the curve on the graph of Wall Street prices would always rise.

The great depression had been a harsh awakening. Every American had learned through bitter experience that success does not necessarily reward either the speculator or even the worker. No man is an island, as Hemingway reminded his countrymen. For whom the bell tolls? Perhaps for thee. Captains of industry, omnipotent the day before, had found themselves in the depression reduced to digging ditches. Wealthy coupon clippers and shareholders, ruined by the slump, had retreated to the country, where life seemed less dear, and there they had seen that the virtual bankruptcy of the farmers to a large measure explained that of the manufacturers. Everybody, or almost everybody, was in need of help. Everybody had discovered that life is tragic, that misfortune lies in wait for every man, and that the butler at the door of a Newport villa cannot protect a banker from it. For the first time, the greater part of the nation had accepted the idea of the welfare state, of the state answerable for the well-being of the outcasts of fortune, at least so far as the essentials of life; for the first time, the nation acknowledged that in a well-constituted society, it was not enough that each should have the right to vote, to speak freely, and to take his chance; it was also necessary that the innocent and unfortunate, the victims of tragedy, should be helped with brotherly kindness and should have the right to be helped, by the entirety of that society.

This continual appeal to the state had its dangers. James Truslow Adams was uneasy at the disappearance of the antique virtues of economy, enterprise, and responsibility. An administrator of the WPA anxiously observed that the many forms of help and its frequency warped the characters of the young and filled them with defeatism. Going clean against the American tradition, many of these young people preferred safety to the struggle for life. But this was not the state of mind of the majority. The great body of the people kept their artlessness and their optimism. The great world's fairs of 1939—the New York fair, dedicated to the World of Tomorrow, with its Trylon and its Perisphere, its modern architecture, its monuments made of concrete and of glass, its Lagoon of the Nations, its dazzling lighting, its countless inventions, its Futurama, its Aquacade (an underwater ballet of bathing beauties), its mixture of eroticism and gigantism; the San Francisco fair, with its Treasure island—were, by their prodigality, acts of faith in the future. Every man was a king as he walked about through these gardens, admiring their wonders. "All these things, the beautiful and the silly alike, reflect in their various ways the one hundred and thirty million people of this land, friendly, inventive, hopeful people, who have found that their lot is cast together."

The visit of King George VI and Queen Elizabeth in 1939 was like a royal tribute to that collective sovereign, Uncle Sam. The King and Queen were given an entirely American bill of fare—clam cocktails and hot dogs; they had Negro spirituals sung to them and the songs of the cowboys. America asserted its 100 percent Americanism. During the first six months of the year, there was an atmosphere of holiday that revived confidence. At last the young people seemed to be getting over the sickness of the depression. J. B. Priestley observed that the Cinderella theme—the secretary who marries Prince Charming—was growing popular again in motion pictures. Some Americans regretted this return of sentimental optimism. "The sad realism of your French films, the hard, hopeless life of the inmates of the *Hôtel du Nord*, is far more valid," they told me. "It is truer, braver, and more human." But the people who spoke like this were New York intellectuals, already infected by European disillusionment. The rest of America went back to its fairy tales. The sorcerers of the New Deal had just written one upon a nation-wide scale.

II

In 1939, the population of the United States reached 130,000,000, as against 122,000,000 in 1930. During this decade, the increase was less by half than the increase over the preceding ten years: the drop was caused by the decline in births (in 1890, the average family had six children; in 1939, two), and by the restriction of immigration. The quotas set by the law of 1921 had reduced the inward flow from 1,218,000 in 1914 to 241,000 in 1929 and to the almost negligible figure of 82,998 in 1939. Yet to some degree, quality made up for want of quantity. Between 1933 and 1939, many of the victims of Hitler's persecution reached America from Germany. Many of these were distinguished scientists (Albert Einstein was among them), engineers, and intellectuals, for whom the United States was playing its traditional role of asylum for exiled liberals, and they, in return, brought the country their knowledge and their capacity for work. The population of the towns was growing faster than that of the country. The newcomers were not farming people, and in any case, farming in America was not a hopeful proposition. The cities were stretching out over the surrounding countryside, and many commuters traveled out to their suburbs every evening.

As far as they could, the Southern Negroes were moving up north. In 1940, New York had as many Negroes as Arkansas, and Chicago more than Kentucky. In 1939, in the automobile center of Detroit, there were more than 150,000 Negroes, drawn thither by the high wages offered by Ford and his rivals. In the South, the racial problem had found no sort of solution: the Negroes were in fact unable to exercise their right to vote. Even in the North, there was still much segregation: the whites did not live in the Negro quarters; most white hotels refused to accept Negroes, even when they were famous men; some unions, such as the railwaymen, were closed to Negroes. The President and Mrs. Roosevelt took every opportunity to show publicly that they did not share prejudices of this kind. Mrs. Roosevelt resigned from the Daughters of the American Revolution in order to demonstrate her solidarity with Marian Anderson, the colored singer whom that society had boycotted. The Negro universities were developing and the level of the colored people's education was rising. The New Deal, through its agency, the United States Housing Administration, had made a great effort to replace the slums of the Negro quarters (which were hotbeds of tuberculosis) with wide-windowed, sunny houses. A third of the houses built by the federal authorities to be let at moderate rents were reserved for Negroes. But on this point, the government was more liberal than the country as a whole. When a Negro family came into a white district, its arrival set off a series of unpleasant incidents.

The chief of the United States Housing Administration, Nathan Straus, stated that in 1939, for the first time in a hundred years, the number of slum dwellings had diminished. Nevertheless, the housing shortage was still a most urgent problem: it was reckoned that there were 4,000,000 dwellings too few. Nearly 2,000,000 New Yorkers were crowded into 59,000 squalid, antiquated buildings. During the depression, the output of the building trade had fallen to a tenth of its ordinary volume, because of the lack of orders. There was little private building to back up the government's efforts. Yet the Metropolitan Life Insurance Company was an exception, for this firm erected a vast complex of buildings in New York called Parkchester, containing in all 12,000 apartments intended for 42,000 people. The company planned to produce several replicas of this standard type of complete town, with its restaurants, libraries, shops, movies, and beauty parlors. Perhaps the right industrial solution would have been the prefabricated house; but this would have been contrary to custom, and it would have displeased the architects, those concerned with the trades, and the unions. However, the WPA provided for landscape architects and town planners, and there was an obvious advance in the management of green spaces and the laying out of avenues and towns.

The New Deal had also attempted country planning. Some farmers had been moved from the poorest ground to better land. Others who were bankrupt were helped to buy and restore derelict farms. After the depression, the agricultural workers had found themselves in a most alarming position. The mechanization of agriculture had put a quarter of them out of a job. Between 1930 and 1939, 1,500,000 young men left the land for the cities. Not only did they find work there more easily, but there were also the lighted streets, the movie theaters, and the clubs that would save a young fellow from loneliness. Before and during the depression, a great number of farmers who owned their land had been obliged to sell it and to become tenants. The sharecropping system that was prevalent in the South barely left them with enough to eat. In those parts, millions of men, women, and children (the "poor whites" described by Erskine Caldwell) still lived in lamentable poverty. Farming was the poor relation in the American family.

Since the depression, incomes had remained low throughout the country. In 1929, at the highest peak of prosperity, they had totaled 87.4 billion dollars; in 1933, this sum had fallen to 39.6 billion. By 1939, it had mounted to 72.5 billion, but this was in devalued dollars, and its value was still therefore well below that of 1929. Toward 1935, says Dixon Wecter, the population was made up of about 39,000,000 "consumer units" (families or single persons) with an *average* income of $1,500. Two fifths of these had less than $1,000, and one third less than $780. This last group could only manage to feed itself with the help of subsidies and relief. But, since the New Deal, this undernourished, ill-clad, ill-housed third could count upon the support of the state for its essential needs. At that time, the Americans were spending 34 percent of their income on food, 20 percent on housing, 10 per cent on clothes, 7 percent on transport, and 1 percent on reading. It is but right to add that although incomes were low, prices were low, too, in those days. Here are some examples, taken from the advertisements in the *New York Times* of July 11, 1939: men's shoes, $6.95; breakfast at Schrafft's, 35¢; lunch at Rockefeller Plaza, 90¢; dinner, $1; a woman's coat, $9.75; a gabardine suit, $35. In September, 1939, the new cars were put on the market: a Hudson cost $670; a Willys, $495. Purchasing power was therefore not so low as the level of wages might lead one to suppose.

The car remained the chief need after the basic essentials— the first object of luxury. Since the depression, people had tended to do without unnecessary things, but not refrigerators, or, above all, cars. Destitute families "who lived on spaghetti or even pickled dandelions" still clung to their old automobile. A relief officer in Connecticut threatened to cut off supplies from one man who insisted on keeping his battered Cadillac. In spite of the depression, the building of the parkways had never been interrupted. Jules Romains described them enthusiastically in 1940: "We have been driving now for miles and miles, and your parkway is still going on! It is still as trim as it was at the beginning, still enclosed in its own landscape—an unsullied landscape. . . . Look at these banks, these grassy slopes scattered with flowers that must have been planted, and the line of thickets up there. . . . It gives you the illusion of being in a little valley ringed with woods. Think of the work of preparation that it all implies. . . . Look at those lamps: they have been given a little countrified air—there is ivy creeping round them. And when posts or fences are wanted, how well they have chosen a material and a design which follows the ancient rule of art and turns utility into delight . . ." He was right: the parkways, like the new towns, lovingly designed and filled with flowers, were the masterpieces of the America of 1939. The other forms of transportation also grew better. On the railways, the ordinary coaches were now air conditioned and shining with chrome, and their comfort was very nearly that of the luxurious Pullmans. The importance of the airplane was continually increasing. Most cities had their landing field or their well-equipped airport. Airplanes with sleeping accommodations linked the Atlantic and the Pacific coasts. In 1939, the Clippers, the Pan American Airways' flying boats, started regular service between Europe and America. In the course of the same year, the airlines on the American continent carried two million passengers. The airplane, as quickly as the motor car not long before, had become a familiar feature of America.

The distant but well-defined aim of the New Deal had been a leveling of the American community. (Yet it was not the richest alone who had to pay taxes. A married taxpayer, without children, with an income of $100,000, paid 52 percent in 1941, as against only 31 percent in 1921; but the taxpayers with no more than $2,000 a year, who paid nothing at all before 1934, now had to give up 2 percent.) The principle of the redistribution of incomes was quite widely accepted. Yet it was, in fact, still no more than a principle. The country was going in that direction; but it was going very slowly. In 1929, the wealthy class (5 percent of the taxpayers) had received 35 percent of the total income; in 1939, this class still had 27 percent; but thirteen years later, in 1952, these privileged people's share was to fall to 16 percent. It appeared to be an irreversible tendency. A furious battle raged around the President, with the moderate New Dealers (like Morgenthau) who wanted to put the brakes on this movement out of prudence, and the thoroughgoing New Dealers, who kept their feet on the accelerators.

The moderate men saw many dangers in this policy:

(a) The discouragement of the businessmen who felt that they were being persecuted, and who said so. In 1933, they had acknowledged the necessity of control, but control is not hostility. They were harassed and brought before commissions of inquiry that were often incompetent, and they no longer dared build up new businesses, undertake fresh construction, or engage labor. They were waiting "bowed under a dark cloud" for the presidential election of 1940. Their anxiety was holding up the recovery.

(b) The unexpected effects of some measures. Companies had been obliged to distribute their reserves, and this had prevented many of them from making the necessary investments. Orders for machines therefore dropped, equipment deteriorated, and unemployment was prolonged. The lawmaker's intentions had been good: the effects of his law, the very opposite of what he had intended.

(c) A dangerous mixture of economics and politics. In some states, relief for the unemployed had turned into subsidies for people who voted the right way. Thousands were put on the WPA lists before an election and struck off immediately afterward. A great many people disliked this policy of "spend-spend, elect-elect." It wounded the moral standing of the New Deal. This was unjust so far as the President was concerned, but others around him went too far; and those who, like Morgenthau, wanted the brakes to be put on firmly seemed to have the facts on their side.

All things considered, a great stride had been made in the direction of an economic democracy. The strength of the unions, backed up by the government, the policy of full employment (even though it was maintained by various expedients), social security, and old-age pensions undoubtedly mitigated the formerly baneful effects of the law of the jungle. Roosevelt's methods were not the result of a monolithic ideology. His opponents said that what he had done was socialism: in fact, he had not nationalized anything whatsoever; on the contrary, he said that he had fought against "that private socialism, the most dangerous of all, which is constituted by monopolies." The truth of the matter is that he liked neither systems nor theories. The American approach is essentially pragmatic, and so the state had assumed responsibility for a task that others were no longer performing, being quite prepared to step down again as soon as private initiative should take its place once more. Roosevelt had created new things but without damaging the fundamental institutions of the country, and he had tried "to reconcile tradition with contemporary realities." It was indeed a "new deal," but a new deal with the same cards. The President, accused of eating "toasted millionaire" for breakfast every morning, replied that he far preferred scrambled eggs. In short, the dragon Business had first been broken, then tamed; the President had put a ring in its nose, but he wanted to keep it alive.

III

Had the fundamental rules of political government in the United States changed during Roosevelt's first two terms? His opponents said that they had. In fact, American politics had always been based upon a few simple principles: the people's participation in the government (by the vote) ; the limiting of the government's powers (by the Constitution) ; the balance and the separation of the three powers; and lastly federalism (the sharing of authority between the government and the states) . These principles had scarcely been modified by the New Deal.

As we have seen, the participation of the people in the government had been increased at the beginning of the twentieth century by the direct election of the senators and by the reform of instituting primary elections. Roosevelt made no new advance in this direction. On the contrary, Congress (that is to say, the representatives of the people) had, to increase the government's efficacy, abdicated from part of its authority in favor of the countless unelected governmental agencies. In the same way, on the local scale, the number of elected officials had been reduced, the nonpolitical choice being almost invariably better. And lastly, in some cities the administration had been taken away from the mayor and entrusted to a city manager, a qualified and more efficient man chosen by the city council.

There were no new restrictions of the government's powers whatever. Those that the Bill of Rights had laid down remained. The general tendency was toward an increase of governmental authority, not through amendments to the Constitution, but by a wider interpretation of that document. Some said that the President had assumed an almost dictatorial power at the expense of Congress and that the executive had reduced the legislative branch to the humble role of a rubber stamp for approving governmental decisions. These accusations were not borne out by the facts. Particularly at the beginning, Roosevelt had undoubtedly had an immense influence over Congress, as Wilson and Lincoln had had before him and as every strong and popular president has had in the past and always will have in the future. By its nature, Congress is cautious: it rarely moves into action except when it is thrust forward by a man of determined character. Nevertheless, nothing would be more inaccurate than a picture of Congress in bondage to Roosevelt. As we shall see, the President found both houses obstinate and tough on the question of neutrality. The Congress elected in 1938 was rather against the New Deal than for it, and it successfully insisted upon financial concessions. Nobody dared attack social security nor the control of Wall Street—in a word, all the obviously useful reforms—but Congress demanded a more efficient and economical administration. The Republican opposition pointed out that after six years of the New Deal the problem of unemployment was still unresolved and that the country's recovery was flagging dangerously. The President himself tried to purge such conservative Democrats as Senator Walter George of Georgia and Senator Millard Tydings of Maryland, but he was soundly defeated in these attempts by the party in those states. The legislative authority preserved its freedom of speech—and its freedom of action.

As for Roosevelt's struggle with the Supreme Court, which stood like a barrier against his reforms, it came to an end not because the President forced a new batch of judges upon them (he had wanted to do so, but Congress would not let him), but because certain of the existing judges, after reflection, suddenly became aware of contemporary necessities. Much of the argument between the Supreme Court and the New Deal reformers had hinged upon the interpretation of two phrases in the holy Constitution. The one was *interstate commerce;* the other, *due process of law.* For half a century, the court had maintained that the Constitutional text, no man may "be deprived of life, liberty, or property without due process of law" meant that neither the federal government nor the states could interfere with the free operation of the economic system. According to the Supreme Court, limiting profits and imposing controls and tariffs would be depriving the citizens of their right of ownership. In 1937, as we have said, a spectacular change of front had reversed this jurisprudence. Finally the court came around to the celebrated opinion of Mr. Justice Holmes, that a law passed by Congress could not be rendered invalid by the judicial power "unless it be said that a rational and fair man necessarily would admit that the statute proposed would infringe fundamental principles as they have been understood by the traditions of our people and our laws." The Supreme Court therefore admitted, as it ought, that it considered itself the guardian of the Constitution, but not of any particular economic theory, still less of the resentments of a single class. That was the end, and the happy end, of the quarrel.

As for the federal structure of America, nobody at any time called it in question. The powers of the federal government were more extensive in 1939 than they had been in 1929, but so also were those of the states. The states had taken in hand the distribution of relief and the control of social security; and they were still the only authorities in the matter of education. The federal government gave them grants-in-aid for these objects, on the condition that they contributed their share, which was considerable. This was not the federal government taking over the authority of the states, but the extension, under the pressure of necessity, of the powers of both. Let us quote a judge of the Supreme Court again, this time Mr. Justice Stone: "The United States and the State of Alabama are not alien governments. They coexist within the same territory. Unemployment within it is their common

185

concern." It sometimes happens, in spite of the obstinacy and foolishness of the greater part of mankind, that common sense wins the day. This is a little more true of the United States than it is elsewhere.

IV

The year 1939 preceded the presidential election, and both parties sharpened their weapons. The Democrats wanted to make the most of the results of their activity; the Republicans denied that any results existed. The former Republican president, Herbert Hoover, said to the writer of this book, who was seeing him at that period, "The business world, instead of being persecuted, needs to be given confidence. Then it will again have the courage to set up new enterprises, and industry will automatically absorb the unemployed. The state's resources will increase because taxes will produce more. You cannot tax wealth that does not exist.... Perhaps gold should also be put back into circulation. In the sixteenth century, the influx of precious metals began a period of prosperity. The behavior of human beings is really very strange at present. At great expense, we dig the gold out of the ground; then, at great expense, we bury it in vaults in Kentucky. It seems possible to imagine a more reasonable economy."

Yet Hoover, like all other Americans, remained faithful to the traditional democracy. "In spite of all its weaknesses, it is the only regime that allows a country to correct its course without violence. In democracy, if an unwise thrust on the rudder has taken a government too far to the left, the mistake is rectified by a thrust toward the right. Or the other way about. The swing of the pendulum is the only form of government that can save us from tyranny. The essential problem is to safeguard our free institutions. They will take care of all the rest. Political power is naturally tyrannical. If in addition it has jobs and pay at its disposal, it becomes too strong."

For their part, Roosevelt and his friends maintained that for the first time since the Civil War a just balance had been reestablished between the government and business. For a long while (said they), the businessmen had been above the law, and throughout the world a dangerous inequality had aroused a justifiable anger. In Europe, the hidden, inarticulate discontent of the masses had begotten totalitarian governments--to correct inequality, they had given up freedom. In America, institutions and traditions had stood up to the test of the most violent economic storm. Once the blast was over, Roosevelt declared that he only had one wish—to help private initiative and not to replace it. He thought that the New Deal had saved liberty: "Democracy has disappeared in several other great nations, not because the people of those nations disliked democracy, but because they had grown tired of unemployment and insecurity, of seeing their children hungry while they sat helpless in the face of government confusion and government weakness. Finally, in desperation, they chose to sacrifice liberty in the hope of getting something to eat. We, in America, know that our democratic institutions can be preserved and made to work."

And indeed the continuity of the American system of government is a remarkable phenomenon. In 1939, it was the oldest in the world. A Constitution, drawn up at the end of the eighteenth century, still retained the country's confidence and respect. In France, since the same period, many different regimes had followed one another. In Germany, a republic had taken the place of William II's empire, and then a dictatorship, that of the republic. In Russia, the Communist Revolution had put an end to the reign of the czars. In China, the emperors had lost their throne. Even in England, the House of Lords was declining, and the monarchy of George VI was no longer that of George III. America, for her part, had adapted her institutions but had never made profound changes in them. She was trying to build up a viable economy, and she was not paying too much attention to such labels as capitalism or socialism. In Iowa, Harry Hopkins, that bugbear of the business world, made a conciliatory speech. He said that the confidence of all was indispensable to a real recovery. He defended the great outlays that the New Deal had made. There were moments when lavishness on the part of the state was the only possible means of supporting industry; but that did not mean that the budget must *always* be unbalanced. The recovery should bring about an increase in receipts and thus a state of balance.

One of the chief complaints of the opposition was indeed the government's excessive spending. "You can no more spend your-self rich than drink yourself sober," said the *New York Times*. In June, 1939, Roosevelt brought before Congress a scheme of great public works (dams, electrification, roads, hospitals, and so on) that amounted to the enormous sum of $3,680,000,000. No private group of interests was to be found that was ready to undertake these investments that were nevertheless considered necessary by the government. Congress rose up in protest and refused to vote funds. And yet there was an example of success—the TVA (Tennessee Valley Authority) that had been set up in 1933 to bring life back to an entire poverty-stricken region by building huge dams in it that would produce cheap electric power. The TVA had not confined itself to this: it had also undertaken irrigation, reforestation, and the building of ferti-lizer factories—in short, it had tried to raise the standard of living, to improve the very nature of the life, of three and a half million exceedingly poor people. With the active participation of the region's inhabitants, it had achieved most of its aims.

It was an undeniable success, but the TVA had aroused the fury of the private companies by selling its electricity at a cheaper rate than theirs. Eighteen of these companies had accused the TVA of illegal competition before the Supreme Court. The court decided against them. The TVA then bought one of the most important of the private enterprises. At the handing over of the check in part payment for the purchase, David Lilienthal, the Chairman of the TVA, met Wendell Willkie, the president of the purchased company. "Thanks, Dave," said Willkie, "this is sure a lot of money for a couple of Indiana farmers to be kicking around." This story was the origin of the popularity of Willkie, an active and likable busi-nessman. He was a specialist in public services run by private enterprise, and he had reservations about the subject of Roose-veltism: "We cannot stay in business against subsidized govern-ment competition." At that time, Willkie was a member of the Democratic party; his struggle against the TVA earned him the support of the Republicans; and this (oh paradox!) was to bring the Democrat Willkie to the doors of the White House as the Republican candidate. The ways of American democracy are in-deed unfathomable.

Another of Congress' (and of the taxpayers') complaints was

the fantastic cost of the WPA. Harry Hopkins delighted in spending, and sometimes he spent money on extravagant schemes. The WPA published tourists' guides and gave excellent performances of the Gilbert and Sullivan operetta *The Mikado.* "But really, you know," said an anti-Rooseveltian to me, "if a French government were to spend thousands of millions of francs just to produce, after six years, a guide to the Corrèze and a fairly good performance of *La Belle Hélène,* you, as a taxpayer, would utter piercing shrieks; and you would be right. Whenever you see the workmen doing nothing on a site but leaning on their shovels and gossiping, it is a WPA site. As for the famous guidebooks, an unemployed intellectual who works for the WPA costs the state much more than when he was simply on relief."

In June, 1939, Congress decided that all the theatrical projects were to be given up, that after eighteen months of WPA the beneficiaries were to be put out of employment for two months, and that any political exploitation of the handing out of jobs should be punished as a crime. In 1939, the WPA still employed 2,578,000 persons (of whom 27 percent were women and 11 percent research workers, literary men, "white-collar workers"); the President promised to try to reduce this number to one million by 1940. Thereupon many of the beneficiaries went on strike. F.D.R. then uttered (another paradox) a phrase very like Coolidge's: "You cannot strike against the government." Power is power. A leader worthy of the name reacts as a leader and not as a member of a party. The WPA was F.D.R.'s child, but it is a father's duty to be severe. In fact, by the end of 1939, a million names had been struck off the lists. The men found their way back into industry. For a long while, on the radio and in the night clubs, jokes about the WPA had been particularly scathing and heartily applauded. In March, the American Federation of Actors forbade its ten thousand members to make attacks of this kind, under penalty of fine and suspension. The union told them that they would be much better employed in setting up a statue with the inscription "To Harry Hopkins, from the grateful theater."

At the beginning of the New Deal, the government had tolerated and even encouraged understanding between manufacturers (that was the aim of the NRA); but, when the law was nullified by the Supreme Court, the government returned to that struggle against the monopolies that had been one of the great preoccupations of Theodore Roosevelt and Wilson. Many administrations and new agencies attempted to bring industry under regulation. So many capital letters had been used up in naming these agencies that the alphabet was not long enough to cope with them all. The number of federal civil servants in June, 1939, was 920,310, as against 528,542 in 1926. And yet it may be said that the relations between government and business were getting better in 1939. Strict control prevented abuses. But the government spokesmen never lost an opportunity of emphasizing the traditional principles of free enterprise, initiative, and private investment. Words and deeds sorted themselves out as best they could.

The President had supported the Wagner Act and the NLRB (National Labor Relations Board), a kind of Supreme Court for labor. Public opinion had considered it just that the workers should have the right of choosing their own unions and that the employers should be obliged to negotiate with the union that won the majority in a ballot controlled by the Board. In the same way, it had approved of the laws that set a minimum wage and a maximum number of working hours and that forbade the use of unfair practices (spies, strikebreakers, and so on) by the employers. The function of the NLRB was not to provide solutions for industrial conflicts but to act as a referee, blowing the whistle for foul play and seeing that the rules of the game were obeyed. Nevertheless, in 1939, its impartiality was disputed, as much by the employers, who said that it was too favorable to the workers, as by the American Federation of Labor, which claimed that it was entirely devoted to the cause of the Committee for Industrial Organization.

The two great trade union movements had not come to terms, nor anything like it. Green, of the AF of L, accused Lewis, of the CIO, of wrecking unionism in order to satisfy his ambition, the real motive of all his actions.

Lewis, an aggressive romantic, shook his leonine mane and asked, in his theatrical manner, "What makes me tick? Is it power I am after, or am I a Saint Francis in disguise, or what?" He counterattacked with the assertion that twenty-five years of Green's administration had led the AF of L from defeat to defeat. More and more Shakespearian, he declaimed, "Alas! poor

Green, I knew him well. He wishes me to join him in fluttering procrastination."

This trial of strength between the two labor organizations, and above all between their leaders, had nothing much to do with the defense of the rights of the workers; and by emulation it led to excesses that the mass of the people disapproved of.

A new kind of strike had come into fashion in France at the time of the *Front Populaire:* this was the sit-down strike, in which the workers occupied the factories. A conflict of this kind broke out between a metal working company, Fansteel, and the CIO. The factory was occupied. The company dismissed the workers who had taken part in the occupation. The NLRB ordered their reinstatement. Fansteel appealed to the Supreme Court that decided the conduct of the workers had been illegal and that consequently they might be dismissed. The right to strike remained inviolable, but it did not cover lawlessness. In letters addressed to "My dear John" and "Dear Bill," President Roosevelt earnestly called upon President John L. Lewis and President William Green to summon a mixed commission and to make peace. In replies addressed to "Dear Mr. President," the two great chiefs promised to try. In April, a new sit-down strike occurred in Philadelphia. A great hosiery works there underwent a seven weeks' occupation. The company sued the Federal Association of Hosiery Workers, which belonged to the CIO, and by virtue of the Sherman Act, it obtained $711,000 in damages, which ruined the union. In his poetical manner, John L. Lewis accused a body of Republicans, strengthened by renegade Democrats, of dancing "a war dance around the chained, prostrate form of Labor." In fact, the new and severe attitude of the federal courts reflected the public's disapproval of certain excesses. On the other hand, all the employers' attempts at evading the law on the minimum wage and the limitation of working hours failed when they came up against the opposition of Congress. The trade union movement was broadening. Between them, the two great organizations had 8,000,006 members. Little by little the balance between management and labor was shifting in labor's favor.

As for the farmers, the government was trying to insure them some degree of stability in their mediocre incomes by the "ever normal granary" (stockpiling of surpluses by the state, restriction of sowing), and also by direct grants to the farmers, whose purchasing power, in spite of these measures, was inferior to that of the period from 1909 to 1914. Agriculture's total income in 1939 was twice that of 1932. On the national market, the farmers had become buyers once more. Seven out of ten of them had a car; six out of ten a radio; one in three some tractors; three out of eight a telephone in the house. In relation to 1930, the improvement in radios and tractors was 100 percent. The average farmhouse had six rooms, and it was worth $1,500. The South remained very poor. In 1939, a drought was feared, a drought of the same dreadful proportions as those of 1934 and 1936. But government insurance against the years of the lean kine had been provided for by the 1938 law concerning agricultural disasters. But in any case the rain came in the end, and the 1939 harvest was good. The problem of overproduction in farming was not solved and could not be solved, for the "ever normal granary" was only kept going by abnormal means. A catastrophe, the Second World War, was to bring about a painful and temporary solution.

V

What was the country's state of mind? What were the Americans of 1939 thinking? During the depression, unemployment, ruin, and stunned amazement had for some years extinguished their traditional optimism. The question was no longer prosperity but ordinary security. "Not a chicken in every pot, but anything at all in the pot." This state of despair did not last long, and what took its place was a gravity mixed with courage. There were only a few unrepentant members of the wealthy class who had learned nothing. The *New Yorker*, that brilliant satirical weekly, aimed many cracks at them. Here are a few: "My son is a Red," says the lady of the house, ringing for her butler. He says that one day I will press on this bell, and no one will come." The mother of a wealthy infant says to the nurse, "I just want baby to learn the first ideas of walking: he will have cars all his life." "Harry wants to take me on a tour of the world," says a young wife, "but I'd rather go somewhere else." These degenerate descendants of the Dinosaurs were growing quite uncommon. Most people, anxious but full of good-will, were searching for another pattern of life.

They were searching collectively. In *Babbitt,* Sinclair Lewis had made fun of the urge that every American feels to belong to the greatest possible number of organized groups—Rotary Clubs, Elks, Boosters, churches, masonic lodges, veterans' associations. But in a moving, unstratified society this is a natural need. Men who continually change their town, state, and trade need to cling to some organization that will bring them together, welcome them, make them eat and talk with other men, where-ever they are. Why do the Americans call one another by their Christian names right away? Because they do not have a great while to make friends before they move house again. Many of them retained an adolescent state of mind their whole life long. The conventions that brought businessmen or trade unionists together in the great hotels were like schools during playtime. "In many ways, the American male of adult years is an arrested small boy, playing with dollars and power as he once did with toys, and matching the violence of his recreation to the intensity of his loneliness." American women felt the same need. In 1939, there were innumerable women's clubs, Junior Leagues, and forums where, as early as ten in the morning, a thousand women and more would meet to listen piously to some lecture, filled with the idea of having done their duty and of having done their part for the community's cultural life.

The depression and its consequences had made the need for escape even greater. The motion pictures had become one of the country's chief industries. In 1939, its takings reached $700,000,000, or $25 for each family. The whole art of the screen had been renewed by the coming of sound. Walt Disney's cartoons filled the need for comforting myths. The famous and heroic three little pigs, who in 1933 sang "Who's afraid of the big bad wolf?" represented the state of mind of the New Dealers face to face with the depression. Some films, such as *Green Pastures,* the Bible seen through Negro eyes, were genuine master-pieces. American comedies attained a graceful naturalness that was then very unusual in the European industry. The films showed the American people their own life in reverse, a fairy-tale world in which everybody was rich, a world in which the typist's honeymoon was spent in a palatial hotel in Bermuda.

In Europe, this America-as-it-was-not passed for the America of sober fact. Escape by way of the movies was not without its dangers. It held up completely false characters to millions of spectators—the brutal businessman, the benevolent Bohemian, the untamed Tarzan. Every boy saw himself as a knight-errant and a righter of wrongs: the American girl, like Emma Bovary before her, expected an impossible perfection from love. Yet some directors were trying to lead motion pictures toward a greater degree of realism or, in some cases, toward social satire. The Catholic bishops and Will Hays, the high priest of decency, tried to limit the more daring sexual flights of the screen, but they never warned the film makers against committing another excess, that of unreality.

The second great form of escape was the radio. During the depression, the unemployed, with their enforced leisure, all listened to it. Between 1930 and 1932, four million families bought radios, and by 1939, 80 percent of homes had a set that was switched on for an average of four hours every day. This gave the news commentators an extraordinary influence over people's minds; and it was particularly true for Franklin D. Roosevelt, the greatest of them all. In 1934, the Federal Communications Commission was set up: this body accepted three principles: (a) radio should remain a private enterprise; (b) it should live on advertisements; (c) it should obey the public regulations concerning wavelengths. There was a serious danger that the radio might oust the book, an infinitely more educative medium, since the reader can turn back to it to understand it better, to criticize it. Some networks tried to stimulate the taste for reading by such programs as "Invitation to Learning," in which, every Sunday, four writers, professors, or critics discussed a great author. But such bold, and unpaying, strokes were rare.

The newspapers kept their public in spite of the radio, but at the price of making concessions. The reader was attracted by comic strips, scandals, crimes, sexy revelations, and enormous headlines. To keep up circulation, the press (a few powerful newspapers excepted) had to carry on in this way—a way that betrayed far more violent instincts in the average reader than anyone would have supposed. In 1909, there had been 2,600 daily papers in the United States; in 1945, there were only 1,750, published in 1,300 different cities. In eleven towns out of twelve, there was only one paper. Politically, it was regrettable; economically, it was understandable. "The advertisers strengthened the papers that were already strong, while the unions weakened those that were already weak." On the national scale, there were magazines of the type of *Time, Life,* and *Fortune,* Henry Luce's empire. Here success was the result of trying to give the ordinary public intelligent news while at the same time amusing it with a sharp, laconic editorial style as well as by very striking photographs. Influenced by the advertisers, practically all the papers and magazines of considerable circulation were hostile to the New Deal. But the elections proved that the political power of the press was less than might have been expected. Readers bought news, pictures, and scandals, and retained their own opinions.

Robert Hutchins, the president of the University of Chicago, and some other professors tried to awaken a love for the masterpieces of literature by evening classes that were built around the thorough reading of mankind's finest books. Hutchins was of the opinion that a total reform of education was called for. The high schools (roughly the equivalent of the English secondary school or the French lycée) provided an inadequate degree of cultivation, he said—an insufficient culture. As for the universities, they did not give a homogeneous education. There was no unity of program whatsoever, and the degrees had different values in different places. In many colleges and universities, there was no solid, thoroughly mastered groundwork of learning. The pupil himself chose his own courses, and the choice available was as varied as it was ridiculous. Teaching wished to present itself as being of practical, immediate use, whereas the essential nature of a well-based education is that it is not a set of instructions for instant employment, not a matter of mere direct utility. Courses upon contemporary events were more successful than history courses. But acquaintance with today's news is not culture. True wisdom belongs to all ages. "The essential virtues," said Robert Hutchins to me in 1939, "are still those that Socrates taught: the men who put Socrates to death are those whom we are fighting today. We teach physics, chemistry, and biology quite well; but although science sometimes gives us the means of compelling nature to do what we want her to do, it does not tell us what we ought to want. Our young people feel this, and your neo-Thomists [Gilson, Maritain] are influential over here for the very reason that they at least try to provide a solution to the great problems."

A recasting of education came up against serious difficulties. It was still the sole concern of the states, and they, jealous of their prerogatives, would not tolerate federal interference. The private universities, of which there were a great many, drew their funds on the one hand from their wealthy benefactors and on the other from the tuition paid by their students. The more intelligent patrons might, in case of great necessity, be won over; but too many students were in search of easy and amusing courses and an athletic and social life. As soon as reforms were mentioned, the reply was, "It would spoil our enrollment." In defense of the universities, it may be said that by their social life and by the way their students looked after their own discipline, they shaped character and formed citizens. Furthermore, even in the less brilliant colleges, there were to be found students with an outstanding freshness of mind who found a way of distilling honey, even from these poor flowers. There were some Americans of the thirties who were men of the highest cultivation—picking at random among the names one may mention Edmund Wilson, Archibald MacLeish, Walter Lippmann, Thornton Wilder.

On the level of artistic creation, the American literature and the American theater of the thirties were both rich and actively alive. Many of the expatriate writers of the twenties were still abroad. Gertrude Stein, one of the chief figures in the new writing, and one who has had a great influence upon the American press by using the spoken language as it was in fact spoken, remained in France, but Hemingway and Faulkner lived in America. Hemingway, nourished on European literature, had formed for himself the personal, sparse, hard style of a great classical writer. He had seen war and death close to, and he was capable of showing them as they appeared to his characters, without any intrusion of the author. He had derived a sensual, brutal nihilism from his experience. He had an utter contempt for the society of his day. He did not believe in the democratic virtues, but in courage, in blood shed needlessly, for the honor of it, in the bullring, in guerrilla fighting, or in love. So he loved boxers, killers, bullfighters. Faulkner has often been likened to

Proust ". . . only Faulkner is lost, and it is because he knows that he is lost that he will take the risk of following his thought out to the end." Proust described a French society that was still on its feet: Faulkner is the poet of a South that is condemned, the poet of the decaying Mississippi. "Hence this harsh and fleshly density, this smell of blood and sweat." Generally speaking, the American novel is tragic. It shows the abyss that separates the American dream from hard reality, and the individual's despair when he realizes the existence of this gulf.

Neither Hemingway nor Faulkner was interested in the reforming passion of the New Deal. John Dos Passos and John Steinbeck, on the other hand, were spiritual descendants of Dreiser. In *Manhattan Transfer,* Dos Passos painted contemporary futility in a series of pictures that melted into one another as they do in the movies. But the Sacco-Vanzetti trial had an immense effect upon him, and in *U.S.A.* he tackled the social problem and wrote the story of what, for him, was a hopeless failure. This period (1920-1940) was the American novel's most creative time, and presently it was to have a great influence upon European writing. As for Steinbeck, his book *The Grapes of Wrath* was the best seller of 1939. It is the epic of a family deprived of its farm by the depression that goes off toward the promised land of California and, after pitiable wanderings, finds only misery there. Disappointment and rage take the place of the pioneer's simpleminded confidence. The state of affairs that it describes no longer exists today, but it is a fine book, like Zola's best. In its time, it had repercussions that matched those of *Uncle Tom's Cabin.* It belongs to the general American tradition of the novel of social protest.

In the theater, Broadway had two currents running down it: plays unpleasant, as Bernard Shaw would have said, and powerful (Lillian Hellman's *The Little Foxes*) ; and plays pleasant, romantic, or amusing like *The Man Who Came to Dinner* or *Life with Father. Swing Mikado,* a parody of the Gilbert and Sullivan opera, had a long run in Chicago and then in New York. Eugene O'Neill, the Nobel Prize winner, was still the great man of the American theater. Robert Sherwood, Clare Luce (*The Women*), Behrman, Wilder (*Our Town*), were successful in London as well as on Broadway. American plays were particularly remarkable for the excellence of their dialogue and for their production. Left-wing propaganda was looked after by Clifford Odets and by the Federal Theater Project, an organization that was dependent on the New Deal. This popular state theater enabled Orson Welles to make Shakespeare's *Julius Caesar* into an anti-Fascist play. It tried to employ out-of-work actors by sending touring companies through regions that had no sort of entertainment at all, but "a vigilant Congress . . . suspicious of Congreve and communism, and not always distinguishing one from the other, ended this adventure."

In music and in painting, America had first called upon all the best that Europe had to offer. The Wagnerian productions of the Metropolitan Opera were as good as those of Bayreuth. Bruno Walter and Toscanini conducted magnificent concerts. The radio broadcast these splendid performances to millions of listeners. In the schools, the love of music was inculcated by recorded concerts followed by commentaries for the children. From the combination of traditional forms with the rhythms introduced by the jazz musicans, Negroes from New Orleans, Chicago, and St. Louis, a truly American music was being born. The tom-tom and the trumpet were a fairly good expression of American life—the monotonous rhythmic beat upon which a Louis Armstrong embroidered the cry of a race and a generation.

VI

On February 24, 1939, at Columbia University, in lecture room 401 of Pupin Hall (the physics building), there was a meeting devoted to the fission of the uranium atom. The speakers were Niels Bohr, a Dane, and Enrico Fermi, an Italian. As the *New York Times* reported the next day, "Three hundred distinguished physicists [were] fascinated by their [Bohr and Fermi] reports on what is being hailed as 'the most sensational discovery in modern physics since the discovery of radioactivity more than forty years ago.'" Since Einstein's work, it had been known that a vast quantity of energy was enclosed in a minute quantity of matter, but it was supposed that this "cosmic treasure" would never be within the reach of man. Only the sun and the other stars could dip into this source of energy. Some months earlier, William L. Lawrence had asked Einstein whether man would ever find the key to the treasure. "No," Einstein had replied, "we are bad shots, shooting at birds in the darkness, in a country where there are very few birds anyway."

By this Einstein meant that to induce a few atoms to give up even a very small part of their energy it was necessary to discharge such a number of atomic bullets at them that the cost in energy exceeded that resulting from the operation. The theoretical possibility that Bohr and Fermi revealed that day at Columbia University was that of chain reaction. The fission of uranium could only be produced by the neutrons, and up to that time, the neutrons had been so firmly linked in the atom's nucleus that there was no hope of obtaining enough of them. But if, as is the case in a chain reaction, each atom of uranium 235 upon breaking were to liberate two neutrons that, in their turn, were to break two atoms, setting free four neutrons, and so on up to astronomic figures, then man would have at his disposal a source of energy of the same kind as the sun's. Even at an ordinary time, this would have been a discovery filled with the richest promise, but in 1939, a year in which war might break out any day, it meant that if the scientists found the secret of chain reaction, Hitler might have in his hands the greatest destructive force that man had ever produced. Unless indeed...

But what hope was there that Congress, at a time when it was so passionately defending the neutrality laws, would authorize the enormous expenditure that such research would call for? From time to time, the Administration was violently criticized for the cost of defense. The United States spent $1,367,978,808 upon the country's safety. This did not prevent the two services from begging for further supplies, making noises like so many penniless orphans. The newspapers ridiculed the ceaseless demands of the rival branches that seemed to make poor work of coordinating their efforts. "We pay without haggling. Our safety, they tell us, is not entirely provided for. But what threatens us? An invasion? It is impossible. Bombers? They cannot cross the oceans. Aircraft carriers? It could only be a scattered attack without serious consequences. Then why so much expenditure?"

To defend the European democracies? In 1939, they certainly seemed in danger. Hitler was bellowing his threats; Mussolini was waiting for the right moment. War seemed likely. "The United States holds the key to peace or war," said Georges Bonnet, the French foreign minister. "If they clearly state that they are on our side, the specter of war will be exorcised." There was no doubt where Roosevelt's sympathies lay: the Nazis' persecution and aggression filled him with extreme horror, and he could imagine what would become of American freedom in a world ruled by the totalitarians. As early as 1937, he had declared that all peace-loving nations should act together against aggressors, or at least put them in quarantine. Yet he was obliged to take public opinion into account, and in America, it was then curiously isolationist. It condemned Hitler; it hated the dictators; it urged France and England to stand firm against them. But the First World War had left the Americans with a profound disgust for European affairs. They had given their blood and their money, only to end up being called Uncle Shylock. "Never again," thought many of them. What is more, they had been induced to believe that their entry into the war in 1917 had been caused partly by the machinations of the bankers and partly by the propaganda of the Allies, and that it had led directly to the great depression. And the moral of that was, "Let us keep out of it. Let us refuse to sell to any of the belligerents, so as not to be involved in a war at sea, and let Europe stew in her own juice."

This feeling took on many forms. Among many people, it caused pangs of conscience, but a small number of fascist groups such as the Nazi Bund and the Knights of the White Camellia openly praised Hitler and Mussolini. In February, 1939, the admirers of Hitler (the German-American Bund) hired Madison Square Garden, the biggest hall in New York, and filled its nineteen thousand seats. Uniformed stewards patrolled it. The speeches were a mixture of anti-Semitism in the Goebbels manner and scandalous attacks upon Roosevelt. The writer Dorothy Thompson was brutally thrown out for laughing at one of the orators.

Some businessmen, obsessed by the New Deal, were afraid of seeing America engaged in a war a few months before a presidential election; they dreaded that in the atmosphere of danger Roosevelt would be reelected. Meanwhile the liberal writers declared that since France and England had abandoned the Spanish and Czechoslovakian republics, they no longer believed in the union of the three democracies. "I find myself filled with a fellow feeling for Pontius Pilate," said one of them to me. "I don't understand anything about your European vendettas. And above all I don't want to get mixed up with them." After a silence, he added, "No one can tell how this country would react if one day Paris or London were really attacked . . . . Probably many Americans would go as volunteers." Another silence, then, "Myself first of all."

In Congress, there was a furious debate upon the law of neutrality, passed in 1937, that required the President, as soon as a state of war was established, to lay an embargo upon all deliveries of arms to the belligerents. Professors of law appeared before the Senate to give lectures upon neutrality. The dean of a girls' college spoke vehemently in favor of neutrality and one minute later expressed her bitter, and totally illogical, regret that the United States had not stopped Japan in Manchuria. Although the neutralist Senator Borah admitted that "there was no sort of doubt as to who was the aggressor; our country has made its choice and its mind is made up." the Senate Committee on Foreign Relations, by the very slight majority of twelve to eleven, decided to adjourn the examination of any amendment. In fact, it was of very little importance which way the Senate voted. The force of circumstances was such that sooner or later it would sweep away all resistance, prejudice, and passion. The visit of the English king and queen provided an opportunity for the mass of the people to show where their sympathies lay.

August, 1939. In the American newspapers, there were to be seen photographs of Paris—the town covering itself with sandbags, air-raid shelters being dug—and of a London surrounded by balloons. The setting of the war was already in place. And yet the American press would not believe that it was near at hand. "For Germany, it would be suicide. Hitler would have to use 1,200,000 soldiers against Poland and 800,000 against Romania. How could he have enough left to stand up against the French army, which the Fourteenth of July review has just shown to be stronger than ever? No doubt he has control of the air, but England has that of the seas, and in any case airplanes do not occupy a terrain. For him to have the slightest chance he would have to have Italy with him, and it would be necessary for the USSR to be at least neutral. Now an Anglo-French mission was in Moscow to negotiate with Stalin . . . ." But it was with Ribbentrop that Stalin signed the nonaggression pact on August 23, 1939. From that moment, war was certain. On September 1, Hitler entered Poland: two days later, England and then France declared war on him. At the Episcopal church, Roosevelt heard a sermon against Hitler upon the text of Habakkuk, "Because thou hast spoilt many nations, all the remnant of the people shall spoil thee." The prophet prophesied truly; but the time for preaching was over.

PART SEVEN

The Second World War

TO every clear-minded observer it was obvious, in August, 1939, that Hitler had made up his mind to go to war and conquer Europe. The vast majority of Americans detested Nazism, with its violence, its intolerance, and its contempt for human dignity. But this same majority was not fully aware of America's potential strength or of her responsibilities. Everything had happened so quickly. Who could have believed, in 1776, when a few English colonies were struggling for their independence, that a hundred and fifty years later they would be the most powerful nation on earth? Yet such was the case. Various causes had produced this great effect: the wealth of a virgin continent; a strong and liberal Constitution; a relative unity between the classes; the huge flood of immigrants. In fact, America's total support, in 1939, could decide the victory. The average American knew that the European democracies were holding the outposts of a way of life and of political institutions that were like his own; he knew that if these outposts were carried by the dictatorships, the United States would find itself isolated in a hostile world. But he still hoped that even if it were isolated his country could live like a hermit on its own continent, averting its face from the corruptions and the madness of the outside world.

I

The American isolationists said that the Russo-German Nonaggression Pact was Neville Chamberlain's fault, and they advised him to throw away his useless sword and take up the Munich umbrella again. For his part, Roosevelt made his last attempt to prevent this monstrous war. In a message to the King of Italy, he invited His Majesty to join him in serving the ideals of Christianity. On August 24 and 25, he communicated with the Führer himself. Poland said that she was ready to accept arbitration. "The whole world prays," said the President, "that Germany too will accept it." But Hitler had very little understanding of prayers. The *Herald Tribune* (August 26, 1939) wrote, "Once more the Americans find themselves face to face with the lesson that they refused to learn during the world war . . . that is to say, that a nation which is armed to the teeth and which thinks of nothing but war, cannot be stopped except by resort, or the threat of resort, to a strength greater than its own. Simple pleas, simple appeals to reason or feeling count for nothing. Mr. Hitler only takes notice of brute force."

And indeed on September 1, Mr. Hitler entered Poland. Two days later England and then France declared war upon him. Roosevelt understood that from that moment onward the freedom of the world was at stake; but he was bound by the earlier decisions of Congress, and on September 5, he was obliged to bring the neutrality law into operation that canceled all the orders made by France and England for munitions. They still had the right to buy raw materials and food but not on credit. Roosevelt was in a tragic position. He was aware of the danger, but he was nearly powerless. This was a presidential election year, so he could not openly tell a pacifist America that she was committing a fatal error. The great body of the country thought, "We got mixed up in the First World War. Shocking ingratitude was our reward. The democratic ideal that we fought for was trampled under foot at Versailles. You Europeans can start once more. That's your business. As for us, never again!" Roosevelt nevertheless had the courage to call to mind the principles of international morality: "This nation," he declared, "will remain a neutral nation, but I cannot ask that every American remain neutral in thought as well. Even a neutral has the right to pay heed to the facts. Even a neutral cannot be asked to close his mind or his conscience."

He prevailed so far as to have the neutrality law at least amended. Where did the risk of war lie? In the fact that if American ships carried arms and munitions and if the Germans sank them, hostilities would automatically break out, as they had in the first war. This would not be the case if the Allies had the obligation of carrying the supplies themselves and of paying with ready money—the system known as "cash and carry." Then there would be no risk to American lives and goods. "There lies the road to peace," said the President to Congress; and Congress passed the amended law, partly out of horror for Nazism and partly because it was obviously in the interest of American industry and American workers to go on selling their products.

The war in Europe, after Hitler's occupation of Poland and Stalin's occupation of Finland, entered into a period of lull. Both sides contented themselves with mere skirmishing. The Maginot Line and Belgium, both untouched, lay between the belligerents. The army theatricals seemed to play a more important part than the guns and the tanks. The Americans called this curious situation (la drôle de guerre of the French) the phoney war. Was it all going to end in a negotiated peace from which Hitler would emerge stronger than ever? Roosevelt was afraid of this, but how could he advise France and England to be more active, at a time when he could not help them? "It was the one crisis in Roosevelt's career," says Robert Sherwood, "when he was completely at a loss as to what action to take . . . a period of terrible, stultifying vacuum." America stood there, motionless and as if unaware, under the threat of an avalanche that was ready to overwhelm her.

In April, 1940, a new crash of thunder shook the world. The German armies invaded Denmark and Norway, then the Netherlands, Belgium, and France. This was Hitler's *Blitzkrieg* that hurtled forward at lightning speed, the Stukas dive-bombing the Allied troops while the armor, the Panzer divisions, having torn a hole in the scarcely defended Sedan front, sowed disorder far behind the lines. The shattering speed of the Nazi victory and the fall of France—that France whose armies the Americans had so admired in 1914—filled the country with an amazed anxiety. In June, Mussolini declared war on France: Roosevelt condemned him with the stinging words, "The hand that held the dagger has struck it into the back of its neighbor." He added that there was only one line of conduct left for America— to provide those who were fighting for liberty with the material means of continuing their struggle and to arm herself for her own defense in case the dictators, drunk with power, should presume to attack the American continent.

Some time before, Churchill had succeeded Chamberlain in England. In France, Marshal Henri Philippe Pétain took power and signed an armistice with Germany. A reduced unoccupied France continued to exist precariously in the center and the southeast; its government settled at Vichy. In England, General Charles de Gaulle created a Free France. Churchill showed himself determined to continue the fight and fortified the English coasts; but he did not conceal the fact that without American aid he would go down. Roosevelt was faced with the most anguishing dilemma. Should it be accepted that Europe was lost and that consequently all the country's strength should be concentrated for the defense of the American continent? Or should the United States help Churchill while there was yet time? Many of the President's military and naval advisers were in favor of abandoning England: all Roosevelt's instincts were for the opposite policy—that of support. In order to carry it out, he sought the Republicans' backing and appointed two of them, Henry L. Stimson and Frank Knox, secretary of war and secretary of the navy, respectively. Both were in favor of England. With their support, Roosevelt could allow himself "to scrape the bottom of the barrel." Between June and October, 1940, he sent the English 970,000 rifles, 200,500 revolvers, 87,500 machine guns, and 895 seventy-five millimeter guns, and he promised 14,375 airplanes by April, 1942. Neutrality was no more than a word. Who could remain neutral as between God and the Devil? Roosevelt was an upright man, and in his eyes Hitler was the Devil.

In July, 1940, Churchill asked America for the gift of fifty old destroyers to defend England from submarines and against the invasion that could be foreseen. The present writer arrived in America from England at that moment, and Adolf Berle, the assistant secretary of state, questioned him at length upon England's capacity for resistance. Could it be taken that these fifty ships would not be thrown away in a hopeless venture? I said that I had had the best impression of the determination of the British, and that support for them would not be in vain. This was indeed the President's opinion, but the law forbade him to transfer to another power any equipment that had not been certified as "not being useful for national defense" by the chiefs of staff. In fact, when a statesman really wants to, he can almost always get around a law. The United States was at that time negotiating with England for military bases in eight British possessions, from Newfoundland to Guiana. Roosevelt suggested that the destroyers should be considered as an exchange for leases on the bases that would allow Admiral Harold Stark to certify, with a clear conscience, that these measures as a whole would strengthen American defenses. Churchill, a man who liked to do things handsomely, did not care for this bartering: he would have preferred that His Majesty's government should give America the bases as a mark of gratitude, not as elements in a sordid haggling. He had to yield, to allay the scruples of Congress, but he did at least succeed in causing two bases, those of Bermuda and Newfoundland, to be free gifts, "generously given and gladly received."

By ceding these weapons and these ships, Roosevelt had taken up a firm position from which there was no retreat; and this, on the eve of a presidential election, was a courageous act. Throughout the whole of the latter part of 1940, he was viciously attacked by the isolationists of the America First Committee that was partly made up of sincere men who thought that non-intervention in Europe was the only way of preserving the

American continent, but that also contained extreme rightists like Father Coughlin and Gerald L. K. Smith. These opponents of Roosevelt were joined by businessmen who were angered by the New Deal, anti-English Irishmen, Germans, Italians, and Protestant clergymen who preached nonviolence. On the other hand, the President's policy was supported by the Committee to Defend America by Aiding the Allies, whose chief was one of the best American journalists, William Allen White. From day to day, there was an evolution, an almost visible evolution, of public opinion toward the idea that a victory for Nazism would endanger American freedom. The whole country turned into a vast forum: the great argument raged in the press, on the radio, in the schools, in every house. The America First Committee noisily preached "an amalgam of isolationism and pacifism, old-fashioned anglophobia and new-fangled anti-Semitism." The White committee fought for the defense of justice and successfully maintained that cowardice does not constitute a policy.

II

While this battle was raging, the electoral campaign of 1940 had begun. It was at first supposed that the two great parties would take opposite sides on the question of the European war, the Democrats supporting the President and the Republicans remaining faithful to their traditional insolationism. Such would have been the case if the Republican convention had chosen Senator Robert A. Taft as candidate. But many of the Republican delegates had evolved—progressed; they would not nominate a conservative of the Harding-Coolidge type. The Republican and liberal Wendell Willkie gained ground with every successive ballot, and in the end, the convention chose him. Willkie had been a Democrat; he approved of a great part of the New Deal; and as for the European war, he proclaimed himself more of an interventionist than Roosevelt. He compared the President to Léon Blum, who, busying himself too much with social reform and not enough with military preparation, had left France weak: he claimed that Roosevelt was partially responsible for Munich and for the French defeat. In fact,

Willkie seemed to be saying, "I shall do the same as he does, but much better." This "me too" policy vexed the professional politicians of the party from the very beginning of the campaign, and they asked him to attack Roosevelt as a warmonger who would send the sons of the American voters to be killed in Europe. In the end, Willkie gave way, against his own convictions, and he went so far as to say that "our young men are already on the troop ships," which gave his campaign a certain inconsequentiality and which terrified those voters who were mothers.

Some of the professionals of the Democratic party had no wish to see Roosevelt elected, against the American tradition, for a third term of four years; but if Roosevelt chose to run, they had no means of opposing him, and they saw themselves, in the case of his defeat, compelled to spend four years in the desert of opposition, where neither grants nor jobs were ever found to grow. In accepting nomination, the President made it clear that his campaign would be in accordance with the dignity of his office: "I shall not have the time, nor the inclination, to indulge in purely political debate." In the beginning, he passed Willkie over in silence, never mentioning his name and obliging him to carry on a one-sided argument. Many times Willkie challenged the Champ, that is to say the President, inviting him to come and defend his title in the ring, as Lincoln had done against Douglas. Roosevelt scornfully let it be understood that he had more important things to do.

Nevertheless, the Republicans had more money for their campaign than the Democrats. The press (and even papers that had until recently supported Roosevelt) was in its great majority pro-Willkie. The Democrats grew uneasy: they begged the President "to come off his high horse" and save the party. Willkie's campaign on the troop ships and "our boys"—a campaign in which Willkie himself did not believe—was making inroads on the country. The letters that poured into the White House at that time astonished Robert Sherwood, who had the job of reading them, by the feeling of collective hysteria that they gave. A wave of terror was sweeping the nation: would it carry Willkie into the White House? The warnings of insurance companies, banks, and doctors competed in frightening the voters. Most of the letters said, "Please, for God's sake, Mr.

President, give a solemn promise to the mothers of America that you will not send their sons into any foreign war."

Roosevelt had at first been attacked by Willkie for execessive prudence; he was now somewhat astonished to find himself accused of warmongering. For some days, he seemed bewildered. On October 28, not long before the election, he made a somewhat ambiguous speech at Madison Square Garden: in the first part, he defended himself against the charge of having left America defenseless; in the second, he almost gloried in the neutrality law that he had so strongly opposed. Never had there been so illogical a campaign. But although Roosevelt loved righteous causes, he also knew that in order to uphold them it was above all necessary to keep in power. There are some situations in which opportunism becomes a duty. Truth would come, but after the political victory. Some days later, at Boston, he thought it right to add this to his prepared speech: "I have already said this, but I shall say it again and again and again: Your boys are not going to be sent into any foreign war . . . . The purpose of our defense is defense." He was elected for a third term by an overwhelming majority—449 electoral votes against 82.

III

From now onward, the President was free to act according to the dictates of his heart and his intelligence. The election had held up his support for Great Britain only too long, and the English were now at the end of their dollar resources. They were ready to give enormous orders—equipment for ten armored divisions, airplanes, cargo ships—but if they had to go on paying cash down, they could not do it. A long letter from Churchill to Roosevelt set forth this position that the President had known and understood for a long while. "Give us the tools," said Churchill, "and we will do the job." Roosevelt prepared a talk. Since it was after his reelection, he could plan without being held back by electoral considerations. Harry Hopkins had provided him with the phrase "We must be the great arsenal of democracy."

He explained that there was only one barrier between the New World and Nazi aggression: the British fleet. For now he could at last call the Nazis by their name and say, "We cannot escape danger, or the fear of danger, by crawling into bed and pulling the covers over our heads." And he explained the credit now about to be extended to the British by the famous statement: "A man would not wait to be paid before lending his hose to a neighbor whose house is burning." Why go on believing in the possibility of appeasement? It, Peace with the Nazis, was only to be had at the price of total submission. And what would life be like, once Hitler's guns were aimed at America? Sherwood says that while Roosevelt was working on this talk he often looked up at Wilson's portrait over the mantelpiece. Wilson's tragedy haunted him. Wilson, in obedience to Christian morality and under inspiration of a noble ideal, had made himself the champion of a peace without victory, maintained by a League of Nations. America had denied him. Hence Hitler and the Second World War. That was what he must avoid at any price.

But he still came up against the same difficulty: how could he break the barrier of legal restrictions that stood there against total support for the English? Someone dug up a forgotten law of 1892, according to which Congress authorized the loan of warlike material when it was "for the public good." From this was born the idea of lend-lease. In order to thrust aside both the barrier of neutrality and the dangerous burden of "war debts," Roosevelt asked Congress to authorize the "loan" of $7,000,000,000 worth of war material to the English. The bill was violently opposed in Congress. But the Administration, strengthened by Stimson and Knox, showed a united front in the battle. Besides, in the presidential election, Roosevelt had had twenty-seven million votes, and that was not an unimportant argument in the eyes of the members of Congress who would have to get themselves reelected in two years' time. In vain did Senator Burton K. Wheeler declare that voting for lend-lease would mean ploughing under "every fourth American boy." Roosevelt replied that that was "the rottenest thing that has been said in public life in my generation." In fact, lend-lease simply meant that it would no longer be necessary to resort to trickery to protect the country's safety. Roosevelt alone, on the advice of his military counselors, would have the right of deciding what would be "for the public good." He considered that as England was occupying positions that were vital for the United States, it was a duty to help the English by all possible means. Churchill wrote, "Our blessings from the whole British Empire go to you for this very precious help in time of trouble." The United States was not yet a belligerent: but it was no longer a neutral.

As soon as one puts a finger in the cogwheels of war, the rest of the arm must go through. Furnishing material implied protecting that material during its journey. In March and April, 1941, the President authorized American dockyards to repair British warships, and he seized the ships of the Axis that were in American ports. He increased the range of action of the "neutrality patrol" that searched for the German submarines and warned the English of their presence. The Germans decided to include the straits between Iceland and Greenland in their war zone and to send wolf packs of submarines into them: this increased the loss of English ships. Consequently the President determined, with the agreement of the Icelandic government, to send United States Marines to occupy the country. Later, he provided escorts for the convoys. The American navy did not limit itself to patrolling; it had orders to destroy "the enemy forces in the western Atlantic." This was an undeclared and limited war; but it was war. Congress had furiously opposed the President's desire to arm American merchantmen sailing for England. The President had won. One after the other, the barriers were falling.

IV

Quos vult Jupiter perdere dementat prius. After the failure of his aerial onslaught on England, Hitler, hungry for victories, gave himself up to the reckless dream of getting rid of his last great rival upon the European continent: Russia. He should have been warned by the example of Napoleon. So long as England kept the command of the seas, all continental conquest would be precarious and vain. But during conversations in Berlin in November, 1940, on an eventual parceling out of Europe, Russia had made her demands so high that they had both disturbed and infuriated Hitler. As early as the following month, he sent out a general order that was his own death warrant: "The armed forces of Germany must prepare themselves to overwhelm Russia in a rapid campaign, before the end of the war against England."

On June 22, 1941, the anniversary of the day upon which Napoleon crossed the Neman, the Führer invaded Russia. He did not intend to occupy the whole of the country, but to paralyze it by seizing the vital regions. This invasion made the USSR the ally of the West. Churchill, boldly forgetting ideological quarrels and concentrating solely upon the defeat of Hitler, welcomed Stalin with open arms, and Roosevelt at once thought of extending lend-lease to the USSR. Who would be entrusted with the negotiations? Harry Hopkins had become Roosevelt's most confidential friend. He, too, had been struck by an illness that had brought him to death's door: the experience had given him a very pure idealism, as well as a profound devotion for F.D.R., who had looked after him most affectionately. He often lived in the White House and played the part of a *de facto* deputy for the President.

Some of the men about the President disliked Hopkins' advanced views and the visionary side of his character. One day Willkie said to Roosevelt, "You surely must realize that people distrust him, and they resent his influence."

Roosevelt replied, "I can understand that you wonder why I need that half man around me. But some day you may well be sitting here where I am now, as president of the United States. And when you are, you'll be looking at that door over there, and knowing that practically everybody who walks through it wants something of you. You'll learn what a lonely job this is, and you'll discover the need of somebody like Harry Hopkins, who asks for nothing except to serve you."

Roosevelt had already, in January, 1941, sent Hopkins on an important mission to England. When Churchill had been told that he was to receive the visit of Harry Hopkins, he had asked, "Of whom?" But no one in London would have asked that question any more by the end of his stay: Hopkins had won the confidence of the English. He passionately embraced their cause; he told them of the anxiety and admiration with which the White House followed their struggle. He gave them the comforting feeling that America was marching at their side and would hold them up if they stumbled.

After the adopting of lend-lease, Roosevelt had appointed Hopkins as its administrator. Above all it was necessary to act fast. Now the President knew how Hopkins dealt with formalities and administrative bottlenecks. The job seemed cut out for him. Stimson, the secretary of war, said, "It's a godsend that Harry Hopkins is at the White House." To the great irritation of Cordell Hull, the secretary of state, Roosevelt communicated directly with Churchill on questions to do with lend-lease, through his intermediary Hopkins. W. Averell Harriman, the leader of the lend-lease mission in London, was one of Hopkins' team. An unofficial, or extraofficial, correspondence between Roosevelt and Churchill grew up, by the medium of Hopkins and Harriman, in whom both the chiefs had entire confidence. In July, 1941, Hopkins went to London to arrange an Atlantic Conference, in midocean, between the President and the Prime Minister. Both leaders were lovers of the sea, and both of them were charmed by the picturesque aspect of such a meeting. But while he was in London, Hopkins became convinced that the conference would be in vain if Russia's position were not better known. He cabled, "I have a feeling that everything possible should be done to make certain the Russians maintain a permanent front even though they be defeated in this immediate battle. If Stalin could in any way be influenced at a critical time I think it would be worth doing by a direct communication from you through a personal envoy." Roosevelt replied, telling him to undertake the mission to Russia. When Hopkins left London, Churchill entrusted him with this message for Stalin: "Tell him that Britain has but one ambition today, but one desire: to crush Hitler. . . . Tell him that he can depend on us. . . . Goodbye. . . . God bless you, Harry."

In Moscow, Harry Hopkins saw Stalin and gave him Churchill's message, adding that Roosevelt's attitude was the same. Stalin said that a certain minimum of morality was essential in the relationships between nations, and that the present German leaders signed treaties when they were determined to break them the next day. "Nations," he said, "must stand by their agreements, otherwise no international society is possible." Hopkins thought these sentiments sound enough. Agreement on basics having been reached, he asked to be told of Russia's immediate and long-term needs. Stalin answered that above all he needed twenty thousand antiaircraft guns, which would allow him to free fighters for battle, then heavy machine guns for the defense of the towns, and lastly one million rifles. His long-term needs were gasoline for his aircraft and aluminum to build them with. "Give us antiaircraft guns and aluminum, and we can hold out for three or four years." Of course, American technicians would be welcome. As for a transit port, Stalin advised Archangel. Later on the same day, Hopkins saw General Yakovlev, and he told him of his surprise at not seeing listed among the Russian needs either tanks or antitank guns; but the general was extremely reticent; and Hopkins understood that Stalin was the only man with whom it was useful to have discussions, since it was he alone who had the power of making a decision.

He therefore saw Stalin again and asked him his opinion on the situation. Stalin replied that he could mobilize three hundred and fifty divisions and that he wanted to put as many as possible of them into contact with the enemy. That was the only way of teaching them that the Germans were not superhuman. "Even the German tanks run out of petrol." Stalin said that the present position of the front meant nothing, because it was not a continuous front. There were Russian troops well in advance of it, harassing the lines of communication. Hitler was finding great difficulty in bringing up his supplies. The Russian roads were not the avenues that the German army had found in Belgium and France. Stalin thought that the seventy-ton German tanks would be completely useless in Russia, where the bridges could not carry them. He added that in his opinion Hitler's weakness was the great number of oppressed nations who hated him and who would be encouraged to resist him if they knew that the United States was on their side. He thought that the morale of the German army and the German people was quite low and that it would collapse altogether the day the United States entered the war; he was convinced that that day would come, because the German power was too great for even a united Russia and England to overcome. Thus in two days Hopkins had, as he thought, obtained all the necessary information about Russia. Henceforward he was sure that Russia would not be beaten easily, or quickly. The exactness of Stalin's knowledge had made a very strong impression upon him. Stalin had not consulted a single note during four hours of conversation. He was an austere figure, in his Russian shirt and boots, with enormous hands, an almost harsh voice and a brief, sardonic laugh; he was terse, exact, and direct; and he would have frightened the American envoy if from time to time he had not unbent with a cold but friendly smile. The fact that he had not been obliged to consult anyone whatsoever had made this total agreement possible in no more than six hours of conversation.

V

Hopkins flew back to London, which he reached just in time to go aboard the *Prince of Wales* with Churchill, who had a rendezvous with Roosevelt off Newfoundland. On August 9, the President's ship, the *Augusta,* loomed out of the fog. That same evening, Churchill dined on board the *Augusta,* the two statesmen being accompanied by their diplomats, soldiers, and sailors. There were two subjects that dominated the conversation during dinner: the threat of a Japanese attack, which was causing the English a great deal of anxiety, and a plan for that declaration of common principles, which was to become the Atlantic Charter. Naturally, Russia was also discussed; but, although Churchill rejoiced at seeing her in the war, he pointed out that the new position, in which any Russian threat to Manchuria was removed, gave Japan a greater freedom to attack elsewhere. The next morning, Roosevelt went to attend a religious service aboard the *Prince of Wales.* There were prayers for the invaded countries, for the wounded, the prisoners, and the exiles, and a prayer that "we may be preserved from hatred, bitterness, and all spirit of revenge."

The English had prepared the text of two parallel declarations, which they hoped that both the United States and Great Britain would address to Japan, warning that country that any fresh encroachment in southeast Asia would compel the one government to retaliate and the other to come to the aid of the victims of the aggression. "For want of a declaration of this kind," said the English, "Japan may use her many cruisers to destroy the

British merchant navy in the Pacific and the Indian Ocean. England would be cut off from her Dominions." Roosevelt did not feel that he had the right to make such a statement. There were some senators who would have seized upon it to call the whole of his policy in regard to Germany in question again. Men one would never have expected to find together, Senator Wheeler, Colonel Lindbergh, and John L. Lewis, were already bitterly decrying aid to the USSR. Later the isolationists reproached F.D.R. with having made secret engagements at the time of the Atlantic Conference. "We wished to God he had!" said the English ministers and diplomats.

As for the Atlantic Charter, its object was to enforce what Roosevelt called the Four Freedoms: freedom of speech, freedom of religion, freedom from want, freedom from fear. The principles of the charter were: no territorial conquests; respect for the right of peoples to choose their own form of government; equal access to raw materials; economic collaboration; renunciation of the use of force in international relations. In the text prepared by Churchill, Roosevelt, Sir Alexander Cadogan, and Sumner Welles, there was this phrase: "They [the United States and Britain] seek a peace which will not only cast down for ever the Nazi tyranny but, *by effective international organization,* will afford to all states and peoples the means of dwelling in security." Roosevelt had the words in italics struck out. Churchill urged that they should stay in. Roosevelt replied that not only would the idea of an international organization arouse disturbance and anger in the United States, but furthermore he himself was not eager to revive the old League of Nations too quickly. He was continually haunted by the specter of Wilson, and he thought it more realistic to entrust the maintenance of peace to the Anglo-American forces, at least at the beginning. Churchill said that this concept would clash with those of the many and powerful British believers in internationalism. The President replied that realism was more important; Churchill admitted that personally he agreed, but. . . . In the end, Hopkins gave his support for a compromise, "a permanent system of general security," and this formula was agreed upon.

The Atlantic Conference had not produced the positive results that Churchill expected (he had hoped to obtain an "iron glove" ultimatum to Japan from Roosevelt), but it had established a deep friendship between the two leaders—a friendship that was to be of immense importance. When two great men meet face to face, things start to move. Yet a hollow, pious declaration of principles was a disappointment for the nations of the whole world, who, for all the secrecy, knew very well that "the cigarette-in-holder and the long cigar were at last being lit from the same match." They were wrong in being disappointed. Roosevelt had set his face against giving the declaration the direct form of a treaty, for that would have obliged him to submit it to the Senate; but he considered himself bound by it. The right of nations to choose their own form of government was to become an essential requirement of American foreign policy. The declaration of a moral principle has this danger—and this advantage—that afterward it has to be applied.

VI

In the Far East, the danger outweighed the advantages. For half a century, American statesmen had been piously declaring principles that could not be faulted (territorial and administrative integrity of China and the "open door" for the trade of all countries) but that took no account of local realities. One of these realities was the weakness of the Chinese government that had almost no authority in some provinces: another was the fact that Japan was stifling on her little islands, as much because of her lack of raw materials as because of her over-abundant population. Hence she was continually tempted to seek room to expand on the Asian continent. After the First World War, a movement had come into being in Japan, and particularly in the army—a movement of the younger men, eager, in a hurry, sure of their strength; a movement whose teaching was somewhat reminiscent of Nazism. The American restrictions upon Japanese immigration had been sharply resented, and from time to time, this resentment broke out in incidents between the two countries. The American reaction was limited to moralizing, fruitless notes. Roosevelt felt that the American people would not have been behind him in the case of effective action, which explains his passivity during this long trial.

When the Second World War broke out, Japan was divided into two parties, the one in favor of the Axis and of war, the other, supported by the Emperor, in favor of peace. America's aim was, by economic pressure, to prevent Japan from entering the war. The Americans' influence might have been great enough, for it was they who supplied Japan with the greater part of her raw materials and above all with the gasoline necessary for her army and her air force. The threat of an embargo was sufficient to keep a moderate government in power for the first half of 1940. But the German successes renewed the zeal of the Japanese soldiers, who longed for expansion. With France helpless, England busy elsewhere, and Holland powerless, it seemed that Japan might set up a "new order" in the Far East, a state of affairs that would in fact be a Japanese domination. She at once asked the impotent government of Vichy for the right to establish bases in Indochina and obtained it. In September, 1940, she signed a tripartite treaty with Hitler and Mussolini, by which Japan recognized the predominance of the Axis in Europe, while Germany and Italy recognized the Japanese "new order" in the Far East. At this time, Hitler was already encouraging the Japanese to seize Singapore. In June, 1941, the German attack upon Russia strengthened the war party in Japan. The Russian government had no longer to be feared in Asia, since from that moment onward, it was too deeply engaged in Europe to fight on two fronts.

In July, 1941, a meeting of the Japanese ministers (Prince Fumimaro Konoye, prime minister; Yosuke Matsuoka, foreign minister, and General Hideki Tojo, minister for war) ratified plans that, five months later, were to bring war with the United States. The imperial government secretly decided to follow a policy that would lead to the setting up of a Greater East Asia Co-Prosperity Sphere (an ingenious euphemism), *whatever the international consequences*. The means were pressure on China, occupation of Indochina and Thailand, mobilization of the nation's entire strength, and preparation of plans against Malaya, Java, Borneo, and the Philippines. From that moment, the Japanese navy began its training for the attack on Pearl Harbor, the great American base. Until then Roosevelt had hesitated over cutting off gasoline and oil even for the Japanese. He justified himself thus: And now there is a nation called Japan.

Whether they had, at that time, aggressive purposes to enlarge their empire southward, they did not have any oil of their own up in the north. Now, if we had cut the oil off, they probably would have gone down to the Dutch East Indies a year ago, and you would have had war.

For two years, the threat had sufficed. On September 26, 1941, the President proclaimed an embargo on steel and scrap iron exports to go into effect on October 16. This appeared to have a great effect in Japan. Matsuoka had to resign. For a long while, the Emperor had been telling his ministers not to take the risk of a war with the United States. Prince Konoye asked for a meeting with the President, either on American soil or at Honolulu. Perhaps at that moment a gesture on the part of Roosevelt might have strengthened the peace party that was still strong in Japan. He did not make the gesture, and later the isolationists said that he had thus deliberately caused the Japanese aggression that he needed in order to enter the war against the Axis. This was not the case. What in fact he feared above all was to be accused of appeasement, a word that had come to have a very ugly ring in America since Munich. On August 28, Konoye promised that if the President agreed to meet him, the Japanese government would evacuate Indochina, would undertake no new invasion in south Asia, and would not consider itself bound by the tripartite pact with Germany and Italy. The obstinate, distrustful secretary of state, Cordell Hull, advised abstention; and Roosevelt followed his advice. Far from wanting war, the President and the State Department supposed that if American policy were firm, the Japanese government would withdraw. But there can be too much firmness.

General Tojo succeeded Prince Konoye as prime minister. The die was cast. The commanders of the American fleet and army in the Pacific were warned, but unemphatically, of the possibility of a Japanese attack. Roosevelt really thought it much more likely that Japan would attack either Thailand or Malaya than the Philippines or Hawaii—the English or the Dutch rather than the Americans. And in any case what could he have done? The isolationists in Congress were saying "Why should any Americans die for Singapore?" just as the French isolationists in 1939 had said, "Why die for Danzig?" Meanwhile new Japanese envoys, Hichisaburo Nomura and Saburo Kurusu, had come to negotiate at Washington, and Hull was working day and night to reach an agreement with them. On December 6, Roosevelt sent an urgent message to the Emperor Hirohito, solemnly appealing to him to keep the peace. But his mind was far from the "inconceivable possibility" that before launching their attack upon the British and Dutch empires, the Japanese would begin by forcing the United States into the war, and forcing it, moreover, in so blatantly insulting a manner that they instantly succeeded in uniting a nation that until that moment had been divided.

On Sunday, December 7, 1941, Hopkins was lunching at the White House with the President when Knox, the secretary of the navy, telephoned to say that a radio message from the American commander in chief at Honolulu had been picked up, and that this message told the forces under his command that an air raid was in progress, an air raid that was in no way an exercise. Roosevelt called Hull, who had an appointment with Nomura and Korusu, and told him to receive them coldly. Hull, like a throughgoing Tennessee mountaineer, went further and told them he did not believe a word they were saying. At twenty-eight minutes past two, Admiral Stark telephoned that the attack was violent and that the fleet had suffered serious losses. Roosevelt called a meeting of Hull and some other Cabinet officers and said that he was going to summon Congress for the next day. It was war. Hull and Sumner Welles at once prepared long messages to inform Congress of the negotiations and to call upon it for a declaration of war. The President was determined not to make use of their drafts, but he took care not to let them know this: he called for beer and sandwiches and went to bed.

The attack had taken place at Pearl Harbor, the great Pacific naval base where the fleet was concentrated. No effective aerial patrol had been provided to give the warning, so the Japanese aircraft carriers had been able to approach with impunity. The waves of Japanese airplanes had bombed the airfields and the fleet. Most of the American planes had been destroyed on the ground. Two hours after the beginning of the raid, the great American port was no more than a heap of ruins: 3 cruisers, 3 destroyers, and 8 battleships were either sunk or out of action; 2,335 soldiers and sailors and 68 civilians had been killed. On this winter Sunday, as on all others, there were millions of

Americans sitting by their radios to listen to light music. Instead of songs, they heard news that at first seemed incredible. When they were forced to believe it, "their incredulity turned into rage and an implacable determination to be revenged."

On December 8, Roosevelt spoke to Congress. He left the drafts prepared by Hull and Welles to one side. To give the session an even greater solemnity, he had asked President Wilson's widow to come with Mrs. Roosevelt to the Capitol. He made a very simple speech: the facts, and nothing but the facts, with one single striking phrase—"a date which will live in infamy." No attempt at disguising the mistakes and negligence of the defense, but a short list of the points attacked: "The facts of yesterday speak for themselves. . . . Hostilities exist. There is no blinking at the fact that our people, our territory, and our interests are in grave danger." There was nothing of the splendid eloquence of a Pericles or a Churchill, nothing of the trumpeting megalomania of a Hitler. An upright man was establishing the fact that the country was in a state of war, without fear but not without disgust. On the radio, he said, "We must face the fact that modern warfare as conducted in the Nazi manner is a dirty business. We don't like it—we didn't want to get in it, but we are in it, and we're going to fight it with everything we've got."

On December 11, Germany and Italy declared war on the United States. Churchill heaved a sigh of relief. "The Lord hath delivered them into our hands," he said.

VII

"We're going to fight it with everything we've got," the President had said. But he was far from possessing the means of carrying out this policy. An Anglo-American conference, held in Washington in December, 1941, showed how huge the task was. It was essential to stand up against the Japanese, to attack the Germans, to keep England supplied, and to go on providing Russia with weapons. Roosevelt at once made up his mind as Churchill wanted on the capital decision of the priority of the Atlantic over the Pacific. It was a difficult decision at a time when the whole country was crying aloud for revenge, but above all, they had to crush Hitler, the dominant leader of the evil coalition. An important attack in France would not be possible until men and arms had been accumulated. Plans for an easier operation were made—a landing in North Africa (its code name was first Gymnast, then Torch) where perhaps the French African troops would join the Americans, and where Rommel's army might be taken from behind. Rommel was threatening Egypt and even the Middle East, which might eventually lead to a junction of the Germans and the Japanese. But even this operation limited to North Africa called for long preparations. For the moment, twenty thousand American soldiers were sent to the southeast Pacific and token forces to Northern Ireland (operation Magnet). A common Anglo-American command, the Combined Chiefs of Staff, was set up at Washington, and production targets were fixed.

The wholehearted cooperation of the American people could be relied upon. An attack upon an English or Dutch colony might perhaps have left them cold—another Danzig. But in one hour, Pearl Harbor had cured the nation of isolationism. No doubt the professional isolationists and Roosevelt's bitterest enemies remained on the alert. "There are," said the commentator Elmer Davis, "some patriotic citizens who sincerely hope that America will win the war—but they also hope that Russia will lose it; and there are some who hope that America will win the war, but that England will lose it; and there are some who hope that America will win the war, but that Roosevelt will lose it." That was true enough, but true only of a minority. In fact, seldom were there soldiers who fought better, seldom was there a more disciplined army, never did producers, both management and labor, work with more intelligent zeal, never was the nation more united. The question of morale never even arose. Not that there was any question of patriotic raving, either, nor even of enthusiasm. It occurred to no one to organize parades, in the manner of the First World War. But the nation was utterly committed to the battle: it was victory or else destruction.

The experts had no doubt about the certainty of winning. For them, victory was essentially a question of productive capacity. Now time was on the side of the United States, whose resources were infinitely greater. There was, however, one condition. The huge machine had to be set in motion quickly. But nothing, or almost nothing, was ready. Since the beginning of the war in Europe, the American government had made some plans for rearmament, but most of the factories were still no more than blueprints. The weapons had gone to England and Russia. During the period 1939–1940, a War Resources Board had been entrusted with the organization of production, but politics had crept in. After the fall of France, Roosevelt had set about uniting all the great national interests—William S. Knudsen, the president of General Motors, Sidney Hillman of the CIO, Chester Davis, to represent farming—in short, men of the highest quality. At the first meeting, Knudsen asked, "Who's boss?" Roosevelt answered, "I am." The essential point was the control of priorities. Who was going to get the money, the steel, the electrical equipment? Which factories would be built first? Roosevelt answered these questions in the American fashion, that is to say pragmatically. Special agencies were set up, and men from every corner of the country were put in charge of them; those that failed were done away with and those that worked were strengthened. Thus, the OPM (Office of Production Management) under Knudsen and Hillman and the OPA (Office of Price Administration) at first under Leon Henderson came into being. Later Donald M. Nelson was put in sole charge of a body called the War Resources Board that superseded the unwieldy OPM. And then James F. Byrnes became a sort of assistant to the President, a supreme ruler of war production. As it always happens, this single head turned out to be more efficient than the divided powers that had preceded him.

One of the difficulties was that of persuading the manufacturers concerned to build new factories. They had only just come out of the great depression, and they were afraid of overproduction. It was necessary to supply them with money and to authorize them to redeem their investment in five years. Congress had granted a billion dollars to build up stocks of strategic materials, but the forecasts were mistaken, and when the break with Japan shut off access to natural rubber, there were no factories for synthetic rubber in existence. At the time of Pearl Harbor, the stocks of munitions were very low. The capacity for *future* production seemed to be very far beyond that of Germany and Japan together: but the chaotic state of that production was still terrifying. Every service, and every arm within that service, was working for itself alone. The merchant ships were robbing the navy of its steel. Locomotive factories were turned into tank factories, and then there was a shortage of locomotives. The priority system was not working, because there was an inflation of priorities. The want of rubber soon became so serious that it was necessary to limit the use of cars and at last to build huge factories for synthesizing it.

The strength of America lies in the fact that when she sets herself to a task she performs miracles. One year later, she was producing more synthetic rubber than all the natural rubber she had ever consumed. As early as 1943, tanks, airplanes, machine guns, landing craft, and merchant ships were being turned out in such great numbers that there was no longer any room for uneasiness. For the transport of troops, one type, the Liberty ship, had been adopted: it was old fashioned, but it was easy to build. The brilliant Henry J. Kaiser succeeded in producing a Liberty ship in fourteen days. Later these were replaced by the better and faster Victory ships. By 1945, in spite of the German submarines, the United States had thirty-six million tons of shipping on the seas. So many contracts, and for such great sums, bred abuses. Corruption and disorder are permanent characteristics of human nature. The Senate War Investigating Committee did its work extremely well and almost completely abolished waste and graft. Its chairman was a senator from Missouri, Harry S Truman, who won a deserved reputation as an honest and efficient man.

Of course, the state of war transformed the country. In 1939, there had still been nine million unemployed: in 1943, there was a shortage of labor. Thirty-one million men had been registered for military service. Fifteen million men and women were called up, leaving great gaps in the factories. Adolescents left school for the workshop. Twenty-seven million Americans changed trade and dwelling place. There were immense migrations. A great many technicians followed the aircraft factories, which were set up in the West; the Negroes and the poor whites of the South moved up toward the North. Overtime (everything above forty hours in the week) was paid at time and a half, and the workers found themselves growing rich. Women and girls worked: this was not without its disadvantages for the children, who, for want of supervision, became accustomed to an excess of freedom. But the general prosperity became a settled thing.

Up until that time, farming had been poor and haunted by overproduction; now it too was given a fresh impetus. The country ate more food, the armed forces being exceedingly well fed and the workers better paid. Furthermore, it was necessary to supply Great Britain and help the USSR. Toward 1945, the surpluses accumulated in the days of underconsumption were no longer enough for the needs of the hungry liberated countries. Between 1940 and 1945, the farmers' net income increased four-fold. The agricultural population saved $11,000,000,000 in four years, although the anti-inflation act had frozen agricultural prices. Prentiss M. Brown and later Chester Bowles, the successive heads after Henderson of the OPA and the supreme rulers of prices, very skillfully succeeded in limiting the rise in the cost of living, between 1939 and the end of the war, to 29 percent in spite of the huge inflation brought about by the government's vast spending. Extremely high taxes mopped up war profits and restrained the upward tendency.

Science worked no less than industry. The war might be won in the laboratory just as much as in the factory. The English had perfected radar. The Americans were trying to find the means of splitting the uranium isotope 235 from its much more plentiful isotope, uranium 238, or transmuting it into plutonium, the only substances from which the atomic bomb could be made. The Americans knew that the Germans were following the same lines of research and that in Czechoslovakia they had at their disposition the richest mines in Europe. Niels Bohr had made known the success of the Germans in splitting the uranium atom experimentally. Laymen were completely unaware of this danger, but among themselves the physicists said that if their German colleagues were to find the secret of initiating chain atomic fission before they did, the war would be lost. Spurred on by the English scientists and even more by the refugees from Europe, they wanted to warn the President. Fermi had tried to interest the American navy, but the unprecedented nature of his scheme had aroused only indifferent interest. The only man who seemed to have the necessary standing to reach Roosevelt himself was Albert Einstein. Leo Szilard and E. P. Wigner conferred with Einstein; and he wrote a letter to the President in July, 1939, which was taken to the President by his friend Alexander Sachs. The President appointed a committee to consider these developments. But it was only at the end of 1941 that research aimed at the manufacture of the atomic bomb began on a big scale. If Einstein's letter had been followed by energetic action as early as 1939, the war might well have been ended much earlier and under far better conditions. But it is only too easy to be wise after the event.

VIII

It was agreed, then, that there should be a landing in North Africa. If the operation succeeded, it would provide a springboard for a subsequent attack upon Sicily and Italy. Stalin was not satisfied, and he noisily demanded the opening of a second front in metropolitan France. The scheme also raised some very delicate problems in Anglo-American relationships. Churchill had welcomed General de Gaulle's Free France, and in his speeches he had expressed his contempt for the government of Vichy. Roosevelt had wished to keep up relations with Vichy, and he sent his most trusted service friend, Admiral William D. Leahy, as his ambassador to Marshal Pétain. This decision earned him sharp reproaches from his liberal associates, who considered the Vichy government a satellite of Germany. Roosevelt held out, and for several reasons. He thought that if he had an embassy there he would maintain a listening post in Europe that would give him information on Hitler's intentions, and he hoped to prevent Pétain from yielding to the demands of the Germans, who were asking for the French fleet and for North Africa. Roosevelt shared the feelings of his friends against some of Pétain's colleagues, but he did not allow his likes and dislikes to direct his policy. Cordell Hull, who looked like a philosopher but who was in fact a forceful man, added to military opportunism a bigger grudge against the Free French, who had seized Saint Pierre and Miquelon, two little islands off Newfoundland, although he personally had given the French Admiral Robert a guarantee that the French possessions should remain *in statu quo*. It was an utterly unimportant wound to his vanity, but it was one that festered and for a long time it poisoned the relationships between Free France and the State Department. For his part, Roosevelt always refused to think of this petty incident as of any importance at a time when a world war was raging.

Leahy's mission was to convince Pétain that France's essential interest called for the defeat of the Axis, and that this defeat was certain. A difficult mission. Pétain was eighty-four, and though he might be clear minded in the morning, for the whole of the rest of the day he would become an easy prey to dangerous advisers. Leahy said that he found Pétain full of feeling, pro-American, fatherly, and determined never to abandon "his children" the French. Admiral Jean François Darlan seemed to Leahy to have only two strong emotions—love for his fleet, which he would scuttle rather than hand over to anyone at all, and hatred for England, chiefly caused by the events at Mers-el-Kebir. Leahy wrote to the President that the majority of the high officials at Vichy hoped for an English victory but did not believe in it. He praised the patriotism and the loyalty of General Weygand, who was in command in North Africa and who was vigorously resisting all German attempts at getting control of this precious bastion—a resistance that was to result in his recall. Pétain admitted that he was powerless to defend him. "I have no force," he said to the American ambassador, "and you know, Mr. Leahy, that when one has no strength, one can do nothing."

Leahy concluded that the Marshal would never leave France but would never give up the fleet or North Africa either. Later he wrote that since America's declaration of war, Darlan was beginning to believe in the possibility of a German defeat. Washington hoped to win Weygand's cooperation for the North African landing, for the whole French army would have obeyed him. Leahy saw him and found him polite and favorable; but the General said that he was bound by his oath to the Marshal and that before accepting he would have to tell him, which he could not do without giving away the secret of the landing. It was at this time that the Americans made contact with General Henri Giraud, a brave soldier known to be hostile to the Axis. For Roosevelt, this opportunist policy was a gamble: he always maintained that it had paid. *Adhuc sub judice . . .*

At the end of 1942, the Anglo-American position seemed full of danger. The results of the submarine war were terrifying. In North Africa, Rommel's Afrikakorps had been checked sixty miles from Alexandria, but it was still threatening. The English urged that an African landing should take place as soon as possible, thus allowing Rommel to be grasped in a pincer movement with Montgomery's Eighth Army on the one side and the Anglo-Americans on the other. Huge convoys were necessary for an operation of this kind, and their crossing of an ocean infested with submarines was not easy. How would the French army in North Africa, bound to Pétain by an oath, welcome the Americans? A small, courageous team of Algerian Frenchmen had met General Mark W. Clark, who landed secretly from a submarine, and they had prepared the operation with him. In fact, there was almost no resistance at Algiers and Oran, though there was rather more at Casablanca, where the French navy played the more important part. The Americans had counted on General Giraud, but at the beginning, he seemed to have little authority over the army in Africa. General Dwight D. Eisenhower, who was in command of the expeditionary force, then fell back upon Darlan, who happened to be in Algeria and who, having full authority, was not bound by the disastrous oath. He agreed to cooperate.

Soon the French African army, which had lost nothing of its fighting qualities and which Roosevelt agreed to rearm with modern weapons, became a valuable auxiliary. It played a great part in the advance in Tunisia. At the beginning of 1943, Rommel had threatened that country: now he found himself squeezed there between Montgomery and Eisenhower. A lightning movement behind the lines, made on the advice of the French General Alphonse Pierre Juin, pinned him at Cape Bon. The German army in Tunisia had to surrender in May, 1943, but Rommel himself was recalled before the final disaster. The Axis had there lost 350,000 men, killed or taken, 250 tanks, and 520 airplanes. It was the first great Allied victory. "The myth of the Nazis' invincibility had been completely destroyed." The English had confirmed their military qualities; the Americans had won battle experience; the French had recovered some of their prestige. Now the campaign in Italy had to be undertaken.

In January, 1943, Churchill, Roosevelt, and their advisers met at Casablanca to plan the future. They had a French problem to solve. Darlan had been assassinated in December. De Gaulle and Giraud remained. Eisenhower thought that the army was more in favor of Giraud, but that the civil population was most enthusiastically for De Gaulle. Churchill stood by De Gaulle, to whom he was committed and who had been the first to join him. Roosevelt had a tendency to think that he was in a conquered country and that he might exercise discretionary powers in it. Eisenhower reminded him that the occupation of Algeria had only taken place because of an agreement with the French army, and that according to this agreement the government was to be French. Roosevelt consented, on the condition that the French should accept the European strategy of the Allies. As to the Giraud-De Gaulle affair, Robert Murphy, the senior United States diplomat in North Africa, told the President that Giraud was ready to cooperate with De Gaulle but not to serve under him. Harold Macmillan, who was representing Great Britain at Algiers, suggested that De Gaulle should play the part of Clemenceau and Giraud that of Foch.

Hopkins advised Roosevelt to induce the two French generals to issue a conciliatory communiqué and to have them photographed together. Churchill undertook to bring De Gaulle. De Gaulle, serene and confident, maintained that Giraud should be under his orders. The President and Churchill came out into the garden, leading De Gaulle and Giraud with them. The photographers were waiting, and they seemed amazed when the President suggested that the generals should shake hands: some of them, taken unaware, missed the crucial moment and asked for it to be done again. In fact, this spectacular reconciliation could have no lasting result. Giraud, an honest man and an excellent soldier, was no sort of statesman—neither was he any match for General De Gaulle. The President then told the journalists that Churchill and he would only accept the *unconditional surrender* of Germany, Japan, and Italy. The advantage of this extreme stand was that it reassured the Russians and encouraged resistance in the occupied countries; but on the other hand it strengthened Hitler's position by depriving the dissident elements in the army and the country as a whole of any hope of compromise. It also threatened to create an absolute vacuum in central Europe, which, after the victory, was inevitably to lead to a struggle among the victors for supremacy in that area.

After the Tunisian victory, the Allies' strategy called for

230

the invasion of Sicily. During the night of June 9, 1943, a great fleet landed 160,000 men, 600 tanks, and 1,800 guns. It was a dress rehearsal for the amphibious operations on the European continent. Mistakes were made: the Allies shot down twenty-three of their own troop-carrying planes; sea water damaged the tanks and trucks. But these were fruitful lessons, and in record time, Eisenhower obtained a protective product for the vehicles from America. By August 17, the whole of Sicily had been conquered. The Germans saw that they could not hold southern Italy. In September, the Allies landed at Salerno. King Victor Emmanuel III then had Mussolini, whom he had never liked, arrested; and he replaced him by Marshal Pietro Badoglio, who was ready to arrange for Italy's alliances to be totally reversed. But the Germans reinforced their troops around Rome and held the Allies at Monte Cassino. In May, 1944, the Allied troops, with General Juin's French divisions among them, at last took Monte Cassino and then in June, 1944, entered Rome. This mountain campaign had been extremely hard. The GIs harassed by the cold, the rain, and the enemy's bombardments, sang bitterly, "Yes, we have no Cassino, we have no Cassino today." Even when Rome was occupied the Nazis still firmly held on to northern Italy where Mussolini, having been rescued by the Germans shortly after his arrest, had been established as a German puppet; but the Allies had the Italian fleet and valuable air bases, and they there immobilized some of Hitler's best divisions. Meanwhile in England the preparations were being made for the great invasion (operation Overlord), and Eisenhower had been given command of it.

IX

In Russia, the Germans had lost the initiative. It was not only General Winter and the vastness of Russia that had put them in danger, but serious faults on the part of Hitler and the patient courage of the Russians. The German soldiers were terrified by the increasing numbers of Russian partisans fighting a guerrilla war. An excessive concentration before Stalingrad created a salient that could only be defended with difficulty. A retreat should have been made, but for political reasons Hitler did not want this: a withdrawal in Russia combined with a defeat in North Africa would have provided too much ammunition for those German generals who were beginning to think of a military coup d'état as a means of getting rid of the Führer. The winter campaign of 1943 was disastrous for the Nazis: they lost two hundred thousand men and irreplaceable material in Russia. Toward the middle of the year, all the foundations of the Axis were giving out ominous cracking sounds. If Roosevelt and Churchill had not endorsed the slogan *unconditional surrender,* it is possible that the Germans themselves would have repudiated national socialism and that Hitler would have been thrown out by his army. But this unhappy formula brought about a tragic conflict of conscience. Germany's enemies forced her to continue the hopeless struggle. One should never become the prisoner of one's own phrases.

Cordell Hull, the secretary of state, went to Russia in October, 1943, to have a meeting with Stalin; he came back convinced that the Russian leader accepted the Wilsonian principles of the Atlantic Charter, and that after the war there would no longer be any need for alliances, balance of power, or "any other of the special arrangements through which, in the unhappy past, the nations strove to safeguard their security or to promote their interests." So in the presence of the harshly realistic Stalin even a Tennessee mountaineer could forget the existence of original sin and believe in a coming Golden Age. Roosevelt said that this meeting had been an immense success. Averell Harriman and Charles Bohlen, who knew Stalin better, retained their doubts. In November, 1943, Roosevelt, Churchill, and Stalin met in a summit conference at Teheran. Roosevelt tried to make friends with Stalin, sometimes even at Churchill's expense, and on his return he told Congress, "We are going to get along fine with him . . . very well indeed." Roosevelt and Stalin asserted that after the war France would be no more than a little nation and that she would no longer count in the world: Churchill took France's part, foretelling that she would quickly rise again.

At the beginning of the Teheran Conference, Churchill delivered the Stalingrad sword to Marshal Stalin. But the object of the meeting was to come to an agreement on operation Overlord, that is to say, the landing in Normandy and the opening of the second front that Stalin longed for so passionately. The question was to know what support the Russians could provide by a simultaneous attack in the East. Before anything else, Stalin asked to know who was to command Overlord. Roosevelt replied that this was not yet decided. Stalin bluntly said that as long as no commander in chief had been chosen, he would not believe that the operation was real. In fact, Roosevelt was hesitating between Marshall, who had the right of seniority, and Eisenhower, who had just succeeded in Africa and Italy. Churchill embarked upon a great speech about the Mediterranean: he would have preferred an attack upon the "soft underbelly of Europe," his favorite target as far back as the First World War, that is to say, the Balkans; all of which Stalin listened to with deep mistrust. For his part, the Russian marshal wanted the landing in France: he wanted a date to be fixed and a commander chosen at once. He asked Churchill to say frankly whether he really believed in Overlord or whether he was only uttering gracious words intended to reassure the Russians. Thus the three Titans stood face to face. Churchill, the most eloquent among them, used all the political skill at his command: to his delicate rapier work, Stalin replied with the blows of a club. Roosevelt acted as referee. At Teheran, he was somewhat shocked by the cynicism of Stalin, who laughed at the rights of the small nations, and also by Churchill's obstinacy in defending his strategic views. But the President remained an optimistic American, ready to trust in men. No doubt he was sincere in writing the last words of the communiqué: "We came here with hope and determination. We leave here friends in fact, in spirit, and in purpose."

So it was to be operation Overlord. Against Hopkins' passionate advice, against the views of Churchill and of Stalin, Roosevelt set Marshall aside in favor of Eisenhower. "I feel I could not sleep at night with you out of the country," he said to Marshall, who from Washington was directing all military operations, both in Europe and in the Pacific, and who, as selfless as he was disciplined, accepted the decision of his commander in chief without a word. In preparation for the great attack, the English and the Americans increased the strategic bombardment of the German industrial centers. They thus killed 305,000 persons and wounded 780,000; and they destroyed 5,500,000 houses. The American historian Arthur S. Link is of the opinion that this bombing alone was enough to convince the Germans that the war was lost. The English General J. F. C. Fuller, on the other hand, thinks that if the Allied air forces had been better used for tactical aims, in closer cooperation with the armies, the war would have been won a year earlier. It is certain that the bombing of Hamburg, for example, not only failed to stop the war factories but even provided them with extra workers by depriving the civilians of any other means of livelihood. But then again, the destruction of aircraft factories, and also that of the many planes that attempted to defend them, prevented the Luftwaffe from offering an effective resistance to the invasion of the continent.

The invasion was to be a gigantic operation, the greatest that history had ever known, and one that called for the most scrupulous preparation. To protect the coast, the Germans had built many defenses. The Canadians' attempt at Dieppe had shown how difficult it was to hold a bridgehead. No doubt the Allies' superiority in the air allowed them to prevent the German reserves from reaching the threatened points by destroying railways and bridges, but to supply their own troops they needed ports. Now the ports would all be knocked to pieces and made unworkable by debris. It was therefore decided to bring two artificial ports from England, each as big as Dover Harbor. This gives some idea of the scale of Overlord. "Prior to the present war," said General Marshall, "I never heard of any landing craft except a rubber boat. Now I think about little else." And indeed, for this amphibious war 3,780 landing craft were needed and 2,876,000 soldiers, sailors, and airmen were to take part in the operation. They were to be covered by 11,000 airplanes. A submarine pipeline (called Pluto) would bring gasoline from England.

The Norman coast, between Le Havre and Cherbourg, was chosen as the point of attack. There, by destroying the Seine and the Loire bridges, it would be possible to pin the German Seventh Army. That army was taken by surprise, having expected the attack in the Pas-de-Calais, where Eisenhower had made a feint. D-day was at first fixed in May, but it had to be postponed until June because of the bad weather. In England, the huge armada was like a compressed spring, ready to shoot out. It was to attack on June 5. A storm made it impossible. On the sixth, in spite of an unfavorable weather report, Eisenhower launched his army. The parachutists and the airborne troops were to land at two in the morning. An aerial and naval bombardment was to follow. And then, at half past six, the landing of five divisions, carried in 4,266 vessels. By the end of the day, 120,000 men had won a foothold in France. "In the whole history of war," said Stalin (laudatory at last), "there has been no undertaking so vast in conception, so tremendous in scale, so masterly in the carrying out."

Ernie Pyle, a journalist who was with the troops, has described the unbelievably busy appearance of this sea, crossed and recrossed by thousands of ships. It might have been the port of New York at its most active but a port stretching right out to the horizon and filling a whole ocean. The ships had to wait their turn. The German shells fell into the sea around them, raising great fountains of water. With their life belts on, the men sat there, playing gin rummy or reading *Life*. On the beaches, there were many dead, both friends and enemies, hanging in the barbed wire. But the match was already won. In spite of difficult moments and a furious resistance during June and on into July, the Allies finally took Saint-Lô. Field Marshal Karl R. G. von Rundstedt began to retreat toward the Seine. It was not only a victory, but a revolution in the art of war. It had been proved that with the coming of airborne troops and artificial ports no nation could any longer trust to the sea for its safety. And incidentally it was also proved that massive bombing of towns did more harm to the civil population than to the army.

France was then liberated "as if by magic." The French Resistance helped the Allied troops in their shattering advance. The American First Army and the French Second Armored Division (under General Leclerc) entered Paris, and at the news New York went mad with joy. On August 15, there had been another landing in the south of France, between Cannes and Toulon. The American Seventh Army advanced up the valley of the Rhone to meet the Third Army that had taken Orleans and Troyes. The Canadians and the English were liberating the west and the north. The Nazis hurried back to take shelter in their own country, behind the Siegfried Line. They attempted a few counterthrusts at Strasbourg and then, during 1945, in the Ardennes; but these were short-lived movements. General de Gaulle, acclaimed at his arrival and now recognized by all, was ruling in Paris.

The Russians had launched a great offensive at the same time as Overlord. They took Warsaw in January, and in February, 1945, they were on the banks of the Oder, only forty-five miles from Berlin. They were occupying Bucharest, Belgrade, and Budapest. The collapse of the Third Reich was from now onward an accomplished fact, but Hitler refused to acknowledge it. On July 20, 1944, a group of patriotic German generals had tried to assassinate him. He had a miraculous escape from a bomb that had been placed under the table at which he and his staff were conferring. In March, 1945, the Allies crossed the Rhine. Churchill wanted to occupy Prague and Berlin as quickly as possible. "I deem it highly important," he wrote to Eisenhower, in his free and easy manner, "that we should shake hands with the Russians as far to the East as possible." In their guileless imprudence, Eisenhower and Bradley were astonished at what they called "Churchill's tendency to complicate military operations by political considerations." Instead of advancing eastward at full speed, they preferred to capture the Bavarian redoubt where it was thought that Hitler would dig himself in for a final battle.

X

There was to be a presidential election year in 1944, and even in time of war the Americans meant to keep up their democratic institutions. Roosevelt was clothed with the glory of victories that were themselves full of promise; but the Republicans had a good candidate in Governor Thomas E. Dewey of New York, whose dynamic youthfulness contrasted with Roosevelt's extreme fatigue. Roosevelt had to choose a candidate for the vice-presidency. Henry A. Wallace, the retiring vice-president, an honest visionary with advanced and woolly notions, frightened the politicians. It was said, by way of joke, that he wanted to extend the New Deal to the entire planet and to provide every Hottentot with a pint of milk. Twenty years later, this wild concept was to become the official policy of the

United States. In ordinary times, the choice of a vice-president is not of very great importance; but anyone could see that Roosevelt's health was sinking, and it seemed likely that if he were reelected, he might not reach the end of his term. The choice of a vice-president in 1944, therefore, was in fact the nomination of the future president. The party would have liked Byrnes, but the unions would have none of him. Roosevelt proposed William O. Douglas, a judge of the Supreme Court, a brilliant, charming man who belonged to the Left in politics; but the South feared Douglas almost as much as it did Wallace. Someone said, "Why not Senator Truman? He has done a very good job on the War Investigating Committee." Truman had no enemies. "Let's go ahead with Truman," decided Roosevelt. But there was one man who had not been consulted—Truman himself. He said, "I am not running." Then, under Roosevelt's urging, he gave way.

It turned out that this was an excellent choice. Truman was a short man with a pleasant face and strong spectacles: he was the son of a Missouri horse dealer, and in the course of his life, he had been a bank clerk, a farmer, an artillery captain in the First World War, a haberdasher, a county supervisor, and a senator. He had passed the greater part of his days in the little town of Independence, Missouri. "I am the poorest of the senators," he said, and no doubt this was true. But he greatly underestimated his abilities. He was a great reader of history, and he had devoured the lives of statesmen and generals. His heroes were Lee, Jackson, the Bonaparte of Arcola, and the great men of antiquity. His other delight was the piano. He played Mozart, Beethoven, Chopin. He had come to Washington a shy provincial, walking on tiptoe. Little by little, he had acquired authority. His senatorial committee had saved $1,500,000,000. Under another chairman it might have become a political tool. Truman quickly won the reputation of being objective and impartial. In him, Roosevelt had an effective fellow candidate.

At the beginning of the campaign, the Republicans were very hopeful: the President seemed to be at the end of his strength. Toward the end of it, he became uneasy at the sight of Dewey winning so much ground, and he made a supreme effort. New York saw this very sick and exhausted man traversing the whole city under the pelting rain in an open car. He won hands down: 432 electoral votes to 99.

In February, 1945, Roosevelt, Churchill, and Stalin met in conference at Yalta. The question was, on the one hand, to draft a plan for a worldwide organization, the United Nations (and on this point Roosevelt, taught by Wilson's misfortunes, did nothing without the approbation of Congress), and on the other, the still more important preparation of the peace. What was to be done with Germany and Japan? How might peaceful cooperation between Soviet Russia and the western democracies be possible? At Yalta, Roosevelt had the look of a terribly shaken man. He might have been a ghost, sitting there wrapped in his cloak, with his ravaged face gray and bloodless. And yet there the President was to make decisions that were to shape the post-war world. Both he and Secretary of State E. R. Stettinius declared they were sure that in the new world there would no longer be spheres of influence or a balance of power. They weakened on the question of Berlin—a question whose importance Roosevelt had understood when he was at Teheran. But the sick Roosevelt was no more than a shadow of his former self. The clearer-minded Churchill wrote, "At the present time, I think the end of this war may well prove to be more disappointing than the last."

The Three came to an agreement upon the occupation of Germany (with France taking her share), upon the trial of war criminals, and upon limited reparations that would not wreck the German economy. Free elections were to decide the fate of the eastern European countries. Roosevelt, and Churchill with him, was strongly critized for having granted useless concessions to Stalin at Yalta, both in the Balkans and in China. In fact, what was called "the tragedy of Yalta" resided less in the letter of the agreements than in the manner of their execution. "I come from the Crimea Conference," said Roosevelt (quoted by Dulles), "with the firm belief that we have made a good start on the road to a world of peace." Later Churchill tried to excuse the risks taken at Yalta: "Our hopeful assumptions were soon to be falsified. Still, they were the only ones possible at the time."

Why the only possible ones? Because the combined chiefs of staff (United States and Great Britain) recommended obtaining massive support from Russia for the final campaign against

Japan. Other advisers, particularly Admiral Leahy, maintained that no campaign was necessary, since Japan was already beaten. The aerial and naval blockade was enough to bring about her surrender. Furthermore, there was the atom bomb that would be ready in 1945; but the chiefs of staff could not reckon upon a weapon that did not yet exist. They urged the necessity of an amphibious operation directed against the territory of Japan itself. MacArthur asked for the support of Russia. It was Admiral Leahy who was right, and we now know that Japan could not have held out, even without the bomb. But upon a vitally important question of strategy, neither Churchill nor Roosevelt would go against the opinion of their technical advisers. Huge concessions were made to Stalin at the expense of China. After Yalta, Churchill continually increased his warnings on the subject of the European frontiers; but he no longer had his wonted partner at Washington. Roosevelt, literally in a dying state, had been obliged to go and rest at Warm Springs. He died there suddenly, on April 12, 1945, of a cerebral hemorrhage. "My Führer," said Goebbels to Hitler, "I congratulate you. Roosevelt is dead." He was in an ecstasy; he believed that the wheel of fate was going to turn.

Truman was called to the White House, where he found Eleanor Roosevelt, brave and dignified. "What can I do to help you?" he asked her—words typical of a citizen of Independence, that is to say, of a little town where neighbors help one another in hard times. And yet it was rather Truman, it seemed, who was in great need of help. The next day he admitted this to newspapermen. "I don't know whether you have ever had a hay bale or a bull fall on your head," he said to them. "Yesterday evening, the moon, the stars, and all the planets fell on me. If ever you pray, pray for me." The first feeling in the country, even among Roosevelt's opponents, was consternation. For these last twelve years, everybody had been used to seeing this great aristocratic-looking Democrat at the head of affairs. On the day of Roosevelt's death, the present writer was in Kansas City. Many people wept. In Missouri, the only feelings for Truman were liking and esteem, but men said "Poor Harry" and sighed.

They thought him inexperienced: they were mistaken. Harry Truman, a man of character, was to show himself an energetic and able president. The new President gladly kept on Admiral

Leahy, the chief of Roosevelt's personal staff, and the admiral said of him, "I soon found out that he had an astonishing knowledge of history. He was very good at discussing a military situation on the map." Nevertheless, he accepted the advice of Marshall and Eisenhower in favor of an attack upon the Bavarian redoubt, which was nothing but an illusion. On April 15, the Russian Marshal Grigori K. Zhukov crossed the Oder: a week later, he was in Berlin. Then the Russian and American troops met on the Elbe, at Torgau. When at last Eisenhower decided to send Patton to Prague, the Russians protested so vigorously that Eisenhower was ordered to let them occupy Czechoslovakia. Stalin exulted. Churchill protested, speaking of the "great failure . . . utter breakdown of what was settled at Yalta."

On April 28, the Italian partisans captured Mussolini (who had been rescued and carried off by German parachutists in September, 1943, and who had set up a Fascist government near Lake Como), shot him, and hung him up by the feet.

The bloody melodrama of Hitlerism ended like a Shakespearian tragedy. Hitler had decided to remain in the Chancellery, surrounded by quack doctors, astrologers, and his last faithful followers. He lived in a bunker under the splendid gold and marble palace that he had built and that had fallen about his ears. He peered at the enormous maps and sent out furious orders to armies that no longer existed. Haggard, drugged, and hysterical, he had become "a shivering specter." He accused Goering and Himmler of high treason. In his last moments, Hitler married Eva Braun in his underground shelter in Berlin. On April 29, he at last acknowledged that all was lost, and he made his will: "To escape the shame of surrendering, I and my wife choose death. . . ." He appointed Admiral Doenitz as his political heir. On April 30, he blew out his brains and the obedient Frau Hitler poisoned herself. Gasoline was poured over their bodies and they were both cremated in the courtyard of the Chancellery. Goebbels, Magda Goebbels, and their six children followed the Führer in death. On May 1, Admiral Doenitz gave the news on the Hamburg radio: then an orchestra played the "Twilight of the Gods."

On May 7, the last German forces agreed to unconditional surrender. Hostilities ceased on May 8, at midnight. Noisy crowds gave vent to their joy in all the Allied capitals. In America, everybody sang and wept: complete strangers kissed one another. The clear-sighted and despondent Churchill, on the other hand, felt the icy shiver of tragedy: "I moved amid cheering crowds or sat at a table adorned with congratulations and blessings from every part of the Grand Alliance, with an aching heart and a mind oppressed by forebodings."

Churchill would rather have had a clear-cut military frontier preserved between the Western allies and the Russians until exact agreements had been reached with the USSR. A lasting friendship must be based upon reciprocal undertakings. The atomic bomb was almost ready, and its makers announced that its destructive power would be unimaginably great. Militarily, therefore, there was no longer any need for Russian support against Japan. But Truman and his advisors wanted to settle all questions with Russia by negotiation rather than by force.

On July 16, 1945, in the desert near Alamogordo, New Mexico, the experimental bomb exploded, with a light more brilliant than the sun and a long roll of thunder. An enormous mushroom-headed column rose into the sky. It towered 41,000 feet. The scientists who were watching the experiment, with their backs turned to the explosion, danced for joy for a moment; but as one of them, Robert Oppenheimer says, "At that moment there flashed into my mind a passage from the Baghavad Gita: *I am become Death, the Shatterer of Worlds.*"

William Lawrence, of the *New York Times,* was there, and he quoted a singular entry in the Goncourts' *Journal:* "April 7, 1869. Dinner at Magny's. Somebody said Berthelot had foretold that in a hundred years man would know what the atom was, and that with that knowledge he would be able to put out the sun like a Carcel lamp, re-light it and turn it up or down as he chose. . . . We made no sort of objection to this, but we are very much of the opinion that when science reaches that point, the good, old-fashioned, white-bearded God will come down to earth with His bunch of keys and say to mankind, 'Closing time, gentlemen.'"

XI

After Pearl Harbor, the war in the Pacific had at first been a series of victories for the Japanese. In six months, they had conquered the Philippines, Malaya, and Hong Kong, sunk two of the finest British capital ships, and forced Singapore to surrender; then, seizing upon all the islands of the south Pacific, they had turned that ocean into an apparently impregnable fortress. In the conquered countries, they found the oil, the rubber, and the metals that they lacked at home. At the height of their career, they had an empire of a hundred and twenty million inhabitants. These people saw their former European masters prisoners in concentration camps, and the sight caused a profound alteration in their state of mind. Whether the Japanese victory were to last or not, European rule in Asia was over. Japan had achieved these extraordinary results with trifling losses —something in the neighborhood of fifteen thousand killed. Their tactics were always the same: the use of islands near the objective as aircraft carriers, attack upon the airfields, then landings from the sea. In the jungle, the Japanese soldier's ability to put up with very little food and the simplicity of his transport easily overcame the English trucks and tanks. He was often helped by a fifth column. The victory was above all that of a country that had made itself ready for war and had an immense material superiority.

But here, as in Europe, the awakening of the United States could be terrible, and its vast industrial power decisive. As Roosevelt had very rightly given the European victory priority, operations in the Pacific were for a long time on a lesser scale; but as early as 1942, the battles of the Coral Sea and of Midway gave America back her naval superiority. From that time onward, the final result was not in doubt. The Americans advanced from island to island toward Japan. It was a strange war, conducted by aircraft carriers and the cloud of little protective vessels all around them. The great armored fleets rarely came into contact, although there were major actions between surface units in the night battles off Savo Island and at Surigao Strait, to mention two of the most dramatic.

In China, the Allies tried to open a line of communication through Burma that would allow them to carry supplies to General Stilwell's divisions. Here there were two opposing factions in direct conflict. General Joseph Stilwell, who was much embittered by the priority given to the European theater, placed his trust in the Chinese Communists, who, in his opinion, fought better against the Japanese. General Claire Chennault, on the other hand, who commanded the Fourteenth Air Force, was in favor of Chiang Kai-shek and his Kuomintang. Roosevelt was exasperated by these quarrels among the generals. He told Marshall that Stilwell hated Chiang, that he sent sarcastic cables about the Chinese, and that the Chinese knew it. General Marshall acknowledged that Stilwell was unwise, but he stood up for him. By a strange kind of musical chairs, Marshall, a moderate, supported Stilwell, who was in favor of the Communists, while Hopkins, in the front row of the progressives, supported the reactionary Kuomintang out of friendship for the Soong family, to which Madame Chiang belonged. From as early as 1944, it could be foreseen that China would get free from the Japanese, but that the country would then be torn apart between the Nationalists and the Communists.

In February, 1945, Manila was retaken. In February, the Marines invaded the island of Iwo Jima, and then in April, that of Okinawa, in spite of a fanatical resistance in which the Japanese lost 3,500 airplanes in suicidal attacks (Kamikaze) upon American ships. The final scenes of the victory at Okinawa were extraordinary. Two Japanese generals, in full uniform, committed hara-kiri in obedience to the code of the samurai. Many officers followed this example, some jumping off cliffs, others blowing themselves up with grenades. Their heroism was beyond argument: their cause was totally lost. Strategic bombing of Japan and the tightening of the blockade had made surrender inevitable. There was a reasonable body of opinion, supported by the Japanese navy and the Emperor, that longed for the war to end. The army still stood out against peace. The Americans were sure of winning, but knowing the desperate courage of the Japanese, the Pentagon still spoke of at least another year of war and of losses as high as half a million American soldiers and sailors. Clearly, there was the atomic bomb; but it was only at Potsdam, where he had gone to confer with Stalin and Clement R. Attlee (the new British prime minister, who had taken Churchill's place after a general election disastrous to the Conservatives), that Truman learned the decisive experiment had succeeded.

Up to the very moment of becoming president, Truman had been utterly ignorant of the atomic project. As chairman of the investigating committee, he had often asked where so many millions of dollars were going, but Roosevelt himself had asked him not to open any inquiry upon that subject, for reasons of national security. As soon as Truman was president, Stimson, the secretary of war, told him of the situation and advised him to set up a committee of scientists to decide whether, with Germany beaten, the bomb should be used, and if so, where and when. "The United States alone," said Stimson, "will be in possession of the secret at the beginning; but the secret cannot be kept. The world will be at the mercy of such weapons, unless an international organization makes of them, on the contrary, an instrument for peace." Truman appointed the most famous scientists to this advisory committee, and General Leslie R. Groves, the director of the atomic project, was also a member, together with General Marshall. The committee unanimously recommended the use of the bomb against Japan. Nevertheless, other scientists, who had worked on the project, but who did not belong to the committee, would have preferred a straightforward technical demonstration to serve as a warning, followed by a ban on its use, since they foresaw the dangers of the future.

At Potsdam, Truman learned of the success at Alamogordo. "This will put an end to war," Marshall said. Truman casually told Stalin that the United States now possessed a new weapon of terrifying destructive power, a bomb twenty thousand times more powerful than any hitherto known. Stalin displayed polite interest, but nothing more. It was later to be discovered that he had known all about the project long before Truman. Truman had no hesitation on ordering the use of the bomb. In his opinion, using it meant the saving of a million human lives, counting the one side and the other. Roosevelt himself had never varied on this point. He was building the bomb to win the war: to win the war he would use it.

On August 6, a B29 bomber dropped the first atomic bomb on Hiroshima. To the duty officer who brought him the message,

Truman said, "This is the greatest thing in history." The effects were terrible. It killed almost a hundred thousand people, some at the moment of the explosion, others after long and horrible suffering. Yet the Japanese army did not yield. Russia hastened to declare war on Japan. Truman was then going back to America aboard the cruiser *Augusta*. On August 9, the second bomb was dropped on Nagasaki. On August 10, the Emperor insisted upon peace. Truman had promised to give back the Japanese nation its freedom. The war was over. It left behind it ruins, corpses, and for the future, the threat of gigantic forces that the human spirit might perhaps be incapable of controlling. Perhaps God, as Goncourt had thought, was already saying, "Closing time."

In front of the White House, a huge crowd shouted, "We want Harry! We want Harry!" He came out on to the lawn. "This is a great day," he said, "it is the day we have all been waiting for; but we have a great task before us." In New York, the sirens filled the city with an enormous din. A flood of paper fell from every window. On Fifth Avenue, on Broadway, the crowds were dancing.

Two years later, on the second anniversary of VJ Day, someone asked the President whether he were not sorry that he had given the order to destroy Hiroshima. "No," he answered, thoughtfully. "doing it horrified me. But I certainly saved half a million men by doing so. It had to be done." Faithful to his local patriotism, he appointed the battleship named after his native state, the *Missouri*, as the place at which the surrender should occur in the bay of Tokyo. That evening he spoke to the American people on the radio. "Liberty," he said, "does not make men perfect; it does not shelter people from all danger. But it has provided the nations with more of progress, happiness, and decent living than the other philosophies in history. Today has just shown that it can also produce more power and strength than mankind has ever possessed." This was the heartfelt philosophy of a citizen of Independence, Missouri. How much influence was it going to have in a new and different world?

PART EIGHT

The Truman Era

THE Truman era—a commonly used expression; and it is a fitting and a discreet tribute to that Harry Truman who, having commanded a battery of artillery in 1918 and having run a not very prosperous haberdasher's shop, suddenly found himself burdened with the world's most important affairs. It means that, unpretentiously, but not without strength, Truman left his own personal mark upon some years of history. He was no Roosevelt who, like Moses, led his people through the desert of the depression and the trials of the war toward an awareness of their social and international responsibilities. Truman's ambi tion was rather to be a Joshua, the faithful lieutenant who, after the prophet's meeting with his God and the proclamation of the Tables of the Law, undertook the application of them. The war was won, the social legislation passed, the Promised Land in sight. He had the right to hope for a presidency during which a lasting peace would reward the American people for the sacrifices they had made.

It is said that the morning after VJ Day, the President changed the little gun that stood on his desk for a miniature plow. He liked artless symbols of this kind. In Independence, it was the simple virtues that counted—honesty, straightforwardness, family affection. He loved accompanying his daughter Margaret, the singer, on the piano, and writing to his ninety-two-year-old mother. The comradeship of the Senate pleased him; so did the feeling that there he had the right to look the most powerful man in the eye, since no one could reproach him with the wrongful gaining of a single dollar. In his heart of hearts, he would have liked to see all the nations of the earth adopt the moral standards of Independence, Missouri. But the nations of the earth possessed neither his common sense nor his humility, and for eight years, he was to learn the ways of a very rough calling. As he says himself, in his *Memoirs,* the vice-presidency had hardly prepared him for it at all. During the year that preceded Roosevelt's death, he had scarcely seen him eight times. But he did hold one trump card—his knowledge of history. He knew how Lincoln before him had dealt with difficult demagogue generals. He knew that all nations sometimes have their fits of hysteria. He had read of the Salem witches and the Ku Klux Klan. He was well acquainted with the life of Andrew Johnson who, like himself, woke up to find that he was the successor of a great president. "History taught me that the leader of any country, in order to assume his responsibilities as a leader, must know the history, not only of his own country, but of all the great countries."

His countrymen, astonished at seeing Truman in Roosevelt's seat, thought of him at first as an average American and nothing more. This was a serious mistake. An "average man" would not have possessed his personality, or his wide reading, or his courage. He began by keeping Roosevelt's favorite advisers, but later he did not hesitate to discard those who, like Byrnes,

Wallace, and MacArthur, tried to oblige him to follow a policy of which he disapproved: on the other hand, when he thought men (Marshall, Clifford, Acheson, and Kennan, for example) good judges of the situation, he accepted their advice. They supplied plans of action: the merit of applying them, in the face of violent opposition, belongs to him alone. The Truman era: yes, the phrase is just, for it was he who guided world events that, without him, would have taken a very different and even more dangerous turning.

I

The victory awoke the glorious but disturbing memories of 1919. More than ever, the shade of Wilson hung over the White House. After the First World War, the country had been sunk under a wave of reaction and intolerance; Harding succeeded Wilson; the liberal intellectuals were harassed; the Senate and the country rejected the League of Nations. Truman himself believed in the necessity for an international organization. Not all Americans agreed with him: Senator Taft and part of the Middle West still maintained that "foreign policy was something you had, like measles, and got over with as quickly as possible." The Senate had been very much struck by the memorable conversion of the Republican Senator Arthur H. Vandenberg. For a long while, he had been a fierce isolationist, but being in London in 1944, he had found himself at the receiving end of the German V2 rockets. He had come to understand that with such weapons, and with those of longer range that would inevitably come after them, the policy of isolation became that of suicide. In 1945, he made his public confession before a Senate struck dumb with astonishment: "I have always been frankly one of those who has believed in our own self-reliance . . . . But I do not believe that any nation hereafter can immunize itself by its own exclusive action . . . . I want a new dignity and a new authority for international law." He was applauded by both parties. Public opinion followed Vandenberg, whom Truman appointed one of the members of the American delegation to the San Francisco Conference that framed the charter of the United Nations.

This charter was not adopted without difficulties. The Western Allies were in disagreement with Russia on the subject of Poland. The United States, like the USSR, wished to see that country ruled by a government "friendly" to Russia; but with a sad and pensive air Roosevelt had said to Churchill, "The Russians do not use words for the same purposes that we do." What exactly was the meaning of "friendly"? Hopkins was sent to Moscow to find a way out of this blind alley and, at the same time, to solve another difficulty with Stalin, one that was holding up the whole of the San Francisco Conference. The new United Nations had been conceived on the same lines as the old League: a security council with the great powers as permanent members and the other countries sitting in rotation; the right of veto for the great powers; an assembly with equal representation for each of the member nations. But in principle the veto was to be applied to all decisions except procedural ones. The Russians wanted the veto to apply to every decision. The conference had almost been wrecked upon this point. Stalin, seeing that the United Nations was going to come into existence in any case, chose rather to join the organization and have influence in it. When Hopkins raised the question of the veto at Moscow, Stalin observed in an offhand manner that "it was an insignificant matter and that they should accept the American position," which strengthened Hopkins in his feeling that it was possible to come to an understanding with the Russians, after all. The charter of the United Nations was therefore signed on June 26, 1945. Henceforward, the United States was irrevocably a member of the concert of nations, for better or for worse.

What was going to be the nature of the relations between the USSR and the West? During the war, Roosevelt had unreservedly cooperated with Russia. He had never doubted but that after the victory she would remain among the democratic nations and on their side. Even the conservative Americans had accepted an alliance that helped to win the war more quickly. In 1945, Truman had his first conversation with Averell Harriman, the American ambassador in Moscow, upon the policy of the USSR. Harriman told the President that the Russians thought they could carry on two policies at the same time. The one was cooperation with the West, the other the extension of Russian control over the neighboring countries. A great many of Stalin's associates took any act of generosity on the part of the United States as a mark of weakness and thought that America could be defied without danger. Truman replied, "I would be fair, of course, and anyway the Russians needed us more than we needed them." Harriman thought it possible to find ground upon which they could agree, but it was essential to give up all illusions about the possibility of the Russians' adopting a foreign policy similar to that of the Western world. Their principles required them to use all means of setting up communism wherever they did not come up against dangerous resistance. In short, according to Harriman, it was one of those cases in which it was necessary to display strength if one wished to avoid having to use it.

The Americans had accepted the United Nations in the vague expectation of universal good fellowship. But what did they see? The United Nations began with quarrels, resounding exits, vetoes. In Europe, the war criminals were being judged at Nuremberg without observation of the traditional, healthy rules of Anglo-Saxon justice: no retroactive laws, no military tribunals for civil crimes, no punishment of soldiers who have obeyed an order. The American people had just given nearly $3,000,000,000 worth of food and other products to UNRRA (United Nations Relief and Rehabilitation Administration) to help the wretchedness of the war-ravaged nations, as well as $5,000,000,000 through other channels. With the Russians, Truman had tried to apply the method that he had found so successful in his political career —that of compromise. "There are many issues that cannot be solved by the surrender of either side, but only through a reasonable compromise which does not sacrifice principles." Yet every time, he was faced with a fait accompli. Without consulting the West, Stalin shaped the governments of Romania, Bulgaria, and Hungary to his liking. For all that, the new secretary of state, Byrnes, persevered in seeking cooperation with the USSR. Roosevelt had imbued him with the idea that agreement of this kind would be the cornerstone of the peace. But as the Americans saw it, agreement implied friendship and respect for settlements. Now international life after the war was nothing but a series of conflicts.

Soon Truman was in complete disagreement on this point with Byrnes. "I am tired of babying the Soviets," he wrote to him. Indeed, the Secretary of State's position was far from an easy one. To speak from a strong position he should, of course, have had strength. But once again public opinion had insisted upon hasty demobilization. The great mass of Americans had no idea that Stalin and Truman were very seriously at cross purposes. They had been taught to consider Uncle Joe as a benevolent sage with a big mustache, an ardent supporter of the United Nations. *"One* world or no world at all," Wendell Willkie had told them again and again during his campaign. They sincerely wanted *one* world, and they would not see that there were two. Everything combined to close their eyes to this ambivalent situation—prosperity, the veterans' happiness in finding their homes, families, and jobs again, and the memory of Roosevelt's speeches.

The first loud, clear warning came from Winston Churchill. The old warrior was no longer prime minister, and hence he had his freedom of speech. There was a college (Westminster College) in the little town of Fulton, Missouri, that had an endowment that allowed it to invite a world-famous speaker. The president of the college offered Churchill a doctorate. Truman backed the invitation and came to Fulton with Churchill. Churchill reminded his listeners that years ago he had foretold the Second World War—so easy to foresee and to prevent—and that no one had paid attention to him. Now, once again, he wanted to warn his friends: "From Stettin in the Baltic to Trieste in the Adriatic an iron curtain has descended across the continent. . . . I do not believe that Soviet Russia desires war. What they desire is the fruits of war and the indefinite expansion of their power and doctrines. . . . From what I have seen of our Russian friends and allies during the war, I am convinced that there is nothing they admire so much as strength, and there is nothing for which they have less respect than for weakness, especially military weakness." He was cheered: the American people love heroes. But once more his warning remained unheeded. The press and the public took up the picturesque *iron curtain:* policy was in no way altered.

In the Far East, Truman possessed the means for taking a firmer stand. America was alone in Japan and essentially had the power to make all decisions. She had every intention of remaining alone. Yet the Russians had profited by their short week of war to get control temporarily of Manchuria and to impose a government of their choice in Korea north of the thirty-eighth parallel.

Another source of friction during this period of ambivalence toward the USSR was the control of atomic energy. The United States, Canada, and England, which were the only countries then in possession of the technology of making atomic weapons, proposed the creation of a United Nations atomic commission. An international High Authority would control the uranium and thorium mines and the factories, as well as research in the atomic field. The United States would turn over to it its entire arsenal of atomic weapons. This High Authority would have the right, not subject to the veto, of ordering sanctions against any state that disobeyed its orders. The Russians answered that the High Authority would in fact be dominated by the United States and its friends, which was true enough. Their counter-proposition was that the making of atomic bombs should be outlawed and that the Security Council (in which they had the veto) should be given the power to punish any contravention. The United States then objected that the veto would do away with all real forms of control. And so vanished all hope of seeing the nightmare of atomic war disappear. The MacMahon Act of 1946 forbade the communication of any information upon atomic research—a measure that was to condemn England and France to enormous and unnecessary expense.

Some thought Byrnes too soft: others thought his approach was not conciliating enough. Among the most zealous of these was Henry Wallace, the secretary of commerce, a former vice-president. In one speech, he accused Byrnes of refusing to offer the USSR compromises that they could accept. "I recognize," said he, "that the danger of war is much less from communism than from imperialism." This raised a great storm. The Secretary of State, who was then carrying on negotiations in Paris, sent the President a teletyped message, offering his resignation if Wallace were not at once ordered to cease all criticism of his own government's foreign policy. Senator Vandenberg, the key-stone of bipartisan foreign policy, said to the journalists, "We can only cooperate with one secretary of state at a time." A week later, Wallace was asked to resign. Was this the end of the period of ambivalence?

II

It was widely held that the transition from a war economy to one of peace could not be made without a serious depression. This had happened after the First World War; and the United States had been even more deeply disturbed and for a longer time by the second. Would a capitalist economy be able to withstand the trial? Stalin expected a crisis in America similar to that of 1929. "It was clear," says Truman in his memoirs, "that his foreign policy was based upon this expectation." Stalin supposed that by delaying settlements he would have a weakened America before him, incapable of helping her allies and ready to make all manner of concessions. This was not bad reasoning. If a major depression had followed the war, it is possible that the Americans might, out of discouragement and bitterness, have turned back to isolationism. But instead of a crisis, the United States was to experience an unprecedented prosperity.

In 1933, the national income was 39.6 billion dollars: by 1940, it had risen to 81.3 billion dollars. It reached 182.8 billion in 1945. There was no unemployment, and savings were abundant. It might have been supposed that the sudden cancellation of war contracts would be a terrible blow to production. But no, everything passed off very well. The needs of the private citizen had been very meagerly served for the last five years, and now that the war was over they were quite capable of absorbing more than the country could produce. Instead of crisis, the threat was rather that of inflation. The people were well off, and they competed for nonexistent goods. There was a shortage of housing and cars, and soon even meat was scarce. Prices rocketed. But the prosperity went on. From 1946 to 1953, during the Truman era, the population increased by 21 percent, the national income by 37 percent, and personal incomes, after payment of taxes, by 20 percent. It had been said, with great anxiety, "Sixty million jobs will be needed after the war." Sixty-two million were available. In spite of the inflation, the people's buying power increased.

It has already been said that the demobilization was too rapid. But how was it possible to resist the pressure of the soldiers and their families, and of the workers whom the war factories had taken far from their homes? The soldiers were tired of military life and the workers of canteens and dormitories, and both rushed back to their houses, their farms, their spouses, and their children. There were positive riots in the army in 1946, when attempts were made to slow down the rate of release. As early as the summer of that year, the huge wartime "armadas" had been reduced to peacetime strength. This hastiness created great dangers in foreign policy. It might also have been supposed that it would do the same for the country's economy, by suddenly throwing ten million men into the labor market. But earlier on, a most prudent law had been passed, a law the public called the GI Bill of Rights. It provided for a great deal of help in many forms for the ex-servicemen: scholarships to prepare for a profession or a trade; four years at a university, with books free; grants of money for those who could not find work; employment agencies; loans for the purchase of houses, businesses, or farms. In short, huge funds to tide over the transition.

The tens of billions of dollars thus spent were the best possible investment for the nation. Good minds that in ordinary times might have been wasted received the education they deserved. There was a feeling that justice had been done, and this appealed to thousands of men who up until then had supposed that the university was a luxury for the rich. The present writer was at that time teaching in an American university. The veterans easily held the lead in all the classes. One of them wrote to him, "It was the army that gave me the only worthwhile education—learning to rely on nobody but myself. Before that I lived in a fictitious world. I loved sentimentality. Now I have moved from the world of words to the world of deeds. It was battle, and not the blackboard, that taught me that the solution of a geometrical problem decided whether I was to come under murderous shellfire or not . . . . It was contact with reality that taught me the difference between a fine book, such as *War and Peace,* and the stupidity of some nondescript piece of propaganda." Another wrote, "The war gave me the opportunity of seeing many different nations in every climate under the sun. I shall never be an isolationist again. I am too well aware how everything in the world links up with everything else."

These men and women came back from the war more devoted to equality than they had been before. Some had suffered from what they called the caste system when they were in the army. One sergeant told how the officers had built a club, in one of the Pacific islands, and had surrounded it with notices "Restricted Area. Officers only"; the enlisted men built a bigger, better club, and wrote on the lane leading to it, "Restricted. Enlisted men only." No one would go back to "underprivileged" jobs. Neither industry nor farming found it easy to recruit laborers. The Truman era was a time of great hopes and of happy dreams. It was thought that the recently discovered antibiotics were going to overcome even the worst diseases. It was foretold that presently new sources of energy would allow men to work shorter hours but nevertheless receive higher pay. This was the time at which Fred Vinson, the director of reconversion, said, "The Americans are in the difficult—and agreeable—position of having to learn how to live half as well again as they have ever lived before." People had not begotten many babies during the great depression: prosperity and the return of the soldiers suddenly set up a new record in this field.

The reconversion of industry, however, raised many difficult problems. As early as VJ Day, Truman had set up a program: the cancellation of war contracts as soon as possible; the freezing of prices and rents until competition should operate again, in order to prevent inflation; the maintenance of wages at their current level, for the same reasons; the retention of wartime controls on production only to the extent necessary to prevent bottlenecks and the cornering of raw materials; and the provision of full employment. It was a reasonable program; but reason is not the prime mover among mankind, and each blamed that part of the program that inconvenienced him. The unions would have liked prices to be frozen while wages were left free. "During the war," they said, "the workers did in fact work overtime. If we are to return to the forty-hour week, with the same pay, our purchasing power will drop." The employers, for their part, maintained that business conditions did not allow them to increase wages and proved that this was so by impressive statistics, to which the unions replied with more statistics, equally impressive.

Truman, torn between the New Dealers in his Cabinet on

the one hand and by some of the conservatives in his party on the other, wavered first this way and then the other. One day, he told livestock dealers that he would maintain price controls on meat; three weeks later, he took them off. The fact of the matter was that $48,000,000,000 of savings and a reduction of $6,000,000,000 in taxes was giving all classes of the population an enormous purchasing power just at a time when there was not much to buy. As for the President, his opponents claimed that he was behaving neither like a real believer in the New Deal nor as an adversary of it, but rather like a man who yields to the strongest pressure at each successive moment. Hence a flood of criticism. "To err is Truman," they said: or, as one might put it, *"Errare Trumanum est."*

In 1946, there began a time of strikes. Some were of no importance, but the long-drawn-out strike of miners made the government uneasy. It appeared to be dangerous, not only for the country, whose factories it might bring to a halt, but for Europe, to whom America had promised coal. The question of pay was complicated by questions of prestige. It was rumored that the former friends of John L. Lewis, of the miners, and Philip Murray, of the CIO, had quarreled, and that if one of them gained a concession the other at once had to get something better. The soft-spoken Murray, a gentle Scot, owed his authority to reason: John L. Lewis, who had the face of a Danton, fascinated the mineowners by his romantic eloquence. "Lewis," said one of these big employers, "speaks an English worthy of Winston Churchill." During the pauses between sessions, he would go to the window, gaze at the trees and the flowers, and improvise a couplet upon spring, scattered with quotations from Shakespeare. Both sides were in agreement upon the most important point, the setting up of a fund to look after the miners' health and security. But Lewis wanted to be the sole administrator of the fund; whereas the employers thought that they too should have a say in its management.

With the midterm election of 1946 in view, Truman maneuvered carefully. He needed the unions. His friends in Independence, Missouri, pitied him: "Poor Harry. He is having a very difficult presidency." Yet in the middle of the strike, he arrived in his airplane "The Sacred Cow" to greet his old mother on Mother's Day. He could understand and direct the most important affairs of the nation, but for all that he remained a small-town man at heart. "Being president is only a beginning for him," said one of his friends. "His real ambition is to be governor of Missouri." An opponent replied, "Under him, Pennsylvania Avenue has turned into Main Street."

But Main Street's intelligence is not to be despised. When in their turn the railways threatened to go on strike, Truman reacted strongly. He requisitioned both mines and railways, and he was in the act of delivering an almost violent message to Congress when he was handed a paper. The strike was over: he had won. It was a bitter victory, and it left rancor behind it. The Americans had accepted compulsory military service but only with great reluctance, and the use of its harsh discipline to prevent a strike seemed to them unconstitutional. On the other hand, the distraction in the railroad stations at the mere announcement of the possibility of a strike proved how right the President had been in dreading an interruption of a public service in this vast country.

Public opinion was turning against him. It objected to Truman's optimism, to what it unfairly termed his platitudes, and even to his filial affection. People said with a sneer, "Every day is Mothers' Day at the White House." The Republicans invented a most successful slogan for the 1946 campaign, the campaign for the election of the Eightieth Congress: "Had enough?" Have you had enough of strikes, of Cabinet officers who contradict one another, of ambivalent policy, of inflation, of expensive living, of atomic bombs? The public opinion institutes, which are no more infallible than weather bureaus but which are reasonably exact in showing a general tendency, had shown 87 percent of Americans as favorable to Truman at the time of his honeymoon with the nation—a record figure. A little before the 1946 Congressional election, the percentage had dropped to 35 percent. To the question "Had enough?" the electors replied, "Yes, we have had enough," and they sent a Republican Congress to Washington. Senator Taft was going to have his hour, unless . . .

III

Unless everything changed. In politics it is almost always forgotten that situations evolve by themselves. Very soon meat became plentiful once more; the housewives calmed down; the strikes stopped because the union leaders felt them to be unpopular. The great body of the citizens were living better than they had before the war, and they knew it. "The American Meat Institute issued the most revealing figures. Before the war, housewives had turned to macaroni, egg, and cheese mixtures, or some other inexpensive dish for half the family meals; in 1947, the average American ate meat five out of seven nights a week." And it was not only the standard of living that was getting better. The average American's dignity and feeling of equality were also increasing. The workers had won solid gains. Truman had caused a very important law to be passed in 1946, the Full Employment Act, under the provisions of which the country was to be divided into economic regions. If, in any of these regions, there was a threat of unemployment, the government would deal with the situation by grants or by undertaking public works. In other words, the government would set about a true planning of the economy. It would not dictate production plans to industry; but, knowing the estimates of private enterprise, it would supplement them with a program designed to maintain full employment. It would be the duty of a Council of Economic Advisers, which the act set up in the executive branch, to tell the President of any signs of weakness in the economy and to suggest means of dealing with them. The Act created also, within the Congress, a Joint Committee on the Economic Report that was to analyze the data contained in the annual report of the council and to initiate legislation on the basis of recommendations by the President.

Equally important was the contract between General Motors, the great car manufacturers, and the United Auto Workers Union. For the first time, a sliding scale of prices and wages was established, with automatic revision every three months, so as to maintain purchasing power. Furthermore, an annual increase in real wages was to take into account increased production: there were also clauses dealing with social security—pensions, medical insurance, and life insurance arranged by the automobile industry. The workers' status was getting better. Strikes were less frequent.

But the Eightieth Congress, with its Republican majority, had come to Washington with the conservatives, so long defeated by the New Deal, thirsty for revenge. These fifteen years past, they had felt a homesick longing for laissez-faire and free enterprise. The war had rendered them powerless. Sadly they had seen a new America, the America of Roosevelt's friends, the intellectuals and the unions, taking on an ever greater importance. Their favorite spokesman was Senator Taft.

The Taft family, which had not long before given the United States a likable and upright president, later chief justice, had for a great while symbolized respectability mingled with culture and a love for tradition in the city of Cincinnati, as the Lodge family had in Boston. Senator Taft, although he had been a brilliant student at Yale and Harvard, refused the label "intellectual" in the disagreeable sense that he attributed to the word. "Basically, Taft amounted to a call for counter-revolution against the half century of revolution." A revolution that had been begun, it may be observed, by the Republican Teddy Roosevelt. Filled with sincerity and an undeniable civic courage, Taft stood up for the old American liberties against all these dubious novelties, these plans, subsidies, and international engagements. In a word, he would have liked to live in 1900, and it was his misfortune to be living in 1946. He was certainly the only man capable of telling the farmers, his electors, that farm prices were too high. "At the height of the furor over meat prices, reporters asked the Senator for his solution, and he replied, "Eat less." It was the purest Taftiana—in its magnificent tactlessness and its bedrock assumption that a real American solved his own problems.

The great aim of Taftism (and of the Eightieth Congress, which was hostile to Truman) was to reestablish the balance between management and workers in the industrial world by restraining "the unions' excesses." In 1946, Truman himself had approved a law that forbade "featherbedding," that is to say, bringing pressure to bear on an employer to oblige him to engage more hands than he needed and paying for work not actually performed. In

1947, Congress passed the Taft-Hartley Act that did not undo all the unions' victories, but that did forbid them to insist upon a "closed shop," in which all workers necessarily belonged to a union. It also forbade them to refuse genuine negotiations, and, more widely, it outlawed all "unfair practices." The law allowed employers to sue unions for breach of contract. It provided for "cooling-off periods," or pauses for thought before a strike, and it authorized the President to use the right of injunction if the strike threatened the health of the nation or the security of the state. It forbade the unions to make grants to political parties and compelled them to submit their yearly accounts to the Department of Labor. The great workers' unions at once protested violently against what they called "a slave labor law." Truman vetoed it. Congress passed the law over his veto. The repeal of the Taft-Hartley Act was to be a major political issue for years. Meanwhile, it did not prevent the unions, which still had the right of negotiating collective contracts, from successfully struggling to improve their members' economic position.

The chief reasons for the relative stability of the American economy after the Second World War was in fact the progress that had been made in the redistribution of income and the huge amount of goods and equipment the Cold War military buildup and economic aid to the war-ravaged countries required. The current that had for so long carried purchasing power toward the same class and that had brought about a dangerous concentration of wealth had been reversed. The current in the opposite direction was not yet a very brisk one, but there was no doubt about which way it was flowing. In 1941, 29 percent of American families had an income of less than $500; in 1947, 8.4 percent. In 1941, only 4 percent of families earned between $4,000 and $5,000 a year; in 1947, 12.8 percent. Poverty, alas, had not been wiped out. The pyramid was not breaking down quickly: far from it. But a vast, slow leveling was really taking place. The welfare of all had become the aim, at least the long-term aim, of most. Crises were still possible, but it seemed that there were compensatory mechanisms that allowed them to be dealt with. Even the farmers, well supported by the government, had recovered, if not prosperity, then at least a position of decent steadiness. It may not have been Paradise, but it was certainly no longer Hell.

After the 1946 election, Truman's opponents had said, "This is not an election; it is a rout." They were wrong: it was only a hard knock, and in the course of his jolting career the President had received plenty of them. The artilleryman decided to correct the range. He adroitly gloried in the opposition of Congress. It insisted upon economies and cut taxes: Truman replied that the savings would be made at the expense of social reforms and the national defense. He proposed a program of greater aid for farmers and equality of rights for racial minorities, thus making sure of important blocks of votes for the presidential election of 1948. "He is not a statesman, he is a politician," said one of his opponents. Truman replied, "You had to have a politician to make a statesman." Foreign policy was to give him the opportunity of showing that he was a statesman as well.

IV

As early as 1947, he had made it perfectly clear that he himself was going to deal with all problems. A newspaperman on the *Herald Tribune* wrote, "Harry Truman is becoming President of the United States." At the time of the 1946 election, one of the President's weaknesses had been the uncertainty of his foreign policy. True, he had got rid of Wallace; but that was no more than a negative solution, and public opinion called for positive action. On March 12, 1947, the President himself came to Congress to read a message in which he clearly laid down what was later to be called the Truman Doctrine, although it was really an attitude rather than a doctrine. It was on the subject of a vote of supplies intended to help Greece and Turkey. For a long while, a civil war had been raging in Greece, and this civil war was one aspect of the struggle for influence between East and West. Great Britain had supported the Greek government both militarily and economically but could no longer bear the heavy burden. If democratic institutions, as the West understood the word, were to be saved in those parts, it was the United States alone that could save them. Now Stalin, faithful to the old czar's dreams of controlling the Black Sea straits, was bringing heavy pressure to bear on Turkey, and he was supplying the Greek guerrillas with arms. It was necessary either to give way or to act.

It was a solemn session of Congress, as important, wrote the *New York Times,* as that in which Monroe had said to Europe, "Hands off the Americas." It opened, as usual, by a prayer. The President, in a blue double-breasted suit, came in, shaking hands with his former colleagues as he passed. Then, in a profound silence, he stated his principles. "I believe that it must be the policy of the United States to support free peoples who are resisting attempted subjugation by armed minorities or by outside pressures . . . . I believe that our help should be primarily through economic and financial aid which is essential to economic stability and orderly political processes . . . . The seeds of totalitarian regimes are nurtured by misery and want. They spread and grow in the evil soil of proverty and strife. They reach their full growth when the hope of the people for a better life has died. We must keep that hope alive." In short, the time for support was past; the time for holding in check, for containment, was beginning. There was some opposition, but Vandenberg brought valuable support: and Congress voted four hundred million dollars in aid to Greece and Turkey.

"We have a rendezvous with Fate," Vandenberg said. The expression was not new: the situation was. The veteran Bernard Baruch added, "Let us not be deceived; today we are in the midst of a cold war." The phrase *cold war,* like *iron curtain,* caught on.

The new secretary of state was another source of invaluable support for the President. Truman had replaced Byrnes, with whom he could not agree, by General George C. Marshall, a man truly admirable for his abnegation, his intelligence, and his energy. Truman said of Marshall that he was "the greatest living American." Eisenhower would have endorsed those words. Marshall spoke little, listened attentively, and, if an argument went on too long, would say, "Gentlemen, don't fight the problem, decide it."

Undersecretary of State Dean G. Acheson says that when Marshall took over his new office, he said to him, "I want you to tell me the whole truth, with the utmost frankness, particularly about myself."

Dean Acheson asked, "Really, General?"

263

"Yes," replied Marshall. "I have no personal feelings, apart from a few that I keep for Mrs. Marshall."

In April, 1947, Marshall came back from Moscow convinced that Stalin regarded the misery of Europe as his surest weapon in the cold war. Now sickness and hunger were ravaging a great part of the European continent. There was deep bitterness in France and Italy. Prompt action was urgently called for.

Marshall had set up a Policy Planning Staff, with George F. Kennan, one of the best American diplomats, at the head of it. Kennan was both a student of the philosophy of history and an observer of the present world. He knew Russia well, and as early as 1945 he had felt that Roosevelt and Hopkins were ignoring the realities of the situation. In Kennan's opinion, the Russian tradition was based upon a feeling of insecurity and distrust that arose from the dangers and the difficulties of their past. This being the case, there were three possible policies: to destroy the USSR, which was something that nobody in the United States wanted; to give way all along the line, which would have been suicide; or to limit the expansion of Stalinism by an open-handed policy toward the unfortunate countries. Marshall naturally chose the third, and he set about putting the wealth of the United States at the service of Europe's reconstruction. Speaking at Harvard in June, 1947, he offered to help all the European nations, including the Communist countries, who would agree to collaborate in a common plan: "Our policy is directed not against any country or doctrine, but against hunger, poverty, desperation, and chaos." He asked only that these nations themselves should initiate a plan and work for their own recovery: "The role of this country [the United States] should consist of friendly aid in the drafting of a European program and of later support of such a program in so far as it may be practical for us to do so." In short, help yourself and America will help you.

Stalin refused, both for Russia and for all the countries on the other side of the iron curtain. But the other reactions were very favorable. In England, Ernest Bevin, the foreign secretary, leaped out of bed when he heard the news and cried, "This is the turning point!" Twenty-two days later, in Paris, all the Western nations welcomed the Mashall Plan. The General would have liked it to be called the Marshall-Vandenberg Plan, for he needed the Senator's support in obtaining the enormous sum of $17,000,000,000 from Congress. The plan was opposed on the one hand by the isolationists and the Taft group, who saw in it a New Deal extended to the whole of Europe: not long before they had foretold that things would end by "every Hottentot being given a pint of milk," and now, they said, that point had been reached. On the other hand, Henry Wallace's friends maintained that it was an anti-Soviet plan and that it would breed war, either cold or hot; and they called it the Martial Plan.

At the beginning of 1948, a small Communist minority seized power in Czechoslovakia: this caused a great wave of feeling in Washington, and all opposition to the Marshall Plan vanished. The plan was one of the most generous political acts in history. It was to succeed. Its success was to surpass the expectations of even those who had worked it out, and it led to Europe's complete restoration. Its success was undoubtedly helped by the general respect that surrounded Marshall, as well as by the personality of the administrator of the plan, Paul G. Hoffman, who, like Vandenberg, was a liberal Republican.

V

Harry Truman had gone to the White House in 1945 not because he had been elected president by the American people but because Roosevelt was dead. To stay there after 1948, he had to win an electoral victory and win it alone. Very much alone, indeed. For his party, with the exception of a few particular friends, did not want him as candidate. "You can't win, Harry," they told him. He had against him the right wing of the Democratic party, the Southerners, because he had shown himself favorable to the Negroes, and, more widely, because they thought him too "advanced." At the same time, certain intellectuals, fellow travelers belonging to the left wing of the party, thought that if Henry Wallace founded a "progressive" party he would win ten million votes. The Democratic politicians, the bosses, asserted that with Truman as their candidate the party was heading for such a defeat that it would never recover. Why this withdrawal from Truman? Because a policy of compromise had disappointed the ultras of either extremity; because many thought he had not the caliber to be a president; and lastly because he had "shot at Santa Claus" by vetoing tax reduction.

The Republican convention made his task harder still by choosing as their candidate not Taft, who had many enemies, but (as in 1944) Governor Dewey, who was more neutral and, like Vandenberg, in favor of a generous international policy; furthermore, Dewey himself was quite near to Truman's social ideas. It was Taft's natural and just ambition to be president, and this nomination, as were the 1944 and 1952 ones, was a tragedy for him. He had sacrificed his career to his principles.

The Democratic convention, which came after, searched desperately for a new candidate. There had been talk among Democrats, including Truman himself in the early days of his presidency, of offering the nomination to Eisenhower. But Eisenhower was politically inclined toward the Republicans. Truman's desire for renomination steadily increased; so nothing came of the Eisenhower draft scheme. When the party realized that the President was determined to run in spite of everybody and everything, it had no choice but to nominate him. Wallace then became the candidate of the new Progressive party, while a Southerner, Governor J. Strom Thurmond of South Carolina, formed the States' Rights Democratic party. The Democrats therefore went into battle divided into three separate parts, the official body unenthusiastically backing a candidate they did not believe in. None of them hoped for victory.

None except Harry Truman. Even if he had to fight alone, he was determined to win. The man who came to the tribune to accept the nomination was no longer the regular guy from Missouri who might have been received with head-shaking commiseration. He was a fighter, an acute tactician. One month earlier, Dewey had promised great reforms and had appropriated the Democratic program. Saying in effect, as Willkie had once indicated, that he would do the same things, only better. Truman very adroitly replied that the Republican party had been in a majority in Congress for the last two years, and that it had done nothing whatsoever. "This do-nothing Congress announces that it is ready to do everything. Very well. I am going to take it at its word, and I shall summon it to Washington for July 28 (which we call Turnip Day in Missouri) and I shall propose to it all the laws it is suddenly showing such a surprising fondness for." It was cleverly turned. Congress met; the atmosphere in Washington was stifling; nothing was done by this "do-nothing session of a do-nothing Congress." Truman had won a point.

The great majority of the press was against him. He decided to appeal directly to the electors, and he undertook a round trip of some 31,700 miles. Three hundred and fifty-six whistle stop speeches addressed to twelve million listeners. His vice presidential running mate, Alben W. Barkley, also did yeoman service in stumping many areas. Truman's speeches were delivered in the stations, while the train stopped. The campaign was directed straight at the Eightieth Congress. It had to be violent. Only repeated attacks could stir the country's political apathy. He had said, "I am going to fight hard. I am going to give them hell." The expectation of a good fight always draws crowds. They came to the railroad stations to listen to "Mr. Missouri." He lashed the Eightieth Congress, and then, when his speech was over, presented his wife and his daughter Margaret: "Here is the boss— and the boss's boss." The Republican newspapers, sure of success, since the public opinion polls gave Dewey 60 percent of the votes, said, "These crowds are made up of people who come as curious spectators, not as electors." They compared the wonderful efficiency of the Republican electoral machine, and Dewey's perfect organization, with Truman's homely, amateur way of carrying on.

Yet the people at the stations cried, "Give 'em hell, Harry." And Harry did so with all his heart. He told the crowds that if they let the Republicans get hold of the White House, they would make America a dependency of Wall Street. He told the workers, "The Republicans voted themselves a cut in taxes and voted you a cut in freedom. The Eightieth Republican Congress failed to crack down on prices. But it cracked down on labor all right." He told the farmers that the Eightieth Congress had given them "a pitchfork in the back," and that a Republican government would abandon the support of farm prices, in order to make economies. To the Negroes, he spoke of their civic rights. He was the first candidate to campaign in the Negro quarter of Harlem. He called the Republicans "gluttons for privilege"; he spoke of cold reactionaries with a calculating machine instead of a heart; he said that it was necessary to choose between a government of the people, by the people, for the people, and a government by the privileged, for the privileged. These resounding speeches awoke some disquiet. But still the bookmakers were giving odds of thirty to one against Truman. Both friends and enemies agreed that Dewey's victory was certain.

Election day arrived. The first results, from Philadelphia and Baltimore, gave Truman a slight advantage. But the Republicans were not worried: the polls could not be wrong. The *Chicago Tribune* brought out a special edition: DEWEY DEFEATS TRUMAN. People waited all night for the final figures. When they came, they utterly confounded the experts. Truman had won 303 electoral votes, and he kept the presidency. Dewey had 189, the Southerner Thurmond 39, and Wallace none whatsoever. The Democrats had regained their majority in the House of Representatives (a margin of 92) and in the Senate (a margin of 12). The unexpected result was heartily welcomed. In life as in the movies, the Americans loved the little man's victory over the giant. Dewey had had a powerful machine at his service; Truman had had to fight single-handed, and almost against his own party. The people cheered courage rewarded. Besides, America rallies to the underdog. Dewey's victory, being certain, would have had nothing exciting about it: Truman's was front-page news. When he came back to Washington, a million admirers covered him with a flood of paper. In the streets, hawkers sold blue buttons reading "I told you so!" This time Truman no longer owed the prophet's mantle to another; he had cut it out for himself.

VI

Truman's inauguration, in 1949, for his second term, was both a triumphant and a homely ceremony. For the first time, Negro citizens were asked to all the celebrations. They had contributed to the victory, and it was but fair that they should be picked out for thanks. The crowds were happy to cheer the man who, by strength of will and nothing more, had been able to pull himself up by his own bootstraps to the highest position in the country. The inaugural message was important. Not only did the President reaffirm his support of the United Nations, and of the free peoples against all aggressors, and the continuation of the Marshall Plan, but he added the famous Point Four: "I believe that we should make available to peace-loving peoples the benefits of our store of technical knowledge in order to help them realize their aspirations for a better life. And, in cooperation with other nations, we should foster capital investment in areas needing development. Our aim should be to help the free peoples of the world, through their own efforts, to produce more food, more clothing, more materials for housing, and more mechanical power to lighten their burdens."

This was help for the underdeveloped countries, in the desirable shape of cooperation and technical assistance, as much as by the provision of capital. Presently the whole of South America was talking about *Punto Quatro*. It took a long while for Congress to transform this fine idea into reality, but by 1951, thirty-three countries, from Peru to Burma and from Iran to Saudi Arabia, were benefiting from Point Four.

Meanwhile the Marshall Plan was producing more spectacular results. Europe had shown the spirit of initiative and unity that America had asked of her, and the OEEC (Organization for European Economic Cooperation) had begun its directing work. From 1947 to 1950, the gross national product of the Marshall Plan countries rose by 29 percent and their industrial production by 64 percent. The plan did not only help the European countries to rebuild their bomb-smashed towns and their destroyed factories but enabled the United States itself to overcome a slight recession that had begun to take shape, raising the number of unemployed to four million—and to overcome it without any serious crisis. Truman asked the Eighty-first Congress for laws intended to deal with the recession: a building program, another for the electrification of the rural areas, a rise in minimum wages, and the maintenance of farm prices—in short, a whole series of measures in favor of the masses, not so daring as the New Deal, but adequate. Truman himself called these measures the Fair Deal. Congress did not pass all that it was asked to; but, still, the military expenditures and the orders for material destined for the underdeveloped countries put an end to the recession as early as the autumn of 1949.

Much of the Administration's success was due to General Marshall; but because of ill health he was obliged to give up the direction of foreign affairs. Dean Acheson succeeded him as secretary of state. Mr. Acheson, a cultivated, remarkably well-informed man, was perfectly suited for the post; but his very perfection vexed some senators. His voice seemed to them to have too much of the ring of Oxford: they thought his clothes a little too well cut. They could not understand how this secretary of state, who had been to Groton, Yale, and Harvard, could have been a New Dealer, nor how he could have been in favor of massive support for the USSR during the war. Although he was "100 percent loyal" and active in the struggle against all forms of aggression and although Truman considered him as one of the greatest secretaries of state the country had ever had, he aroused a great deal of opposition. "I look at that fellow," said Senator Hugh Butler of Nebraska, in a furious outburst, "I watch his smart-alecky manner and his British clothes, and that New Dealism, everlasting New Dealism, in everything he says and does, and I want to shout: Get out, get out! You stand for everything that has been wrong with the United States for years." Meanwhile the Secretary of State, unmoved, stroked his mustache and warned the nation that the outward ills from which it was suffering would last the lifetime of this generation: "We have got to understand that, all our lives, the danger, the uncertainty, the need for alertness, for effort, for discipline will be upon us. This is new for us. It will be hard for us."

Yes, it was hard for a peace-loving, open-handed, good-humored nation to be continually obliged to defend its rights, or the rights of others, against an opponent that untiringly probed the weak points of the western positions. One of these points was Germany. Averell Harriman warned the President that the German economy was going to collapse: "Industry is using up its spare parts and stocks. Transportation has cannibalized bad-order locomotives, in order to keep others running . . . . We cannot attain our basic objectives unless we are ready to move rapidly to reconstruct German life, from its pitiful and chaotic condition." In 1947, Great Britain and the United States, followed a little later by France, came to an agreement to set up a Federal Republic of West Germany. Stalin instantly reacted. During the summer of 1948, he forbade all traffic from Western Germany to Berlin. This was aimed at forcing the Allies either to abandon Berlin or their plan for West Germany. Truman at once stated that the United States would stay in Berlin. But rather than send armed convoys by road, which would have led to fighting and perhaps to war, he decided to send in supplies by air. General

Lucius Clay devised and put into operation the greatest airlift in history. There began an unceasing flow of planes, coming and going. It was a positive miracle of logistics. Altogether the English and American planes made 277,000 flights and carried 2,500,000 tons of supplies. Little by little, the stocks built up again. As early as August, Berlin had thirty days of food in hand and twenty-five of coal. The population showed a great deal of calmness and courage. In 1949, the realistic Stalin acknowledged the fait accompli and raised the blockade.

On their side, some of the nations of Europe were uniting for their defense. The Council of Europe was founded in January, 1949. As the American Senate had approved of the principle of it, Ernest Bevin approached the Americans with a view to including the United States in this European alliance. The negotiations turned upon the nations that were to be included; upon the kind of obligations that each would incur in the case of an attack upon its allies; and upon the idea that each country should give up its military autonomy so as to insure the existence of a well-balanced whole. The Constitution of the United States did not permit an unconditional engagement, since only Congress might decide upon the country's entrance into a war. Canada suggested a compromise. Any attack upon a member country would be considered an attack upon all the others. But, instead of automatically entering into a state of war, each nation would come to the help of the victim according to its own particular constitutional methods.

In April, 1949, the North Atlantic Treaty was signed at Washington by the representatives of the United States, Great Britain, France, Italy, the Netherlands, Belgium, Canada, Iceland, Luxembourg, Denmark, Norway, and Portugal. In December, 1950, the Atlantic Council in Brussels announced the appointment of General Eisenhower as Supreme Allied Commander in Europe. During the war, Eisenhower had shown that he possessed the qualities necessary to command combined forces, and he was popular in France. Truman wrote to the General, "First time you are in town, I wish you'd come in and see me. If I send for you, we'll start the speculators to work." Eisenhower came to the White House and accepted the task that was offered to him. Like Truman, he firmly believed in the necessity of uniting the European nations and of doing it as quickly as possible.

VII

The nation had agreed to undertake a policy of international cooperation; but its history had accustomed it to quickly won and certain victories. Now it was faced with a difficult, obscure situation, in which the danger, like the ghost in Hamlet, would move about under the ground, to come up again in unexpected places. China went over to the Communists. As early as 1946, Truman had sent Marshall there to negotiate a truce between the two armies. But it was an impossible task. The corrupt, unpopular government of Chiang Kai-shek had not the least chance of survival. By 1949, the Communists controlled the entire country, and Chiang, with his remaining followers, had to flee to Formosa. In August, 1949, the State Department published a White Paper that threw the responsibility for the defeat upon Chiang. "Nothing that this country did or could have done, within the reasonable limits of its capacities, could have changed that result . . . . It was the product of internal Chinese forces." That was true enough: but a quarter of the world's surface had thus become Communist. It was a severe shock for the Americans. In September, they had another. Charles Ross, the President's press secretary, called the newspapermen of Washington together and handed out mimeographed slips: "We have evidence that, within recent weeks, an atomic explosion occurred in the USSR."

Of course it had always been known that one day Stalin would possess the atomic bomb. The physicists had given the warning that its principle was known and that the only secret was the precise manner in which it was made—the "know how." The Americans had at least been able to hope that it would take the Russians a long while to find out how to make a device that they could use. The optimists said 1955: the pessimists 1952. The Russians had knocked three years off even the pessimists' estimate. How? It appeared to be certain that spies had given them very valuable information. In 1945, the OSS (Office of Strategic Services) had discovered some of their most secret documents in the offices of a Communist magazine. In 1946, the Canadians had been obliged to announce that to their deep regret twenty-three Canadians, holding confidential positions, had provided Moscow with atomic secrets and samples of uranium. One can understand the intense anxiety that seized those who knew that they were responsible for the country's safety.

In 1947, Truman ordered an inquiry into the loyalty of all federal employees. The measure was contrary to the country's traditions, and many liberals protested. But in Congress, the Un-American Activities Committee displayed rigorous severity. Truman had both to cover himself politically and protect the country's military secrets. The vast investigation went forward. Fourteen thousand doubtful cases were reported; two thousand employees resigned rather than submit to the interrogation; two hundred and twelve were dismissed. In 1950, the President went further and authorized the heads of ten services, classed as "sensitive agencies," to dismiss any persons who appeared to them to be bad security risks. These assumptions, these guesses were to lead to very serious mistakes, and they were to ruin more lives than one.

But the danger was real enough. Soon the English discovered that Klaus Fuchs, a naturalized German scientist whose position made him familiar with the most important secrets, had betrayed them, and it was discovered in the United States that Julius and Ethel Rosenberg had been passing important atomic secrets to the USSR. Before the House Un-American Activities Committee, Whittaker Chambers, an editor of *Time* and a former Communist, accused an outstanding member of the State Department, Alger Hiss, of having at one time given him secret papers. Alger Hiss, who had become head of the Carnegie Endowment for International Peace, denied the charge; and he was backed up, in all good faith, by powerful friends. The President himself said that the whole thing was a red herring. Feelings and prejudices that had nothing to do with the actual case came most violently into play. Hiss belonged to the fashionable world of the Social Register, the "striped pants, British accent" world that so irritated those members of Congress who spoke with a broad Midwestern twang. Two Americas stood in opposition: that of the farmers and the pioneers, which disliked the East and which was always to say that the bankers of Wall Street and the "parlor pinks," the drawing-room Communists, were all one; and that of Harvard and Yale, no less American, no less patriotic, but more restrained.

Whittaker Chambers had the backing of Congressman Richard Nixon, and he brought forward evidence: the State Department documents had been copied on a typewriter that was identified as one that had belonged to Hiss. Chambers produced a microfilm that had been kept in a pumpkin in his garden and that, according to him, dated from the time when he and Hiss belonged to a spy ring. At Hiss's first trial, the jury could not agree on a verdict; but at a second, he was condemned for perjury. This dramatic turn of events gave the public the idea that the New Deal administrations—Truman's as well as Roosevelt's—would not recognize the Communist danger and did not defend the country against subversion. Eleven Communist leaders were brought before the federal courts and accused of having advocated the violent overthrow of the government of the United States. The Supreme Court upheld their convictions. Fred M. Vinson, the chief justice, reconciled this judgment with the right of free expression that was guaranteed by the Constitution with the assertion that a "clear and present danger" existed. America was now united, almost in spite of herself, and she was making ready for her defense. Once again, a decision of the very first importance was announced to newspapermen by the President's press secretary in a simple mimeographed note: "It is part of my responsibility as commander in chief of the armed forces to see to it that our country is able to defend itself against any aggressor. Accordingly, I have directed the Atomic Energy Commission to continue its work in all forms of atomic weapons, including the so-called hydrogen or superbomb."

It was legitimate that a president, anxious for the security of his country, should do his utmost to protect it from spies: it was not legitimate that a popularity-hunting senator should make use of the country's reasonable fears to poison its entire moral atmosphere. At one time, in the America of the Puritans, witch hunting had caused hideous judicial errors: now a senator from Wisconsin, Joseph R. McCarthy, a person notorious for his coarse violence, seized upon the Communist infiltration of the State Department. He made a trial run in February, 1950, when he charged that there were Communists in the State Department. The country's peril, he would say, lay less in the possibility of a foreign invasion than in the treachery of those whom the nation had treated so well. And who were the worst culprits? The young men born with silver spoons in their mouths. The Senator contended that the whole State Department was riddled with Communists.

At the beginning the accusation seemed ridiculous, but then this idea of a huge conspiracy on the part of the "striped pants" to ruin America captivated the minds of the simple and led them astray. The Senator was utterly unable to prove a single one of his assertions, but the violence of his language made up for the weakness of his evidence. A wave of hysteria flowed over the country, drowning it. For some, McCarthyism became a faith: others regarded it as a shameful disease. As chairman of a Senate committee, McCarthy paid little attention to the constitutional rights of the witnesses he called; he violated all the principles of democratic freedom; he brought about the reign of suspicion and terror. The systematic intolerance that went by the name of McCarthyism did the reputation of the United States the utmost damage abroad, without in any way improving its internal security. Presently Korea was to give the Senator from Wisconsin even greater strength.

VIII

The Far East had for a long while been a source of continual anxiety to the President. He was in a position, with regard to the Far East, not unlike that in which Roosevelt found himself in 1939–1940, with regard to Europe. Public opinion blamed his want of firmness, while Congress, the mouthpiece of that opinion, refused to vote the war materials and the troops that would have allowed a stronger policy. Hence perpetual half measures: in Roosevelt's case, ineffectual messages to Germany and Italy; in Truman's case, limited financial help for Chiang Kai-shek and the sending of Marshall and Wedemeyer to China. The solution in both cases was an aggression that caused the country to close its ranks behind the President.

Yet Truman was in a better position than Roosevelt had been. Major public opinion now accepted the country's international responsibilities; and the existence of the United Nations reconciled action abroad with respect for international law, a very important point for the American conscience. But after Marshall's journey, the President seemed to despair of China. He

275

feared Mao's Communists, but he had little confidence in Chiang. "If he is a generalissimo," said Senator Tom Connolly of Chiang, "why doesn't he generalize?" General Wedemeyer, sent to China after Marshall, confirmed that Chiang was not in the least degree popular: Wedemeyer nevertheless advised that Chiang should be helped to improve his regime. Congress, the President, and the State Department as it turned out, refused to support him. "Supplying Chiang with arms," they said in Washington, "is a backhanded form of lend-lease for the Chinese Communists." After Chiang's flight, Mao Tse-tung and Chou En-lai set up the People's Republic of China in Peking.

What was to be done now? Was the right course in the Far East to adopt the policy of containment that had been tried in Europe? The United States would accept the conquests that the Communists had made, and that could not be remedied, but would draw a line that it would not allow to be passed. In January, 1950, the Secretary of State announced that the United States would protect a "defensive perimeter" running from the Aleutian Islands to Japan and the Philippines, but excluding Korea and Formosa. The last two were to see to their own defense, with the eventual help of the United Nations. The danger of this policy was that it might encourage attacks upon those countries that were not protected.

And indeed the aggression was hardly delayed at all. On June 24, 1950, the President was at Independence, Missouri, for a family gathering, and Dean Acheson was staying at his old farm in Maryland, when a news agency, the United Press, warned the State Department that the North Koreans had crossed the thirty-eighth parallel, the frontier between North and South Korea. Could the State Department confirm the news? At that moment it could not; but presently General MacArthur cabled from Tokyo: South Korea had been invaded. The United Nations Security Council was called. It recognized that North Korea had launched an armed attack, and it required both armies to cease fighting. On Sunday, Truman was at his brother's farm at Grandview, looking at a milking machine, when Acheson telephoned to say that the North Koreans were advancing in six columns and that they were certainly not paying any attention to the United Nations' injunctions. Truman left the milking machine, ordered his private airplane, and flew to Washington.

Truman decided upon making a firm stand, and as soon as he arrived he held a conference at Blair House, where he was then living, as the White House was undergoing renovation. Since aggression had been committed, everything must be done to stop it. MacArthur was ordered to send arms to the South Koreans; the Seventh Fleet sailed for Formosan waters. Then, as the news from Korea became worse and worse, the Secretaries of State and Defense advised that the American ships and airplanes should go to the help of the South Koreans, but without crossing the thirty-eighth parallel. The whole country was raised up upon an extraordinary wave of unity. In his memoirs, Churchill says of Truman, "His celerity, wisdom, and courage in this crisis make him worthy, in my estimation, to be numbered among the greatest of American presidents." When Truman's declaration was read in the House of Representatives, everybody stood up and cheered. In the Senate, a few cross-grained Republicans asked whether the President were assuming to himself the right of declaring war without the consent of Congress; but the Republican Senator William F. Knowland stated that the decision to support the free nations deserved the solid backing of Americans of all parties. He was heartily applauded.

Still, Truman very much wished to be the soldier, or one of the soldiers, of the United Nations. His moral position, both with regard to all the other nations of the world and to Congress, would be so much the stronger for it. Now the situation in the Security Council was most uncommonly favorable. The Soviet delegate had stopped coming to its sittings, as a protest against the presence of Nationalist China. There was therefore no veto to be feared. Yugoslavia voted against, Egypt abstained, but the majority voted for Truman and called on the other member nations to join the United Nations in collective action to oppose the aggression. In the Senate, Taft threw the responsibility for the attack upon the Administration's earlier weakness; but in his peroration, he supported the President's policy of intervention with all his usual courage. "My God!" said Charlie Ross, "Bob Taft has joined the United Nations—and the United States." Was the United States at war? No, said Truman: this was a question of a police operation undertaken by the United Nations. But it looked so very like a war that it was extraordinarily difficult to tell the difference.

In the Western world, and in India as well, there was a great feeling of relief. Aggression was no longer to be accepted as a means of solving international disagreements. Truman's opponents admitted that whatever one might think of the past, the theory of a "conspiracy in the State Department" was disproved by the facts. The nightmare of another Munich disappeared. But in the beginning, the war in Korea was terrible. In spite of the fiction of a United Nations operation, the United States was fighting almost alone: however brave the troops provided by the other countries may have been, they were no more than token forces. Once again, a misconceived economy meant that so far as defense was concerned, the country was deprived of almost everything. The North Koreans' Russian-built tanks met little to stop them, and they reached the neighborhood of the port of Pusan that had become a bridgehead in South Korea. Then the wind turned, and hope changed sides. Slowly MacArthur built up an army. A very ably conceived and executed amphibious operation allowed him to land at Inchon behind the enemy, who was obliged to flee in disorder. The thirty-eighth parallel was reached and then crossed. MacArthur went as far as the Yalu River, the frontier between Korea and China. He did not believe there would be any important Chinese reactions. He was wrong. Twenty-six Chinese divisions (250,000 men) threw the forces of the United Nations back below the thirty-eighth parallel once more. Already the casualty figures for the Korean war amounted to 120,000. The American people gradually longed for the end of it.

MacArthur, stung by this grave setback, asked for permission to bomb the Chinese bases in Manchuria, suggested a blockade of the Chinese coast, and support for a Chinese Nationalist invasion of the mainland. Truman firmly maintained that he had undertaken a purely defensive action to preserve the integrity of South Korea. Making war on China would not be in conformity with the United Nations charter. MacArthur urged his point: a long message that he sent to the Veterans of Foreign Wars was published, in which he said that the Oriental mind would only be impressed by a forceful aggressive policy, and that nothing could be more mistaken than appeasement in the Pacific. In short, he called for a determined strategy, one based in part on the use of Chiang's troops on Formosa. It was an open challenge to the policy of his commander in chief, the President of the United States. In like circumstances, wrote Truman, "General Mac-Arthur—and rightly too—would have court-martialed any second lieutenant." In a letter to Congressman Joseph Martin, Mac-Arthur confirmed his opposition to the government's policy. On April 11, 1951, America was astonished to learn that Harry Truman had removed the Commander in Chief of the American forces in the Far East and of the United Nations forces in Korea. MacArthur was replaced by General Matthew B. Ridgway.

In the United States, among many others, the Asia First group became very angry. There was talk of impeaching Truman and Acheson. The coarse-mouthed Senator McCarthy said that the decision must have been taken during a night of "bourbon and benedictine." Seventy-eight thousand telegrams arrived at the White House, twenty supporting MacArthur for every one against him. When the dismissed general landed at San Francisco five days later, splendid and youthful-looking in his service cap, slim and distinguished in his trench coat, the very picture of a hero, the crowd's enthusiasm exceeded anything that the town had ever known. In a triumphal parade through New York City, he was acclaimed by six million people. In Washington, a thousand Daughters of the American Revolution took their hats off to him as the highest possible mark of respect, and three hundred thousand people escorted him along the way. He appeared before Congress. "I address you," he said, "with neither rancor nor bitterness, but in the fading twilight of life, with but one purpose in mind: to serve my country." Many Congressmen wept: others thought that MacArthur would be the next president of the United States. He then undertook a tour throughout the country —an enterprise that his friends called a crusade and his enemies a vendetta—during which he behaved like a candidate who was in favor of a return to a traditional America.

Truman followed Disraeli's policy of giving the man rope enough and time. After six weeks of silence, the Joint Chiefs of Staff gave evidence before the Senate. They stated that on many occasions MacArthur had opposed the government's policy; that if his advice had been followed, America would have engaged all her forces in the vast expanse of China, leaving Russia mistress of the world. Public opinion, always fickle, changed direction. At the moment of MacArthur's return, the polls had shown 69 percent of the population in favor of him: now the figures went into a vertical decline. Who spoke about MacArthur as president any more? The country was experiencing an extraordinary degree of prosperity, partly caused by the expenditure for the Korean war. There were 7,600,000 GIs who had been through universities, thus acquiring a profession or a calling, and they felt all the better for it. Meanwhile Japan signed a peace treaty with the United States, and the war in Korea resolved itself into a near stalemate only a little in favor of the Allies.

The Truman era ended upon a mixed note. Truman had certainly allowed mistakes to be made; but he had strengthened collective security. On the home front, he brought about the reconversion of the economy without a crisis. Yet in 1952, he was violently attacked. The coming of a presidential election always opens the scandal-hunting season. Truman himself was of an unquestionable integrity, but corruption existed in a few of those around him. One aide-de-camp accepted a deep freeze, another a mink coat, to mention two of the best-publicized incidents. Senator Kefauver's inquiry into gangsterism alarmed the vast television public that gazed, fascinated, at the killers' hands upon the screen. McCarthy, more violent than ever, poured out his everlasting denunciations. Where was America bound? The opposition snatched at every possible weapon—juvenile delinquency, the war in Korea, communism in high places. The Republicans promised to clean up Washington, if the presidential election brought them into power. In their time, the Democrats had used just those very words.

PART NINE

The Days of Eisenhower

THE Republican party had spent twenty years in the wilderness: twelve years of Roosevelt, eight years of Truman. It hoped that in 1952 it would at least have a chance of power. An administration that has reached the end of its term never wants for enemies, nor for critics. Truman was blamed for his inability to wind up the Korean affair, for "communism" in high places, the "corruption" of Washington, the budget deficit. Senator Taft supported McCarthy's complaints, if not his methods. For many Americans, this was a time of longing for the past and of distrust for intellectuals. But at the same time, the better-informed Republicans—

Senator Henry Cabot Lodge of Massachusetts, for example, or Governor Sherman Adams of New Hampshire—knew that Taft and the Old Guard of the party could never bring over the mass of the people. But Dewey or Harold E. Stassen, more liberal candidates, would be opposed by the Old Guard. What was wanted was a new, untarnished man. Now this spotless knight did exist: he was General Eisenhower.

I

After his victory in Europe and his triumphal entry into New York, Eisenhower had served a tour as army chief of staff and had finally retired from the army and had then accepted the presidency of Columbia University, where he remained until, at Truman's request, he went to France to take over the command of the NATO forces. There he had shown the same qualities that had distinguished him during the war—capacity for work, straightforwardness, and the art of making himself liked and of causing people to get on well with one another. He was sincerely modest: he loathed high-flown words and gestures. Life had taught him that isolationism is impossible in the modern world: he believed in the cooperation of the Western nations, and he had himself successfully organized it. On this point, he was not in agreement with the Old Guard, but he was in agreement with the mass of the people who, having also been to the war, understood the situation. The people liked Eisenhower because he shared their feelings, because it was clear that he was both religious and tolerant, because he was a "Kansas farm boy," and because this general was known to hate war.

In short, he would have been the ideal candidate for either of the parties; but would he run? Truman had already promised him the presidency in 1945, at the Potsdam Conference. Eisenhower had laughed: "I'm a soldier and I'm positive no one thinks of me as a politician." On several occasions, in the course of the years that followed, influential Democrats had tried to tempt him. In vain. "It is my conviction," he wrote, "that the necessary and wise subordination of the military to civil power will be best sustained . . . when life-long professional soldiers, in the absence of some obvious and over-riding reasons, abstain from seeking high political office." Besides, although he had been the instrument of Roosevelt's and of Truman's foreign policy, he was not a Democrat. Speaking to his friend Roy Roberts, of the powerful *Kansas City Star,* he said, "Why, Roy, I am just a good Kansas Republican like yourself." After having worked with him for a long while, his assistant, Sherman Adams, came to the conclusion, "I don't think he has any politics."

Numbers of Republican politicians appeared at his headquarters at Louveciennes, near Paris, and tried to convince him. They assured him that if he ran, Truman would not stand again. In fact Truman had told his friends of his decision as early as 1950: "In my opinion, eight years as president is enough and sometimes too much for any man." In 1951, Taft had announced that he would be a candidate. For his part, Senator Lodge stated that he would propose Eisenhower's name, without the General's consent, at the New Hampshire primaries. Eisenhower issued a statement in which he said that he would remain at his post at SHAPE, that he did not seek nomination, but that he acknowledged the American citizens' right "to place before me next July a duty that would transcend my present responsibility." In other words, "Prove to me that the majority of the Republicans want me as their candidate, and I will stand." For him, the basis of the whole question was the unity of the West: he knew the state of the world, the current situation, too well to allow isolationism to take over the command. Taft had given his support to the idea of "Fortress America," the Gibraltar of freedom. Eisenhower could not admit that a wise man could cling to the notion of an isolated, free America.

The primary elections showed that Eisenhower was immensely popular. In their homely way, the electors wrote "Ike" upon their ballots. "I like Ike," and "We want Ike," became favorite slogans. Eisenhower came back from Europe on July 3: the next day he gave up his general's retired pay ($20,000 a year) because he was entering politics. What was he going to support? "The great problem of America today is to take that straight road down the middle." He wanted to keep equally far from the right-wing extremists (McCarthy, and even Taft, although Eisenhower had a high opinion of him) and those of the party's left, such as Stassen, with whom he was nevertheless in complete agreement on the subject of foreign policy. He was opposed, both by his nature and his education, to the New Deal and to any kind of coddling by the state. He had once said, harshly enough, "If all the Americans want is security, they can go to prison." He was more careful during his campaign. Was he against the war in Korea? Yes, but he blamed no particular man, only pledging himself to put an end to it if he became president. Did he disown the Republican Senator McCarthy? He supported all Republican candidates, but he did not approve of un-American methods; he wanted the party to be clean and decent. Yet when McCarthy, during the presidential campaign in Wisconsin, trying to ride on his coat-tails, climbed onto his train, Eisenhowed suffered but tolerated the intrusion.

When the Republican convention opened at Chicago, the underlying mass of the party supported Eisenhower: Taft, as a professional politician who controlled the convention machinery, hoped to win over the majority of the delegates. This was an illusory hope, and it quickly vanished. The Taft-Hartley Act had alienated the unions, and as John Kennedy says, that gave the general impression that Taft could never win a presidential election. It appeared to be a close struggle, but when it came to voting, Eisenhower carried the day on the very first ballot. He at once went to see Taft, who said, "I want to congratulate General Eisenhower. I shall do everything possible in the campaign to secure his election." Verbal magnanimity is customary in American politics; but Taft kept his word. His friends hoped that Eisenhower would offer him the vice presidency, but the General chose Senator Richard M. Nixon of California, who was chiefly known to the public for his activity in the Hiss affair. The choice of such a relatively minor party leader caused a certain amount of surprise.

The Democrats chose Adlai Stevenson, the governor of Illinois, as their candidate, and they chose him almost in spite of himself, for he apparently refused many times. He was a most cultivated and intelligent man, one who would have delighted the New Dealers of 1932: he was little known in the country as a whole, but his first speeches made a deep impression. "Let's talk sense to the American people," he said, and he reminded them of their history, their freedom, and their duties, speaking gravely but also with a great deal of wit. He was amusing and attractive on television. He maintained that "the Republican party has been

284

devoid of new ideas for almost seventy years . . . . As to their platform, well, nobody can stand on a bushel of eels." He observed that Eisenhower accepted the greater part of the New Deal. "I've been tempted to say that I was proud to stand on that record, if only . . . the General would move over and make room for me." The Democratic program included the repeal of the Taft-Hartley Act, equality of civil rights, help for farmers, and the continuation of Truman's foreign policy.

At the beginning, the General's speeches were disappointing. "Now he's crossing the thirty-eighth platitude again," sighed the reporters. The hesitating liberals, who had favored Eisenhower as against Taft, were very much displeased at the way he humored McCarthy. "It's not a middle-of-the-road policy," they said. "It's the middle of the gutter." But the Republican columnist Joseph Alsop used a particularly striking (and unkind) image for the kind of intellectual who supported Stevenson: "A large, oval head, smooth, faceless, unemotional, but a little haughty and condescending." "Sure," he said, "all the eggheads are for Stevenson, but how many eggheads are there?" The word egghead caught on at once. In the popular mind, the eggheads joined the striped pants of some years before. Once again, the average American was afraid of outstanding thinkers and of cultivated voices that would bring back wildly extravagant spending, foreign political ideas, and war. Stevenson lost ground.

Meanwhile Eisenhower's speeches grew better. Little by little, he became an excellent candidate. He was, after all, a chief of staff by profession, and he knew how to organize a campaign. It was said that the chemical formula for this one was K_1C_2, that is to sal, Korea, Communism, Corruption. "Americans," said Eisenhower, "wanted an end to the war in Korea. . . . Americans wanted a government thrifty and frugal with the country's money. They wanted a stop to the endless rise in taxes, taking more and more of the family income to support an overgrown Washington bureaucracy . . . . Americans were determined to eliminate penetration by the Communist conspiracy, in our government and in our whole society." Eisenhower did not attempt to compete with Stevenson in the matter of wit. "There is nothing to laugh at," he said gravely, in reply to his opponent's epigrams. It would no doubt be amusing to make jokes: "Frankly, I have no intention to do so. The subjects of which we are speaking these days, my friends, are not those that seem to me to be amusing. . . . Is it amusing that we have stumbled into a war in Korea? That we have already lost 117,000 of our Americans, killed and wounded? Is it amusing that war seems to be no closer to a real solution than ever?" The electors were of Eisenhower's opinion that these things were not in the least amusing.

During the campaign there was a curious incident: it concerned Nixon alone, but it was distinctly awkward for a party that was struggling against corruption. A Democratic paper, the *New York Post,* accused the vice presidential candidate of having secretly received $18,000 for his election expenses from a club of Californian millionaires. There was an uproar, and Nixon was called upon to withdraw. He had no feeling of having acted wrongly at all: he had spent the money on posters, stamps, and secretarial staff. "Yes," answered the hostile papers, "but where should we be if every representative of the people accepted 'gifts' from people who would afterward come and ask him for favors?" Eisenhower became very angry: he would only support Nixon if Nixon's hands were utterly clean.

The national committee of the Republican party decided to buy time on television (it cost $75,000) to allow Nixon to make his explanations to the American people. It was a moving spectacle. This young husband, the father of two little girls, came forward to tell the story of his life. He was the son of a Californian grocer: he had married Pat, "who is here, right by me." He had fought in the Pacific. He had never become rich and all he had was his car and life insurance amounting to $4,000. His house was mortgaged. What about this money? He had not spent a penny of it on himself. The only personal gift that he had ever received was a dog, a cocker spaniel for his little girls. "I should say this: that Pat doesn't have a mink coat, but she does have a good Republican cloth coat, and I always tell her that she'd look good in anything." By the end of the program all America, including Mrs. Eisenhower, was in tears. The General sent a congratulatory telegram to Nixon but reserved his decision until they should meet. At their meeting, he grasped Nixon in his arms and said, "He is not only vindicated as a man of honor, but as far as I am concerned, he stands higher than ever before."

This put the last strokes to the legendary picture of the Eisenhower-Nixon tandem, an image of two worthy average Americans, loving their families, fearing God, and free from any taint of ideology. Eisenhower went on promising economies, particularly in the military budget. He stood up for NATO and the United Nations, but above all he stressed the necessity for peace in the atomic age. "The only way to win World War III is to prevent it." And who could prevent it better than the man who had won World War II? His past inspired confidence, his smile affection. When the balloting was over, Eisenhower had 442 electoral votes. Stevenson 89. But in the Senate and the House of Representatives, the Republicans retained only the smallest majority. It seemed that the new president was far more popular than his party. He owed his success partly to his virtues of honesty, simplicity, kindness, and decency, and partly to the Southern whites. But an even more important factor was Korea. A great many of the votes cast represented the people's impatience at the dragging hostilities there that kept so many American boys far from home.

II

During the campaign, Eisenhower had frequently stated that the new Administration's first task would be to bring the war in Korea to an honorable end. "That job requires a personal trip to Korea. I shall make that trip." This spectacular promise had contributed a great deal to his success. There is always a blank period between the election of a President, in November, and his inauguration, in January. Eisenhower flew to Korea, visited the snowy battlefields, took note of what the soldiers had to suffer, and then returned across the Pacific aboard the cruiser *Helena*.

He was joined by some of his future colleagues aboard the *Helena*: John Foster Dulles, who was to be his secretary of state; Charles Wilson, secretary of defense; Chairman of the Joint Chiefs of Staff General Omar Bradley; and Admiral Arthur Radford, whom Eisenhower thought of as a replacement for Bradley, who had reached the age limit. Eisenhower took advantage of the long voyage to set out his policy. He told them that he considered that the American citizens did not need to be controlled and directed in every act of their lives. Government's role was to act as a referee, and also, by its credit policy and its management of the budget, to insure the stability of the dollar. This implied a defense policy that would not be ruinously expensive. Eisenhower thought that a country's strength lay not only in its arms but also in its wealth, the prosperity of its industry, and its agriculture, and in the loyalty of a contented population. He said that a crushing military budget, because of its repercussions upon the economy, nullified the measures it financed.

John Foster Dulles, the most important member of the coming administration, was a lawyer, "the best-paid of the big business legal counsellors." He had always given the closest attention to foreign affairs, both from family tradition and personal inclination. He was one of the principal architects of the Japanese peace treaty, had been a consultant on foreign policy to the State Department under Truman and also an adviser to Dewey. He was a cold, slow man, severely, doggedly moral, and a great worker: he impressed the President by his knowledge of the problems and at the same time pleased him by his rigid principles. Dulles wanted the country's foreign policy to be inspired by the imperative requirements of former times, "openness, simplicity, and righteousness." Eisenhower was entirely in agreement upon this point. Dulles sometimes bored him with his oracular, dogmatic way of speaking; but he respected him, and he needed to respect those he employed. Eisenhower could never, like Bonaparte, have made use of a Talleyrand, utilizing and despising him at the same time. "If anything happened to Foster, where could I find a man able to replace him?"

Upon other points, Eisenhower had the same trust in the judgment of Admiral Radford. The Admiral held that the United States had undertaken too many local engagements, particularly in Asia. America was everywhere, but everywhere she was weak; and he would rather have the country concentrate its forces in one powerful strategic reserve in its own territory or not very far from it, relying upon native forces elsewhere—forces that it would arm and that it would support with its strategic reserve in serious cases. Dulles agreed with Radford. He thought that the two great wars of the twentieth century had been brought about by mistaken calculations on the part of heads of state (William II and Hitler), who had supposed that the other nations would put up with something that in fact they could not tolerate. It was therefore necessary to make a clear statement of the circumstances in which the United States would go as far as war.

On his return, the President was inaugurated at Washington, and in his speech he promised a strong policy: "In the final choice, a soldier's pack is not so heavy a burden as a prisoner's chains." Then he formed his Cabinet; and its composition showed his intention of pursuing a "neo-conservative" policy. The Cabinet would have been roughly the same had Taft been president. Ike gave the Department of the Treasury to George Humphrey, the president of the powerful Hanna Company that controlled coal, minerals, chemicals, and banks. Humphrey was the very prototype of the big business man, active, agreeable, convinced of the hellish wickedness of the New Deal (his mother had always written *roosevelt* with no capital). Shortly after Humphrey entered the Cabinet as secretary of the treasury, a reporter asked him whether he had read Ernest Hemingway's *The Old Man and the Sea*. The Secretary replied, "Why would anybody be interested in some old man who was a failure and never amounted to anything anyway?"

As secretary of defense, Eisenhower chose Charles E. Wilson of Detroit, chairman of General Motors. The Senate made a certain amount of difficulty about ratifying this appointment. How could Charles E. Wilson make unbiased deals with his own company (which had an important share of the government's orders) when he himself owned shares to the extent of $2,500,000? The Senators said that the situation brought about a conflict of interests that was contrary to federal law. When Wilson gave evidence upon the subject before the Senate committee, he said, "I thought what was good for the country was good for General Motors, and vice versa." This unfortunate remark was taken up, and often distorted, by the Democrats. Stevenson observed, "While the New Dealers have all left Washington, to make way for the car dealers, I hasten to say that I, for one, do not believe the story that the general welfare has become a subsidiary of General Motors."

Wilson promised to get rid of all his shares before April 1, and the Senate confirmed his appointment.

Herbert Brownell, the attorney general, was a wealthy lawyer. Arthur Summerfield, the postmaster general, and Sinclair Weeks, the secretary of commerce, both directed important business concerns. Ezra Benson, secretary of agriculture, was a "professional churchman," one of the twelve apostles of the Mormon church. At first he declined the office: besides, he had campaigned for Taft, as he had not wanted to see a general in the White House. He had started life as a missionary, then he had turned to farming, in which he had shown himself skillful and fortunate. He had no political ambitions. Eisenhower said to him, "I didn't want to be president, frankly, when the pressure started. But you can't refuse to serve America. We've a great job to do, and I want you on my team." In the event, Benson proved to be a brave, efficient, unpopular secretary.

As a secretary of labor, Eisenhower picked Martin Durkin, the president of the Plumbers and Pipe Fitters Union. Taft considered this an "unbelievable" appointment. Durkin had been a Democrat and a friend of Truman; he had campaigned against Eisenhower and for the repeal of the Taft-Hartley Act! Yet the President very much wished to include in his Cabinet a labor leader who could, in the event of a crisis, win the support of the unions; and he had promised Durkin to propose some liberal amendments to the Taft-Hartley Act. Durkin resigned in 1953 because the amendments were too long delayed. But at the beginning, it could be said that Eisenhower's Cabinet consisted of "nine millionaires and one plumber." The plumber raised protests from a group of senators, but the President would not yield.

In 1953, a new department was set up—the Department of Health, Education, and Welfare. The word *education* must not be misinterpreted: public instruction remained the concern of the states. A woman, Oveta Culp Hobby, was the first secretary. She was the wife of a governor of Texas, and she had run a newspaper and a radio station and been head of the WACs during World War II, as well as having been in politics since her youth. Although she was a Democrat, she had brought Texas around to Eisenhower, which had earned her the President's gratitude. She was a prudent, reserved woman; yet she ran into serious difficulties over the recently discovered Salk vaccine against poliomyelitis. In some lots of the vaccine, fully active viruses were found; some children were infected, and a panic ensued. Oveta Hobby drew much criticism upon herself by saying that "no one could have foreseen" such a demand for the vaccine. It was observed that a Cabinet officer is there to foresee. She resigned in 1955, much to the President's regret.

Eisenhower was used to having a chief of staff at his side, and he appointed Governor Sherman Adams of New Hampshire as president's assistant. Adams dealt with a great many problems for his chief, and his political experience was of the greatest value to a president who was so little of a politician. C. D. Jackson, a brilliant journalist of the *Time* and *Life* group, became special assistant, with the cold war as his province. Every week, Eisenhower himself had conferences (stormy ones, on occasion) with the leaders of the party; on Thursday, he conferred with the National Security Council; on Wednesday, with the press; on Friday, with the Cabinet. Every Monday, he saw his economic advisers and the Joint Chiefs of Staff. This changeless, exact timetable suited his nature. As he had done during the war, he acted as a link between the various teams, and he infected them with his optimism.

III

March, 1953, saw an event of the first importance: the death of Stalin. Eisenhower was awakened to be told the news. "Well," said he, "what do you think we can do about this?" At the nineteenth party congress, Stalin had appointed Georgi Malenkov as his successor. From his earliest pronouncements, the latter spoke of peaceful negotiations to solve the differences between East and West. America listened with the utmost attention. Was this interminable, ruinous cold war going to stop at last? The peaceable American nation and its peace-loving president hoped so wholeheartedly. There were two opposing attitudes: President Syngman Rhee of South Korea wanted the Chinese and their friends to be thrown back beyond the Yalu River by the waging of total war and, if necessary, by the use of atomic weapons. Eisenhower wanted a compromise: he thought that total war would alienate the United Nations and most of the United States' allies.

Talks upon an armistice in Korea dragged along slowly, because of the question of prisoners. Some North Koreans did not want to be repatriated. The suggestion of asking neutral countries to look after them was being discussed when Syngman Rhee, without authority from the United Nations, liberated twenty thousand of them, which held up the talks again. Rhee would not accept the reinstatement of the thirty-eighth parallel.

"And what will you do if we leave Korea?"

"We shall die," he said.

Eisenhower sent him a messenger who obliged him to renounce this heroic solution, worthy of Corneille. Dulles also promulgated the doctrine of "massive retaliation."

At last, on July 27, 1953, an armistice was signed at Panmunjom. This did not put an end to the tension between the two Koreas. "Don't forget where you put your gun," said the American soldiers when they heard of the armistice, "you'll need it next week." In America itself, the armistice raised economic problems for Eisenhower and his Cabinet. The war orders were going to dwindle. Would this lead to a depression? A Republican administration, more than any other, was unable to accept that risk. It was a government dedicated to the free-enterprise system: what would be said if, under their leadership, business declined—and declined before the Congressional election of 1954? Secretary of the Treasury George Humphrey had at first restrained credit to protect the dollar; but he soon reversed this policy. Taxes were cut by $3,000,000,000; unemployment payments rose by $640,000.

The difference between these methods and those of the New Deal was by no means clear. The President paid close attention to the economist Arthur Burns, who told him, "It is no longer a matter of serious controversy whether the government should play a positive role in maintaining a high level of economic activity." There was no doubt at all that crises should be controlled. The only questions were those of timeliness, the choice of the moment to intervene, and the extent of the intervention. This directed, or half-directed, economy smelled of heresy to Republican noses, but in fact it succeeded for Eisenhower, and from 1954 the recession changed into prosperity. Wages and dividends rose, and as prices remained steady, purchasing power increased. In order to prevent "prosperity strikes," some manufacturers of their own accord offered their workers new benefits. The car industry accepted the sliding scale. In case of unemployment, Ford guaranteed 65 percent of a man's pay for four weeks and then 60 percent for twenty-two. Some firms, such as American Can, went so far as a guaranteed annual wage.

Only the farmers were not happy with the "Eisenhower prosperity." Science and machines raised their productivity, but since the consumers could not take up their surpluses, farm prices went down while industrial prices went up. The number of farmers diminished: so did their incomes. "An Iowa banker pointed out that a packing-plant worker, who earned $6,000 a year taking the bones out of hogs, was receiving more than twice as much as the man who grew them." The government bought the surpluses, but could only sell them at a loss. If it stored them, they deteriorated. Ezra Benson was still one of the true believers in free enterprise, and he wanted to lower the guaranteed price for butter. He was called to the White House, for the milk producers were shrieking with rage. "Ezra," said the President, "I think maybe we went a mite too far this time." The stockbreeders had urgently desired the government to leave them and their affairs alone the year before; they now indignantly called upon the authorities to keep the prices up.

One curious thing about the Eisenhower Administration was the fact that the President had been elected against the wishes of the conservative wing of the party, and that having defeated Taft, he surrounded himself with Taftists, whose two chief aims were to reduce the budget and to avoid setting the state in competition with private industry. Another paradox was that gradually this middle-of-the-road president, with his conservative Cabinet, and with the agreement of Taft (a far less uncompromising man than he was said to be, or indeed than he thought himself), took measures not at all unlike those of their Democratic predecessors—the making of roads, the building of schools, the extension of health insurance and social security. Even in agriculture, they were to set up a soil bank to indemnify farmers who would agree to reduce their acreage. What did this fence-sitting policy amount to, then? To tell the truth, it was governed by events, by facts, which are what they are, and which never accommodate themselves in the least to the men in power. But the President tried to find a name for his economic policy that would please everybody. Dynamic conservatism? Progressive moderation?

Adlai Stevenson did not let this opportunity for wit go by.

"I have never been sure what progressive moderation means, or was it conservative progressivism? I have forgotten, and I am not sure what dynamic moderation or moderate dynamism means. I am not even sure what it means when one says he is a conservative in fiscal affairs, and a liberal in human affairs. I assume what it means is that you will strongly recommend the building of a great many schools, to accommodate the needs of our children, but not provide the money." The audience rocked with laughter. The last sentence was not fair, for Eisenhower's social program was to cost $4,000,000,000 more than Truman's. But what of the balancing of the budget that had been so highly extolled? The crowning paradox was that this great military leader was to carry out his economies at the expense of the armed services. On one occasion, he said that if as president he did nothing but leave a balanced budget, he would think his time at the White House well spent.

One of the Eisenhower Administration's most difficult problems was that of domestic security—the question of the citizens' loyalty, particularly those of them who were employed by the government. One of the arguments used against the Democrats in the election campaign had been that they were too soft with disloyal public servants. Eisenhower thought the idea of loyalty too indefinite and decided to use instead the notion of "security risk." Without having any treacherous intent, a man might constitute a risk by reason of his ideas, his conduct, or his vices. An alcoholic or a drug addict was a potential danger. The head of each department was required to "clean it up."

In October, 1953, the government announced that 1,456 undesirables had been dealt with. The Democrats protested, saying that this arbitrary figure gave the impression that the Truman Administration had left the services infested with spies. Eisenhower himself, always fair minded, said that he much disliked this playing with figures. But McCarthy and his friends on the right wing of the party were not satisfied. They brought about the dismissal of the great physicist J. Robert Oppenheimer, a very well-known scientist and a most highly respected man, upon the claim that he had had Communist friends. Unhappily the 1952 election had made McCarthy one of the most senior senators and he was therefore chairman of the Committee on Government Operations, which made him very powerful. He tried to prevent the nomination of Charles Bohlen, one of the best American diplomats, as ambassador, because he had been among Roosevelt's advisers at Yalta—a conference that had left disagreeable memories behind it. With Taft's support, Eisenhower prevailed, however.

But McCarthy had begun an investigation into the information services (Voice of America and libraries abroad). Two of his agents, Roy Cohn and David Schine, toured Europe, detecting "subversion" on the wing as they made their brief halts at the various capitals. They took all books by leftist authors out of the libraries and, furthermore, books by such men as Foster Rhea Dulles, an admirable historian and the Secretary of State's cousin, and Clarence Streit, an outstanding liberal. Some librarians burned the condemned volumes. This angered Eisenhower. In a speech to the students at Dartmouth he said, "Don't join the book burners. Don't think you are going to conceal faults by concealing evidence that they ever existed . . . . How will we defeat communism unless we know what it is, what it teaches, why it does have such an appeal for men?"

Yet he did not dare to attack McCarthy directly. But when one of McCarthy's followers began on the churches and the army, public opinion was roused against him. An army dental surgeon was accused of being a security risk, and in the course of a hearing, McCarthy insulted a general. For the extremist senators, the President of the United States himself was suspect. The White House published a communiqué that stated no individual had the right to set himself above the law as McCarthy was doing. In this inquiry, the army's legal adviser was an able Boston lawyer, Joseph N. Welch. McCarthy tried to discredit him by accusing him of employing a young man called Fisher, who, he alleged, had belonged to a suspect body, the Lawyers' Guild, long before. Welch exploded. He asserted that Fisher was brilliant and loyal: "Let us not assassinate this lad further, Mr. Senator. You have done enough. Have you no sense of decency, Sir, at long last? Have you left no sense of decency?" Prolonged applause greeted this reproof.

The demagogue muttered, "What did I do wrong?"

He never knew: but he had done too much. In December, 1954, he was censured by the Senate, 67 senators against 22 disavowing him. He took to drink. He desperately tried to attract attention and blamed himself for having supported Eisenhower in 1952. He was finished. On May 2, 1957, he died of an inflamed liver.

IV

During their 1952 campaign, some Republicans had maintained that Truman's policy of containing the advance of communism was too passive, and that a "roll back" policy should take its place. They had taken care not to say how this policy was to be brought to bear. From the beginning of his administration, Eisenhower stated specifically that he had only peaceful methods in mind: he also said that he would not repudiate the engagements made, rightly or wrongly, by his predecessors at Yalta and Potsdam. There were some ultraconservatives who hoped to see Roosevelt and Truman condemned, but Eisenhower, after all, had been the military instrument of their policy. In the Administration's strategy, therefore, there was at no time any question of attacking the rim of the Communist world, or of liberating "the enslaved people." Peace remained the primary aim.

Nevertheless, the new Administration's policy had to have a "new look." The Eisenhower-Dulles team wanted to play the part of a good neighbor in the world, standing for peace and general good will; but it was a necessary condition that they should have another good neighbor to deal with. They certainly wanted to keep up the best possible relationship with all countries; but they also intended to be ready to hit back, instantly and powerfully, against any sort of aggression. Once again, how was this to be accomplished? Dulles let a certain amount of mystery veil the subject. So that the promise to balance the budget could be kept, he wanted the United States to do "more with less." Not too many military or financial engagements, therefore and the country was not to allow itself to be led into local wars. "The way to deter aggression," said Dulles, "is for the free community to be willing and able to respond vigorously, at places and with means of its own choosing."

Dulles chose that the outline of the "new look" should be vague. Critics wondered whether he meant to reply to any peripheral aggression by a violent attack upon the vital centers of the

East—to use "atomic holocausts to counteract brush fires." Dulles certainly had no intention of dropping bombs on Moscow if the Russians tried to subvert and annex some little state in the Middle East; but from the earliest days, he acquired the reputation of being tough, and it may have been useful. His adversaries spoke of his "brinkmanship," that is to say, of his way of going to the very edge of the precipice. He himself said, "We shall not be the aggressors, but we and our allies have and will maintain a massive capability to strike back."

After Stalin's death, the problem was modified by the rhetoric about peaceful coexistence. In Russia, the ruling team changed several times. In 1953, Lavrenti Beria was put to death: in 1955, Malenkov lost his place as premier. Then there began the long partnership of Nikita Khrushchev and Nicolai A. Bulganin, who traveled over the whole world together. In February, 1956, at the twentieth party congress, Khrushchev announced that the cult of personality would henceforward be abolished and replaced by group direction. Once again the emphasis was upon peaceful coexistence. The Eisenhower Administration had therefore to adopt an ambivalent policy. On the one hand, it was necessary to make a sincere reaffirmation of the fact that above all the United States wanted peace throughout the world and the prosperity of all nations; and on the other, the cold war, which was going on on the other side of the screen of coexistence, had to be dealt with.

The "peace offensive" could not fail to please the American nation, so utterly tired of world wars. As soon as Stalin was dead, Eisenhower held out the olive branch to Russia's new leaders. He invited them to join with the United States in making war together on "the brute forces of poverty and need." This speech (February, 1953) was published in *Pravda*. Then, in December, 1953, he and the leaders of the Western world (Churchill, Eden, Laniel, Bidault) discussed the idea of setting up a "bank" of atomic materials, whose stock would be provided by all the producing nations that were in favor of the peaceful use of atomic energy. After this he made a dramatic speech in the United Nations to support the program called Atoms for Peace. It was very long in getting under way, and the International Atomic Energy Agency's charter was not approved until 1956. Unfortunately Atoms for Peace did not do away with Atoms for War. The H bomb had been successfully tried out over the Pacific in 1954.

There was, alas, no want of subject matter for the cold war. In Indochina, France was fighting a difficult battle, and the end of the conflict in Korea allowed the Chinese to take part in it. Eisenhower saw the consequences plainly: "You have a row of dominoes set up, and knock over the first one, and what will happen to the last one is a certainty that it will go over very quickly." Vietnam was the first domino. Which was to be the next to fall? Laos, Burma, Cambodia? The situation was so threatening that Vice-President Nixon stated that he personally would not hesitate to send "our American boys" to Indochina. Dulles and Radford went to London and Paris to set out a plan for common action. But the English were against any decisive measures before the conference with the Russians and the Orientals that was to take place at Geneva. Eisenhower did not like to act on his own, and he did not send American airplanes to relieve Dienbienphu. France was defeated in Indochina and in 1954 the creation of two independent Vietnams was decided upon—one in the north, associated with the Communist bloc, and one in the south, supported by the United States.

In China itself, Formosa was still a burning question. Eisenhower decided that the Seventh Fleet should no longer stand in the way of an all-out attack by Chiang upon the Chinese mainland. This was a decision of purely academic interest, however, since Formosa did not possess the military equipment for an attack upon China, and in any case had bound herself not to make one without America's consent. The islands of Quemoy and Matsu, close to the mainland, were not covered by the treaty. So far as they were concerned, Eisenhower adopted an attitude of "deliberate ambiguity." He would defend Quemoy and Matsu if an attack upon these islands appeared to be a preparation for an invasion of Formosa. There followed a peaceful interval, lasting three years. At the end of this time, in August, 1958, the Chinese started shelling Quemoy and Matsu again. Now Dulles turned to a threatening form of ambiguity. The shelling stopped, then began again, but only every other day. It was an odd sort of compromise, but the peace of the world was preserved.

Eisenhower had asked for a tangible proof of peaceful coexistence. In the spring of 1955, the Soviets agreed to the conclusion of a peace treaty with Austria, and this seemed to be a first sign of slackening tension. It appeared to be a favorable time for the holding of an East-West summit conference. This took place at Geneva, in July, 1955, the four great powers being represented by Eisenhower, Khrushchev and Bulganin, Edgar Faure, and Anthony Eden. Eisenhower seemed radiantly hopeful. He affectionately welcomed his wartime comrade, Marshall Zhukov, and gave him a wedding present for his daughter. The most dramatic moment occurred when Eisenhower proposed that the United States and Russia should exchange plans of all their military installations, and that this exchange should be followed by an "open sky inspection," each of the two countries granting the other the right to fly over its territory. The delegates heard this with astonishment: they were very much moved. While the President was speaking, a flash of lightning cut off the electricity, and the lights went out, which made the moment even more dramatic. At the end of the speech, Edgar Faure said, "I wish the peoples of the world could have been in this room to hear the voice ... speaking from great military experience. ... They would believe that something had changed in the world. ... I am sure this conference has scored its first victory over skepticism."

In point of fact, nothing at all was settled at Geneva. Bulganin would not give an inch on the German question. Eisenhower wanted free elections that would lead to the reunification of the country. The Russians said that West Germany's membership in NATO made all discussion upon the subject pointless. They proposed a European treaty for collective security that would replace both the Atlantic Pact and the Warsaw Treaty. Eisenhower very much wanted to end on a positive note: "I came here because of my lasting faith in the decent instincts and good sense of the people who populate this world of ours. I shall return home tonight with these convictions unshaken and with the prayer that the hope of mankind will one day be realized." He had never supposed that a week of meetings would be enough to do away with the gulf that separated the East from the West, but in his mind, and in the minds of the somewhat comforted nations, the "spirit of Geneva" remained as a symbol and an example.

Toward the end of that summer, in September, 1955, the President had a serious heart attack. He was at Denver, staying with his mother-in-law, and he had been playing golf. A violent pain in his chest woke him up. The doctors sent him to the hospital with all possible speed. There was a clot blocking an artery near his heart. Would he recover? In any case, it would take a long time. Vice-President Nixon was told. He called a meeting of the Cabinet, and Dulles set forth the international situation. It was very disturbing indeed, particularly in the Near East. The great body of the Arabs were turning against the West. In Egypt, Gamal Abdel Nasser, who had taken the place of General Mohammed Naguib, was obtaining arms from the USSR. Nixon wanted the government to limit itself to carrying out decisions that had already been made, until the return of the President, whose health was improving.

V

Health returned to the President more quickly than calm to the Near East. In June, 1956, when the last British officer had left Egypt, Nasser invited Russian foreign minister, Dmitri T. Shepilov, to come and join the celebrations. He obtained the promise of Russian financial support for the building of the Aswan Dam that would provide irrigation for a great deal of desert land. Yet at the same time he had meetings with Eugene Black, the president of the World Bank, which gave the impression that he was negotiating with two sides at once. Or even with three, since he also conferred with the neutralists Tito and Nehru. The United States was not hostile to neutralism. "We were a young country once, and we were neutral," said Eisenhower, in his good-natured way. At the beginning of July it seemed that Egypt and the West would soon reach agreement. The World Bank, the United States, and Great Britain in their turn promised to pay for the construction of the huge dam.

Suddenly everything went wrong. Had Nasser's flirtations with the USSR and China made Dulles lose his patience? Were the American cotton growers uneasy about the great rise in production that the dam would make possible? Was it that the future of the whole thing seemed unsure, because Egyptians had not been able to come to an agreement with their neighbors on the use of the Nile water? Or was it because the Egyptians themselves were unable to contribute to the expense, since they had taken to exchanging their cotton for arms from the Communist countries instead of selling it for money? Was Dulles afraid that Nasser, with the weapons and the experts supplied by the East, was going to try to crush Israel? All these factors had their influence. Congress was intensely irritated by Nasser's behavior and would certainly not have voted the money. It was abruptly announced that in the present circumstances the United States would not take part in the project.

Nasser flew into a terrible rage. He hurled insults at the Americans and seized the Suez Canal. "I look at you, you Americans, and I say to you, 'May you choke with anger.'" In a three-hour speech at Alexandria, he said that Egypt would run the Canal by herself, since American financial support had no other aim than buying nations, reducing them to slavery, and robbing them of their sovereignty. There was strong reaction in England, France, and Israel. Eden and Guy Mollet said that the seizure of the Canal was the first step toward a new Hitlerism. What was to be done? Dulles suggested a plan for making the Canal international but did nothing to realize it. For a while he seemed to favor an economic boycott of Egypt, but this dwindled to a vague scheme for sending the oil from the Middle East around by South Africa. In despair, Eden and Mollet took the matter before the Security Council of the United Nations. They got no satisfaction there, and it appeared to them that they had no remedy left but force.

Israel had for a long while been engaged in border skirmishes with Egypt. On October 29, 1956, she invaded the Sinai Peninsula, and her armies reached the Canal, but the Egyptians had had time to block it. English and French expeditionary forces, coming from Cyprus, supported the Israeli armies. In theory, they were throwing themselves between the Egyptians and the Israelis, according to the right given them by a tripartite declaration of 1950. But the undertaking could succeed only if it were brought to an end so quickly that it presented the world with a fait accompli. This did not happen. President Eisenhower was angry at not having been told beforehand, and he was even angrier at seeing his own allies guilty of violating the United Nations charter. It was true that Nasser had committed the first aggression in seizing the canal, but the infuriated Eisenhower ordered the Sixth Fleet to take up positions along the Egyptian coast. "For we do not accept the use of force as a wise and proper instrument for the settlement of international disputes." In the United Nations, the United States denounced the military intervention and voted with the USSR. Bulganin threatened France and England with his atomic rockets. Under this double pressure, to which must be added the British Labour party's disavowal of the operation, a cease fire was ordered. For some time, the Western Alliance seemed in grave danger. On both sides, there was very strong resentment. Eisenhower thought that his allies had failed to live up to the spirit of Geneva: the French and English said that they had exhausted all peaceable methods before recourse to arms, and they blamed Dulles, who could have brought them legal support.

Taking everything into account, Eisenhower's popularity in his own country remained at the highest pitch. He had not only got over his heart attack, but also, in June, 1956, an operation. As early as July, he was sufficiently recovered to announce that his doctors would allow him to run for reelection. He was advised to jettison his vice-president; but he was steadfast in his friendships, and he kept Nixon. The Republican convention at San Francisco therefore remained faithful to the Eisenhower-Nixon ticket. In the opinion of the American masses, Geneva had been a triumph for the President; they were grateful to him for having maintained peace. In home affairs, the party proudly recorded the undeniable "Eisenhower prosperity" and hoped that the partnership between the government and private industry would go on.

The Democrats met at Chicago, and in spite of pressure from Truman in favor of Averell Harriman, they once more chose Adlai Stevenson as their candidate. They attacked the Republicans for their "dawdle and drift" policy over Suez—their "dead dog" policy. It may be observed, in passing, that this dead dog had in fact shown only too many teeth. As for agriculture, the Democrats promised the farmers a 90 percent guarantee of parity prices. There is always a great deal of eloquent support for the American farmers at election time. As for the partnership between the government and industry, it was in fact, according to the Democrats, no more than the pillaging of the public's wealth by private interests. Both parties undertook to support civil equality—they were both competing for the Negro vote. Stevenson emphasized the country's need of a leader: and according to him, the President was only capable of part-time leadership.

No argument could make headway against the personal popularity of a man who so exactly embodied the average American's ideal of a president, an honest, smiling, modest, religious man; nor against the general approval of a policy that still maintained the peace. Stevenson won no more than the electoral votes of six Southern states, 73 in all, while Eisenhower had 457, an overwhelming victory. On the other hand, in both houses of Congress the Democrats retained their majority, although it was indeed a very small one. The American public liked Ike, but the New Deal and the Fair Deal still kept their charm.

VI

One of the Eisenhower Administration's chief problems in home politics was that of the Negroes' civil rights. The three amendments to the Constitution that guaranteed the Negroes all the civil rights of citizens and the vote had remained a dead letter since the Civil War. The Negroes in the South were separated from the whites in the schools, in public transport, in business, and even in places of amusement. Even the Supreme Court, in 1896, had appeared to give segregation its blessing by stating that there might be different schools for the two races, providing that in those schools the children received equal treatment.

In 1954, the Supreme Court, under the presidency of a new chief justice, Republican Earl Warren, unanimously decided that segregation in schools was contrary to the Fourteenth Amendment. The psychological effect of segregation on the Negro children, said the court, was of such a nature as to engender a feeling of inferiority: whatever the degree of material equality, it was impossible, in these circumstances, to speak of "equal treatment." The Supreme Court acknowledged that integration should come about gradually, for these tendencies were so deeply rooted in the South that it was clearly impossible to change them from one day to the next; but it ordered that integration should be carried out "with all deliberate speed."

The President had nothing to do with this decision; but he gave his backing to a program of desegregation that made rapid progress in Washington, for example, and even in the White House. He nevertheless recognized an emotional opposition to the court's ruling. "You cannot change the hearts of the people by law," he said.

In certain Southern states, there was a violent reaction. Some tried to evade the law by closing the public schools and subsidizing the private schools reserved for whites. The head-on encounter between the federal government and the South took place at Little Rock, Arkansas, in September, 1957. The federal court had approved a plan for gradual integration in the Central High School of Little Rock—a plan that was subsequently to spread to the other schools. Nine young Negroes (out of two thousand pupils) were to be admitted to the Central High School. Orval E. Faubus, the governor of Arkansas, announced that to prevent bloodshed he would have the school surrounded by the National Guard. On September 4, nine Negro students presented themselves: the soldiers barred their way.

Governor Faubus, having promised to obey the orders of the federal judges, was received by the President. On September 23, the nine Negroes tried again. A crowd of five hundred shouted "Where are the niggers? We'll lynch them!" Then there was a riot. One Negro child barely escaped from the mob. The police sent the others home. Eisenhower grew angry: he loathed the idea of sending troops to Little Rock, but he very seriously observed that if once a president allowed might to become right, the result would be anarchy. He stationed a thousand parachute troops at Little Rock, and under their protection the young Negroes were able to get into the school. The federal troops remained in Arkansas for many months. Next year, at the beginning of the September, 1958, term, Faubus closed all the high schools: they stayed closed for a year, the children carrying on their education as best they could. The people began to grow tired of this fruitless struggle. When the Little Rock School Board dismissed forty-eight teachers who were in favor of integration, the voters got rid of the anti-integrationist members of the board. By the autumn of 1959, the ground was prepared for integration. Farther to the north, the State of Virginia declared that it was determined, albeit against its will, to obey the federal judges. The more sanguine minds thought that this example would be followed and that integration was now only a matter of time.

As for the actual practice of the Negroes' right to vote, until 1957 Congress had obstructed all bills dealing with the subject— every time, the Southern senators organized a filibuster to wreck the debate. But in 1957, the climate of Congress had changed. Eisenhower's attitude on civil rights had brought many colored voters over to his side; and now some Republican senators joined the Northern liberals. The NAACP (National Association for the Advancement of Colored People) had carried on an intelligent, restrained campaign in favor of a law concerning guarantees to free vote. Two Southerners, Senator Lyndon B. Johnson (leader of the Democratic majority in the Senate) and Sam Rayburn, the Speaker of the House of Representatives, both Texans, caused a compromise law to be passed. "Let us make this session of Congress," said Johnson, "an historic session. We must all give in a little if we want to find a reasonable solution, rather than exacerbate extremist convictions." Wisdom was gaining ground.

This law set up a Civil Rights Commission, whose duty it was to make inquiries in all states where the Negroes complained of being kept from the ballot box. This commission was empowered to call for prosecutions in the federal courts that would henceforward have the right of issuing an injunction against any person guilty of having deprived Negroes of the right to vote. The measure withdrew this type of case from the Southern juries that invariably acquitted the accused whites. In 1960, Congress passed still another law that (a) gave the federal authorities the right to take over the supervision of the enrollments on the electoral lists from the local registrars in those sections in which Negroes were refused the right to vote; and (b) ordered the preservation of the registers for twenty-two months, so that they might be inspected by the Department of Justice.

There was no doubt of the progress; but many Negroes thought it too slow and turned to other methods. At Montgomery, Alabama, they boycotted public transport until segregation in it was abolished. They then successfully made use of passive resistance, chanting the Lord's Prayer and the national anthem. This peaceful movement, after the fashion of Ghandi, made a great impression. There was a widely distributed manual of passive resistance: "Don't strike back or curse back if abused. Show yourself friendly and courteous at all times." The day when the Negroes would let themselves be overawed was past: they were now advancing toward integration. But there were still to be many setbacks.

VII

The next very important factor in home politics was the relationship between the government and the world of labor. The workers had acquired new strength since the union of the two great federations, the AF of L (American Federation of Labor) and the CIO (Congress of Industrial Organizations) in 1955. The new body included more than 15,000,000 members, the biggest unions being the United Auto Workers, 1,239,000 members (CIO), the Teamsters, 1,418,246 (AF of L), and the Steel Workers, 960,000 (CIO).* The railwaymen remained independent. George Meany (AF of L) was president and Walter Reuther, of the automobile workers (CIO), vice-president. It was Walter Reuther who negotiated the famous annual wage contract with Ford, Chrysler, and General Motors in 1956.

These gigantic unions had very large sums of money at their disposal. It was of importance both to the workers and the government that the funds should be honestly managed. The AF of L–CIO did its best to get rid of suspect leaders, but in the case of the Teamsters, the Senate had to take a hand. Dave Beck, the president of that union, was found guilty of having appropriated $400,000 of its money. He had bought $94,000 worth of shirts, radios, and golf balls. "I don't think he plays golf, so he must be very generous and give away his golf balls," said the union's legal adviser. He had induced the employers to present him with a car and a chauffeur. As he had cheated the tax gatherers in the bargain, he was sent to prison for five years. Before this, George Meany had expelled the Teamsters from the AF of L–CIO federation. A Labor Reform Act, upheld in the Senate by young John F. Kennedy of Massachusetts, tried to establish a kind of Bill of Rights for the mass of ordinary union members, so that they would be able to exercise control.

* 1958 figures.

Eisenhower was most scrupulous in all matters to do with honesty, and he did his utmost to protect his own administration from any kind of corruption. He was very fond of Sherman Adams, his assistant, who took a great deal of work off his shoulders and who, during his illness, had dealt actively and intelligently with current affairs. But in 1958, Sherman Adams resigned, accusing himself of imprudence for having accepted presents from his old friend Bernard Goldfine. As it happened, Goldfine had difficulties about this time with the Securities and Exchange Commission: Adams telephoned to find what it was all about. No more was needed to start Congressional inquiries. Eisenhower was ready to defend his assistant, and he publicly expressed his high opinion of Adams. But Adams felt that Caesar's assistant must be above suspicion, and he resigned. The President and the Cabinet very much regretted his going. But no doubt severity of this kind is healthy enough.

Another case was the Dixon-Yates contract. The right wing of the party had long wished to be rid of the TVA, the state enterprise that distributed electric power. "Pure socialism," said the orthodox Republicans. It was suggested that the TVA's contract with the Atomic Energy Commission should be transferred to two private firms, whose presidents were Edgar Dixon and Eugene Yates. The Democrats cried out, and shouted even louder when they learned that a man employed by Dixon and Yates as a financial agent had taken part in the government conferences on the contract in his other capacity of consultant to the Bureau of the Budget. Eisenhower felt more strongly about straight dealing than anything else whatsoever, and he ordered the contract canceled.

He remained constant to his middle-of-the-road policy; and while he still set his face against "socialism," he continued to give the government's support to public works and to do his best for unemployment insurance, so important for dealing with any eventual recession. In 1958, there were signs of weakness in the country's economy, with the number of unemployed rising to five million, or 7.5 percent of all the workers. The now classic machinery of credit and assistance for the workless was successfully set in motion. The recession did not last long; yet it was important enough to give the Democrats a majority of 281 to 153 in the House of Representatives and 62 to 34 in the Senate in the elections of 1958. The President was as much loved as ever, but it was now the Democrats who passed his measures. The great question was still the budget. He had promised to balance it and at the same time to lower taxes: the international situation made this a very difficult promise to keep.

VIII

The foreign policy of the United States had become largely isolationist after 1815, and it had remained predominantly so until 1917; then, during both world wars, it had been idealist. Now it was rapidly becoming a struggle for life. Atomic bombs and H bombs were so powerful that they could destroy vast countries—perhaps, indeed, the whole human race. For some time America had been able to rely upon her superiority in long-range bombers, but for reasons of economy their construction had been slowed down. "We're operating on half burner," said Air Force Chief of Staff General Nathan Twining. Furthermore, intermediate-range and intercontinental ballistic missiles were reaching a high state of perfection that made the danger even more urgent.

The spirit of Geneva, which might have exorcised the danger, was rapidly fading away. East and West were unable to agree about Germany, about disarmament, about freedom of exchange between the two worlds. Yet there was a different tone since Stalin's death. The tough Vyacheslov Molotov had had to yield the foreign ministry to Dmitri Shepilov. In 1955, the Soviet Union announced that the Russian army would be reduced by 640,000 men. Admiral Radford brought forward a plan that would cut the effectives by 450,000, reducing the numbers in Europe by 180,000. This alarmed the United States' European allies as well as some Americans. "The huge Soviet army," said this school of thought, "can stand such a reduction better than ours, which has already been very much cut down." John Foster Dulles, who was in favor of defense by nuclear deterrent, agreed to a partial demobilization; but Congress, on its own initiative, took the most unusual and surprising measure of increasing the military appropriations that Eisenhower asked for, by $900,000,000. He did not spend these additional sums. He had commanded the greatest army that history had ever known, and he did not care to be advised by senators. Resignedly he observed, "Now they want a nuclear carrier, enormously expensive and useless in a big war. Congress seems to be going on the theory that we have to have all of everything everywhere all the time." In his opinion, what the country's defense needed far more than extra supplies was closer cooperation between the three services, the air force, army, and navy. "It is not a question of defending generals, but the American people."

Presently the attitude of the USSR hardened again. Andrei Gromyko replaced Shepilov as foreign minister. An "antiparty group" was eliminated, and then Bulganin himself. Khrushchev became prime minister. It seemed that for the time being the Soviet "new look" was to be abandoned. In 1957, the London Disarmament Conference bogged down as usual on the problem of inspection. Meanwhile the United States was growing uneasy at the sight of Russia winning new allies, without war, particularly in the Middle East.

The United States' policy at the time of Suez had helped settle Nasser firmly in his place, but without making a friend of him. In January, 1957, the President set forth an "Eisenhower doctrine": he spoke "of building a peace with justice, in a world where moral law prevails.... The United States has a deep involvement and responsibility in events that may lead to controversy or conflict in every part of the world, whether they touch on the affairs of a vast region, the fate of an island in the Pacific, or the use of a canal in the Middle East." It should not be supposed, added the President, that the Middle East would not be defended in the event of armed aggression, for, were that to occur, the United States would be bound to take forcible measures. It was no longer a question of the "massive retaliation" dear to John Foster Dulles, but rather of local campaigns, if they became necessary.

As early as 1956, Nasser's supporters had successfully organized a coup d'état in Syria. On February 1, 1958, Egypt and Syria decided that henceforth they should form a single state, the United Arab Republic. The aim was to frustrate the Baghdad Pact, whose members were Turkey, Iran, Iraq, Pakistan, and Great Britain, and which Nasser called "an instrument of colonialism." In July, 1958, a whole flood of events brought the Middle East onto the front pages of the entire world's newspapers. In Iraq, Nasser's supporters overturned the government; in Lebanon, President Camille Chamoun complained of infiltration by Syria. He had appealed to the United Nations in vain; as a last resort he called upon the United States.

Eisenhower had just said that he accepted great responsibilities in the Middle East, and he was obliged to act: he did so rapidly, for he was afraid that "operation domino"—by which he meant if one country fell it would topple others in succession—might once more succeed only too well. Covered by the Sixth Fleet, 1,700 United States Marines suddenly landed in Lebanon, while the English sent 2,000 men into Jordan. Ten thousand parachute troops followed and peacefully took up positions around Beirut. Furthermore, the State Department announced that the United States would become a member of the Baghdad Pact. The USSR brought the Lebanese question before the United Nations. Eisenhower made a speech to the Assembly, explaining that his country could not remain unmoved by an indirect aggression, that he had acted in the name of the United Nations, and that he would withdraw his troops as soon as the United Nations was capable of insuring the maintenance of peace in that region.

It appeared that John Foster Dulles had thoroughly implemented the doctrine of containment; for the whole globe was now covered by three defensive pacts—NATO (North Atlantic Treaty Organization), METO (Middle East Treaty Organization), and SEATO (South East Asia Treaty Organization). A treaty of mutual defense had been concluded between the United States, Great Britain, France, the Philippines, Australia, New Zealand, Thailand (formerly Siam), and Pakistan. Each of these countries promised, with the reservations made necessary by the workings of its particular constitution, to resist any armed attack in the zone covered by the treaty. A separate agreement extended the protection to Laos, Cambodia, and South Vietnam.

The American continent itself provided problems of its own. In 1954, the regime of President Arbenz of Guatemala showed a strong leftist tendency with evidence of increasing ascendency of Communist elements. Under cover of the Organization of American States, the United States armed Guatemala's neighbors, Honduras and Nicaragua. A "counterrevolution" brought Guatemala back to the side of the West. But the Department of State was growing uneasy at the latent hostility toward the United States in Latin America. The mass of the people there were exceedingly poor, and this favored revolutionary propaganda: what is more, at the time of the "little recession" of 1958, the United States had cut its imports of lead from Peru, of coffee from Brazil and Colombia, and of wool from the Argentine and Uruguay, which caused discontent and resentment.

When the new Argentinian president, Arturo Frondizi, was to be installed, Eisenhower sent Vice-President Nixon to make a good-neighbor tour in Latin America. He was received with violent hostility. In Peru, students stopped his car and threw stones and eggs at him. Nixon shouted: "Are you afraid to talk to me?" A stone then hit him in the neck: he courageously shook his fist at the mob and cried, "Cowards! You are cowards, afraid of the truth!" The Lima papers deplored these incidents. But the warning was clear enough to the State Department: Congress had made a serious mistake in raising tariffs and reducing the aid to foreign nations. In so divided a world, no short-term electoral policy was allowable. In March, 1960, Eisenhower himself in the course of an extended tour in Latin America made a powerful declaration in Montevideo upon the necessity of strengthening both economic cooperation and democratic institutions.

But in order to strengthen one must first of all be strong. In October, 1957, the Russians put their sputnik, the first artificial satellite, into orbit, thus proving that they could launch huge devices and launch them with precision. Eisenhower maintained that the country's essential defense was still adequate because the bombers of the Strategic Air Command, on the one hand, and the intermediate-range rockets, on the other, provided an effectual deterrent. But there was strong and mounting criticism. Senator Lyndon Johnson affirmed that control of space gave control of the world. General James Gavin, the director of research, resigned from the army after having strongly criticized the inadequacy of the defense program: "Do more or we will be out-distanced." Gavin thought that it was essential to be prepared not only for a world war but also for limited operations with tactical nuclear weapons. He was also in favor of larger supplies for research and experiments to do with space.

"Most of us," admitted the President, "did not anticipate the intensity of the psychological impact on the world of the launching of the first satellite." Yet it might have been foreseen. Sherman Adams says that the Administration was not trying to score points in an interplanetary game of basketball. But it was not only the spectacular side of the launching of the sputniks that counted: there was also the precision of the space machines—the proof of the scientific ability of the men who built them. Eisenhower took steps to improve scientific teaching in America, and he also did his best to put an end to the rivalry of the three services (army, navy, and air force) that were quarreling over the missiles. Belatedly, on January 31, 1958, the United States sent its first satellite, Explorer I, into space from Cape Canaveral. Now America was in the race, although with a certain disadvantage, both in the matter of time and of size. In November, 1958, there came the successful launching of the intercontinental rocket Atlas that hit its target area 6,325 miles away. More and more American satellites revolved about the earth. The two countries aimed at reaching the moon, Venus, and Mars. The Americans set up a National Aeronautics and Space Administration to cordinate their projects.

In 1959, John Foster Dulles died of cancer, working bravely until the last moment. Even those who had suffered from his obstinacy admired his fortitude in those days. As secretary of state, he had flown some five hundred thousand miles, visiting forty-seven different countries. People spoke of his "infinite capacity for taking planes," but few today would deny that he had labored mightily and with a considerable measure of success to shore up the free world's defenses against communism. Christian A. Herter, who came after him, inherited a difficult task. Once more the Russians had raised the question of Berlin. They asked for a conference in order to demilitarize Germany; and they said that, if it were not held, they would conclude a separate peace with East Germany that would thenceforward be the only authority competent to deal with the status of Berlin. Now the Western Allies had never recognized East Germany. There was a general feeling that the only way of breaking this deadlock was another summit conference.

Khrushchev launched his peace offensive. His right-hand man, Anastas Mikoyan, visited the United States in 1959 and made himself particularly agreeable. "Are both of us so sick of the burdens we have to carry," asked Eisenhower, "that we want to find a way out of this dilemma?"

Mikoyan made jokes: he shook the hands of bankers and boot blacks. "Why can't we get along?" he cried, on a variety of occasions. The USSR and the United States exchanged exhibitions.

Frol R. Kozlov, the vice-premier, came to New York to open the Russian exhibition.

Vice-President Nixon went to Moscow to open the United States counterpart. There he found a lowering atmosphere. The Berlin question, the failure of the foreign ministers' conference at Geneva, and above all a "Captive Nations Week" that the United States had organized at this untimely moment, had all contributed to put the Russian prime minister into a bad temper.

Nixon was accompanied by his wife, Pat, Dr. Milton Eisenhower, and Admiral Hyman Rickover, the father of those atomic submarines that had recently passed under the ice pack of the North Pole—a superb feat, but scarcely the one best calculated to delight the Russians. At the airport the welcome was frigid, although Nixon handed out chewing gum to the children and shouted "Long live peace" in Russian. Khrushchev spoke woundingly of the representative of the panic-stricken capitalists, who had come to look at the "captive nations."

Then they went to see the American exhibition—cars, supermarkets, ideal homes—and as they went around they talked together.

Khrushchev: Russian newly built houses have all this equipment right now, yet you say we are the slaves of communism.

Nixon: To us diversity, the right to choose, is the most important thing.

Khrushchev: On political problems, we will never agree.

Nixon: When we sit at the conference table with you, it cannot be all one way; one side cannot put an ultimatum to the other.

Khrushchev: Who is raising an ultimatum?

Nixon: We will discuss that later.

Khrushchev: If you have raised the question, why not go on with it while the people are listening?

The exchanges were sharp enough, but for all that both men seemed to be enjoying themselves. James Reston of the New York Times cabled, "The Vice-President and the Premier acted like politicians conscious of the gallery . . . like what would have happened if Mr. Nixon and Mr. Truman had made a trip together through a country fair."

On the whole, Nixon's tour was a success. He faced down planted Communist hecklers while visiting Soviet industrial plants. And he was wildly acclaimed in Warsaw, Poland.

In September, 1959, Khrushchev visited the United States. He was at the top of his form and in an excellent temper: coexistence had never seemed so peaceful. In Washington, he bowed his head as he passed before the Lincoln memorial: "A truly great man," he said. In the course of his tour around the United States, he often spoke of his plan for complete disarmament in four years: he also extolled the Soviet economic system and endeavored to reduce the force of his famous remark "We shall bury you" without actually withdrawing it. It only meant, he said, that the objective historical process would insure the rule of communism. Many times, in California, he hurried over to the crowd and shouted "Spassibo! Thank you!" At San Francisco he said, "Now, if I were to use a somewhat poetic word, you have virtually charmed us here. You really are charmers, magicians; you have managed to charm me, a representative of a Socialist state . . . . You have charmed my heart, but, in my head, I still think our system is a good system. You evidently think that your system is a good one. Well, God be with you! Live under it."

At Los Angeles, someone threw a tomato. "It may have been a very good tomato," said Khrushchev, "but the fact is it hit the car in which the chief of police was driving, so he decided to show us his power and deprived us of the pleasure of visiting the city of fantasy, Disneyland, which we were scheduled to visit." He had a tolerably rough encounter with Walter Reuther, when he met the union leaders and called them "capitalist lackeys." He said to Reuther, "You are like a nightingale. It closes its eyes when it sings and sees nothing and hears nobody but himself."

But his good humor returned when he reached a farm in Iowa, where he walked happily about the fields, discussing corn and pigs with the journalists and observing that Henry Cabot Lodge, who was accompanying him and whom he used to call "my capitalist," had "never experienced such smells as these." The journey ended with a stay at Camp David with Eisenhower, during which a summit meeting was arranged for May, 1960, in Paris. The talks were open and cordial. The spirit of Camp David was akin to that of Geneva: everything seemed for the best in the best of divided worlds.

But the spirit of Camp David was not enough when the pilot of an American U2 high-altitude reconnaissance plane flew over Russia, got himself shot down, and admitted that he was there on a spying mission. The handling of the incident was inept: but in fact neither of the two countries was ignorant of the fact that the other was spying on it. What then was the real meaning of all the fury? Had Khrushchev come to the conclusion that too friendly a reconciliation with the capitalist world was a danger for the public mind? Had the Chinese intervened? Or was this a cold, calculated anger, dictated by a political technique that was exceedingly good at disconcerting the other side by blowing now hot, now cold. The Americans who had let themselves be seduced by the charms of Khrushchev the traveler were dumbfounded when he refused to discuss the agenda at the second summit conference in Paris, in May, 1960, upon the pretext of the U2 incident. Khrushchev broke up the conference: the cold war began again.

There was no want of ideological battlefields. In Cuba, a revolution had brought Fidel Castro to power: he at once seized property owned by Americans. By way of retaliation, Eisenhower cut down the purchases of Cuban sugar and broke off diplomatic relations. The Communists fell upon such an opportunity, offering both weapons and contracts to Cuba. Then there was the Congo that had become independent in July, 1960, and that seemed to be going from colonialism into anarchy, despite the United Nations' attempts at bringing the opposing factions together. In Asia, there was Laos, the most exposed of the "dominoes," a continual source of acute anxiety to the State Department. During the autumn of 1960, the glass-walled palace of the United Nations was a noisy, apprehensive Tower of Babel. In the center of the stage, there was Khrushchev; and all around there were the other statesmen, vainly trying to guess his real intentions. He embraced Castro, interrupted Macmillan; and then for a moment he was the charmer of Camp David once more. Not a single problem was solved. Meanwhile the end of Eisenhower's second term was drawing near.

IX

In October and November, 1960, the present writer traveled through the American continent. The presidential election was not causing much of a stir. There were two dominant feelings: personal affection for the retiring president and doubts about the United States' standing in the world. As has been already said, the U2 affair had been thoroughly badly handled by the Administration—denied, denied again, and then avowed—and it had presented the East with a unique opportunity for propaganda. The strength of the dollar was in question; intercontinental defense seemed inadequate. The rate of increase in the economy seemed too slow. The country had never had a more prosperous appearance, but in 1958, a sudden uneasiness had brought a tidal wave of Democrats into both the Senate and the House of Representatives. It was a sign—and a warning.

Yet had Eisenhower stood again, he would have been reelected. "I like Ike" still interpreted a great deal of the country's feeling. But Ike did not want a third term, and was constitutionally debarred from one even if he desired it. He gave his support to Richard Nixon. The liberal Republicans would rather have had Nelson A. Rockefeller, but he could not command enough party support. From then onward Nixon, Eisenhower's heir, was sure of the nomination, at least. On the Democratic side, there was no lack of candidates for the presidency—Stuart Symington, Hubert Humphrey, Lyndon Johnson, Adlai Stevenson. The young Senator John F. Kennedy at once drew ahead of the main body, and he never lost his lead. He was the descendant of two financially and politically powerful Boston-Irish clans, the Fitzgeralds and the Kennedys, and he had "a jet-powered bandwagon" consisting of the glamorous Kennedy family, the professionals of the party, and a brain trust such as had not been seen since the days of Franklin D. Roosevelt. To mention just a few, Arthur M. Schlesinger, Jr., and John Kenneth Galbraith, among the most provocative minds at Harvard, were his advisers.

The experts maintained that the Democratic candidate's weakness was his Catholicism, and they recalled the failure of Al Smith. But the experts were wrong. Times had changed. There were many more Catholics in America now, and they made up a very useful addition to the vote. Other minorities also backed Kennedy, and he won many of the primaries. Long before the two national party conventions, almost the whole of the country was of the opinion that the battle would be fought out between Nixon and Kennedy. In July, the Democratic convention gave Kennedy an immense majority. As he had included civil rights in his platform, which was bound to annoy the South, he restored the balance by choosing Senator Lyndon Johnson of Texas as vice-president. The theme of his acceptance speech was the New Frontier, the frontier of unknown opportunities and of hopes that had not yet been realized.

Some Republicans still hoped that Nelson Rockefeller would change his mind: he had publicly criticized Nixon, saying that he marched toward the future carrying a banner with a question mark as its sole device. Nixon saved himself by a brilliant political maneuver. He had talks in New York with Rockefeller that lasted for eight hours, and there emerged a document that was called the Fifth Avenue Treaty and that by implication adversely criticized the retiring Administration, promising greater efforts in national defense and social security. On that day, Rockefeller succeeded in turning his party toward a more liberal policy. Nixon was in a false position, since as vice-president still in power he was prevented from dissociating himself from the Administration; but he had succeeded in causing Rockefeller to put into words all that he could not utter himself. The Old Guard, now led by Senator Barry Goldwater of Arizona, said that Nixon had surrendered, and that this was the Republican party's Munich; but the agreement was signed. The danger was that Eisenhower might be angered by it, and in fact he did say, "You are saying that you and I haven't done a proper job." But he continued to support Nixon, who was adopted as the Republican candidate on the first ballot. Nixon offered the vice-presidency to Henry Cabot Lodge of Massachusetts, an able politician with a great political name and heritage in the Republican party.

There was a general want of precision in the main lines of the campaign. Kennedy asserted that the United States' prestige had declined. At an earlier time, Teddy Roosevelt had carried a big stick and had talked softly: the motto of the present Administration, Kennedy said, seemed to be "Talk tough and carry a toothpick." Kennedy asked for more money for defense, for the workers (a minimum hourly wage of $1.25), for education, and, widely speaking, for welfare. The USSR was turning out 125,000 engineers a year, three times as many as the United States. John Foster Dulles' foreign policy, said the Democrats, had alienated many countries. "We have pinned medals on the chests of hated dictators." At the beginning of the campaign, some of the voters seemed to be disturbed by the question of Kennedy's Catholicism. An assembly of Protestant ministers reminded the people that he belonged to a church whose headquarters were in Rome. Was he going to consult the Vatican before every decision? But Eisenhower and Nixon very honorably undertook never to raise the question of religion during the campaign, and they kept their promise.

By October, the election campaign was in full swing. It was an odd battle—one in which the two opponents were defending almost the same program. Both said that they were in favor of giving the underdeveloped countries the American farm surpluses for nothing; both were for the retraining for new jobs of the surplus agricultural workers. Nixon accused Kennedy of weakness in foreign policy because he had said that the United States should have apologized for the U2 incident. Kennedy regained the advantage in the first of several televised debates, a new feature of this campaign. Thanks to the little screen, the American people, like the peoples of the ancient world, could all assemble in the Forum: a hundred million watchers on television could hear and see the two youngish men (Kennedy was forty-three; Nixon, forty-seven) seriously discussing serious questions. Nixon, who had recently been unwell, seemed nervous and pale during the first debate. Kennedy was less known to the public, and he had the opportunity of showing his self-possession, his keen intelligence, and his maturity. Reporting these debates, that severe judge *Time* praised "the cool objectivity, the freedom from hoopla. There was no place to hide, no occasion for sonorous platitudes." However, Nixon showed to much better advantage in the subsequent television confrontations of the series.

Kennedy criticized Eisenhower for the inadequacy of his moral guidance on the question of civil rights, for the insufficiency of the United States' aid to underprivileged regions, and for

318

having taken too little notice of the needs of Latin America. Nixon contested his rival's harsh judgment upon the standing of the United States in 1960. He asserted that the country's standing was very high indeed. Amidst all the campaigning, the Assembly of the United Nations continued its sittings and its debates in New York, to the sound of the sirens howling in front of official cars and in the middle of an incredible multitude of police, while from the balcony of his country's embassy Khrushchev harangued the crowds on Park Avenue.

Gradually the tone of the televised dialogues grew sharper, but not to excess. Kennedy said that it was impossible to defend Quemoy and Matsu, and this allowed Nixon to win a point. "There was a principle involved," he said. "If we surrendered the two islands, a chain reaction would occur." For his part, Kennedy criticized the economic embargo against Cuba. "Too little and too late," he said. Nixon counterattacked by blaming Kennedy for a remark on the support to be given to the anti-Castro forces. As the present writer followed these debates in four different universities, he found that the dons among whom he was staying were very hesitant. "I'm still undecided," said the greater part of the watchers. Yet Kennedy's fetching ways, the quickness of his replies, and in a word his charm, seemed to foretell his victory.

On Election Day, the gap between the two candidates was so narrow that in some states the votes had to be recounted. The final reckoning gave Kennedy 34,084,289 votes and Nixon 33,881,866. Very nearly a draw. The Southern ultras had voted for a third candidate. Kennedy had 303 electoral votes against Nixon's 219. He owed his narrow victory to the television, the Catholics, the other minorities, the still-Democratic Southern states, and above all to his youthfulness. John Fitzgerald Kennedy was therefore president of the United States, with a mandate to do more than the preceding administration for defense, education, social security, and the country's prestige. The country itself, after the election, seemed solidly behind its new leader. Nevertheless, his majority had been too slight to justify any sudden changes, alterations like those that had characterized Franklin Roosevelt's Hundred Days.

PART TEN

The United States in 1960

Variety in laws, races, and religions, but fundamental unity. A way of life.

AMERICA is quite as much a continent as it is a nation. The differences between Alabama and New Jersey or between Arizona and Minnesota are certainly as great as those between Spain and Sweden. Neither customs nor laws are the same. For Negroes and whites to travel together was a crime in Mississippi until recent federal rulings forced a change; in the buses of New York, it is perfectly commonplace, accepted by everybody. Impotence in a husband is grounds for divorce in Indiana, but not in Iowa; alcoholism will do in California, whereas in Louisiana it will not. There are countless reasons for divorce in Nevada: in the state of New York there is but adultery alone. So a remarried couple may be guilty of bigamy in New York and innocent in Reno. Wendover is half in Utah and half in

Nevada: one half of the town may gamble and drink, the other may not. America is a continent peopled by all the races of the world. Twenty million citizens have black or yellow skins. In a Los Angeles hotel, the chambermaid may be black, the head waiter Japanese, the elevator boy Puerto Rican, the receptionist Scottish.

In 1960, the population of the United States reached about 180,000,000. Between 1950 and 1960, it had increased by 28,000,000, a record; and that in spite of the fact that the annual immigration no longer exceeded 300,000. If this rising curve of births were maintained, in fifty years the United States would have as many people as the India of today. This "baby boom" is not due to prosperity alone since poverty-stricken nations have a high birth rate, but to the feeling that "the pursuit of happiness" implies the possession of a family, of children.

In America, all religions are freely practiced. The country is impregnated with an imprecise, diffused religious feeling. "I do not know," wrote Tocqueville far back in the nineteenth century, "whether all the Americans believe in their religion, for who can read men's hearts. But I am certain that they believe it necessary for the maintenance of republican institutions." The president of the United States takes his oath on the Bible and goes regularly to church. Eisenhower never missed a Sunday, and at present Kennedy hears Mass before meeting Khrushchev. Sessions of Congress, union conventions. Sometimes even political banquets begin with a prayer, everybody standing, with lowered eyes. The open atheists in the country do not amount to 1 percent of the population, although there are many citizens who are not members of any church. A survey made in 1957 counted more than 35,000,000 Catholics, 60,000,000 Protestants in all, and 5,500,000 Jews. It is possible that religion in the United States may be more of a social than a metaphysical phenomenon; but it is still the basis of all morals.

Black or yellow, German or Italian, Jew or Catholic, they all proudly say, "I am an American." What do they mean by that? They do not have the quasi-religious bond of a sovereign, a single person, that the Canadians and the British have. In America, there is no revolutionary mystique common to all, as it is common to all the various republics of the USSR. Unlike the French, the Americans are not bound together by the soil

322

of their country and by history, for many of them were born in other lands. Yet nevertheless all of them strongly feel the immense pride of belonging to a very great country and a certainty that there exists an American way of life that, by means of a freedom that respects the law, in the long run solves all problems. The tension, among so many national groups, rarely becomes dangerous. They feel themselves united by the Constitution and by television, by football and baseball, by automobiles and the presidential election, and also by something deeper, which is the love of peace, a genuine wish to act well, a philosophy that tucks tragedy away between brackets, and an optimism that is based upon faith in mankind.

I

Have Americans changed much since 1914? Their essential characteristics are still the same. The first of these is their mobility. The migration from east to west is still going on. Between 1951 and 1960, the State of California alone has gained five million inhabitants, one fifth of the total increase. As Arnold J. Toynbee has said, it is the New World's New World. The center of population of the country as a whole has moved westward since 1920 by 142 miles. Everyday, the sprawling city of Los Angeles receives a thousand new citizens, and its long suburbs run farther out toward the ends of the valleys that surround it. "Six suburbs in search of a city," writes one commentator, not unacquainted with Pirandello. Downtown Los Angeles, the center, is studded with skyscrapers; and all around it there is to be seen a vast plain, bigger than Paris or London, covered with blue, red, green electric signs, perched on little low buildings. Laundries, real estate offices, cheap or expensive restaurants —it is a jungle with no apparent plan, a one-storied Broadway, a world in the act of being born. If a traveler asks the way, the native may reply, "First on the left, second on the right, and straight on for twenty miles." Great main roads, expressways, reach right to the heart of the city: people scarcely move about at all except by car.

Phoenix, in Arizona, is even more surprising. The town stands on the edge of a desert composed of sand and dried mud.

It has a marvelously healthy climate, with a warm, dry winter; and rheumatism melts away like snow in the sun. Five hundred Americans a day come to live there, building elegant, comfortable houses in the desert. After them come the shopkeepers. The university is overflowing with cheerful young people. This desert, with its sand changing color as the sun moves over it, is turning into a metropolis. Some truly nomadic Americans live there in trailers that they tow behind their cars. They choose their climate and their neighborhood, and they set up their homes there in a camp. Thus the spirit of the pioneers of 1860, the pioneers with covered wagons one sees in Western movies, is still alive in 1960; and the Indians themselves are not far away, behind the ever-changing hills.

This mobility is not only a survival from the days of the frontier; it is also enforced by circumstances, by the conditions of life. There are huge organizations, such as General Electric, Du Pont, and so on, that have offices and works all over the country, and they move their people about according to the requirements of promotion. The "organization man" may be sent from Pennsylvania to California. Everywhere he will find branches of the same shops, interchangeable neighbors, nearly similar universities for his children. If the steel works of Ohio operate at only 40 percent of their capacity in 1960 because light metals and plastics have partly replaced steel, the engineer's wife says, "What of it? What if my husband is going to lose his job? We will move, and he will do something else." The growth of air travel has done away with distance. Every year the number of people traveling by air goes up. Even the little towns have their airports. People take planes as they once took buses, although the journey may be short. Very soon the jets will bring Los Angeles within three hours of New York.

The next persistent characteristic is the goodwill of the great body of Americans. The pioneers of the heroic days helped one another because it was utterly essential to do so. Generosity has remained a tradition. The phrase that a foreigner in difficulties hears most often is "May I help?" No doubt there are hard and grasping Americans, as there are hard and grasping people in every country, but the average American is still a kindly man whose intentions are excellent even though his actions may seem a little clumsy. He is said to be a materialist because he feels strongly about the possession of certain machines—his car, his refrigerator, his electrical household gadgets. But the machine liberates him in two ways; on the one hand, it frees the worker from heavy manual labor, and on the other, it frees him from feelings of inferiority. The possession of the same machines brings the people of all classes and all callings closer together. The immigrant who has become an American does not buy a bathtub in order to bathe in it, but to be in a position to take a bath if he chooses. "We are a nation of twenty million bathrooms," writes Mary McCarthy, "with a humanist in each bath." I would prefer "with an idealist in every bath." For what is an idealist but a man who believes in the possibility of making the ideal take its place within the real—of inserting it in the real? That is the American's attitude of mind. The need for a happy ending, which is so strongly felt by those who read magazines or go to movies in America, must, in real life, be associated with a certain generosity. When an entire nation wants a happy ending, it will work with all its heart to make the story end happily.

A country's choice of its great men is both a testimony and a trial. Who was ever less self-seeking than Lincoln? Einstein was respected in America because he was a scientist, a musician, and in politics, a poet. The man in the street knows the name of Mark Twain; he does not know the name of the president of the National City Bank. The American, far from being a materialist, is a disappointed idealist, and he sees himself as the Don Quixote of our day. As a righter of wrongs, he left his village to set the invaded nations free—France and Belgium. For these causes, for these foreigners, he gave his blood and his treasure, though primarily he was fighting to keep his own country free of the danger of such invasion. He has met with many reverses and with very little gratitude. Why? In the first place, because gratitude is not a very widely felt emotion. Secondly, because he had little knowledge of the customs and wishes of those he went to help, and so he spent his time tilting at windmills. And lastly, because he had a natural tendency to rush to extremes.

The Englishman likes compromise. In America, any political attitude quickly becomes utterly rigid. There is a certain kind of American liberal for whom big business is the devil; its interests are opposed to those of the people; and, if you discern the slightest worth in it, it is obviously because big business has bought you. For a certain kind of conservative, on the other hand, it is the politicians in Washington and the egghead professors who are the devil. Until quite recently, the average American was convinced that the problems of the modern world could all be solved "with the help of a few elementary truths landed at Plymouth Rock by the first pilgrims." It was this conviction that made such unheeded prophets of Woodrow Wilson and John Foster Dulles.

The America of 1960 is still uneasy; not uneasy about her economy that on the whole is prosperous; nor about the dollar that is steadily finding its strength again; nor about her institutions that she still considers the best of all possible institutions; but about peace. The outside world dismays her. She once had a period of total isolation in which she was quite unconcerned by European affairs and in which the Monroe Doctrine kept the Europeans at a distance. Then she intervened in the outside world, with the certainty (then sound enough) that her weight would suffice to turn the scales in the right direction. In 1918 and in the 1940's, she contributed a very great deal to the winning of two great wars; and she came out of the second all the stronger for the exclusive possession of the atom bomb. The invincibility of America was then, and for some years, a universally held and temporarily true dogma; but it was a dangerous one, because it begot complacency. America's virtues prevented her from profiting from her superiority, as she so easily might have done. At the time when her strength would have allowed her to threaten, her morality forbade her to do so.

It is an uncertain, wavering world in 1960. In the East, a group of nations throws almost as great a weight as America's into the other pan of the scales. Two political, two economic systems stand face to face. Each has the power of coming close to annihilating the other, if it chooses to run the risk of being itself annihilated by the selfsame blast. It is a situation that seems to call imperatively for peaceful coexistence, and America certainly wants it. Yet the countries of the East continually eat away at the neutral third of the world. Without any hot war, some of the bastions in Africa and in Asia have fallen, one after another. Must so large a part of the work and the wealth of a peaceful nation then be devoted to the making of means of destruction? This is an outlook that horrifies the Americans, who want not the triumph of an ideology, and still less the twilight of mankind, but happiness, mutual goodwill, and peace.

"A civilization is the picture that a nation makes of itself." The American nation does not make an imperialist image of itself, nor an aggressive, nor a cruel one. What is "the American way of life" as they see it? It is a democracy founded upon a belief in the perfectibility of man and of society, a democracy that turns utterly away from cynicism. It is an optimism based upon faith in progress. It is a thoroughly rooted trust in the virtues of work and in the possibility of opening the way, by means of technical progress, to spiritual progress, to equality and freedom.

The American loves the word freedom: what does he mean by it? First of all he wants the freedom of being hail fellow well met with the pompous and the lofty and of calling them by their Christian names. If any man tries to presume because of his superiority in wealth, birth, or office, the American will say, "Who do you think you are?" and put him back in his place, which is the same as that of everyone else. This is what Piovene calls "the liberty of irreverence." Next the American wants the liberty of changing his job and of moving about. He will not put up with any sort of physical restraint, and he wants to be able to set himself free from all social trammels by going to another part of the country. Lastly, to the basic freedoms, such as those guaranteed by the Bill of Rights—freedom of conscience, of thought, and of speech—he now adds, with Franklin Roosevelt, freedom from want and freedom from fear.

II

The American economy has evolved rapidly. There is an out-of-date tradition that calls for the separation of industrial countries into two groups—the capitalist, or free-enterprise, countries, and the collectivist countries of state enterprise. The facts do not accord with this simple division. In reality, the American economy is a mixed economy. Private enterprise flourishes there, but the state does take certain economic functions upon itself. Sometimes it undertakes production—for example, the Tennessee Valley Authority, Columbia River Authority, at Hoover Dam, and the Atomic Energy Commission. Sometimes it works by means of controls, as in the case of the currency and credit, and even by the regulation of the output of oil, metals, and farm products. The state at present intervenes to regulate the production of oil according to its consumption. It was made quite clear, by the cases of General Electric, Du Pont, and General Motors, in 1960–1961 that the antitrust laws do restrain firms' freedom of action to a considerable extent.

The most important share of both industry and commerce is now in the hands of huge companies that cover the country with their networks of factories and selling outlets: United States Steel, the American Telephone and Telegraph Company, chain stores such as Woolworth's or the Atlantic and Pacific food stores, mail-order houses like Sears, Roebuck—and a hundred others of various kinds—are great industrial and commercial empires. A concern like General Electric, for example, may control a hundred factories, scattered over the whole territory of the United States. Each factory is an autonomous business with a manager who is responsible for it, but all depend upon one central organization that weighs the results, decides whether to close down or add to any particular line, and looks after scientific research. Some laboratories, such as the Bell Laboratories of the American Telephone Company, employ thousands of researchers.

The manager of each factory has a financial interest in the profits of his own undertaking, which makes up its account independently, but also in the profits of the entire concern: this is intended to insure that all cooperate in the global plan. Who owns these industrial empires? An investigation has been made into their financing over the last twenty years. The greater part of a firm's resources come from within the enterprise itself that plows back a large proportion of its profits into research, equipment, and building. The principal shareholders are corporations —insurance companies, investment trusts, pension funds. Individual shareholders no longer account for anything but a small proportion of the nation's investments. The capitalist of classical economics, the man who takes a personal risk to build up an industry, rarely plays an important part nowadays.

What, then, is the nature of these great companies that do in fact hold economic sway in the United States? They have been defined as "private public services": public services, because managed by officials, positive civil servants, in the interest of the enterprise and not according to the wishes of the shareholders, who have scarcely any say in the matter; private, since they retain their autonomy, subject to the state's control. They are apparently independent; but there is scarcely any real difference between Régie Renault, the car factory that is run by the French state, and any given great American corporation. Yet the verbal taboos remain: the words "private enterprise" are still holy. There are still orators who raise tear-filled eyes to Heaven when they speak of Washington's undue interference with business. But this is only a pious form. Free enterprise does play its part; it keeps the taste for risk alive; it makes bold undertakings possible; it brings the qualities of character into play. But the sphere in which it can come fully into action is limited.

Is the American economy better armed against cyclical crises than it was? It seems that this must be the case, since the end of the Second World War and demobilization were not followed by important slumps. The curve has gone up and down: Wall Street has recorded rises and falls, but no spectacular catastrophes like the great depression of 1929. In 1961, the national production exceeded $500,000,000,000. It doubles approximately every twenty-two years. From now onward, the Administration has not only the classical methods (credit, bank rate, public works) at its disposal, but also close supervision of the stock market and increased unemployment benefits. In so great a body of workers, it is normal that there should be from 4 percent to 5 percent unemployed—seasonal movement, the shifting and change-over of industry account for this. For example, more steel was needed to make tanks than is required in the manufacture of rockets. Automation, too, eliminates some jobs. The employers and the workers are studying the problems of redistribution and absorption together. The immediate requirement is to insure that the unemployed can live decently and remain within the body of consumers.

It should be possible; for, in Galbraith's words, the American economy is an affluent economy. This does not mean that the country produces too much, but that its production of such basic needs as food, clothing, and transportation would be amply sufficient if it were better distributed; and that the "marginal urgency" is diminishing. This is proved by the fact that intensive publicity is needed to convince the buyers that they want the products that are offered for sale. From this Galbraith concludes, not that total production is enough (during the last few years its annual increase has only been 3 percent, which is too little), but that it would be better to spend more on schools, hospitals, roads, and housing, all fields in which there are unsatisfied requirements. Such a program, with other added activities, would be a means of reabsorbing the unemployed. It must, however, be pointed out that there are many eminent economists who do not agree with many of Galbraith's theories and appraisals.

About a sixth of the population (during his campaign President Kennedy said 15 percent) are still poor and find it difficult to provide the essential requirements of a family. This group is chiefly made up of Negroes, farmers, the "poor whites" of the South, and recently arrived immigrants. Many old people have very low incomes, but old-age insurance is beginning to have its effect, and their condition is steadily improving. If the income-tax returns are examined (there were some sixty million taxpayers in 1959), it will be seen that incomes between $3,000 and $20,000 account for more than half the total (about thirty-two million returns). The incomes of more than $100,000 represent about $2,000,000,000 out of a total of $282,000,000,000; but to the resources of the richer people there must be added gains on the stock exchange and the appreciation of shares, which are taxed at only 25 percent, as well as certain sources of income that receive tax allowances such as oil wells. These exemptions explain the sudden fortunes made in Texas. The average wage of the industrial worker was $54 a week in 1948: by 1960, it had risen to $90.

A striking fact is the power of the great unions. They have hundreds of employees working in their enormous buildings. They have their own social institutions, their own banks, and their own statistical departments. They understand the industrial market and their financial position quite as well as boards of directors. But automation looms increasingly large as the most terrifying problem to labor in the next few years. One of its probable effects will be to reduce the number of working hours— hence greater leisure and a movement away from industry, the secondary group of occupations, toward the tertiary, such as trade, the liberal professions, and those to do with the movies, the theater, and so on. Entertainers, Hollywood actors, funny men on television, have become national heroes, as the great businessmen were in former times. Publicity, with its train of experts, pollsters, and psychologists, has an extraordinary importance.

The workers on the land, the farmers and their kind, who once dominated the electorate, now no longer amount to even 10 percent of the population. No government has succeeded in solving the problem of agricultural surpluses. The farmers have been paid to reduce the area they cultivate. In vain. Technical progress has enabled them to produce more on the reduced acreage. The production of wheat increases while consumption goes down. The government buys the surplus, but the stocks pile up. Such are the maladies of affluence.

III

American society has inspired two contradictory myths: according to the first, it is a classless society, in which any workingman may become president of General Motors; and according to the second, it is a closed society, with a little group of capitalists standing guard at the gates. As is invariably the case, the truth is not so plain and straightforward. American society, like all other societies, has its ranks, its hierarchy. But the classes in America are not closed castes: they allow individuals to rise—and to descend.

The first American upper class was a religious one. Then the great merchants and shipowners made something resembling an aristocracy in the East, while in the South the planters formed an exclusive caste, with deeply rooted prejudices. This caste was partially ruined by the Civil War; and after the war the nouveaux riche appeared, first in the North, then the Middle West, and then the West itself—bankers, manufacturers, oil men, and railway men. These men had started from scratch: it was not birth that counted, but work and success. The generations that came after began to take a pride in their ancestors. Some families adopted the royal way of adding an ordinal to their surnames. People spoke of Cornelius Vanderbilt, II, just as they might have said Henry II of England. There is today a Social Register that enshrines the status of the families named within it or the splendor of their connections. It will not include a multimillionaire unless he comes up to certain snobbish requirements. But after some generations, wealth, purified by support of culture and sanctified by charity, does at last give the right to an entry.

Have those families that grew so immensely rich between 1860 and 1920 been able to form a stable plutocracy? Only partially. No doubt the newcomers find it hard to build up fortunes comparable to those of the Astors, the Vanderbilts, the Rockefellers, and the Goelets, because of the high level of taxation. But many of the old families have lost the economic power that they once had. Unless the son of the house is talented, he must give way in the family business to a technician who is capable of running it. Besides, firms have become so enormous that they have gone beyond family control. In 1960, the real power in America is in the hands of six groups that are not always allied, nor anything like it: they are the White House; the Congress; the managers, or heads, of the great corporations, who are sometimes called to high positions in the government because of their knowledge of organization (Robert McNamara, of Ford, for example, has become the secretary of defense); the Pentagon that governs not only the three services but also a great deal of the scientific research; the men who guide opinion, that is to say, the owners of certain papers, the presidents of great foundations, and universities, and the group that is called Madison Avenue because it is in that street of New York that the lords of the radio, the television, and publicity have their being; and finally the chiefs of the great unions, who talk to the five others as equal to equal.

Each of these powers is kept in check by the collective strength of the others. The White House can do nothing without Congress; Congress is always anxious about the coming election, and it pays attention to the pressure groups; Wall Street would be powerless to bring about the reelection of a senator. Has wealth kept its political power? David Riesman, a brilliant analyst of modern America, thinks that this power is both threatened and reduced. To him, the future seems to belong to the trade combinations of small firms; to legal and financial counselors; to the soldiers, whose influence affects not only defense but also foreign policy; to the union leaders, who partially control the workers' vote; to the Poles, Italians, Jews, and Irish who exercise a powerful influence through their religious, cultural, and racial organizations; to the Catholic church, very united and therefore very strong; to the editorial writers of the important papers and the television commentators; and to the farmers, who, incidentally, are often at war among themselves, since their products and their interests are at variance. It is difficult to place real power in America; it is, at any given moment, the result of a great many different pressures.

Where do the country's many and varied rulers come from? Some from rich families: Kennedy, for example, and Nelson Rockefeller. Others have come up by way of Congress, for the Senate often leads to the highest positions. Nixon is an example of this, and so is Lyndon Johnson. Most of the generals in the Pentagon are of humble origin. Sometimes the big Hollywood and Madison Avenue tycoons are recently arrived immigrants. The powerful, then, form neither a caste nor a party. It may happen, as it did in the days of the New Deal, that big business joins in a body to oppose the White House. But once he has passed a certain degree of wealth, some intelligent Americans grow liberal. Nelson Rockefeller represents the Republican party's most advanced wing. Meanwhile, both Congress and the army offer their chance to those men who have to make their own fortunes.

"My son is a colonel in the air force," a taxi driver told me proudly, in 1960. This son had been well educated: he began his career as a skillful pilot, and he had been deservedly promoted. Tomorrow he might be a general and even (who knows?) president. Does this mean that a classless society is becoming a fact in America? No. In America, as in every other country, it is a very great advantage to have been brought up among the top people. A man who "belongs" knows everybody who will be useful to him by family connection: their ways and their tastes are the same as his. In 1950, there was an investigation that covered eight thousand big business executives: it showed that 23 percent owed their position to family friendships; 48 percent did not come from the business world, but their fathers had belonged to the liberal professions; 10 percent were the sons of workmen or farmers. So although birth gives advantages and connections, which in any case is true in every society, there does remain a margin of hope. As Franklin Roosevelt put it in 1935, "The freedom and opportunity that have characterized America's development in the past can be maintained, if freedom and opportunity do not mean a license to climb upward by pushing other people down."

And what is the margin of hope for the Negroes? For a long time it did not exist, and even today it is too narrow; but it is widening. In some of the Southern states, racial prejudice is still unbelievably violent. The recent troubles in Alabama and Mississippi have shocked the conscience of the entire world. The situation is better in the rest of the country, and President Kennedy has been able to appoint Negroes to important positions. The National Association for the Advancement of Colored People, a powerful organization that is run with intelligent moderation, says that it is confident about the future. A great deal of ground has already been won. The Negro vote is important in the North, and both parties seek its support. It is a capital fact that the Supreme Court has stated that segregation is unconstitutional, even though the federal government's decisions are not completely effectual in the South. The prestige of the new black republics in the United Nations will have a favorable influence for the American Negroes. The senators who have visited Africa and Asia have observed that the racial prejudices of the South hinder America's foreign policy dangerously. Slowly all these influences will have their irreversible effect. In possibly thirty or fifty years, there will be complete racial equality. It may be said that thirty or fifty years is a long time; but there are very ancient prejudices that have to be overcome. One generation has to pass away and a fresh one must rise up: meanwhile there will be a continuous progress, because that is in the nature of things.

IV

Since the prosperity of all is no longer an insoluble problem in the United States (not that that means it has been solved), the country's two outstanding problems are security (foreign policy and defense) and education. They are, in any case, bound up together. In the modern world, security depends upon certain scientific techniques. It is important to know whether the United States is willing to take the necessary steps to produce a sufficient number of physicists, chemists, and biologists, and whether scientific research is developed efficiently.

We have already seen how difficult any kind of educational reform is in the United States, because of the lack of centralization. The European traveler is struck by the rapid increase in the numbers of universities and colleges, by their comfort, and by the intense activity of their social life. Thirty-eight percent of young men and women enter some institution of higher educaton and stay there until they are twenty or twenty-two: this is a very much higher proportion than in Europe. The reasons are the national love of equality (every citizen has the right to all the education possible) and the abundant supply of labor that makes the unions anxious to keep the young out of the market.

The Americans ponder anxiously about the quality of this education. Pessimistic critics say that the young American is two years behind his European contemporary equivalent; that in a world in which a knowledge of the other nations has become essential, he neither knows history well, nor foreign languages; and that the colleges turn out neither enough engineers nor enough doctors. More hopeful observers reply that the best American universities are quite as good as the best in Europe, and that it is ridiculous to compare those universities that are meant for the masses to those that are intended for the chosen groups of European students, who are far fewer in number.

"The places that correspond to your Sorbonne in our country," says the sanguine American, "are our graduate schools, where the student goes for further study after the university; or else our specialized institutions, such as MIT or Cal. Tech. In the mass universities, we are not trying to make either scientists or scholars, but citizens. At college, our young men learn to live together—to live in a community." The critical American answers this by saying, "They would learn just as well by following better-conceived programs. Our mistake is in setting up intellectual cafeterias, where the student decides upon his bill of fare for himself, and if he likes may read for a bachelor's degree in television or for a diploma in business management or for a doctorate in real estate."

The European traveler then asks, "But why doesn't the government in Washington insist upon unified programs?" He is told that Washington has no say in matters of education, apart from compiling statistics; that the schools belong to the states; that some universities are privately owned, that others belong to religious bodies, that still others are state universities—of Missouri, Texas, or California, for example—but that none is a federal university. "It would be impossible," he is told, "to uproot so ancient a tradition. And in any case, would it be a good thing? Mississippi needs are not the same as Minnesota's. Our private universities are very valuable to us because of their independent spirit. They are the nation's conscience for the very reason that they are not dependent upon the government. You think that these universities are unequal in value? No doubt they are; but then so are the students. As well as brilliant universities for brilliant students, we need ordinary universities for ordinary students. If you don't follow that, it is because you are not a democrat."

This passion for equality is carried very far. In an aggressively democratic system of education, all, whatever their capacities may be, are treated in the same fashion. In France, the years spent at the lycée are a continual trial of strength. At the end of every term, examinations point out a first and a last. Then comes the time of the competitive examinations. In Europe, there is no end to being classed, compared, and judged. The secret ideal of many people in America is that the last should feel himself the equal of the first. In extreme cases, when it is quite necessary, a stupid boy may be made to stay in a class for a second year; but this is done regretfully, since there is the danger that he may contract an inferiority complex because he is older than his companions. It is a kindly feeling; but it is not by means of kindly feelings that good students are made.

Now today the Americans find themselves in continual competition with the Russians in scientific matters. From both the military and the industrial points of view, it is essential for them to keep up. They have some brilliant scientists; but the number of engineers and researchers is important, too. This implies a mathematical training for the children as early as the primary school: it also implies the existence of teachers of physics, chemistry, and biology in the high schools. These reforms, together with the increase in the population, will make it necessary to recruit two hundred thousand new teachers in the next ten years. In order to attract them, their salaries will have to be increased and their social standing, too. In the future, they will be required to know more, and in exchange they will insist upon greater rewards and a recognition of their rightful place in the community. John Galbraith says that the teachers must henceforward share far more widely in the prosperity of America, and he is right.

On the other hand, scientific and technical instruction should not overshadow the importance of classical studies. Schools and universities are there to hand on the patiently accumulated culture of the centuries to the younger generations. If one does not study Homer and Plato, Shakespeare and Molière, Dickens and Tolstoi, in one's youth, it may well be that one will never read them at all. If a student neglects history in favor of current affairs, he will never know any history; and he will never understand anything about current affairs. It is not the role of a school to dispose of current affairs, but to initiate its pupils in eternal affairs—in matters of permanent importance. Professor Whitehead has said "that there can be no successful democratic society till general education conveys a philosophic outlook." And indeed, it is according to his philosophy, or his faith, that a man may make either a good or an evil use of the terrible strength that technology has put in his hands. America needs (a) engineers who know how to apply the new techniques; (b) researchers who are capable of improving them, and of invention; and (c) philosophers to teach the art of placing material efficiency at the service of wisdom.

Scientific research in America is no more centralized than education. It is carried out by very different organizations—universities, private research institutions, industry, and government agencies and laboratories. It is necessary to make a careful distinction between pure research, which is defined by the National Science Foundation as "systematic and intensive study directed toward a fuller knowledge of the subject studied," and development, or applied research. For the fiscal year 1959–1960 pure and applied research together received $12,400,000,000; but of this sum only $800,000,000 at the most went to pure research. Application, in the form of missiles, rockets, and new kinds of airplanes, calls for prodigious quantities of money. Scientists are of the opinion that it would be easy to raise the allocation for

337

pure research to $1,500,000,000, and they think that nothing is of more urgent importance.

Would it be desirable to submit so many varying institutions to an overall plan for research, conceived either by the National Science Foundation or the Scientific Adviser to the President? Some think that it would, but the majority of American scientists hope that freedom of research will continue. No doubt it would be impossible to give grants to every comer for research into every subject under the sun; but it is surely not impossible to work out a compromise between excessive planning and regulation on the one hand and complete laissez faire on the other. Qualified bodies should strike a balance between the spectacular projects and the less dramatic but more important studies. There is no foreseeing discovery: it is often made by an isolated researcher who is investigating something else. If Alexander Fleming had been sharing in a strictly planned program, he would have left penicillin on one side.

The university laboratories, in which some discoveries of the first importance have been made, need grants from the Department of Defense or the Atomic Energy Commission. But it is useful, too, that they should go on receiving local subsidies, according to the American tradition. These allow a more adventurous kind of research, less bound by Washington's millions. Some industrial concerns, such as the Bell Telephone Company, carry on pure, disinterested research that may pay very high dividends indeed. The National Goals Commission has recommended (a) that biology and the other sciences to do with life should be given a larger share (at present 80 percent of the grants go to physicists and engineers); and (b) that the Defense Department should not have the distribution of so large a proportion of the total sums allocated to research. The Defense Department sets itself definite, limited goals—an attitude that does not encourage the free play of the more original minds. "We should avoid like the plague the enticing danger of too much and too concentrated planning of our national scientific development. The great majority of scientists agree that the supposed benefits of centralized planning are an illusion." In science, a researcher rarely finds what he is looking for; but, because he has searched, he often finds something.

V

Is the America of 1960 more cultivated than the America of the earlier generations, or less? I think that her culture is above all becoming more her own. The language itself, vigorous and racy, continually adding new, image-making words, is a proof of the vitality of American minds. The creators of this language are nearly all people of European culture; but, as soon as one has read a few sentences, it is impossible not to recognize them as true Americans. Their influence on the younger European writers has often been acknowledged, and it is indeed profound.

George Gershwin and Leonard Bernstein are great, essentially American, composers. Europe likes (and copies) their mixture of jazz and symphonic music. The musical is a peculiarly American form; and when it is found in perfection (*My Fair Lady, West Side Story*), it unites an admirably disciplined choreography to the Dionysiac stimulation of jazz. The ballets of Jerome Robbins are admired all over the world, and they have given new life to the art of the dance. In painting, the war of 1939—1945, by cutting the New World off from the Old, set free a violent art that corresponds with the innate feelings of the Americans. They buy Calder's mobiles; and they do so not out of snobbery, but from a genuine love for "these blue, red, and silvered objects that turn like the necklace of a delirious black magician."

The American reader wants to be shocked. Every literary tendency is represented in 1960: Norman Mailer and John Hersey are carrying on the neo-realist tradition; whereas others owe more to Henry James and Kafka. Most of the best sellers are short-lived. The writing that will last is to be found elsewhere. Criticism is producing some admirable pieces of work in the United States. Biographies and historical books find almost as many readers as novels. Professor Schlesinger's brilliantly written and provocative study of the times of Franklin Delano Roosevelt has had a wide circulation. The American public likes to be told about itself. Books on political economy, like those of Galbraith, and on sociology, books like those of William H. Whyte, David Riesman, Vance Packard, make works of literature out of scientific studies.

The paperbacks have brought about a revolution in reading. Until quite recently, the American book was bound, printed on fine paper, and often illustrated with plates: it was therefore expensive and out of the reach of the masses. Suddenly a great flood of paperbacks (perhaps imitated from the English Penguin books) poured over the country. Prices dropped from $4 or $6 to $1 or even 25 to 50 cents, while printings rose from a few thousand copies to hundreds of thousands.

In the early days, the paperbacks were often sexy novels or detective stories, but now a great many of them are rapidly evolving toward quality and seriousness. In the station and airport newsstands and in the drugstores, one now sees Plato and Tocqueville, Balzac and Tolstoi, Melville and Henry James, as well as many works on science and history. For a trifling sum, the best culture is put at the service of the best minds. It is a phenomenon of prime importance. The same thing has happened, furthermore, in Russia. In both countries, printings of five hundred thousand, a million, or even two million copies have become possible. This is very much better than the old way that made a book a luxury. Yet the public library still plays its part, offering the reader a great range of works and allowing him to choose those he would like to read. But it is of capital importance that even the poorest should be able to have their own private collection of books. The only books a reader knows really well are those that he possesses and that he can return to.

"It should be added, for perspective, that despite their astronomic sales, paperbacks are bought by something less than 10 percent of the American population." Clearly, it is not the entirety of America that reads Stendhal and Plato. The great mass of the citizens fill their leisure not by reading but by listening to the radio or watching television. Now both are commercial enterprises: their money comes from the advertisers, who, for their part, want as wide a public as possible. They are not talking so much to the reading 10 percent as to the 90 percent who do not read, who like coarse, commonplace jokes, and tales of emotional crime, and whose heroes are film stars or baseball players. A great danger for radio and television in America is that they are continually obliged to interlard their programs, to dilute the emotions that the programs may have aroused, with the advertiser's praise of his soap, his pudding, or his lavatory

340

paper. But for all that, in the long run both radio and television have a positive effect upon the country's culture. Into homes that were formerly cut off from the life of the outside world, they bring pictures, news, and a vocabulary. "Actually, the movies and jazz, radio and television, the paperbacks and the spectacle arts have reinforced one another, because their vitality is contagious rather than sterilizing."

America played a great part in the beginnings of the motion picture industry: she gave the world original artists—Charlie Chaplin, for example, and Walt Disney. The American movies in 1960 seem hampered by the need for producing spectacular and enormously costly films (*Ben Hur, The Ten Commandments*) to mark the difference between itself and television, as well as by the rigid code of Hollywood that forbids too much boldness in the matter of morals or sensuality. But the public requires the movies to provide what life denies, so it hurries off to the European films, which are unaffected by the law of Hollywood, and long queues form in front of the places that (in 1960) show *Never on Sunday, Hiroshima Mon Amour,* and *La Dolce Vita.* Nobody, even in Hollywood, has ever been able to make men shed their passions entirely.

In architecture, America has found salvation in liberating herself from a tradition that was foreign to her. The architects of the older American universities derived their inspiration from Greece and Rome; and this was not the natural, instinctive culture of a people that was essentially northern in its origins. The builders of the old colleges put up Greek temples and Gothic dormitories. They would hoist a renaissance château onto the top of the early skyscrapers. The effect was hideous. The soul of modern America is to be seen in the great glass and steel buildings that adorn Park Avenue, or in Frank Lloyd Wright's colored roofs. In 1940, Fernand Léger was afraid that America might become insipid through adapting its tastes too much to those of Europe. The present development is reassuring. The Americans of 1960 have more style than they ever had before, in art and in writing, in furniture and in architecture; and more and more, their style is their own.

VI

There has been a great development in the foreign policy of the United States between 1917 and 1960; and yet a moral Puritanism is still its foundation. Wilson abandoned isolationism only at that moment when Right and the cause of the Allies appeared to coincide. He entered the war because "right is more precious than peace," and he had hoped to crown the victory with the creation of a world that would be safe for democracy. Where Wilson had failed, because he was too sure of himself and too much alone, Roosevelt believed that he had succeeded. But, when he died, he left behind him a situation full of danger. After Yalta, America no longer had the choice between isolationism and alliances. The world has become "a bipolar system in which the two sides surround themselves with satellites and dependents. Only a single one of Roosevelt's ideas has proved unquestionably right—the colonial empires have been destroyed. But this very destruction itself has taken place in a world in which the magnetic pull of the two great powers is obvious to all. Wilson prepared the destruction of the balance of power in Europe; by following a comparable line of conduct, Roosevelt helped to open a Pandora's box," said Duroselle.

The young and courageous President Kennedy wants to remain faithful to the American feeling for morality. "We are on the side of freedom." He does not want force to be used for the protection of interests. "Our unfulfilled task is to demonstrate to the entire world that man's unsatisfied aspiration for economic progress and social justice can best be achieved by free men working within a framework of democratic institutions." A modest and sincere profession of faith. This country, which lives by an eighteenth-century Constitution, uses the vocabulary of the eighteenth-century enlightenment with genuine emotion. In foreign policy, the American remains an idealist, in Plato's sense of the word. He sees the essences (liberty, democracy) better than the concrete realities. If he has no moral arguments to justify his actions, he feels guilty and unhappy. This accounts in part for the prime importance, in his eyes, of the part played by the United Nations. For a long while, he has hoped to see therein the parliament of a worldwide democracy. He would be very much hurt if ever he were obliged to acknowledge that the United Nations was made use of for the defense of "immoral" interests, contrary to the principles of American democracy.

But harsh realities insistently remind this idealistic country that they are there. The first is the existence of a huge and powerful Communist world, with which the United States would like to live in peace, so long as that peace does not have to be bought at the price of both honor and freedom. Peaceful coexistence calls for a balance between the military strengths of the two sides; sensible negotiations without unprofitable threats; and the acceptance of ideological differences. It is essential for each to abandon the illusion of a sudden change of heart in the other. The Americans will not become Marxists, and the Communists will not stop being Communists, at least not until shrimps have learned to whistle, as Khrushchev puts it. By definition, peaceful coexistence implies the desire to live in peace with the other nations *as they are*.

The second reality is a world made up of "haves" and "have nots," that is to say, of comparatively prosperous nations and of nations that lack everything. In the United States, Western Europe, and the USSR, production is increasing as quickly as the population, and the essential requirements are more or less satisfied. But in the Middle East, Southeast Asia, tropical Africa, and most of the South American continent, the masses are very ill provided for. In some countries, this poverty is caused by an improper distribution of the available wealth, in others by a drop in the prices of the raw materials that they export, by the lack of industries, and by the lack of capital. Whatever the cause, the contrast is unacceptable. Long ago Lincoln said that a country cannot live half in slavery and half in liberty. That is also true of a planet. There can be no peace throughout the world unless throughout the world there is justice.

America understands this, and she comes to the help of the underdeveloped nations. In doing so, she sometimes has the Communist bloc as a competitor; and in certain countries, the Communists have the better hearing, sometimes because of the peoples' resentment of the former colonial powers and sometimes because of their distrust of the great American companies who own land, mineral deposits, or oil wells. America accounts for only 10 percent of the population of the "free world": she consumes 50 percent of its raw materials. She may therefore both charm the foreigner by her standard of living and at the same time arouse his envious dislike. President Kennedy is aware of the extent of these difficulties; and he clearly sees that technical assistance should in every case be accompanied by social reforms, particularly in the ownership of land.

The American's natural impulse would also be to make sure that the form of every government that receives help should be democratic, in the Western sense of the word. The average American has never thought it right that from motives of convenience or interest the Administration should (as it sometimes has) support dictatorial regimes. Yet there are those who advise caution: they say that it would be pointless and dangerous to present a parliamentary system to a country that is used to tribal loyalties and in which 90 percent of the people cannot read. And no doubt the United States would be mistaken in making use of economic aid to insist upon the adoption of its own form of government. Every state has the right to decide upon the institutions that suit it for itself. But it would be an equally serious mistake to repudiate or disavow liberal civilization: "Democracy is doomed if the leading democratic countries behave with diffidence about their fundamental values," says Henry Kissinger. But this is not what is happening, and President Kennedy is not a man to pocket his principles.

VII

We have shown the nature of the American dream as it was at the beginning of the century—a great hopefulness and expectation; the pursuit of happiness. Have the hopes and expectations been fulfilled? Has happiness been caught? Put like this, the questions are badly set. America is not, and never will be, something that is finished, but (in Joyce's words) a work in progress. This great work cannot build itself up with a steady continuity. It has encountered very grave impediments—two world wars, an immense depression. But, like most great works, it has profited by the difficulties and has made unlooked-for progress because of them. In fact, although absolute happiness has not been reached

(and how could it ever be?), the great body of citizens has benefited from the unceasing advance of science and technology, from
the increase in production, and from the rise in the standard of
living. It is perfectly true that material welfare is not everything,
but the nations that do not possess it complain bitterly. America
is achieving it.

Then again, the American feels that he has set up a social order
that is satisfactory, perhaps not for everybody, but at least for
the immense majority. He knows that this order should be improved, and that some gross inequalities still exist. But taking
everything into account, he has a feeling of success. His purchasing power is increasing; his hours of work are going down; his
wife has been set free from many unpleasant household tasks.
The wishes that the poor immigrant made for his children in
about 1910 have been more or less fulfilled. The visitor who
contemplates the life of the universities and the schools can have
no doubts about the happiness of the young people, nor about
the opportunities that are offered them. There are, and there
always will be, some unfortunate characters who cannot adapt
themselves to life in a community. But generally speaking, student life in America is egalitarian, warm, and cheerful. It forms a
healthy preparation for civic life. The parents are proud of their
children's brand-new knowledge. The astonishing results that
research has produced in the last twenty years reassure the American as to the consequences of the rise in population in his country
that is much more likely to suffer from overabundance than from
famine. He has an understandable tendency to suppose that there
is no limit to the possibilities of progress, and that it will make
man's daily life something more than merely tolerable.

He also finds grounds for pride in the efficient working of his
institutions. It is a fact that the system set up by the Founding
Fathers has lasted, although the country has expanded to become
a continent, although its population has increased beyond all
measure, and although immigrants of every race have come to
swell the numbers of the first little group of Anglo-Saxon settlers.
Even in times of grave crisis, even in war, the regime has never
ceased to function. The Civil War threatened it but did not bring
it down. The President of the United States remains an august
and respected figure; and except at election time the people are
usually united behind him. The fact that he has in addition to

345

this assumed a worldwide role as the leader of the most powerful of the Western democracies has made his standing even greater. The fundamental, moving ideas of this Republic, the essential liberties, have for their part also retained their almost religious character. Although the Americans belong to many and various churches, liberalism is the common factor that runs through their spiritual life. Conservatism has sometimes been represented, in America, by upright men of moderate views persuaded of the truth of their beliefs, such as Wendell Willkie and Dwight Eisenhower; but, when this happens, the boundary between conservatism and liberalism grows somewhat vague. It only becomes sharp and distinct when, as Max Lerner says, conservatism lets itself "be invaded by furious reactionaries." But the country never listens to these people for long.

It might well have been asked, during the great crisis of 1929, whether an economy based upon free enterprise and buying and selling could continue to exist in the modern world. The experience seems to prove that if it submits to a certain degree of state regulation and voluntarily sets up controlling mechanisms of its own, such an economy does work and does work well. In present-day America, most freedoms are safeguarded without any sacrifice of production. The citizens of the United States are perfectly aware that in the East a completely different system is also producing remarkable results. They think that only the future will tell which of the two methods insures its people more well-being, freedom, and happiness; and they want this competition to be peaceful, for if it is not, both East and West must perish together, going down in massacre and anarchy.

Bibliography

Part I

ALLEN, FREDERICK LEWIS. *The Big Change*. New York: Harper & Row, 1952.

BEARD, CHARLES A. *The Rise of American Civilization*. New York: The Macmillan Company, 1933.

BENNETT, ARNOLD. *Your United States*. New York: Harper & Row, 1912.

BROGAN, D. W. *The American Character*. New York: Alfred A. Knopf, 1944.

BROOKE, RUPERT. *Letters from America*. New York: Charles Scribner's Sons, 1916.

DANIELS, JOSEPHUS. *The Wilson Era*. Chapel Hill: University of North Carolina Press, 1946.

FAULKNER, HAROLD U. *The Quest for Social Justice*. New York: The Macmillan Company, 1931.

GARRATY, JOHN A. *Woodrow Wilson*. New York: Alfred A Knopf, 1956.

GOMPERS, SAMUEL. *Seventy Years of Life and Labor*. New York: E. P. Dutton & Co., 1925.

HERRIOT, EDOUARD. *Impressions d'Amérique*. Lyon: Audin, 1923.

KAZIN, ALFRED. *On Native Grounds*. New York: Reynal & Co., 1942.

LINK, ARTHUR S. *Wilson*. I. *The Road to the White House;* II. *The New Freedom*. III. *The Struggle for Neutrality*. Princeton: The Princeton University Press, 1947.

LINK, ARTHUR S. *Woodrow Wilson and the Progressive Era*. New York: Harper & Row, 1954.

MYERS, GUSTAVUS. *History of the Great American Fortunes*. New York: Modern Libraries, 1936.

NEVINS, ALLAN. *Ford*. New York: Charles Scribner's Sons, 1954.

PARRINGTON, VERNON LOUIS. *Main Currents of American Thought*. New York: Harcourt, Brace & World, 1939.

PAXSON, FREDERIC L. *The New Nation*. Boston: Houghton Mifflin Co., 1915.

SANTAYANA, GEORGE. *Character and Opinion in the United States*. New York: George Brazillier, 1955.

SULLIVAN, MARK. *Our Times.* New York: Charles Scribner's Sons, 1936.

WALWORTH, ARTHUR. *Woodrow Wilson: American Prophet.* New York: Longmans, Green & Co., 1958.

WALWORTH, ARTHUR. *Woodrow Wilson: World Prophet.* New York: Longmans, Green & Co., 1958.

Part II

BLUM, JOHN M. *Joe Tumulty and the Wilson Era.* Boston: Houghton Mifflin Co., 1951.

GRATTAN, C. H. *Why We Fought.* New York: Vanguard Press, 1929.

HOOVER, HERBERT. *The Ordeal of Woodrow Wilson.* New York: McGraw-Hill Book Co., 1958.

MILLIS, WALTER. *The Road to War.* Boston: Houghton Mifflin Co., 1935.

PERSHING, JOHN. *My Experiences in the World War.* New York: Stokes, 1931.

SEYMOUR, CHARLES, ED. *Intimate Papers of Colonel House.* Boston: Houghton Mifflin Co., 1926-1928.

SEYMOUR, CHARLES. *Woodrow Wilson and the World War.* New Haven: Yale University Press, 1921.

WHITE, WILLIAM ALLEN. *The Autobiography of William Allen White.* New York: The Macmillan Company, 1946.

Part III

ADAMS, SAMUEL HOPKINS. *The Incredible Era: The Life and Times of W. G. Harding.* Boston: Houghton Mifflin Co., 1939.

ALLEN, FREDERICK LEWIS. *Only Yesterday.* New York: Harper & Row, 1931.

HOOVER, HERBERT. *Memoirs.* New York: The Macmillan Company, 1951.

KEYNES, JOHN MAYNARD. *The Economic Consequences of the Peace.* New York: Harcourt, Brace & World, 1920.

NICOLSON, HAROLD. *Peacemaking, 1919.* London: Constable, 1933.

SCHRIFTGIESSER, KARL. *This Was Normalcy.* Boston: Little, Brown & Co., 1948.

SEYMOUR, CHARLES. *Woodrow Wilson and the World War.* New Haven: Yale University Press, 1921.

SLOSSON, PRESTON W. *The Great Crusade and After.* New York: The Macmillan Company, 1930.

TUMULTY, JOSEPH P. *Woodrow Wilson As I Know Him.* New York: Doubleday & Co., 1921.

Part IV

ADAMS, SAMUEL HOPKINS. *The Incredible Era: The Life and Times of W. G. Harding*. Boston: Houghton Mifflin Co., 1939.

COOLIDGE, CALVIN. *Autobiography*. New York: Cosmopolitan, 1929.

FAULKNER, HAROLD U. *From Versailles to the New Deal*. New Haven: Yale University Press, 1950.

HOFSTADTER, RICHARD. *Age of Reform*. New York: Alfred A. Knopf, 1955.

HOOVER, HERBERT. *Memoirs*. New York: The Macmillan Company, 1951.

LEIGHTON, ISABEL. *The Aspirin Age*. New York: Simon & Schuster, 1949.

MUZZEY, D. S. *A History of Our Country*. Boston: Ginn & Co., 1948.

SCHLESINGER, ARTHUR M., JR. *The Age of Roosevelt*. I. *The Crisis of the Old Order*. Boston: Houghton Mifflin Co., 1957.

SCHRIFTGIESSER, KARL. *Gentleman from Massachusetts*. Boston: Little, Brown & Co., 1944.

SCHRIFTGIESSER, KARL. *This Was Normalcy*. Boston: Little, Brown & Co., 1948.

SOULE, GEORGE. *Prosperity Decade*. New York: Rinehart & Co., 1947.

Part V

ALLEN, FREDERICK LEWIS. *Since Yesterday*. New York; Harper & Row, 1953.

CRANE, MILTON. *The Roosevelt Era*. New York: Boni & Gaer, 1947.

FREIDEL, FRANK. *Franklin D. Roosevelt: The Triumph*. Boston: Little, Brown & Co., 1952.

LILIENTHAL, DAVID. *T.V.A.: Democracy on the March*. New York: Harper & Row, 1953.

PERKINS, DEXTER. *The New Age of Franklin Roosevelt*. Chicago: University of Chicago Press, 1957.

PERKINS, FRANCES. *The Roosevelt I Knew*. New York: Viking Press, 1946.

RAUCH, BASIL. *History of the New Deal, 1933-1938*. New York: Creative Age Press, 1944.

ROOSEVELT, ELEANOR. *This I Remember*. New York: Doubleday & Co., 1949.

ROOSEVELT, FRANKLIN D. *On Our Way*. New York: John Day, 1934.

SCHLESINGER, ARTHUR M., JR. *The Age of Roosevelt;* II. *The Coming of the New Deal*. Boston: Houghton Mifflin Co., 1957; III. *The Politics of Upheaval*. Boston: Houghton Mifflin Co., 1960.

SHERWOOD, ROBERT. *Roosevelt and Hopkins*. New York: Harper & Row, 1950.

349

TUGWELL, REXFORD G. *Battle for Democracy*. New York: Columbia University Press, 1935.

WECTER, DIXON. *Age of the Great Depression*. New York: The Macmillan Co., 1948.

Part VI

ALLEN, FREDERICK LEWIS. *Since Yesterday*. New York: Harper & Row, 1940.

BROGAN, D. W. *U.S.A.* New York: Oxford University Press, 1941.

EINAUDI, MARIO. *The Roosevelt Revolution*. New York: Harcourt, Brace & World, 1951.

ROMAINS, JULES. *Salsette découvre l'Amérique*. New York: Editions de la maison française, 1942.

SHERWOOD, ROBERT. *Roosevelt and Hopkins*. New York: Harper & Row, 1940. *Time*.

Part VII

BRADLEY, OMAR N. *A Soldier's Story*. New York: Holt, Rinehart & Winston, 1951.

EISENHOWER, DWIGHT D. *Crusade in Europe*. New York: Doubleday & Co., 1948.

FEIS, HERBERT. *Road to Pearl Harbor*. Princeton: Princeton University Press, 1950.

GREW, JOSEPH C. *Ten Years in Japan*. New York: Simon & Schuster, 1943.

CORDELL HULL. *Memoirs*. New York: The Macmillan Company, 1948.

JANEWAY, ELIOT. *The Struggle for Survival*. New Haven: Yale University Press, 1951.

LEAHY, WILLIAM D. *I Was There*. New York: Whittlesey House, 1950.

NEVINS, ALLAN. *The New Deal and World Affairs*. New Haven: Yale University Press, 1950.

PRATT, FLETCHER. *War for the World*. New Haven: Yale University Press, 1950.

PYLE, ERNIE. *Brave Men*. New York: Holt, Rinehart & Winston, 1943.

PYLE, ERNIE. *Here Is Your War*. New York: Holt, Rinehart & Winston, 1943.

SMITH, WALTER BEDELL. *Eisenhower's Six Great Decisions*. New York: Longmans, Green & Co., 1956.

STETTINIUS, EDWARD R., JR. *Roosevelt and the Russians*. New York. Doubleday & Co., 1949.

WELLES, SUMNER. *Seven Decisions That Shaped History*. New York: Harper & Row, 1951.

Welles, Sumner. *Time for Decision*. New York: Harper & Row, 1944.

Willkie, Wendell. *One World*. New York: Simon & Schuster, 1943.

Part VIII

Allen, Frederick Lewis. *Since Yesterday*. New York: Harper & Row, 1940.

Byrnes, James F. *Speaking Frankly*. New York: Harper & Row, 1947.

Campbell, John C., et al. *The United States in World Affairs, 1947-1948*. New York: Harper & Row, 1946.

Goldman, Eric. *The Crucial Decade*. New York: Alfred A. Knopf, 1956.

Goodman, Jack, ed. *While You Were Gone*. New York: Simon & Schuster, 1946.

Koenig, L. W. *The Truman Administration*. New York: New York University Press, 1956.

Truman, Harry S. *Memoirs*. Vols. I and II. New York: Doubleday & Co., 1955.

Part IX

Adams, Sherman. *Firsthand Report*. New York: Harper & Row, 1961.

Donovan, Robert J. *Eisenhower, the Inside Story*. New York: Harper & Row, 1956.

Freidel, Frank. *America in the Twentieth Century*. New York: Alfred A. Knopf, 1960.

Goldman, Eric. *The Crucial Decade*. New York: Alfred A. Knopf, 1956.

Kennedy, John F. *Profiles in Courage*. New York: Harper & Row, 1961.

New York Times, The.

Pusey, Merlo J. *Eisenhower the President*. New York: The Macmillan Company, 1956.

Rovere, Richard H. *Senator Joe McCarthy*. New York: Harcourt, Brace & World, 1959.

Part X

Allen, Frederick Lewis. *The Big Change*. New York: Harper & Row, 1952.

Duroselle, J. B. *De Wilson à Roosevelt*. Paris: Librairie A. Colin, 1960.

Gorer, Geoffrey. *The American People*. New York: W. W. Norton & Co., 1946.

Lerner, Max. *America as a Civilization*. New York: Simon & Schuster, 1957.

Riesman, David. *Individualism Reconsidered*. New York: Free Press of Glencoe, 1954.

Taft, Philip. *The A. F. of L.* New York: Harper & Row, 1959.

General

Adams, James Truslow. *The Epic of America*. Boston: Little, Brown & Co., 1933.

Allen, Frederick Lewis. *Only Yesterday*. New York: Harper & Row, 1931.

Dulles, Foster R. *Twentieth Century America*. Boston: Houghton Mifflin Co., 1945.

Dulles, Foster R. *The United States Since 1865*. Ann Arbor: University of Michigan Press, 1960.

Faulkner, Harold U. *American Economic History*. New York: Harper & Row, 1931; eighth edition, 1960.

Freidel, Frank. *America in the Twentieth Century*. New York: Alfred A. Knopf, 1960.

Link, Arthur S. *American Epoch*. New York: Alfred A. Knopf, 1955.

Morison, Samuel E., and Henry S. Commager. *The Growth of the American Republic*. New York: Oxford University Press, 1951.

Parrington, Vernon Louis. *Main Currents of American Thought*. New York: Harcourt, Brace & World, 1939.

Personal Interviews.

U.S. Census Bureau: *Statistics of the United States.*

Index

ABC Powers, 48
Acheson, Dean, 249, 263, 269, 270; speech omitting Korea, 276
Adams, James Truslow, 14; disappearance of economy, enterprise, responsibility, 177
Adams, Sherman, 282, 283, 291, 307
Afrikakorps, Rommel's, 288
agencies, government, taking authority from Congress, 183-184
Agricultural Adjustment Administration (AAA), 153; declared unconstitutional, 163; new act, ever normal granary, 164
agriculture, mechanization of, and overproduction, 21
airlift, Berlin, 270-271
Alamogordo, first atom bomb, 241
Alexander I, Czar, 46
Alexander III, Czar, 3
Alexandria, 229
alphabet soup bureaucracy, 158
Alsop, Joseph, 285
Amalgamated Clothing Workers, 164
America First Committee, 207, 208
American Federation of Actors, and WPA, 189
American Federation of Labor, 92, 151, 164, 165; differences with CIO, 190, 191; union with CIO, 306
American Mercury, 93
American Telephone and Telegraph Company, 328
Anti-Saloon League, 94-95
appliances, 1920's, 114
Arbenz, of Guatemala, 310
Archangel, 215
aristocracy, Southern, destroyed by Civil War, 6; Northern nouveaux riches, how produced, 6-7

armaments limitation, rival, agreement between five great powers, 102
Armstrong, Louis, 198
Arnold, Thurman, 163
Asquith, Herbert Henry, 61
assembly line, changes resulting from, 20
Astor family, 7, 8-9
Astor, Mrs. William, 8
Aswan Dam, 300, 301
Atlantic Conference, 214, 216-217, 218
Atlantic & Pacific Tea Company, 115, 328
atom, fission of, 198, 199, 226; control of, 253
Atomic Energy Commission, 327, 338
Atoms for Peace, 297
Attlee, Clement R., 244
Augusta, 216, 245
Austria, 51, 52, 56; frontiers in peace treaty, 80; separate treaty, 89
authoritarianism, accepted as result of depression, 137
automobiles, 1914, 12, 20; Model T price, 20; 1919 and 1926, 114; first need after basic essentials, 180-181

Babbitt, 193
Bainville, Jacques, 82-83
Baker, Newton D., 66
Balfour, Arthur James (Lord Balfour), 66
Bank of England, 128
bank holidays, 138, 144
banks, reform of, 153-154
Barkley, Alben W., 267
Barton, Bruce, 113
Baruch, Bernard M., 64, 147, 152, 156, 263; cold war, 263
Beck, Dave, 306

353

rivalry, 312; church attendance, 322, 346

Eisenhower, Milton, 313

elections, 1912, 32; 1916, 58; 1920, 97-98; 1924, 111; 1928, 125-126; 1932, 136; 1934, 159; 1936, 167; 1940, 210; 1944, 237-238; 1948, 268; 1952, 287; 1956, 303; 1960, 319

electricity, rural (REA), 161

Elk Hills, oil reserves, 103

England, 50, 52; Wilson in London, 74; League of Nations and Treaty of Versailles, 77-84; depression in, 133; changes in government of, 187, 200; declared war on Germany, 202; see World War II

equality, pioneer, end of, 6

escapism, kinds and extent, 1914, 12-14

Fair Deal, 269

Fall, Albert B., 87-88; Secretary of Interior, 103, 104

Fansteel, 191

Far East, half measures, 275-276, 298

Farewell to Arms, A, 93

Farley, James A., 145

farmers, marginal, 159, 161

farmers, problems of, 21-22, 117-118, 152-153; improved income of, 158, 163, 192, 226

Faubus, Orval E., 304

Faulkner, William, decay of aristocracy in writings of, 93, 196-197

Faure, Edgar, 299

Federal Association of Hosiery Workers, 191

Federal Communications Commission, 194

Federal Farm Board, 132

Federal Republic of West Germany, 270

Federal Reserve Bank, 42-44, 123, 127, 138

Federal Theater Project, 198

Federal Trade Commission, 44

Ferdinand, Archduke, 50-51

Fermi, Enrico, 198, 199, 226

Field, Marshall, 7

Filene, Edward A., 114

fission of atom, uranium 235, 198, 199, 226

Fitzgerald, Scott, writings of, 93

Fiume, 80, 82

Fleming, Alexander, 338

Florida boom and collapse, 117

Foch, Ferdinand, Marshal, 65, 70

food administration, World War I, 64-65

Forbes, Charles L., 103, 104

Ford, Henry, assembly line and five dollar day, 20; and prohibition, 94; low selling prices, rise in living standards desired, 113; the Model A, 114; factories in Europe, 116

foreign relations, varying attitudes toward, 1920's, 119-122

Fortune, 146, 162, 195

Four Freedoms, 217

Four Horsemen of the Apocalypse, 167

Fourteen Points, 63; Wilson and, 73

France, 51, 52; ports, 69; and peace treaty, 77-84; accord with England and U.S., 82; accord not signed, 89; depression in, 133; changes in government, 187, 200; declared war on Germany, 202; see World War II

Frankfurter, Felix, 161

Free France, 206, 227; seized Saint Pierre and Miquelon, 227

French Resistance, 235

Freud, Sigmund, influence on youth, post-World War I, 94

frontier, end of, 6

Fuchs, Klaus, 273

fuel, administration of, World War I, 65

Full Employment Act, 259

Fuller, J. C. F., General, 234

Galbraith, John Kenneth, 316, 329, 330, 337, 339

gangsters, 95-96

Gaulle, Charles de, General, and Free France, 206, 227, 229, 230, 236

Gavin, James, General, 311

General Electric Co., 126, 324, 328

General Motors, 123, 125, 165, 224, 328, 331

George, King, and Queen Elizabeth, visit to U.S., 1939, 177

George, Walter, 184

Gerard, James Watson, 50, 51

German-American Bund, 200

Germany, 45, 50, 51, 52, 55, 56; mistakes about U.S., World War I, 61, 67; League of Nations and Treaty of Versailles, 77, 79-84; separate treaty,

and Treaty of Versailles, 83, 84; Wilson's disfavor, 88
housing, need for, 179
Hughes, Charles Evans, 58, 99, 139, 167
Hull, Cordell, 145; and South America, 157-158; in World War II, 214; advises against Roosevelt meeting Japanese, 220; meetings with Nomura and Korusa at time of Pearl Harbor attack, 221; prepared message for Congress, 221; and Free French, 227; interview with Stalin, 232
Humphrey, George, 289
Humphrey, Hubert, 316
Hundred Days, The, 148
Hungary, frontiers in peace treaty, 80; separate treaty, 89; government set by Stalin without consulting West, 251
Hutchins, Robert, educator, 195-196
Hyde, James Hazen, 8

Ickes, Harold L., 145, 161
ideologies, distrusted, 24
illiteracy, of immigrants, 4; in 1900, 13-14
immigration, German and Irish, 1840-1880, 2-3; Italian, Austro-Hungarian, Polish, Russian, 1840-1860, 3; restriction of, 101-102; in 1914, 1939, 178
imperialism, 16
Imperial Wizard, 96
incomes, 1900, 9; 1910, 10; 1913, Ford workers, 20; 1929, 119, 127; 1939, 180; 1945, 254; 1953, 254; 1947, 261
Indians, destruction of, 5
Indochina, 219
Industrial Board, 90
Industrial Workers of the World, 92
industrialization, changes from, 22
inequality, by 1900, 6
International Atomic Energy Agency, 297
International Court of Justice, 120
International Harvester Co., factories in Europe, 116
"Invitation to Learning," 194
iron curtain, 252
Israel, 301
Italy, secret treaties concerning, 77, 201; declares war on U. S., 222

Jackson, C. D., 291
James, Henry, 339

Japan, and California, 45; and Russia 45; and China, 47; in World War I, 59, 71; attack on Manchuria, 122, 133; against Shanghai, 133, 201; given freedom by attack on Russia, 216; conditions leading to moves for new order in Far East, 218-219; attacks Pearl Harbor, 221; wide conquests, 242; defeats, Carol Sea and Midway, 242; at Savo Island and Surigao Strait, 242; Stilwell and Chinese Communists, 243; Chennault and Kuomintang, 243; Iwo Jima, 243; Okinawa, 243; Hiroshima, 244; Nagasaki, 245; war ends, 245
Java, 219
Jellicoe, Admiral J. R., 68
Jerome, Jenny, 8
Jerome, Leonard, 8
Jesus of Nazareth, 113
Joffre, Marshal J. J. C., 66
Johnson, Hiram, 58, 84, 87, 333
Johnson, Hugh S., 147; administrator for NRA, 150, 151
Johnson, Lyndon B., 305; on control of space, 311; candidate for presidency, 316
Juin, General Alphonse Pierre, 229
Julius Caesar, 198

Kafka, Franz, 339
Kaiser, Henry J., 225
Kaiser, the, Wilhelm II, 50, 59
Kansas City Star, 283
Kefauver, Estes, 280
Kellogg-Briand treaty, 122
Kennan, George F., 249, 264
Kennedy, John F., 284, 306; candidate for presidency, 316; campaign, 317-319; church attendance, 322; quoted, 330, 333, 342, 343, 344
Keynes, John Maynard, 74, 79, 82, 83, 171-172
Khrushchev, Nikita, 297, 299, 309, 312; to U.S. and U.N., 314, 315, 319; and talk with Reuther, 314, 322
Kleagles, 96
Knights of the White Camellia, 200
Knowland, William F., 277
Knox, Frank, Secretary of Navy, World War II, 206, 211
Knudsen, William S., 224
Konoye, Prince Fumimaro, 219, 220;

offers halt in expansion activities for meeting with Roosevelt, 220

Korea, Russian-established government, 252-253

Kozlov, Frol R., 313

Kredit Anstalt, 133

Krock, Arthur, 139

Ku Klux Klan, 32; the new Klan, 96; in 1924 election, 111, 248

Kurusu, Saburo, 220

labor laws, 164, 165

Labor Reform Act, 306

La Follette, R. M., and elections, 26; and filibuster, 59-60; attempt at presidential nomination, 111; nominated by third party, 111

Lamont, Thomas, 128

Landon, Alfred M., 166, 167

language, 1900, 4

Laniel, 297

Lansing, Robert, 76, 80

Latin America, U.S. relations with, 121-122; loans to, 138; relations with, 311

Lawrence, D. H., 31

Lawrence, William L., 198-199, 241

League of Nations, Fourteen Points, 63; Hoare and Wilson on, 73; Wilson presents in Europe, 74-80; Permanent Council, International Court of Justice, Labor Office, Council of Mandates, 80; and Treaty of Versailles, 81-84; Senate failure to ratify, 84-89; avoided by Harding, 1920 campaign, 98; at Atlantic Conference, 217; charter of, 249-250

Leahy, William D., Admiral, 227, 239, 240

Léger, Fernand, 341

Lehman, Herbert, 138

lend-lease, 211; Hopkins as administrator, 214

Lenin, 79

Lerner, Max, 346

Lewis, John L., 92, 164, 165, 166, 167, 190, 191, 217, 257

Lewis, Sinclair, 193

Liberty Bonds, 91, 126

Life, 195, 235

Life with Father, 197

Lilienthal, David, 188

Lincoln, Abraham, 325

Lindbergh, Charles A., 217

Link, Arthur S., 233-234

Lippmann, Walter, 196

Little Foxes, The, 197

Little Rock, 304

Litvinov, Maxim, 157

Lloyd George, David, 68, 69, 75, 77, 78, 81, 82

Lodge, Henry Cabot, and Woodrow Wilson, 48-49, 61, 76, 81, 84-89

Lodge, Henry Cabot, II, 282; nominated for vice presidency, 317

London, Jack, 27

Long, Huey, 159, 160, 166, 167

Longworth, Alice Roosevelt, 99

Louvain, 53

Luce, Clare, 197

Luce, Henry, 195

Ludendorff, Erich Friedrich Wilhelm, 59

Lusitania, sinking of, 55

Lyon, Mary, 30

McAdoo, W. A., 65, 97; presidential nomination attempt, 111

McAllister, Ward, 8

MacArthur, General Douglas, 131, 249, 276, 277, 278, 279, 280

McCarthy, Joseph R., 274-275, 279, 280, 283, 284, 285, 294-296; death of, 296

McCarthy, Mary, 325

MacDonald, James Ramsey, 157

McKinley, William, 16

MacLeish, Archibald, 196

MacMahon Act, imposed secrecy on atom research, 253

Macmillan, Harold, 230

McNamara, Robert, 332

McNary-Haugen bill, twice vetoed by Coolidge, 118

Madariaga y Rojo, Salvador de, 16

Mailer, Norman, 339

Malaya, 219

Malenkov, 297

Man Nobody Knows, The, 113

Man Who Came to Dinner, The, 197

Manhattan Transfer, 197

manipulation, in business, 17

Mao Tse-tung, 276

Marines, in Lebanon, 310

Marshall, General George C., 233, 234, 243, 244; on atom bomb, 244, 249; replaces Byrnes, 263-265; Marshall Plan, 264, 268, 269; to Far East, 275

Martin, Joseph, 279
Matisse, 31
Matsuoka, Yosuke, 219, 220
Max of Baden, Prince, 70
Meany, George, 306
Mellon, Andrew W., 99; as secretary of treasury, 116-117, 127
Memoirs, Truman, 248
Mencken, Henry L., ridicule in writings of, 93
METO, 310
Metropolitan Life Insurance Company, housing built by, 179
Metropolitan Opera, 198
Mexico, 47-48, 59; D. W. Morrow attempts at adjustment with, 121-122
Meyer, Eugene, 138
Mickey Mouse, first, 125
Mikoyan, Anastas, 312, 313
millionaires, 1914 and 1926, 113
Mirabeau, Octave, 112
Missouri, 245
Moley, Raymond A., 145-146, 157, 160-161, 165
Mollet, Guy, 301
Molotov, Vyacheslov, 308
Money Trust, 18, 41
monopolies, struggle against, Theodore Roosevelt, Wilson, New Deal, 189-190
Monroe Doctrine, and Roosevelt, 45
Monte Cassino, 231
Montgomery, Field Marshal Bernard Law, 229
Montgomery, Ward & Co., 115, 126
morality, Wilson preoccupation with, in foreign relations, 47
Morgan, J. P., 7, 9, 10, 18, 22, 24, 57
Morgan Bank, 18, 128
Morgenthau, Henry, Jr., 143, 182
Morocco, 45
Morrill, J. S., 29
Morrow, Dwight W., 121
motion pictures, as escape, 193
muckraking, 27-28
Murphy, Robert, 230
Murray, Philip, 257
music, 198
Mussolini, 199, 200; declares war on France, 206; arrested by Victor Emmanuel, 231; death of, 240

NAACP, 305, 334
Nagasaki, 245

Naguib, Mohammed, 300
Napoleon, 7
Nasser, Gamal Abdel, 300, 301; seizes Suez Canal, 301; with Syria, forms United Arab Republic, 309
Nathan, George Jean, 93
NATO, 310
Nation, The, 90
National Goals Commission, 338
National Industrial Recovery Act (NIRA), 151, 152, 153
National Labor Relations Board, 164, 165, 190
National Science Foundation, 337, 338
National Security League, 100-101
National Union for Social Justice, 167
National Youth Administration, 161-162
Nazi Bund, 200
Nazism, 203
Negroes, movement to North, 178, 179; civil rights of, 303
Nelson, Donald M., 224
Nevins, Allan, 157
New Deal, 135, 143, 144, 175; land planning, 179-180
New Freedom, 30; explained by Wilson, 40; to be exported, 46
New Republic, 90, 134
newspapers, as escape, 194-195
New Yorker, The, 192-193
New York Post, 286
New York Times, The, 76, 139, 198-199, 241, 263
New York World, 28
Nicaragua, difficulties with, 121-122
Nicolson, Harold, 77-78, 79
Nixon, Richard, 274; nominated for vice president, 284; *New York Post* story, 286, 298, 300; in Argentina and Peru, 311; to Russia, with his wife, to open Moscow exhibit, 313; talk with Khrushchev, 313; nomination for presidency, 31; campaign, 317-319; 333
Nomura, Hichisaburo, 220
Norris, Frank, 27
North Africa, landing in, 223, 227
North Atlantic Treaty, 271
North Korea, aggression of, 276; police action against, 277-280; armistice, 292
Northern Securities, Theodore Roosevelt action against, 24

Odets, Clifford, 198
Office of Price Administration (OPA), 224
Office of Production Management (OPM), 224
Office of Strategic Services (OSS) secret documents in office of Communist Magazine, 272
old, the, 159
Old Man and the Sea, The, 289
On Our Way, 158
O'Neill, Eugene, 31, 197
Oppenheimer, Robert, 241, 294
Organization of American States (OAS), 310
Organization for European Economic Cooperation (OEEC), 269
Orlando, Vittorio, 69, 78, 82
ostentation of wealthy, 1900, 7-9
Outlook, The, 39
Overlord, invasion of the continent of Europe, 232; artificial ports, 234; D-Day, 234-235; advance into Europe, 235-236
overproduction, by farmers, and its problems, 117-118

Pacific, war in, Pearl Harbor, 221; Japanese conquests, 242; battles for Coral Sea and midway, Savo Island and Surigao Strait, 242; Burma Road, 243; General Joseph Stilwell, supported Chinese communists, 243; Manila retaken, 243; Iwo Jima, 243; Okinawa, 243; Hiroshima, 244; Nagasaki, 245; war ends, 245
Packard, Vance, 339
Page, Walter Hines, 49, 59
painting, 198
Palmer, A. Mitchell, 92-93
Panmunjom, armistice signed at, 292
Papen, Franz von, 56
Paris, Conference of, 77-84
parties, political, 24-26
Pearl Harbor, 219; destruction at, 221
pensions, ex-servicemen, cut in, 148-149
people, participation in government by, 26
Perkins, Frances, 142, 145
Perry, Matthew C., Commodore, and Japan, 45
Pershing, John J., General, 67
Pétain, Marshal Henri Philippe, 68;

signs armistice with Germany, 206, 227, 228, 229
Philippines, 16, 45, 219
phoney war, 205
Piovene, 327
Pirandello, 323
Plumbers and Pipe Fitters Union, 290
Poincaré, J. H., 120
Point Four, 268-269; 53 countries benefit from, 1951, 269
Poland, 201, 250
policy, economic, post-World War I, 100
Polish corridor, peace treaty and, 80
politics, corruption by business, 17-19
population, 1790, 2; 1840, 2; 1930 and 1939, 178; 1960, 322
ports, artificial, Operation Overlord, 234
ports, French, World War I, 69
power, of president, strengthened by Wilson, 39-40
presidency, symbolism of, 108
prices in 1939, 180
Priestley, J. B., 177
Prince of Wales, 216
Princip, Gavrilo, 50-51
principles of U. S. politics, 183
profit sharing, 1924, 113
Prohibition (Eighteenth) Amendment, 94; effect of, 94-96; favored by Southern Democrats in 1924, 111
propagandists, German and Austrian, blunders of, 56-57
Proust, Marcel, 197
public works, 150
Puerto Rico, 16, 45
Pulitzer, Joseph, 28
Pupin Hall, 198
Puritan in Babylon, A, 108
Pyle, Ernie, 235

Quemoy and Matsu, 298

Radford, Admiral Arthur, 287, 288, 308
radio, as escape, 194
Radio Corporation of America, 123, 126
radios, 1922 and 1929, 114
railways, influence of, 5, 6, 14; and Interstate Commerce Commission, 18-19; administration of, World War I, 65
range, western, and cattle industry, 5
Raskob, John J., 125

Rayburn, Sam, 305
reconstruction, 90-96
Reconstruction Finance Corporation, 132
reconversion, post-World War II, 254-257
recovery, beginning of, 156
Reed, James A., 84
reforms, proposals for, 2; how achieved in U.S., 24
Régie Renault, 329
registration and draft, World War I, 66-67, World War II, 225
Réjane, 8
relations, foreign, and Roosevelt, 45-46; and Wilson, 46-49
religion, early, 3; in 1900, 4; expansion of, 1911, 31
Reparations Commission, 83
Reston, James, 313-314
Reuther, Walter, 306
Rhee, Syngman, 291, 292
Rheims, 53
Ribbentrop, Joachim von, 202
Richberg, Donald, 139
Rickover, Admiral Hyman, 313
Ridgway, Matthew B., 279
Riesman, David, 332, 339
Robbins, Jerome, 339
Robert, Admiral, 227
Roberts, Owen J., Mr. Justice, 168
Roberts, Roy, 283
Rockefeller, John, 7, 8, 10, 25
Rockefeller, Nelson A., 316, 317, 333
Rogers, Will, 130, 148
Romania, secret treaties concerning, 77, 201; government set by Stalin without consulting West, 251
Romains, Jules, on highways, 181
Roosevelt, Eleanor, 134, 222, 239
Roosevelt, Franklin Delano, 1920 elections, 97; wanted Hoover as Democratic candidate for presidency, 124, 134; personality of, 134-135; refusal to cooperate with Hoover, 136, 137; New Deals, 137, 143, 144; bank holiday, 144; administrations of, 139-241; claimed liberty saved by New Deal, 187; message to King of Italy, 204; *see* World War II; death of, 239; cooperation with Russia, 250; quoted, 333
Roosevelt, Theodore, first prosecution of a trust, 25; and muckrakers, 28; and

reform, 30; 1912 elections, 34; reforms carried on by Wilson, 44; foreign relations, 45-46; not candidate 1916, 58; World War I, 67; on Fourteen Points, 76; to Franklin Delano Roosevelt, 142; status of his reforms in 1939, 172
Root, Elihu, 76
Rosenbergs, The, 273
Ross, Charles, 272, 277
Ruhr, occupation of, 120
Rundstedt, Karl R. G. von, 235
Russia, new government recognized by U.S., 60; second revolution, 67
Russian offensive, 236
Russo–German Nonaggression Pact, 204

Saar, plebiscite for, in peace treaty, 80
Sacco-Vanzetti Case, 101, 197
Salem witches, 248
Salk vaccine, 290
Samoa, 102
Santo Domingo, 47
Sarajevo, 51
satellites, U.S., 312
Schine, David, 295
Schlesinger, Arthur M., Jr., 316, 339
Schwab, Charles, 65
Scripps, E. W., 28
Sears, Roebuck, 115, 328
SEATO, 310
Securities and Exchange Commission (SEC), 154
security, collective, idea of League of Nations, 80-81
Security Council, vote on North Korean aggression, 277
Senate Committee on Foreign Relations, 201
Senate War Investigating Committee, 225
Serbia, 51, 52, 54
sex, emphasis on, post-World War I, 93-94
Shanghai, attacked by Japanese, 133
sharecroppers, 159
Shepilov, Dmitri, 300, 308
Sherman Anti-Trust Act, 19, 43, 90, 163
Sherwood, Robert, 141, 142, 147, 155, 197, 205, 209, 211
shipping, World War II, 225
Simmons, William J., Colonel, 96

Sims, W. S., Admiral, 68
Sinclair, Harry F., 103
Sinclair, Upton, 27, 159
Singapore, 219
Smith, Alfred E., attempt at presidential nomination, 1924, 111; nomination for presidency, 1928, 125; personality of, 125; campaign against, 1928, 125; quoted by F.D.R., 142; opposed radicalism of New Deal, 158
Smith, Gerald L. K., 208
Smith, Jesse, 103
Smuts, Jan Christian, General, 81, 83
Social Security, 162-163
Sonnino, 82, 83
Sophie of Hohenberg, Duchess, 50-51
South, backwardness of, 31-32
Spain, 16, 45, 200
speculation, late 1920's, 126-128
spending, complaints against, 188, 189
Sputnik, first, 311
stabilization, effect of talk of, 157
Stalin, 214-216; demanded second front, 227; interviewed by Hull, 232; on United Nations, 250; U.S. attitude toward, 252; expected crisis like 1929 in U.S., 254; pressure on Turkey, 262; stopped traffic into Berlin, 270; death, 291
Standard Oil Company, 18, 27; factories in Europe, 116
standard of living, 1947, 259
Stark, Harold, Admiral, 207, 221
Stassen, Harold E., 282
states' rights, 158
Steel Workers, 306
Stein, Gertrude, 31, 196
Steinbeck, John, 197
Stevenson, Adlai, 284, 285, 289, 294, 302, 316
Stimson, Henry L., and Japanese occupation of Manchuria, 133; secretary of war, World War II, 206, 211; told Truman of atom bomb, 244
Stettinius, E. R., 238
Stilwell, Joseph, General, supported Chinese Communists, 243
Stone, Harlan F., Mr. Justice, 185-186
Straus, Nathan, 179
Streit, Clarence, 295
strikes, 191, 257, 258
Suez Canal, 301, 302
Summerfield, Arthur, 289

surpluses, farm, during and after World War II, 226
Sun also Rises, The, 93
Supreme Court 16, 23, 25, 119, 151, 159, 163, 164, 167; F. D. Roosevelt attempt to pack, 167-168; adjustments by, 183; 191; school integration, 303
Swing Mikado, 197
Symington, Stuart, 316
Szilard, Leo, 226

Taft, Robert A., 208; personality and philosophy of, 260-261; approves Korean action by Truman, 277; 283, 290
Taft, William H., 32, 33, 34, 76; chief justice, 99
Taft-Hartley Act, 261, 290
Tarbell, Ida, 27
Tardieu, André, 66, 69
tariff, reduction of, under Wilson, 40-41
tax, federal income, 41
taxes, New Deal, 162, 181-182
Taylor, Frederick W., 20
Teamsters, 306
Teapot Dome, oil reserves, 103
Teheran Conference, 232-233
Tennessee Valley Authority, 188, 327
Thailand, 219
Thompson, Dorothy, 200
Three R's Program, Relief, Reform, Recovery, 174
Thurmond, J. Strom, 266
Time, 138; on NRA codes, 151, 195
Tirpitz, von, Admiral, 50, 59
Tocqueville, Alexis de, 322
Tojo, Hideki, General, 219, 220
Toscanini, 198
Townsend, Francis E., and Townsend Clubs, 159, 160, 167
Toynbee, Arnold J., 323
transportation, improvement of, 181
Truman, Harry S, 225; nominated for vice presidency, 237; becomes president, 239; prefers negotiation with Russia, 241; and atom bomb, 244; personality of, 247-248; and United Nations, 249-250, 251; adjustments with Stalin, 251-253; reconversion, 254-258; seizure of railroads to prevent strike, 258; Republican Congress, 1946, 258; Doctrine, 262, 263; elected,